Praise for *Socialnomics*

"People with a passion for something can be infectious. It's obvious that Erik Qualman's passion is social media."

—Dan Heath, *New York Times* Best Selling Author of *Made to Stick* and *Switch*

". . .people are hot for social media . . . Erik Qualman who has written a book called *Socialnomics* says it's about listening first, then selling."

—*Forbes*

"The Social Media revolution has raised new and important questions and is now interwoven into our lives. Whether you are an executive, a parent or a basketball coach, Qualman's *Socialnomics* is a great guide for these issues."

—Tom Izzo, Basketball Coach of Michigan State University

"Erik Qualman has been doing his homework on the social media phenomenon."

—*Huffington Post*

"In *Socialnomics*, Qualman brilliantly prescribes that the key to social media success is doing rather than deliberating. This is a must read for anyone trying to leverage the social graph rather than be squashed by it."

—Steve Kaufer, CEO, TripAdvisor

"The day I met Erik, I met his mom. You learn a lot about someone from how they treat their moms. Erik is a trustworthy guy."

—Chris Brogan, *New York Times* Best Selling Author of *Social Media 101* and *Trust Agents*

"Qualman is to social media what Demming is to quality and Drucker to management."

—Scott Galloway, Professor of Marketing, NYU Stern School of Business & Chairman, L2 Think Tank

"Erik Qualman has a very bright future."

—Angelo Pizzo, Award-winning writer and producer of *Hoosiers* and *Rudy*

"Social Media isn't just for the Next Generation—it's for every generation. Whether you're an entrepreneur, a media professional, a college student or a mom, Social Media will shape your future. Don't be overwhelmed by it; read Qualman's book instead."

—Jane Wooldridge, Award-winning journalist, *The Miami Herald*

"Social Media is one of the most popular activities online today offering opportunities for both businesses and individuals to connect with a new audience. Qualman's book, *Socialnomics*, helps readers understand this emerging behavior."

—Chris Maher, President, Hitwise

"Marketing is experiencing a profound paradigm shift. In the old paradigm, marketers controlled the conversation with consumers through commissionable media—television, radio, newspapers and magazines. In the new paradigm, marketers risk being marginalized in the electronic dialogue now taking place real-time. Erik Qualman's *Socialnomics* offers valuable insights that will help marketers in regaining control in the perplexing world of modern communications."

—Dr. Eli Cox, Marketing Department Chair, McCombs School of Business

"Marketing and research are just the tip of the iceberg when it comes to tapping the wonderful world of *Socialnomics*. Social media is so powerful that we've seen it drive spikes in search behavior in Google. Qualman's book will provide you with a navigational map and allow you to prioritize your Social Media initiatives."

—Kevin Lee, CEO, DidIt

"Qualman makes a powerful case that social media has forever changed the way we live and do business. *Socialnomics* helps make sense of it all."

—Dr. Stuart Levy, Professor, George Washington University

"If you need to know Digital/Social Media in business, then you need to know Erik Qualman."

—William Hawkes, PhD, CMO, AmericasMart

"Right now an online conversation is happening about you, your brand and the things you care about. Erik Qualman's book—*Socialnomics*—will help you and your organization join and benefit from that conversation."

—Harry J. Gold, CEO, Overdrive Interactive

"We live in a world where engagement with your consumer is critical. The one-to-many paradigm is gone. Are you prepared? If not, this book is a must read."

—Robert J. Murray, CEO, iProspect

"Qualman's intelligence on Social Media is a necessity for business and individuals. A 'Socialnomics Strategy' should be put in place for every person and company."

—Todd L. Young, President and CEO-ProspX, Inc.

"I am convinced Qualman can contribute to driving change towards embracing and utilizing social media with any size of company in literally any business."

—Bjorn Ulfberg, Vice President of Marketing, Nokia

"Qualman's lively presentation fascinated the audience and the messages were a great start for our FTTH conference alongside the Prime Minister of Portugal."

—Dr. Hartwig Tauber, Director General—FTTH Council Europe

SOCIALNOMICS

HOW SOCIAL MEDIA TRANSFORMS THE WAY WE LIVE AND DO BUSINESS

REVISED and UPDATED

ERIK QUALMAN

John Wiley & Sons, Inc.

Published by John Wiley & Sons, Inc., Hoboken, New Jersey.
Published simultaneously in Canada.

For general information on our other products and services or for technical support, please contact our Customer Care Department within the United States at (800) 762-2974, outside the United States at (317) 572-3993 or fax (317) 572-4002.

Wiley also publishes its books in a variety of electronic formats. Some content that appears in print may not be available in electronic books. For more information about Wiley products, visit our web site at www.wiley.com.

ISBN 978-0-470-63884-2 (paper) ISBN 978-0-470-90120-5 (ebk);
ISBN 978-0470-90121-2 (ebk); ISBN 978-0-470-90122-9 (ebk)

Printed in the United States of America.

10 9 8 7

CONTENTS

FOREWORD

From Main Street to Wall Street and from school rooms to board rooms, there is a revolution happening. It is being driven by a fundamental shift in how we communicate and it is enabled by the unprecedented rise of what is commonly called "social media." Now, one may argue that we've always interacted with each other through dialogue and debate, but there's no question that the platforms and tools that are freely available to us are taking this to the next level. It's one-to-one and one-to-many discourse in a public setting. And while we may only be at the beginning of this revolution, the effects are palpable. The historic invisible "walls" of the Internet are being broken down daily, locally and globally.

Social media touches nearly every facet of our personal and business lives. In business it isn't just for the Marketing and Public Relations departments. Rather, it is imperative for social media to be an integral part of a company's overall strategy. Whether a business is large or small, its overall success will be partly owed to its success within social media. Social media is living and breathing and it touches every part of an organization from Customer Service to frontline sales, even Human Resources and Information Technology. It's wherever and however your customer chooses to reach out to you. Social media is your customer today, customer tomorrow, employees, etc. Companies properly engaging with the social graph have already seen the power and the payoff. At Ford Motor Company, we have seen this firsthand and it's not the result of one person, but rather the result of an entire movement.

The currency in social media isn't euros, pesos, or dollars; meaningful engagement, participation, and value creation rule the day. The Web is being categorized by billions of users across the world, and if individuals or businesses want a say in how they are categorized, they need to participate with the appropriate currency. And just as in the real world, true givers are rewarded handsomely.

For those willing to forge ahead into this new frontier, the opportunities are real and scalable. We've seen it work at Ford: the Fiesta Movement, in which we gave 100 euro-spec Fiestas to digital influencers for six months, yielded amazing results. We let them do what they normally do: tweet, blog, post videos and photos, and tell everyone they know about their experience. We let their content flow through to our site in real time, unfiltered and uncensored. The results? Over 7 million views of their YouTube videos, 750,000 views of their Flickr photos, more than 125,000 hand-raisers on FiestaMovement.com, 11,000 vehicle reservations and an awareness rate of 60 percent—equal to that of vehicles that have been in the market for two to three years. All through social media.

Radical shifts in business models are also occurring elsewhere: Pepsi bypassed a Super Bowl advertisement for the first time in 20 years in order to shift those millions of dollars into social media. At Ford we've adjusted our marketing budget so that 25 percent is digital and social media. These changes aren't only for businesses. The world of politics has seen its fair share of social media influence, from the oft-used example of the Obama campaign to the rise of conservatives on Twitter with their #TCOT (top conservatives on Twitter) hashtag that has fueled the Tea Party movement.

In the United Kingdom, management of the BBC has mandated that their staff use social media tools since they believe that if their employees aren't using them, they aren't doing their jobs as effectively as possible.

When the Iranian government shut off all outgoing communication channels, a revolution within the country was made known to the world via Twitter. Relief efforts poured into Haiti via texted donations and digital applications. Disasters from the flu to fires, and terrorist attacks to earthquakes, are being tracked and disseminated to mainstream news more quickly than ever. The first photo of the US Airways plane in the Hudson River? It was uploaded to Twitter.

It's also heartening to see that many of the most popular applications and widgets are those that help people easily donate to various causes and charities. The great paradox is that this swath of society that is seemingly narcissistic and navel-gazing is also one of the most collaborative and community-minded when it comes to cause-related efforts. They want to be part of something bigger than themselves. They want to make a difference in the world, and they believe in the collective power of the crowd. To put in perspective just how powerful this can be, if Facebook was a country, it would be the third largest in the world only behind China and India. Yet, some argue that China's social networks (QQ, Renren) will be even larger than Facebook.

The winners in a socially driven world are numerous: good companies, good products, employees, consumers, democracy, entrepreneurial talent, and the environment—all creatures great and small. However, it doesn't come without a price; the majority of what we consider to be our personal privacy may be a thing of the past. This opens up new challenges that may be resolved over time, but Andy Warhol's famous statement about fame may very well be flipped on its head and read something like: "In the future, we'll all have 15 minutes of privacy."

Socialnomics succeeds at helping us make sense of it all. A strength of this book is Qualman's ability to take complex issues and break them into easily digestible takeaways through the use of real world examples and analogies. He also peers into the future—seeing a world where products and services will find us via our social graph.

An item unique to this book is that as a reader you are encouraged to NOT read the book from start to finish. Instead, you're encouraged to "jump around," looking for the items most relevant to you. Helpful summaries of the key points at the end of each respective chapter make this easy.

Fittingly enough, this is similar to our social media usage behaviors. As Qualman correctly points out, we no longer search for the news; rather, the news finds us. Even though you as a reader have the ability to skip sections of this book, if you're like me, you will find most of the constructs and future models in this book are relevant and necessary to achieve success today and tomorrow. Enjoy!

Scott Monty
Global Digital Communications
Ford Motor Company

ACKNOWLEDGMENTS

Socialnomics could not have been completed without the help of many friends and family members. First and foremost, my beautiful wife Ana Maria served a dual role of sounding board and support coach. My immediate family of Dad, Mom, Jay, Helene, Matt, Mary Alison, and my loving grandparents made certain to tell me when things weren't up to standard, but were also my greatest supporters. Encouragement came from my newest family members, the Lozanos: Fernando, Margarita, José, and Stephanie. A special thanks goes out to my Wiley team, Shannon Vargo, Matt Holt, PJ Campell, Nick Snyder, Linda Indig, Amy Scholz, and Beth Zipko, for having both the skill and patience to make this happen. To talented authors Tim Ash and Brian Reich for introducing me to John Wiley & Sons, Inc.—a truly class outfit. The Muellers and Youngs for their moral support. The legal mind of Chris Norton. Julie Jawor's artistic eye. And finally, to numerous friends and family who kept giving me positive reinforcement and ideas, just when they were needed most—you know who you are and it meant more than you know.

ABOUT THIS BOOK

This book does not need to be read from start to finish like a sultry novel, nor should it be. Rather, it provides useful insight into changes in macro trends, behaviors, and constructs as a result of social media. Just like social media itself, this book is written in sporadically digestible sound bites, and by the magic of my wonderful editors Shannon Vargo and Beth Zipko, is arranged so that you, the reader, can easily select an example, particular topic, or case study that is relevant to you or your company. So, while this work will not win any Grammar Girl awards, I hope you find it informative, educational, and entertaining.

Updates and augmentations to this book can be found at www.socialnomics.net.

I love hearing from my readers at twitter@equalman or equalman@gmail.com—feel free to disagree or shower me with affection. I adhere to my promise of personally responding.

INTRODUCTION

It's a People-Driven Economy, Stupid!

In 1992, James Carville coined the phrase "It's the economy, stupid."[1] This simple phrase was a major driver behind why Bill Clinton became our forty-second president. Much has happened since 1992, with the most powerful change being the ubiquitous adoption and assimilation of the Internet. The Internet has revolutionized almost every facet of our business and personal lives. This last statement about the Internet is hopefully not news to anyone reading this book.

What is news, however, is today, we are in the early stages of yet another far-reaching revolution. This revolution is being driven by people and enabled by social media. That is why nearly two decades later we are taking liberty with Carville's famous quote by adjusting it to: "It's a *people-driven* economy, stupid." Although only a slight modification of words, it's a drastic adjustment in philosophy and in how people and businesses are changing and will continue to evolve in the coming years.

Socialnomics is the value created and shared via social media and its efficient influence on outcomes (economic, political, relational, etc.). Or, more simply put, it's Word of Mouth on digital steroids. A subset of this is in the future we will no longer search for products and services, rather they will find us via social media.

Barack Obama understood it was now a people-driven economy, and he rode this philosophy and strategy all the way to the White House. He was able to leverage social media to mobilize the young and old alike, to go from an unknown senator in 2004 to the most powerful man in the world four short years later. In his historic victory speech, he acknowledges this:

> *I will never forget who this victory truly belongs to. It belongs to you. . . . We didn't start with much money or many endorsements. Our campaign was not hatched in the halls of Washington. . . . It was built by working men and women who dug into what little savings they had to give $5, $10, and $20 to the cause.*[2]

Socialnomics is a massive socioeconomic shift. If Facebook were a country it would be the third largest country in the world behind only China and India. Yet, some of the core marketing and business principles of the last few centuries will still apply, whilst other basic practices will become as extinct as the companies that continue to try to force them on the unwilling public. Businesses don't have the choice on whether or not they do social media, the choice is on how well they do it.

We are already seeing the economic potential of social media in its ability to reduce inefficient marketing and middlemen. Million-dollar television advertisements are no longer the king influencer of purchase intent. People referring products and services via social media tools are the new king. It is the world's largest referral program in history. There is also less need to subscribe to costly newspapers when consumers are pushed more relevant and timely free content from their peers via social media. The news finds us. All of this can be done easily from the comfort of home or while on the go with mobile devices. These paradigm shifts, along with many others, are discussed in the forthcoming pages. The end result is that everything from purchasing a baby carriage to drafting a last will and testament is easier and cheaper for the consumer and more profitable for the seller.

Social media also eliminates millions of people performing the same tasks (multiple individual redundancy) over and over. If a new father sees, via social media, 14 of his closest friends have purchased the same brand and model baby seat and they all express glowing reviews, he will not waste hours on research; this research and review process has already been done by people he trusts. This recaptures billions of hours that can be redistributed toward the betterment of society. Today's winners are not the result of Madison Avenue, blueblood political parties, or monopolistic distributors. As a result of the ease and speed with which information can be distributed amongst the social graph, the winners today are great products and services—which ultimately means people win. Companies can elect to do business as usual at their own peril. We are at the start of a newer and brighter world for consumers and businesses; this is the world of Socialnomics.

CHAPTER ONE

Word of Mouth Goes World of Mouth

Ask any Fortune 500 executive, small business owner, or sole proprietor what their most effective form of marketing is and I guarantee their answer, without hesitation, is Word of Mouth. Word of Mouth is not a new concept, but what happens when this is taken to another level? What happens when Word of Mouth goes to World of Mouth?

As depicted in Figure 1.1, an oversimplified historic model of Word of Mouth works something like this: Joe User has a great experience with his Dell computer; then he tells his friend Kelly about it and why he likes it. Kelly in turn tells her friends about it and so on down the line. This is a great model. However, no model is perfect. A few shortcomings of this model are: (1) the news/information can be slow to spread; (2) the original information can be altered as it changes hands; and (3) Kelly's friends may not know much about Joe. The beauty is that social media helps Word of Mouth overcome these imperfections.

While traditional Word of Mouth can be slow to spread, the opposite is true for Facebook status updates. These updates are

Figure 1.1 Difference between Word of Mouth and World of Mouth

pushed via news feeds to all friends in the network. Or, to an even greater extent, a platform like Twitter gives you access to 85 million users who have the ability to read your tweets. This scales much better than an individual telling a few friends a week about the new product or service she enjoys.

Also, social media is global in nature; one of its biggest benefits is enabling users to stay connected with friends and family who are geographically separated. This global connectivity extends to positive and negative messages relating to products and services.

Also, since your opinion is in digital format, it is less likely to be misunderstood or diluted over time. Think about the children's game *telephone*. This is the game where you sit in a circle and start with a phrase like "light weight knickers" and it is passed around the circle via whispers or Word of Mouth from child to child until it reaches the last child and she squeals "bright white Snickers." While traditional Word of Mouth doesn't suffer the same degree of degradation as a children's game, the message, over time and distance, does lose meaning and context. However, when that message is passed digitally, as is the case with social media, it is less likely to lose its original intent. That digital string is passed intact. Along with the benefit of the message remaining intact, the viewer/reader can also see who was the originator of the initial thought. Beyond this, one can often see helpful information about the originator like age, education, hobbies, location, and so forth.

Is Social Media Just a Fad?

Why is there even a need for social media? In less than three years it became the most popular activity on the Web,[1] supplanting pornography for the first time in Internet history. Even search engines weren't powerful enough to do that.

Remember years ago when the last three to four seconds of many television commercials prompted viewers to use various AOL keywords? You don't see or hear that anymore do you? What do you see? People are sending this traffic to social networks. A good example of this is CBS, which sends a majority of its March Madness basketball traffic not to its own website, but to www.facebook.com/brackets.

Why has social media's popularity been so meteoric? Its rapid ascent is due in large part to its ability to help people avoid *information indigestion.* At first glance, this would seem counterintuitive because inherently, social media (e.g. status updates, tweets, social bookmarks, video sharing, and social media's photo commenting), actually produce more content and information. Because of this increase in information, you would think that it would cause more confusion, not less. But, when we dive deeper, we can see why this is not the case.

In his groundbreaking book, *The Long Tail,* Chris Anderson succinctly describes the ability of the Internet within free markets to easily and effectively service small interest groups:

> *The great thing about broadcast is that it can bring one show to millions of people with unmatchable efficiency. But it can't do the opposite—bring a million shows to one person each. Yet that is exactly what the Internet does so well. The economics of the broadcast era required hit shows—big buckets—to catch huge audiences. Serving the same stream to millions of people at the same time is hugely expensive and wasteful for a distribution network optimized for point-to-point communications. Increasingly, the mass market is turning into a mass of niches.*[2]

As we have seen, this is powerful stuff. This is great for individualism, but it greatly fragments the market. Life was much simpler when we knew that all our world news would come from *Time* and *Life* magazines. Fragmentation can be stress-inducing for people.

As human beings, we have the dichotomous psychological need to be an individual, yet feel connected to and accepted by a much larger social set. Accordingly, people are willing to keep *open running diaries* as a way to stay connected and accepted. In Maslow's Hierarcy of Needs Study, he indicates that after the basic needs of survival and security, humans greatest need is to feel accepted. Being social animals by nature, we were highly receptive when social media came along.

However, as humans we experience an ongoing struggle between protecting our privacy and being accepted by others. As a result, there is often give and take when it comes to privacy and acceptance and much depends on the individual and factors including age, race, ethnicity, religion and location. Often this struggle is resolved by balancing the acceptance we receive with the privacy we sacrifice:

> *If you can make something more relevant to me by having less privacy, well that is a small price to pay.*
>
> —*Bill Tancer, General Manager, Global Research, Hitwise*

Everyone has a different "privacy tolerance," but whatever that level may be, most of us still have a yearning to understand what other people are doing.

It was much easier to know what the majority was doing when all you had to do was tune into Casey Kasem's *American Top 40* to find out the latest and greatest in music, or to flip through *Vogue* magazine to quickly grasp fashion trends.

Who Cares What You Are Doing?

Why do I care if my friend is having the most amazing peanut-butter-and-jelly sandwich? Or that someone is at her kid's dance recital? These types of questions are often posed by someone who doesn't understand social media, rather than by someone who hasn't embraced social media; there is a difference. These questions are usually posed by people who are frustrated, because they don't understand what social media is about.

Heavy social media users actually don't care about every little thing happening in their friends' lives all the time. Yes, there are the exceptional few who view every post, photo, tweet, or comment. Individual users make personal choices about how they establish their settings (privacy being one big item here) and, more importantly, viewing behavior.

This is similar to a BlackBerry, Android, or iPhone where users can customize their settings so that the unit vibrates every time a message comes in or they can disable that setting and download messages at their leisure, thereby avoiding *crackberry* syndrome (addictive immediate response to every incoming message).

The key with social media is that it allows you to easily stay abreast of people you want to stay connected with via casual observation. Someone might argue, "Well I already don't have enough time in my day; how can I possibly follow anybody else or keep those following me informed? I can't waste my time like that!" This is a fundamental misunderstanding. One of the key maxims of this book is that *investing time on social media actually makes you more productive.* Let's look at an example with a fictitious character dubbed Sally Supermarket.

We find Sally Supermarket at her favorite place and namesake. It's Fourth of July weekend, so all of the checkout lanes are congested. It's going to be a 10-minute wait until she reaches the cashier. During these 10 minutes, she can:

A. Ruminate about how upset she is that she has to wait in line for 10 minutes, for which she definitely doesn't have time.
B. Flip through a magazine she has no interest in.
C. Be rude and place a call on her cell phone, most likely annoying the others in line around her and potentially the person receiving the call as well, because it's loud in the supermarket, and she might have to hang up the call at any time.
D. Check on updates from her friends/family via social media.

Sally chooses option D, and here's what occurs:

- *Sally's status:* "Bummed that the supermarket is out of mayonnaise—I was planning to make my cold chicken curry salad for the annual picnic tomorrow."

- *Friend 1's status:* "Excited to be boarding a plane to DC for the weekend!"
- *Friend 2's status:* "Who knew my kids would love mandarin oranges in a can?"
- *Friend 3's status:* "I'm pregnant!"
- *Sally's daughter's status:* "Excited! Got an A on my psychology exam—off to get a Frappuccino to celebrate!"
- *Friend 4's comment:* "Sally, plain yogurt is a great substitute for mayo—use a third more curry than normal to kill the bitterness. I recommend Dannon. It's healthy, too!"
- *Friend 3's status:* "Going in for first ultrasound. We've decided not to find out if the baby is a boy or a girl ahead of time."
- *Friend 5's post:* "Great video on bike decorating for the Fourth of July is found here: www.tinyurl.com/4th/."

After reading the status updates from her friends on her phone, Sally still has about four minutes before she'll be at the front of the checkout lane, so she runs to get some plain yogurt (per Friend 4's recommendation). While checking out, she sees a $10 gift card for Starbucks hanging above the magazines. She purchases this gift card with the intent of mailing it to her daughter as a congratulatory surprise for doing well on her exam and to let her know she's thinking about her.

Sally will see Friend 3 tomorrow at the picnic and be able to congratulate her on her pregnancy. Staying up to date on Friend 3 means that Sally won't spend time speculating whether Friend 3 was just putting on extra weight. Sally can also avoid asking if the couple knows whether the baby will be a boy or girl because Sally already knows that they are waiting based on Friend 3's last updated social media message. Sally knows from firsthand pregnancy experience how tiring answering the "Do you know if it's a boy or girl?" question can become—if only she had social media back then!

On the way home, Sally's husband calls her.

"Hey, honey, I'm on my way home from the supermarket—how are you?"

"Struggling—Jack and I are trying to decorate his bike, but it's not looking so hot, and the crepe paper keeps tearing in the spokes."

"Not sure if this will help, but Friend 5 just bookmarked a video about bike decorating—maybe you could check it out for some ideas."

This Sally Supermarket example is a little played up for the purpose of illustration, but it certainly isn't far-fetched. This "10-minute-snapshot" is just one simple example of why social media is a time *saver* rather than a time *waster*.

Like many others, my wife and I experienced firsthand the ability of social media to help save time and stress. We were in Austin, Texas, for the SXSW Conference when my wife's departing JetBlue flight on Sunday was cancelled due to weather in Boston. In fact, all flights to the Northeast on all airlines were delayed due to the extreme weather conditions. My wife tried calling JetBlue and a few other airlines that operated out of Austin, but most of the hold times were in excess of two hours. In our dismay we turned to JetBlue's Twitter account and posted the following:

"Wife's flight cancelled to Boston, what are our choices?"

JetBlue normally has exceptional customer service on Twitter. However, due to the high volume on this day, they couldn't get all the thousands of tweets pouring in, including ours. We witnessed several others that tweeted almost the same exact question that we posted. While JetBlue couldn't get to the tweet, some fellow Twitters could. In the next few minutes we received several tweets from different users, but most were similar to this one:

"Got thru to JB. First JB Flight isn't until Thursday. If you need to get back BOS use Continental out of Houston. DFW soldout too."

This allowed us to hang up on the phone call and start taking action to try and book a flight on Continental Airlines out of Houston. It also saved us the hassle of figuring out our potential options out of Dallas (DFW), since several people had told us (via Twitter) that DFW was not an option. For JetBlue, it also helped reduce their call volume as we weren't the only ones with the question about how to get back to Boston. Several other people were able to hang up their phones. As a reminder, it wasn't JetBlue that answered the question, it was other JetBlue customers. However, JetBlue enabled this to occur by having a robust Twitter presence so that people knew to turn there for viable information; whether that information came directly from JetBlue or JetBlue customers is immaterial.

Foreign Friends Are Not Forgotten

This depiction by German-based social media user, Christoph Marcour, is a quick example of how social media can easily keep us globally connected:

> *One thing I enjoy the most about social media is staying in touch with my friends in America. Before, I would occasionally travel to the United States for work; primarily to New York and Houston. I was generally very busy leading up to these trips and often didn't have time to e-mail or call my friends—all of whom lived in Indianapolis. My friends from Indy also traveled for work quite a bit. So, ironically, we'd often be in the same city at the same time and not know until months later.*
>
> *However, today, we are more likely to meet up if I'm traveling to the United States. It's primarily the result of the fact that even if I'm not directly reaching out to them if I put in my status "packing for New York" or "Bummed that my flight to Houston is delayed," they see that, just as I see similar items that they are updating.*

Geo location tools like Gowalla and Foursquare also come in handy for people attempting to stay in touch with others' whereabouts. These tools are especially helpful when attending massive conferences or conventions.[3]

Search Engines and Social Media

The Internet's greatest strength—rapid and cheap sharing of information—is also its greatest weakness. Search engines have and will continue to help users quickly access the one morsel of information they need out of the trillions of bytes of data. The inherent fault of search engines is that users need to know what they are looking for in the first place. For example, if users type in "Great Father's Day Gift" they do receive some helpful nuggets, but the results are often an overwhelming sea of confusion. And, if what you need is not on the first results page, it might as well not be anywhere because only roughly 5 percent of users go to the second page. In 2010 the Chitka Network reported that going from the 11th spot to 10th sees a 143 percent jump in traffic, proving that a very small percentage of users click through to the second page whilst searching online.

With the excess of information on the Web, people require a tool to make sense of it all. Social media is that mechanism.

Search engines are getting better and better at understanding our individual search needs. Search engines have advanced technologically to recognize that when my 13-year-old cousin searches for "Paris Hilton," she is looking for the pseudo-celebrity, but that when my mother searches for "Paris Hilton," she wants a hotel room in the City of Lights.

While these are nice improvements, if the searcher types in generic terms like "chocolate" or "shoes," the results will be relatively the same as everyone else's results. So, even though search results are getting better, you still can't type in "best rib-eye steak in New York" and quickly get what you are looking for. The advancement in semantic search will largely depend on who wins the search engine wars. If a virtual monopoly exists (e.g., Google), the advancement in search technology could potentially be slow. Someone could argue that the core offering and search engine results have not advanced much in the past five years. This isn't surprising given Google's relative dominance of the space over this time period. Can one blame Google for not changing things too radically? Why would they try to *fix* something that is making record profits for their shareholders? This isn't a book about search, but we touch on it because social media and search are so closely tied to each other.

In fact, search engines are, rightfully so, viewing social media sites as competition—people are already going to wikipedia.org directly if they are on a fact-finding mission and starting to search within Facebook for celebrities and other people. For the best articles on a subject, they may search Digg, Delicious, or other social bookmarking sites. As we discuss in Chapter 5, consumers will soon receive relevant information from Facebook, RenRen, Vkontakte, Twitter, and so on for products and services they want to research and/or purchase (part of social commerce). So, Google's strongest competition may not be other search engines (Yahoo!, MSN, Ask, etc.), but social media, instead.

Google and other search engines are recognizing this shift, and they are trying to make their offerings more social. Google introduced Google SearchWiki, giving users the ability to hit buttons that either promote a search (place it higher in that individual user's rankings) or demote a search result. This is a good advancement. Previously, if a user disagreed with the search results, there was nothing he or she could do about it. The most exciting feature, one that gives further credibility to what we discuss throughout this book, is that Google introduced the ability for users to post comments about specific search results. All searchers can see these comments. Google's success in the social media space (e.g., SearchWiki) will be dependent on user uptake (just like Wikipedia wouldn't be successful if only 200 people contributed). Old and new players alike are racing to win the battle of social search. The competition will be fierce because much of social search will be directly tied to social commerce. Social commerce will be counted in billions of dollars.

In 2009, Google also introduced a new collaborative communication tool called Wave to better integrate e-mail, IM chat, wikis, and so forth. Time will tell if Wave is too bleeding edge, rather than cutting edge. One of the reasons for Facebook's rapid ascent is that young and old users find it simple to use. As of the writing of this book, Wave appeared a bit too obtuse for the common user to grasp.

In 2010, Google Buzz was released in the hopes of offering a Twitter-like micro-blogging tool that was deeply integrated with Gmail accounts.

It's nice to see that social media is pushing technology incumbents like Google to innovate. Time will tell if this competition morphs into more co-opetition. As of this writing, deals were solidified between Google and Twitter and Microsoft Bing and Facebook. Specifically, social results are being shown alongside search results, and search functionalities within social media sites are being dramatically improved. We discuss in later chapters the significance of this for business and consumers.

We No Longer Search for the News—It Finds Us

We no longer search for the news; rather, the news finds us. This is evident when looking at key newspaper statistics. According to third quarter 2008 data from the Newspaper Association of America, advertising revenue for newspapers declined 18.1 percent, national advertising sales fell 18.4 percent, classifieds sank 30.9 percent, and online advertising sales dropped 3 percent.[4]

During the 2008 U.S. presidential election, one of *Saturday Night Live*'s (*SNL*) cast members, Tina Fey, was a dead ringer for Republican vice presidential nominee Sarah Palin. There were several skits done by Fey mimicking the vice presidential hopeful, and some argue that it played a large role in the election itself. The most popular of these episodes was the premier. What was interesting about this five-minute video was: (1) the popularity of it and (2) where people watched the video clip.

NBC estimated that over 50 million viewed the "Palin Skits." According to research conducted by Solutions Research Group, more than half of the people who saw this *SNL* video viewed the clips over the Internet.[5] Many viewed it on the popular social video network YouTube, while the majority of others had it pushed to them and played right within their social media network.

As a result, *SNL*'s television viewership increased more than 50 percent over the previous year (2007), allowing NBC to profit from both ends of the spectrum (online exposure and TV ratings). The power of Socialnomics isn't just online; it can also drive activity in the opposite direction—to the offline world. This makes sense because the roots of social media and the social graph come from an offline world (book clubs, men's clubs, garden clubs, athletic clubs). Technology has enabled us to go to a whole new level with our networks or clubs when they become digitized. As an aside, it's important to note that these Sarah Palin skits are another good example of social media being a time saver rather than a time waster. Historically, a viewer would have to sit through 90 minutes of *SNL* content, a majority of which may not be germane to that particular viewer. Instead, with the help of social media tools, the relevant five minutes (e.g., Palin Skits) of that particular *SNL* episode are pushed the viewer's way by like-minded friends, which in turn saves 85 minutes that can be repurposed accordingly.

Old marketers used to conjure up 30-second commercials that were so entertaining they would be discussed around the watercooler. However, what happens when the watercooler now exists for the sole purpose of dispensing water? Watercooler conversations are now happening online in real time.

There's no longer a need to wait until Monday morning to catch up because the speed of social media already has us all well informed. By seeing a few updates from various social media tools or from an aggregator, your friends probably have a good idea about where you were, how the weather was where you were, if you had any travel complications, whether you got a new puppy, whether you watched or attended a major event, whether you liked it, whether you had a fun weekend, and so on.

Newspapers and Magazines Diminish in Power

People will still catch up around the watercooler, but the conversation will be a little more detailed and specific rather than the traditional small talk. This, on a whole, is a good thing because it helps you learn more about people by getting more information all the time. You don't need to ask them how the weather was on their trip or what their new puppy looks like because you probably have seen their updates, photos, or videos. Instead, you can ask about the characteristics and personality of the puppy, and so on. This allows for the establishment of a quicker and more profound connection between individuals.

If we are no longer walking down to the end of our driveways in anticipation of reading what is going on in the world, and if we are no longer even going onto our favorite Internet news sites to find the news, what does this mean for the various news outlets and the businesses that support them?

We have shifted from a world where the information and news was held by a few and distributed to millions, to a world where the information is held by millions and distributed to a few (niche markets). This has huge ramifications for traditional newspapers. The Internet caused major newspapers and magazines to rethink their business models. While these traditional mediums were still trying to grasp how to handle the upshot of blogs and user-generated content, social media suddenly came along, causing yet another significant upheaval in the status quo. In 2008, it was estimated that traditional newspapers would see a drop of 23.4 percent in revenues.[6] And 2009 can almost be labeled as the year the traditional newspaper died. *PC Magazine* is a good example of a periodical that experienced this macroshift firsthand. Launched in 1982, *PC Magazine* was such an icon in the tech world that at one point advertisers lined up in droves. (Sometimes causing certain issues to exceed 600 pages!)

PC Magazine closed the doors on their print version in November of 2008, moved all of their operations online, and renamed their online publication *PC Mag.* The move was necessary, even though they were in a relatively good position with revenue still in the tens of millions of dollars and digital already accounting for 70 percent of the *PC Mag* brand's revenues. Their online revenues have grown an average of 42 percent since 2001. *PC Mag* brand's revenues grew 18 percent in Q3, 2008.[7]

Traditional newspapers and magazines need to recognize that people are having their news pushed to them from friends and automated free subscriptions. This means newspapers and magazines need to change what their content delivers—otherwise the decline will continue. Newspapers should no longer be reporting the news; instead, they should be commenting on the news and what it means. Even if they do this, their chance of survival may still be slim and only a few, if any, will survive.

In fact, it was interesting to see legendary advertising and marketing columnist Bob Garfield start his 2010 presentation at the SXSW Interactive conference by announcing "I and traditional marketing and advertising are . . . [slow reveal to a presentation slide] Fu%#ed!"

While I am a huge social media Kool-Aid drinker, I still believe that social media is more of an "and" thing than an "or" thing.

A quick ironic example is that as more and more companies cut down on direct mail (expensive to print; slow; environmentally damaging; more difficult to track than digital; etc.), the few companies that continue direct mail pieces may actually see an uptick in results, because there is less clutter in the mailbox.

This book is actually a microcosm of the "newspaper/magazine" phenomenon. By the time this goes to print, many of the news items and examples in this book will be outdated; in fact, some websites listed in this book will no longer be market leaders or even exist at all. There may only be a handful of paper newspapers left, as well. Hence, the importance for the material in this book, as well as in newspapers and magazines, is to provide helpful commentary on what the news means and be able to identify constructs that have occurred before and will potentially occur again. Please note that new examples and updates to this book can be found at www.socialnomics.com. The irony is, that it begs the question: With eReaders, iPads, tablets and the like, why can't I as an author simply continually update the digital version of the book you are currently reading? I see this coming soon.

This digital shift will continue to present an uphill battle for traditional magazines and newspapers because they still need to maintain the best and brightest columnists and experts. But how do they retain these experts when their platform is no longer as strong as it once was? In the past, newspapers had almost full control because they managed the distribution. Today, the experts (i.e., writers, journalists, reporters, bloggers) have increased leverage because the price to entry for them to gain mass distribution is close to zero. While it still means something to have the *Wall Street Journal* on your résumé, it doesn't mean nearly as much as it once did. In fact, in the technology world it probably means more to have a Mashable byline than to be the technology writer for *Newsweek*.

Playboy and the *Sports Illustrated* Swimsuit Issue Are Stripped Down

A salient example of this is the once famed *Sports Illustrated* Swimsuit Issue. People in the 1980s and 1990s used to talk in anticipation for weeks prior to the Swimsuit Issue landing in mailboxes across the country. The most popular person in school or the office that week was whoever received the magazine and brought it in. *Sports Illustrated* was able to charge up to three times its usual rates to advertisers.

As a supermodel, landing on the cover of this issue was life changing. That was then; this is now. The luster of this issue quickly faded with the seemingly limitless photographs and videos on the Internet. When's the last time you heard the *Sports Illustrated* Swimsuit Issue in a conversation? It went from part of pop culture to irrelevance. Even Hugh Hefner's venerable *Playboy* in 2009 reduced its guaranteed magazine subscriber base by 13 percent, from 3 million to 2.6 million. Christie Hefner, daughter of the founder, stepped down as CEO at the start of 2009.[8]

Craigslist, LinkedIn, Monster, CareerBuilder, The Ladders, and many others have eviscerated the one-time newspaper monopoly in recruitment advertising since the technology bubble burst, resulting in a loss of $4.9 billion, or 56.3 percent, of classified revenues between 2000 and 2007.[9] In turn, LinkedIn will most likely make HotJobs, Monster, and CareerBuilder obsolete. This is how fast business cycles move these days. Today, 80 percent of all companies use social media tools to recruit, and of these, 95 percent use LinkedIn (2009 Jobvite Social Recruitment Survey).

The first step that some major periodicals took was to place their content online; this was a logical step. Of course, they still needed to make money, and the model that they understood was subscription based. This worked well for a few years for major publications like the *New York Times* and *Wall Street Journal;* but if you have a good understanding of Socialnomics, you can see how over the long haul this is a somewhat flawed strategy. To effectively leverage the social graph, every company needs to understand that they need to make their information easily transferable.

Idaho Bloggers Are Better than New York Reporters

It's important to free your content from being trapped in a "walled garden" because people have quickly grown accustomed to the news finding them, and there is no turning back. That is a key construct of the book: the world as it was, no longer is. Good, bad, or indifferent, it is a fact that will not change.

People expect and demand easy access to their news; any hurdle, no matter how small, can kill potential distribution. If distribution is limited, then the eventual effectiveness and ultimate viability will be doomed. So let's quickly showcase an A to B comparison of how this works in Socialnomics.

News Site A

Site A is one of the world's largest and known newspapers. Historically, they have generated revenue from print advertising, as well as paid subscriptions. In the past decade, they have put even more information on their website, along with additional video content, multimedia, and so on. They have seen tremendous growth in their online revenue, but it's not enough to offset the loss incurred by their traditional offline revenue model. They still have a large staff of expensive writers, large office buildings that need to be maintained, along with trucks and various overhead to distribute the paper. As a result of these large costs, they require a paid subscription and login for their online content in the hopes of generating enough revenue to offset these costs.

Blog Site B

Jane the Blogger works out of her house in Boise, Idaho. She has plenty of time to write because she works only three days a week in the state courthouse. She uses a popular free blogging tool (e.g., WordPress, TypePad, Tumblr, Blogger) and pays $20 per year to have the vanity URL www.idaho-senators.com. She likes to stay current with events outside of Idaho and pays for a subscription to News Site A. Her husband is a big Boise State football fan and gets a free subscription to the *Idaho Statesman,* and Jane enjoys reading the political section. Her only other cost is the time she spends reading the political section. One could argue that in this instance this is no cost at all because she finds intrinsic value in (aka enjoys) discussing the political topics on her blog about Idaho's senators.

To keep abreast of the latest news on her two senators, she uses free social media tools and alerts to push the news her way when either of the two senators' names is mentioned. She also carves out time to review and edit the various wikis (e.g., Wikipedia) across the Web on each respective senator. Her interest started when her high school friend, Julie Patterson, was elected to the senate seat. Patterson still holds her senate seat in Idaho.

Situation

The other Idaho senator (i.e., not Patterson) is involved in a drunk driving accident early one Saturday morning where he is at fault. There was one other passenger in the car—the senator's babysitter—and she was killed in the accident. The driver of the other car is a Supreme Court judge who was in Idaho on vacation. The Supreme Court judge is in critical condition at a local Boise hospital. As you might imagine, this is going to be big world news coming out of Boise, Idaho.

Jane the Blogger finds out about the accident from one of her friends from the courthouse prior to it appearing on local or national news. Surprisingly, no citizen was there with their digital phone to send a picture off via Twitter, Facebook, etc. Jane is already intimately familiar with the Idaho senator, so no background is required; in fact, she knows that he has a history of overindulging with booze and has had a previous DUI incident that went through her courthouse a few years before he became a senator.

Meanwhile, News Site A's field reporter for that area is on vacation, and so they assign it to a reporter who sits in their Manhattan headquarters. This reporter is not at all familiar with the Idaho senator and immediately goes to her favorite search engine and types in the senator's name. Guess whose site comes up in the top five rankings on the search engine? You guessed it: www.idaho-senators.com. The reporter reads background information on the senator and then hops on a flight to Boise. While on the flight, she begins writing the story. Jane the Blogger and the reporter both post stories about the event. Because of her background and experience on the subject matter, Jane the Blogger posts her story an hour or two before News Site A. Not only that, to pre-sell her more in-depth story, she originally breaks the news she received from the courthouse via a micro-blogging tool like Twitter. She immediately becomes the recognized expert on this story. Microblog posts were the first to break such noteworthy news events as the 2009 U.S. Airways water crash landing in New York and the 2008 California forest fires, and will continue to grow in importance in the reporting and consumption of breaking news.

The purpose of this Jane the Blogger example isn't to showcase who produces better stories—bloggers or traditional reporters; there are plenty of great articles about that. This example demonstrates the availability of free, great content on the Web and the fact that some of the most qualified people to write a story are bloggers who actually do it for free—because they enjoy it! Most of these people aren't doing it for advertising revenue or subscription revenue; they are doing it because they want to be heard. It's not just for news stories, either. As we cover later in this book, this has ramifications on commerce transactions. In a study conducted by Jupiter Research in 2009, it was found that 50 percent of Internet users consulted a blog prior to making a purchase.[10] A Nielsen Study indicated that an astounding 81 percent consulted reviews prior to their holiday purchases. 78 percent of us trust peer recommendations (July 2009 Nielsen Global Online Consumer Survey) while only 14 percent of us trust advertisements (*Marketing to the Social Web* by Larry Webber, Wiley Publishing, 2007).

Pundits try to broad-brushstroke bloggers and microbloggers (e.g., Twitter, Facebook) as "all bad and uninformed" or "regurgitating the same news and facts" when in fact there are varying levels of quality in the blogosphere. There are certainly bloggers who act as leeches, can't source a story, and don't fact check properly, but there are many who provide invaluable original content and information.

Later in this book, we discuss how social media helps pinpoint the good sources of information from the bad ones. Understandably traditional journalists that bad-mouth bloggers have a biased opinion; after all, these new outlets are stealing their journalistic jobs.

Not All Bloggers Are Bad

Getting back to World of Mouth, let's continue with this example to show why the public turns to nontraditional outlets.

During this scenario, for argument's sake, let's assume that the stories of News Site A and Blog Site B are exactly the same in terms of quality. There are three reasons that the Jane the Blogger story has a higher chance for success than News Site A:

1. She is the most qualified expert on this particular niche subject.
2. She posted first.
3. She has Socialnomics on her side.

The first two are self-explanatory and have been touched on in other publications, so let's look at the Socialnomics aspect by continuing our story example with Trevor in San Francisco, California. Trevor is an avid follower of politics, and has used some social media tools to alert him once a day about stories that are related to senators. He receives these two stories (Jane the Blogger's and News Site A's) in his daily newsfeed via real simple syndication (RSS) technology. Trevor has no idea how the technology works; he just knows that his favorite stories show up on his MyYahoo!, iGoogle, and Facebook home pages. Let's see what happens to each story. If these tools inform him, the stories would be pushed his way by his friends and peers via social media tools like Twitter.

News Site A's Story

Trevor looks at the link for News Site A and likes the catchy title and brief summary of what the story contains. He notices "subscription required" listed next to the link, but he has seen this before and sometimes he is able to get enough of the story before hitting the pay wall. Keep in mind that many readers would have stopped here as soon as they saw "subscription required"—they would not have bothered to click on the hyperlink to the story. However, Trevor is hopeful, clicks through, and the page promptly displays a login screen for subscribers only. News Site A has put a hurdle in Trevor's path. As a result of this hurdle, this is the end of Trevor's experience with News Site A for this particular story and most likely for future stories.

Quick recap of Trevor's experience:

1. He clicks on the headline within his feed for News Site A.
2. He notices "subscription required" for News Site A.
3. The end.

Jane the Blogger's Story

Trevor still wants to read about the drunk-driving senator so he clicks on the next related headline in his feed, which is Jane the Blogger's post. He also sees a link to this same story in his Twitter account. Here's what happens:

1. He clicks on the headline within his feed.
2. He reads and enjoys the story.
3. He posts to his 245 friends on Facebook and 45 followers on Twitter.
4. Forty of his friends/followers read the story.
5. Twenty of his friends/followers who read the story also repost it.
6. Ten of his friends/followers rate and tag it on social media bookmark sites (e.g., Delicious, DIGG, Reddit).
7. A few other websites and blogs link to this story.
8. Steps 1 through 6 continue in recurring multiples like Russian nesting dolls.

Search engines read these social bookmarks and hyperlinks and rank the article high in their organic rankings for news around the keywords "senator drunk driving." It's important to note that a key aspect of social media is the ability to tag items. In this example, anyone reading the story could add a tag such as "Idaho senator" or "drunk senator," similar in concept to a tag you would use when organizing a manila file folder in a steel filing cabinet. This is done for quick reference later, but it is also extremely helpful in cataloging the Internet for other potential readers. This is instrumental in social media; via tagging, users help other users make sense of all the information available on the Web. (People tell search engines what various pages and articles contain by the tags they apply.) Other forms of tags may include *#idahosenators* for tools like Twitter. This is called a hashtag (#) and hashtags are helpful in categorizing conversations: #ford, #bpoilspill, #jokes, #doughnuts, #etc.

So, as we mentioned in our opening pages of this book, even though social media helps produce more content, it actually causes less confusion and helps make sense of the morass of information on the Web for everyone across the globe. Search engines rightfully look for and aggregate these tags as well as the names of the links to help in ranking items.

Jane the Blogger receives tons of direct traffic from the various direct links to her story. She receives even more traffic from the search engines because so many "voted" for her by social bookmarking it, reposting it, re-tweeting, or linking to it. She has thousands of eyes looking at her story that a marketer would be happy to pay decent money for. Her gain is News Site A's loss.

As reported by Facebook, the average person on Facebook has roughly 130 friends—there is a lot of viral potential when one person posts a story or video.

Barriers to entry, like required subscriptions, can cause an unfavorable ripple to cascade into an inevitable crescendo of failure. This example isn't to show that subscription-based news models are a bad thing, although we anticipate by the time you read this book there will be limited subscription-based content models on the Web, but rather it is to indicate that most companies need to fundamentally rethink their business models. The mindset of, "we've always made money this way for the past 100 years, and we are going to stubbornly keep doing it this way" is flawed. Just as flawed is thinking, "Let's 'digitize' our current offerings but use the same business model" (in this example, putting newspaper content online but charging the same subscription price). This model isn't going to work in a time where competitive free Web offerings have similar content. It also hasn't worked as evidenced by Tribune Company filing for bankruptcy at the end of 2008. Tribune is the second largest newspaper conglomerate and has such well-known properties as the *Los Angeles Times* and the *Chicago Tribune.*

We see this type of flawed thinking time after time, and it keeps repeating itself because companies are having a difficult time understanding how to leverage the social graph. Rather than attempt to understand, many forge ahead and try unsuccessfully to impose outdated business models on the social graph. The end result of this type of approach is not pretty.

In 2009, the Associated Press asked Google not to feature its content in the search results. Other companies and publishers pay search experts to help get high in the rankings because they want more traffic. Yet, the AP did the exact opposite. They were telling Google not to list their articles at all. They were putting up a distribution hurdle, which as we previously mentioned, is a bad idea.

The AP's decision is similar to cutting off your nose to spite your face.

More progressive thinking is what the *New York Times* has done. They have a monthly subscription-based model that automatically downloads to eBook readers like the Amazon Kindle, Sony eReader, Apple iPad, and so on. At the time of this writing, they are charging $12 per month. It is too soon to tell if this type of model will work, but it has a better chance than the models that are attempting to cram a square peg into a round hole. The *New York Times* did a smart thing by looking at the success of Apple iTunes' charging 99 cents per song. There is no need to recreate the wheel if you can just as easily learn from the mistakes and successes of the past. History repeats itself because nobody listens the first time.

There are no physical fees (printing press, website maintenance, delivery trucks, paper, ink, shipping, and so on) for the *New York Times*, but most importantly, it meets the users' desire to have news pushed to them in real time to their preferred mobile device. We don't know if this new model will work, but we do know that the old model does not.

Free and Faster Information

Tim Russert was the well-known anchor of the popular television show *Meet the Press* for 17 years. When he unexpectedly passed away in 2008, his Wikipedia page was updated before Fox News announced it. Entertainment Blog TMZ and Wikipedia also scooped the untimely death of Michael Jackson. The online newspaper-subscription model works well if you are the only one holding the information. However, it breaks down if free and faster information is available. Social media enables this "free and faster" information to exist. Online newspapers would argue that their information is more credible, and that Wikipedia isn't a reliable source.

While this argument may hold true for smaller niche topics, it's not likely to hold true for the more popular topics. Ironically, major media outlets are designed to cover the big news stories, not the minor niche ones. This makes sense because these niche stories were historically reserved for the local media outlets.

Our major media outlets are now competing against Wikipedia and other social collaborative sites, and these outlets continue to increase in power and relevance. As far back as

December 2005, studies were conducted showing the accuracy and viability of Wikipedia. One such study was conducted in the journal *Nature* and posted by CNET.

For its study, *Nature* chose articles from both *Encyclopædia Britannica* and Wikipedia in a wide range of topics and sent them to what it called "relevant" field experts for peer review. The experts then compared the competing articles side by side—one from each site on a given topic—but were not told which article came from which site. *Nature* collected 42 usable reviews from its field of experts. In the end, the journal found just eight serious errors, such as general misunderstandings of vital concepts, in the articles. Of those, four came from each site.[11]

Back in 2005, when Wikipedia wasn't fully vetted, this study was showing that it was as accurate as *Encyclopædia Britannica*. One could debate (and many have) the validity of this study, but one thing that is very telling is that Britannica itself launched its own version of a Wiki (however, they do censor and have final approval) in 2009. Wikipedia should be more accurate for major topics—if you have 1,000 experts contributing, versus 3 to 5 experts, the social graph will win every time. However, conversely for niche products, where you have 2 to 3 contributors versus 2 to 3 encyclopedia experts, the experts, in most instances, will provide more reliable information. Wikipedia is successful as a result of scale and self-policing. As a result of the success of Jimmy Wales's Wikipedia experiment, others have started to leverage the social graph.

One prime example of free and faster information is the site zillow.com. Zillow allows users and realtors to investigate the estimated values of various real estate properties. It aggregates various public data (most recent sales price, up-to-date selling prices of the surrounding houses in the neighborhood, asking prices, quality of schools, etc.) into an algorithm to obtain the estimated property value. To augment this third-party data, Zillow allows its user base to update various aspects. For example, a user can update the number of rooms or bathrooms in a particular home. If you are the homeowner and you renovated it by adding a bathroom in the basement, who is a more qualified expert than you (the homeowner) to update the listing?

Google Maps offers a similar wiki functionality by allowing users to move items on the maps so that they are more accurate, such as updating a store that may have gone out of business in the last few weeks. This model works well. Google establishes a baseline product offering (map of the area) and then allows the public to help fine-tune and grow it.

This is a slightly different but just as effective model as Wikipedia. The difference is that Wikipedia doesn't produce a baseline; rather, everything is developed from scratch. In January 2008, Facebook introduced the Translations application, effectively turning the translation process over to their users. And why not? The users are the people who understand Facebook and their languages best. Even Facebook was blown away by the success. The site was translated into Spanish in two weeks; French followed soon after and was translated in just 24 hours. At the start of 2010, Facebook is available in more than 65 languages, all translated by Facebook users using the Translations application.

Wikipedia proves the value of collaboration on a global basis. The output of many minds results in clarity of purpose and innovation. The lesson to be learned is that if collaboration among strangers across the Internet can result in something as useful as Wikipedia, think about how collaboration among colleagues can transform business. Many businesses are even starting to use social media collaboration tools like Yammer in the workplace. The theory behind tools like Yammer—a social networking tool for use inside companies—is that employees communicate via e-mail, which is antiquated. Social media tools offer the possibility of better collaboration in the workforce. Please note at the writing of this book that there weren't too many proven success stories using social tools to collaborate in the workforce. It's important to keep in mind that not all uses of social media are golden, so this may be an instance where social media doesn't prove successful. Time will tell. While social media will play an important role in most of our lives, it's certainly not a panacea for everything.

A Touch of Bacon Salt on Your Social Media

The success of Bacon Salt is a great example of how the social graph can even cause a product to be made. Bacon Salt was an idea that was born out of the minds of two Seattle buddies, Justin Esch and Dave Lefkow, who over a few beers jokingly posed the question—"Wouldn't it be great if there was a powder that made everything taste like bacon?"

The genesis of their success was when Lefkow started a MySpace profile dedicated to Bacon Salt. They then used data openly available on MySpace to seek out people who had mentioned bacon in their profiles—they found over 35,000 such people. They began reaching out to these people to gauge their interest in Bacon Salt, and not only did they find interest, they started receiving orders when they didn't even have a product yet!

World of Mouth took over from there, and as Lefkow describes it, "It was one person telling another person, telling another person. It was amazing and scary at the same time. We weren't prepared for the onslaught." The viral aspect of this experience branched into non-social media channels, and they even received a free endorsement from the Gotham Girls Roller Derby team. It's one thing to get buzz about your product, it's another thing to sell it—and sell it they did. The spice that made everything taste like bacon incredibly sold 600,000 bottles in 18 months. "We didn't even have a product at the beginning; instead, we bought cheap spice bottles, printed out Bacon Salt logos and Scotch taped them onto the bottles."[12]

The Bacon Salt product and brand was built entirely using social media. Similar to JetBlue, Zappos, and Comcast, the founders of Bacon Salt started following what people were saying about their product and responding to them. They did other activities, but as Lefkow and Esch readily admitted, they wanted to keep some of their social media insights to themselves and indicated, "We don't want them (big companies) to get on our gravy train."

Micro-Revenue Streams Huge for Social Media

The Bacon Salt case study is a good example of a potential revenue stream for the social networks. For a small business owner, it is still very daunting and cumbersome to figure out how to set up a website for a small business. As evidenced by Lefkow and Esch, you can get a fan page, profile page, group page, and so on up and running on your favorite social network in literally minutes. The best part is that as of this writing, the social networks don't allow for much customization.

How can non-customization be a good thing? For small business owners, this places everyone on a level playing field, which means it comes down to the product you're selling versus the glitz and flash of your website.

The future functional solution that social networks will provide is the ability to have an automatic shopping cart and transaction model easily established. The social network will take a "small percentage" of all transactions. This is similar to what Obama excelled at—small payments that add up to millions of dollars. Ninety-two percent of Obama's donations were less than $100.[13] Essentially, this is almost a micro-payment model for small businesses. Small businesses can be up and running in a few hours on a social media storefront, and the fractions of pennies that the social media platform captures from transactions would hardly be missed by that small business, but would be a huge revenue generator for the social media platform when they collect from thousands of businesses. Companies like the T-Shirt supplier Threadless are already successfully completing transactions on social networks.

Dancing Matt—Something to Chew On

Later in this book, in more than one example, we show how companies try, some in earnest (TripAdvisor—"Where I've Been") and some halfheartedly (Hasbro—Scrabble) to leverage existing successes. These efforts often fall short, and as a result, companies often develop their own similar marketing programs—sometimes to grand success and other times to failure.

One company that was able to leverage an overnight sensation was chewing gum brand Stride (Cadbury). The story begins with Matthew "Matt" Harding, born September 27, 1976. Harding was an American video game developer from Westport, Connecticut, who had stints at Cutting Edge Entertainment and Activision. Many of these games were primarily *shooter* games. Saying he "didn't want to spend two years of my life writing games about killing everyone," Matt quit his job and began traveling, which lead to the production of his first "dancing" video.

All of us are known for something peculiar or quirky amongst our friends. Harding was known for a particular dance. So, while traveling in Vietnam, his travel buddy suggested he do his dance, and they filmed it. The video was uploaded to his website for friends and family to enjoy, and they loved it! "The dance can probably best be described as a five-year old on a Halloween sugar rush.

Harding decided to perform his unique dance whenever he was visiting an exotic location on his journey. After the trip, Matt was able to string together 15 dance scenes in exotic locations.

All the scenes had him center frame, with the background music "Sweet Lullaby."

The video was passed around by e-mail and eventually became *viral,* with Matt's server getting 20,000 or more hits a day as it was discovered country by country. The beauty of the video is that there are no language barriers; it's simply Matt dancing in various locations.

It was a natural fit for Matt to upload it to YouTube. Stride Gum saw a huge opportunity and approached Matt, offering to help sponsor his travels. Matt was delighted because he had been traveling on a shoestring budget—originally using a college travel company (STA) tour. With the help of Stride, Matt was able to produce a third video in June 2008.

This video was the result of traveling to 42 different countries over the prior 14 months and included shots from 70 different cities and locations.

One of the founders of YouTube, Jawed Karim, states that Matt's video is his favorite. Karim said that he particularly likes the "Dancing Matt" video because it "illustrates what YouTube is all about—namely that anyone who has a good idea can take that idea and make it happen." When told that Harding has been hired by Stride Gum to go dance around the world, Karim said, "Sounds good to me."[14]

This sounds good to Stride Gum as well. As of April 2010, over 42 million people had viewed Matt's two most popular videos on YouTube.[15] Keep in mind that this doesn't include all the ancillary videos like "How the Hell Did Matt Get People to Dance with Him?" and "Where the Hell Is Matt's Girlfriend?". That video also produced a few million views.

If you typed in "Matt" in Google, he shows up for the top 5 results (organic). He was voted a Top 40 Internet Celebrity by VH1, and he made guest appearances on *Good Morning America*, *The Ellen DeGeneres Show*, *Jimmy Kimmel Live*, and *Countdown with Keith Olbermann*, just to name a few. For the nominal fee of sponsoring Matt's travel costs, Stride was paid back in millions of dollars worth of brand equity. The best part is the video is still being viewed by the millions, which is completely different from a *one and done* television commercial. In fact, as of March 2010, this video was being showcased on one of the giant flat screens in New York's Times Square.

A main reason the campaign was successful was that Stride kept the integrity of the original concept—it was always about people; it wouldn't be prudent to all of a sudden make it about gum. In fact, Stride helped Matt improve on his original formula by suggesting that Matt try to surround himself with locals also joining in the dance, whereas previously the somewhat reserved computer programmer would have, at most, one or two people in the video with him. This resulted in some genius results—one of the most inspiring being Matt surrounded in Poria, Papua New Guinea by a tribe (Huli Wigmen) dressed in their indigenous garb. The beauty of this sponsorship is that Matt and his girlfriend Melissa continued to do all of the legwork.

Prior to the third video, Matt sent out communications to the various cities he'd be visiting so that he would have people to dance with. He received over 25,000 responses, and he needed to get release forms signed prior to the filming. This is quite a bit of legwork that could easily get bogged down in the legal department of a large corporation. In this instance, Matt and his girlfriend were continuing to produce the videos from point A to point Z.

Stride could have also made Matt wear a Stride t-shirt and pass around free samples of gum, but they were smart enough to leave well enough alone. Instead, they had a tactful message at the end of the video (i.e., post roll) and also had a discreet logo in the upper right of some of the videos. Stride showed how successful a brand can be by simply associating itself with social media that is already virally successful, which gives other brands something to chew on.

Flying the Not-So-Friendly Skies

A good example of the *viralness* of social media can be seen in this American Airlines example. In April of 2008, over the course of four days, American Airlines had to cancel 3,000 flights as a result of a large percentage of their jets not meeting the maintenance requirements mandated by the Federal Aviation Administration. This was not the result of bad weather or security threats; it was pure negligence on the part of American Airlines. A spokesman for American Airlines expressed their strategy in handling the situation:

> *We fly over 100 million passengers a year, and they are all important to us. A large percentage of them fly with us exclusively, so the most important goal was to stay in contact and let them know what was going on. And we used every communications channel we have available to us.*
>
> *This included some new plays, including monitoring blogs, as soon as the crisis started. That was an important part of our strategy. And we felt, in general, that the information was generally correct and balanced enough to where we didn't have to get involved in the conversation. Some of the remarks were tough to take and on some blogs people were actually defending us.*[16]

I underline two important pieces in this statement. The first is that "we used every communication channel available to us," yet there is no specific mention of social media. The second is "we didn't have to get involved with the conversation." As an individual or company, you should feel compelled to become part of the conversation; people want to hear from you. A strategy based on only entering a conversation if it "gets ugly" is generally flawed logic in the sense that the damage will be done before one can react. This is similar to trying to time the stock market; it's very difficult.

Website complaints to www.aa.com increased 25 percent over the same period as the year before and 9 percent over the previous week.[17] American asked consumers with complaints about the cancellations and inconveniences to e-mail them. This caused a 13 percent increase in e-mail complaints. What jumped out was a 74 percent increase in downstream traffic to social networks.[18] This is compelling in the sense that users were most likely going to social media to vent and widely disseminate their own personal issues with the crisis. This large increase couldn't only be caused by teens because teens index low on travel volume. Also, as noted in the previous quote, there was no mention of specifically monitoring social media outlets—only blogs. This type of rabid activity on social media can affect an airline's brand equity, yet as stated by the American Airlines spokesman, they weren't using the popular social media tools, listening to what was being said, and attempting to address it. They chose to ignore these important conversations. Later in this book, we will show how JetBlue has correctly taken the appropriate measures to make sure they are listening and responding within social media to disgruntled consumers.

Chapter One Key Points

1. Despite niche fragmentation caused by the Internet, people still desire an understanding of what the majority is doing. Social media is that mechanism.
2. Spending time on social media makes you more productive. Social media is the mechanism that allows users to avoid "information indigestion." Recall the Sally Supermarket example where she uses social media to turn 10 minutes of historically wasted time into 10 productive and enjoyable minutes.
3. Business models need to shift. Simply digitizing old business models doesn't work; businesses need to fully transform to properly address the impact and demands of social media.
4. Traditional magazines and newspapers are struggling for online survival because some of the most qualified people to write a story are freelance bloggers who write for the sheer joy of it! They aren't writing in hopes of subscription revenue; they are posting free content (opinions, videos, facts, etc.) because they want to be heard. It's tough for traditional journalists and publications to compete with *free*.
5. We no longer look for the news; the news finds us.
6. A key aspect of social media is the ability for millions to tag items just like you would label a manila folder. This helps catalog the information on the Web and makes it easier for all users.
7. Not all great viral marketing ideas need to originate in the marketing department. It is prudent to team up with already successful grassroots programs (e.g., Stride Gum and Dancing Matt).
8. World of Mouth is an advancement of Word of Mouth as: (1) it disseminates the information quickly and globally;

(2) its digital aspect allows the original integrity of the message to remain intact; and (3) it is traceable to an original source

9. Google's main competition today is social media. People want to know what their friends and peers think about products and services. Social search drives social commerce.
10. Businesses don't have a choice on whether or not to DO social media, their choice is how well they DO it.

CHAPTER TWO

Social Media = Preventative Behavior

We covered in Chapter 1 why there is such a thirst and demand for social media. But what does social media demand from us? While hundreds of millions of people have discovered the benefits of social media, some people and companies have also experienced the potential pitfalls of such mass transparency.

More than a few students have been kicked out of universities for collaborating on Twitter, hi5, Facebook, MySpace, and the like on assigned individual school projects. It's old news that potential employers haven't hired some people because of inappropriate content or associations on their LinkedIn or Facebook pages. Or, how about the teachers who have been asked to step down for overtly sexual content within their social networks? There's also the famous Jeff Jarvis blog post about Dell's inadequate customer service.

So what does this all mean? Are social networks powerful enough to cause an adjustment in personal and corporate behavior on a macro-level? You bet your camera phone they are. This is why we are seeing governments starting to step in to help try and regulate social media. Hopefully the social media suppliers can self-regulate as much as possible.

The 20-something now thinks twice about getting so drunk that she blacks out and can't remember how she wound up in the hammock of a stranger's backyard. Cameras document everything, and technologies like Facebook's Mobile Upload and "tagging" can disseminate a naked keg stand to your network faster than you can count to five.

Sure, many still have the desire to put their deepest and darkest thoughts and behaviors into a black box, but they are less likely to be able to keep their actions secret.

Staying in Touch with Your Teenagers

When you get home from a hard day at work and ask your kids what happened in school, many respond with the same answer that you did when you were a teenager—"nothing." They aren't intentionally being difficult (at least most of the time); they are just teenagers being teenagers. They do not understand that the fact that their classmates Holly and Suzy were pulling each other's hair in gym class is incredibly intriguing. Or, the fact that the substitute teacher went an entire class period not knowing she had toilet paper on her shoe would provide much needed levity to a parent returning from a stressful or monotonous day at the office.

In many instances, social media can help bring families a little closer by enabling parents to unobtrusively follow their kids' lives. Oftentimes in today's busy world, parents and teenagers share time only around the dinner table, and then everyone goes about his or her own life. Many families don't share the luxury of sitting down together at dinner.

To some extent, social media can bring families together—it connects parents to their kids like never before. "I think one of the real beauties of social media is the passivity of it. Unlike e-mail that requires a response, a mother or grandmother can passively observe the whereabouts and activities of their children or grandchildren," indicates Steve Kaufer, CEO of TripAdvisor.

While ignorance can sometimes be bliss, social media provides insight for parents into the day-to-day activities of their children. But you shake your head and say there is no way that kids would allow their parents to spy like that. You would be right, but it's not universally true. Although some junior high students don't mind being seen with their parents at the movies, others would rather be dead than be spotted with their parents in public. Also keep in mind that some parents will not bless their children's social media usage unless they are a part of their child's network. Sixty-nine percent of parents indicate they are "friends" with their kids on Facebook (The Social Media and Personal Responsibility Survey). The same study revealed that the vast majority (73 percent) of parents believe it's acceptable for their child to have a Facebook or MySpace account. However, those same parents claim they will monitor their child's social media profile until they are 18 years old.

Obviously, if their parents are in the social network, then teenagers will be taking on preventative behaviors. Keep in mind that teenagers will also take on preventative behaviors not only for their parents, but also for some of their classmates. For example, if a rowdy, partying guy was trying to impress a particularly prudish and reserved girl—his behavior in the social network might be a little more refined after she becomes a part of his network and is privy to his activities and behavior.

There is also "Facebook Dating." Facebook dating is where teenagers change their profile to reflect who they are dating. However, in the "real world" they aren't really dating, have never held hands, or even kissed. Simply put, if a girl likes a boy she can simply change her profile to reflect she is dating the dreamy guy in her geometry class.

Preventative Behavior for Business

The great thing about technologies like Twitter (microblogging) for businesses is that this is a tool that enables a company to search for a brand name like "Hershey" or "Prada" and see what millions are talking about. Good companies do this, but savvy companies take it one step further and act on it.

Comcast, who has notoriously terrible customer service, did a progressive and great thing from the beginning when it came to microblogging. Comcast assigned a person to monitor conversations for any mention of the term "Comcast," and more importantly, they also gave that company representative the authority to respond and act. This first came to the public's attention when famous blogger Michael Arrington of TechCrunch had his service down for over 36 hours and was getting no help from customer service over the phone. He ranted on Twitter about how much he despised Comcast's service, and pals like Jeff Jarvis ("Dell Hell") started reposting the story. To Arrington's surprise, he was contacted within 20 minutes by a Comcast representative who was following rants on Twitter, and his issue was resolved by the next day. Another example of Comcast's progressiveness was posted by C. C. Chapman on the blog "Managing the Gray":

> *I just had an amazing experience in customer service from Comcast. . . . With all the flack they have gotten over the years, I've actually been very fortunate to have a mostly good experience with them and the last 24 hours really proves that when a brand pays attention to the conversation happening out on the Web about them and actively works to engage in that, good things can happen.*
>
> *. . . last night I made a snide remark about the lackluster quality of my HD picture on Comcast during the Celtics game. Comcast saw that and tweeted me back minutes later. This morning I got a call from their service center. This afternoon*

someone came out. Now my HDTV rocks! THAT, my friends, is customer service and how it should work all the time.

Brands need to wake up to the fact that "new media" isn't going away and in fact, I'd argue that it isn't new anymore, but is here and at the forefront so you either wake up and pay attention or you lose business to the company that is paying attention.[1]

JetBlue also engaged in trying to keep a pulse on its customers. When a company starts to follow you on Twitter, it may seem a little too Big Brother, but if the company is transparent, then the consumer's concerns about too much information-sharing go away. For example, this is a typical response from JetBlue:

Sorry if we weirded you out by following you on Twitter. @JetBlue isn't a bot, it's merely me and my team keeping our ears to the ground and listening to our customers talk in open forums so we can improve our service. It's not marketing, it's trying to engage on a level other than mass broadcast, something I personally believe more companies should try to do.

Because corporate involvement in social media is a new and evolving discipline, I also take a specific interest in conversations revolving around our role here. I'd have messaged you directly if you allowed direct messages, so please also forgive me for following the link on your twitter page here to send you this note.

You and Lisa are no longer being "followed" as you indicate.

Again, my apologies.
Morgan Johnston
Corporate Communications
JetBlue Airways[2]

Notice what Morgan says, "It's not marketing, it's trying to engage on a level other than mass broadcast."

In another use of Twitter, authors are constantly doing vanity searches on Twitter to determine if people are talking about them or about their books. One author says, "I was doing a vanity search on my name within Twitter when I saw a post out of Billings, Montana, that had happened in the last two minutes and the exchange went something like this."

Author: My husband just handed me a book by Tim Ash called *Landing Page Optimization.* Is this any good?
Tim Ash: Yes, it's a great book.
Author: Aren't you the author?
Tim Ash: Yes, I am.
Author: Well, if I don't like this book will you refund my money?
Tim Ash: Yes, I'm so confident that you will like the book that I will refund your money if you don't.

As you read this, you may say wait, this isn't necessarily new; good companies have been responding to comments on message boards for several years now, especially after popular blogger Jeff Jarvis flamed (no pun intended) Dell in his "Dell Hell" post in 2005.[3]

The concept of responding to customer unhappiness is certainly not new and especially not new on the Web. The difference with social media is the speed and ease in which this occurs as well as the sphere of influence.

A post on a message board can take a company quite some time to find (i.e., time measured in days), if they find it at all. This can also be a labor intensive and costly process for companies to follow. The key problem is that it is often very labor intensive for the user to post a complaint. To post on a message board, you generally are required to set up an account for that particular message board. Message boards are sometimes difficult to navigate to a particular topic area, and so on.

In the past, millions of frustrated customers didn't bother to comment. According to a study by the Strategic Planning Institute, historically 96 percent of dissatisfied customers don't bother to complain. An astounding 63 percent of these silent dissatisfied customers will not buy from you again.[4] Hence, companies didn't know they had hundreds of frustrated customers. Now, it is so much easier to provide feedback from anywhere (in particular from your mobile device) that more and more customers are doing it. With programs like Facebook Connect and Friend Connect (Google), one can use an easy-to-remember login (Facebook or Google) no matter what site you happen to be on, whether it's cnet.com or cbssportsline.com. Or, if you don't feel like posting a comment with one click of a button you can simply Facebook "like" a particular website, brand, or company.

With social media tools, you can post a comment or video in seconds directly from your laptop or most likely your mobile device. This is critical because it allows frustrated customers to instantly post their exact feelings at the point of frustration. They haven't had time to ruminate, so it is unbridled. Similarly, the posts are easy for companies like JetBlue and Comcast to see. It's not laborious at all to find problems; in fact, they can assign one person to help handle most situations, which means they have more time to focus on the solution rather than spending time finding the problem.

This gets to another point on how savvy companies philosophically approach critical posts on the Web. Ineffective companies, that aren't in touch with their customers, view negative posts as nuisances. These companies approach negative feedback by attempting to figure out how to technically scrub or manipulate it by means of posting bogus "good" user comments or applying pressure to the site(s) via anti-trademark infringement laws to remove the post.

Effective companies and people relish critical online feedback. They use this information to make themselves more competitive by improving their products and services in the eyes of the consumer. These companies don't waste their time attempting to manipulate online systems; rather, they spend their time (like in the JetBlue Twitter example) trying to resolve the issue with the disgruntled customer and learning from it. Good companies view it as an opportunity to prove to that customer they are willing to go the extra mile for them. From the previously mentioned Strategic Planning Survey, of the 4 percent of unhappy customers who do complain, 7 out of 10 will do business again with the company so long as their concerns are handled properly, and 19 out of 20 if the grievances are dealt with swiftly. Rapid response is even more critical when it comes to tools like Twitter, where 10 minutes is considered a lifetime.

A good everyday analogy of constructive feedback is a friend who lets you know when you have an unsightly poppy seed stuck in your teeth prior to a big blind date. This friend is much more valuable to you than the politically polite and silent friend. Perhaps the biggest difference between these examples and traditional message boards doesn't have anything to do with the tactical or the technology. It has to do with the sphere of influence of the person posting.

If the fictitious Peter Poster places something on a message board, he doesn't know whom he is reaching, and the reader most likely doesn't know who Peter is. With social media, Peter posts a status update on Facebook, LinkedIn, Twitter, and so forth. This status update is sent to people within his network who all (personally) know him. By knowing Peter, they can readily identify with the position Peter is coming from.

If Peter complains about a Boston cream doughnut from a particular bakery, his followers may discredit it and say "That Peter is always so fickle when it comes to eating. It's rare if he likes any food item that his mother doesn't make." Conversely, if Peter complains about the poor customer response from a phone provider, a follower may say, "When it comes to eating, Peter is fickle, but he is very patient and forgiving otherwise, so if he says his phone company has poor customer service, I'm going to make certain that I steer clear of that phone company."

> *Someone who has stayed only at five-star hotels will rate a five-star hotel differently than a honeymooner staying at a five-star for the first time.*
>
> —*Bill Tancer, General Manager, Global Research, Hitwise*

One step would be to find someone you don't know on general review sites who seems to have similar tastes; however, the next logical and more rewarding approach is locating a person in your social network who you know and who you are confident (via personal knowledge) has the same preferences you do.

Let's perform a quick calculation based on the average number of people that a person on Twitter has following them to underscore the importance of social media. The old rule of thumb was that a person who had a bad experience would tell 6 to 10 people about it. The average person on Twitter follows 100 people. If you take that and assume that 10 percent of the people following someone will pass it along, then you get to the number 10 ($100 \times 0.10 = 10$). Ten people will be influenced directly. If those 10 also have 100 followers and only 5 percent pick it up, then another 50 individuals will be influenced indirectly, and so it goes on down the line. That's quite an impact.

Chapter Two Key Points

1. Businesses and people are willing to have open diaries within social media as a way to stay connected because their ultimate desire is to feel a part of something larger than themselves. With this openness comes responsibility for both businesses and individuals.
2. What happens in Vegas stays on YouTube.
3. Individuals and companies are starting to lead their lives as if their mother or board of directors were watching their every move because they probably are. While there are downsides to these behavioral changes caused by social media, overall it's beneficial to society.
4. Social media connects parents to their kids like never before.
5. Social media enables customers to instantly post what they like and don't like about anything from products to government.
6. Negative comments and posts are easier for companies to find with social media. Hence, those companies have more time to focus on the solution rather than spending time finding the problem.
7. Effective companies and people embrace critical feedback. Digital comments that identify areas for improvement are invaluable.
8. Ineffective companies spend time attempting to obfuscate or manipulate negative comments within social media. Good companies spend time addressing and resolving customer complaints.
9. Try to use social media to get hired vs. fired.

CHAPTER THREE

Social Media = Braggadocian Behavior

The second, more exciting behavioral change is braggadocian behavior. As people continue to microblog, and update their status via social media, it often becomes a competition of who's doing the coolest thing. What once took place only periodically around the watercooler is now happening in real time.

Would you rather post "I'm watching reruns of *Saved By the Bell*" or post "Just snowboarded down a double-black diamond run at Aspen and highly recommend it for those who love Colorado snow!" Over time, each of these posts contributes to *your* individual brand or social tattoo.

As a society, this is a good thing. It allows people to take stock of their collective lives and what they're doing throughout the day, rather than letting years go by and looking back on their wasted youth, saying "what did I do with my life?"

People are actually living their own lives rather than watching others. As a company, it's imperative that you produce products and services so that people not only want to be associated with your brand, but also take ownership of it.

Social media is in.
Out: Reality TV.
In: Reality social media.

Just Do It, Did It

Nike understood how to take advantage of users' appetites for competition as well as users looking to brands for helpful tools (creators of content). That is why Nike created an avatar named "Miles" that people can place on their desktops. Miles helps users by tracking the miles they run or their jogging patterns compared to others inside and outside of their network. Miles encourages you to run and keeps you aware of local weather, running events, and promotions. This can easily be used wherever you are (iPod, social network, desktop, etc.).

Companies need to focus on providing content and tools to consumers, which is the opposite of traditional marketing. Instead of providing consumers with a one-way communication stream, companies today need to focus on supplying something of value. People are grateful that Nike is able to provide them with a tool to track how many miles they run and to tell them which songs from their iPod playlists seem to stimulate them to run their best. Also allowing users to see what songs stimulate other runners is a tremendous help to the Apple consumer.

This social media technique also helps align Nike and Apple with additional revenue. More songs will be downloaded and more shoes will wear out and need to be replaced. Every time a person's running profile is updated it broadcasts this to their social graph, helping increase Nike brand awareness. In fact, joggers are encouraged to challenge others to virtual races in which their respective performances are tracked via the tracking technology placed in the shoes.

Other stationary spinning and bicycle manufacturers have picked up on the social aspect of exercising and the ability to enable connections via social media technology. Some of these bikes that have built-in monitors with connectivity to the Internet allow Joe in his gym in New York to compete against Suzy in her spa in Santa Fe. Looking at the digital screen, you see real-time avatars of other people cycling across the world and you can virtually pass or be passed by these cyclists.

This also allows for the introduction of celebrity athletes; yes, you could be virtually competing against Lance Armstrong. This is a huge opportunity for advertisers, who can sponsor the Lance avatar or could even sponsor Joe from New York if he became the most proficient within the virtual racing world. Many of the world's top gamers are currently sponsored—they are treated similarly to successful athletes. Some even make a living from professional gaming.

Social Media Is the New Inbox

The "killer" tool of the first part of the Internet boom was e-mail, and then along came e-commerce, e-care, search, music, video, and now social media. E-mail has held on through the years as, arguably, the king of the Internet, used by the old and the young. However, the new Inbox is shifting toward social media.

"I have a 16-year-old cousin, and she listed her favorite websites and applications and failed to mention e-mail, so I asked her about it. I was shocked by the incredulous look on her face and even more shocked at her response that she didn't use e-mail that much since it was too formal; she would rather use instant messaging tools on her phone or post comments based on people's activities in social networks," said Mike Peters, 37, of Detroit, Michigan. It turns out that Generations Y and Z find e-mail antiquated and passé, so they simply ignore it.

While this is shocking to some generations, it fits within the scheme of Socialnomics. E-mail isn't entirely going away; it just may not be the first means of digital communication in a Socialnomic world. Messaging is much easier to manage within social media versus e-mail because it acts like a real conversation amongst friends.

"As a salesperson, I see social networks like LinkedIn and Facebook as invaluable tools. It doesn't necessarily shorten the sales cycle, but what it does is keep the information flow more open and also allows for a much deeper relationship than e-mail. I've started relationships and signed contracts exclusively within social networks. It is revolutionary for sales; it's much easier than telephone calls and e-mails," said Allison Bahm of Response Mine Interactive Agency.

Whereas e-mail functions in a non-fluid manner:

"How are you doing?"
"Fine."

Open conversations within social media have an easier flow to them and replicate a normal conversation. Also, the conversational content is broken down into bite-size chunks and is associated into more easily recognized compartments rather than just a long and daunting slew of 45 e-mails that you need to wade through systematically.

Kids today prefer one-to-many communication; e-mail to them is antiquated.

—*Bill Tancer, General Manager, Global Research, Hitwise*

People are updating their status: "I'm depressed," or "I got a new job," and it is much easier to read this and stay connected than to send a series of e-mails asking how someone is doing or what that person is up to. In a sign of the times ahead and for the first time since e-mail was invented, Boston College will not be giving out e-mail accounts to incoming freshmen for the class of 2013. On the flip side, Seton Hall announced they would be giving out Apple iPads to some of their students for classroom use in 2010.

"At Apple, we generally hire early adopters. That being said, I was still blown away when we recently hired a 22-year-old and he had literally never sent an e-mail. Via his iPhone he had always communicated with his friends either by instant messenger, text, phone call, or comments within Facebook. I believe he is not alone and this is a trend we will continue to see with the next generation," said a director of Apple.

"Are You on Facebook?" Is the New "Can I Get Your Phone Number?"

The most underlying factor for this new inbox may be the seismic shift in the way people exchange information. Let's take a quick look at the evolution of dating over the past 10 years. First, people used to give out their home phone number. Then, people began to give out their e-mail address instead.

At first it seemed odd to ask someone for a date over e-mail, but then it became quite natural. Then we progressed to mobile phone numbers because some people didn't have landlines anymore. Besides, it was easier to text message one another—it was less intrusive and awkward: "What are you doing tonight?"

Today with social media, when people meet, it's common for one of them to ask the other person, "Are you on Vkontakte?" "Are you on Facebook?" or "Tu estas en Orkut?" Just as people use the word Google as a verb—Google it—they are starting to use phrases like "Facebook me or send me a Tweet." People are no longer exchanging e-mails; they are exchanging each other's social media information. In many instances, people wouldn't give out their e-mail for fear of SPAM (broken marketing model). Today, if they desire an e-mail communication stream, social networks have inboxes of their own that replicate and replace e-mail.

Executives are still holding hard and fast to the concept of the traditional inbox. In a survey of 180 Chief Marketing Officers of $1 billion corporations that was conducted by GfK Roper Public Affairs and Media, they found that while 70 percent were decreasing their marketing budgets, the area in which they were least likely to make cuts was e-mail.[1] You can't necessarily blame them for this type of thinking. This has been one of their best performing channels for years, and they've spent money building and managing their databases.

Now and in the future, marketers need to adjust their way of thinking because it's no longer about building out the existing database. Instead, you could be in communication with fans and consumers on someone else's database (Facebook, YouTube, Foursquare, Twitter, etc.). Yet, many companies fail to grasp this new concept. They build elaborate YouTube or Flickr pages, placing callouts and click actions that send the user outside the social site, often to their company website or a lead capture page. These companies still believe they need to get users into their prospecting databases in order to market to them. They are doing a disservice to their loyal fan base and in turn a disservice to themselves.

It's analogous to meeting a pretty girl in a bar and asking if she would like a drink. When she responds "yes," rather than ordering a drink from the bartender, you grab her and rush her into your car and drive her back to your place; because after all, you have beer in your fridge. This is not a sound courtship strategy, nor should companies employ comparable social media strategies in "courting" potential customers. It is best to be patient rather than to rush into things, because without consumer confidence, just like in dating, you have nothing.

Deep Dive into Dating 101

Let's digress back to our dating scenario on social media. Social networks are fantastic for meeting new people and dating. If a girl meets a guy out on the town and they exchange names and connect within a social media network—it's a virtual gold mine of personal data.

The more friends you have in common within a shared social network, the more secure you feel knowing the other person isn't some form of lunatic. Photos are helpful, especially if the night before was a bit wild and a little fuzzy. If you are listed in a network for "Star Trek Fanatics" or "Dracula Oprah," that will be even more telling about who you really are. What you do, who you work for, where you live and have lived, provides additional insight into your personality.

If all checks out fine, that first date is more like a fourth date; you don't have to ask questions like "Where did you go to college?" or "What are your hobbies?" You will still probably ask these questions to show a polite interest or to avoid coming across as a stalker, but it is a completely different dynamic than the world in which Baby Boomers, or even Generation Xers, grew up. Social networks make it easier to stay in touch with someone new before you are at the "Let's grab a drink" stage. It's easier than face-to-face because you avoid awkward silences, you don't have to worry about who is going to pay the bill, and you don't experience potentially embarrassing situations (poppy seed between the teeth anyone?).

Geographically locating mobile tools like Foursquare and Gowalla alert you when people of interest are in your area. Going one step further, some tools recommend locations based on your mood. Instead of listing the top-10 restaurants in the SoHo area of New York, it lists the top-10 romantic restaurants or the top-20 hip, laid-back restaurants; so, if it was your first date, it wouldn't be awkward being at a place with white-glove service and dining by candlelight.

The benefits of these types of relationship-building tools certainly hold true from business to consumer, as well. Businesses capture more information via social media about their consumers than ever before. Good businesses realize that the relationship they have with their consumer still needs to be cultivated (e.g., the grabbing the girl from the bar analogy). Good businesses realize that it's not all about the instant win of getting someone into a database. Rather, it is cultivating that relationship via social media. If it's done correctly, you will have a relationship that lasts a lifetime.

Assess Your Life Every Minute

The examples presented in this section stress a crucial maxim of this book. Social media allows individuals to take real-time inventories of their lives and helps answer the age-old question, "What am I doing with my life?"

Bill Tily, 83, says:

> *I actually made a habit of physically printing out my social media updates from the previous month and going through them one-by-one and highlighting updates that weren't necessarily contributing to a "full" life. Over time, I reduced the amount of "waste" and actually became so cognizant of it during the actual act of updating my status that I'd recognize in that specific moment in time what I would deem an "unfruitful activity" and cease engaging in it immediately. My life is much more fulfilling because of this! I wish these social media tools were around a long time ago!*[2]

Heather, a mother of three, has her own story about how social media is helping her lead a more productive life:

> *I had a close friend who was married without children. One day she confided in me that she didn't know if she was ready for children. She thought she was but then she mentioned something that floored me; the conversation went something like this:*

"Heather, I'm just not sure that I'm up for it. I mean you are probably the most with-it person that I know and it seems like your kids are all that you can handle."

To which I responded, "Yes, having kids is life-changing and presents its new challenges, but it's not as bad as people let on; for every one thing my kids do bad, they do nine things that light up my life."

"Really? That's good news to hear and helps alleviate some of my concerns, but to be blunt, it's also a little surprising given the social media status updates I receive from you."

I was obviously surprised to hear this revelation from one of my closest friends, and I didn't think it had much validity. So, later that day, I wanted to prove it was unwarranted. I pulled up the last several weeks of updates, which didn't take me too long since I only did one or two updates per day. There it was staring back at me in black and white; my friend was exactly right! While my kids were the greatest joy in my life, you would never know it from reading my updates. My kids provided 90 percent of all the new wonders and happiness in my life, yet I was conveying the exact opposite in my status updates. For every one positive status update about my kids, "Lilly gives the best hugs" or "I posted Will's beautiful finger painting on the fridge," I'd post nine negative ones, "Have a massive headache from the kids nonstop screaming" or "Not sure I can handle a full day at the zoo with the kids again."

The reality of the situation shocked me, and I was afraid that there was a possibility that I was also projecting this negative attitude onto the kids. The answer to this came sooner than expected. For the next few weeks, I made a concerted effort not to post anything remotely negative on the social media platforms I used. Or at least [to] have it reflect my reality, nine positive posts for every single negative post. Then one day, about two weeks into practicing this experience, it really hit home when my four-year-old tugged at my shirt and looked up at me with her big blue eyes and said, "Mommy, you seem a lot more happy, and I really like it."[3]

Updating your status or microblogging about what you are doing are immediate reminders of exactly that! And, if you pause, like Bill, and look back over a day, week, or month of what you posted, it is extremely enlightening because it shows you how you are spending what precious time you have.

Millennials—All about Giving Back

In 2008, Millennials (Generation Y) showed up in record numbers to vote. In comparison, jaded Generation Xers never stepped out to vote when they were in their early 20s, despite all the Rock the Vote hoopla on MTV at the time.[4]

In 2008, the most popular Facebook application wasn't a fancy game, music, or TV show. It was an application called "Causes," with almost 20 million active monthly users.[5] The application was quite simple in its description: Causes lets you start and join the causes you care about. Donations to Causes can benefit over a million registered nonprofit organizations. Not surprisingly, this was a far cry from the 1980s' "Me Generation." Recall that one of the popular songs of that era was Madonna's "Material Girl."

Generation Y is a byproduct of the 1980s, and after witnessing the horror that can be caused by narcissistic behavior, they want to do everything in their power to correct it. They don't want their kids to grow up as latchkey kids. The social community aspect simply doesn't stop at discussing the hottest young pop star. No, Generation Y has a strong sense for making the world a better place.

While the majority of this book stresses the many positive aspects of social media, we'd be misleading if we didn't highlight the potentially negative aspects as well. One trend we are starting to see is Generation Y and Z's difficulty with face-to-face interactions.

The Next Generation Can't Speak

The desire and ability to meet new people has rapidly eroded so much that humans fear public speaking more than death. This led comedian Jerry Seinfeld to quip, "According to surveys on what we fear . . . you are telling me that at a funeral, most people would rather be the guy in the coffin than have to stand up and give the eulogy?"[6]

Difficult and awkward subjects are much easier to deal with when hiding behind instant messaging or social media tools than when confronting them face-to-face.

And even written skills have eroded from living in a 140-character world.

A study by the nonprofit group that administers the SAT and other placement tests (National Commission on Writing at the College Board) found:

- 50 percent of teens surveyed say they sometimes fail to use proper capitalization and punctuation in assignments.
- 38 percent have carried over IM shortcuts such as LOL or U.
- 25 percent of teens have used :) and other emoticons.
- 64 percent have used at least one of the informational elements in school.[7]

So yes, there are downsides to not having as much face-to-face interaction and that's a challenge these two generations and future generations face because technology is an intrinsic part of their lives, but the positive aspects are plentiful.

They have an understanding of their place in the global community and are more creative and collaborative. They don't mind challenging the status quo—which is much different than simply not respecting it. They expect a better work-life balance, are better at prioritization, and are adroit at multitasking. On the flip side, these generations need more guidance in management skills, project planning, and business communication.

They are also less likely to understand boundaries, whether that is answering e-mail from a friend during business hours or taking e-mail from a manager at 11 P.M. To them, things are just more fluid; it's not a 9-to-5 world, it's a 24/7 world, and it's up to the individual to properly balance the hours in the day. Generation Xers and Yers think it's laughable that a company would block Facebook or YouTube during work hours—you are either getting the job done or you are not getting the job done. Aside from that, these blockers aren't very effective since most can access what they need via their mobile phones. Workers realize that if they play during the workweek they will have to work on Saturday to complete the necessary tasks. But that is a conscious decision they make.

Let Kids Take Ownership of Your Brand

The "Young Adults Revealed" global survey conducted by Synovate in partnership with Microsoft was designed to find out how much young adults interact and engage online with brands on a daily basis. The research included 12,603 people 18 to 24 years old from 26 countries. The survey revealed that 28 percent say they talked about a brand on a discussion forum, 23 percent added brand-related content to their IM service, and 19 percent added branded content to their home page or favorite social sites.[8]

The research concluded that young adults are more than willing to add brand content to their instant messenger services, Web home pages, and social networking sites. The researchers found that respondents spent an average of 2.5 hours online daily in nonworking-related activity. Synovate's global manager of syndicated research, Julian Rolfe, indicates:

> *The research shows that young people are not only comfortable with the idea of branded content and branded entertainment, but also reveals they are openly willing and eager to engage online with brands.*

> *They clearly feel their opinions about brands are important, they want to associate themselves with brands they see as "cool" and this is why we see them uploading clips to their social networking sites and IM services.*[9]

Synovate found that one in ten said they passed along viral ads and marketing clips.[10] For brand marketers, this should be welcome news. Your consumer wants to have a relationship with you and even help out where they can. All it takes is honesty, transparency, listening, and reacting. Because not every company can do these well, the ones that do will win decisively.

Kids Ages 2 to 17 Don't See Advertisements

A 2008 Nielsen study found that kids ages 2 to 11 endure the least amount of advertisements on the Internet. The group experiencing the second lowest ad exposure is the next age group in succession (12 to 17). The amount of ads someone was exposed to was somewhat correlated with age; the 65 and older demographic sees the most ads.[11]

This speaks to the infancy of social media, because this is where a lot of teens spend the majority of their time. It also speaks to the fact that social media companies realize that they shouldn't "force fit" an old advertising model into a completely new and different space; insert square peg into round hole here. The limited ad exposure of kids under 12 years of age is due in part to protection laws coupled with the fact that many of the more popular kids' sites (e.g., Webkinz) carry few, if any, advertisements.

The upside to this as a marketer is that if you are able to integrate your content (note we say content rather than advertising), then it will have a better chance to stand out since there is less clutter.

Turning Lemons into Lemonade with Fizzle

A salient example of companies less steered by their legal departments is the Diet Coke and Mentos experiment. This started with two scientists experimenting in a laboratory one day and discovering that if you dropped five Mentos (chewable gum-like candy with a hard outer shell) into Diet Coke, a fairly volatile chemical reaction would ensue. They perfected these geysers and determined that five Mentos on a fishing line dropped into a two-liter bottle of Diet Coke with the cap on and a tiny hole at the top would result in the most dramatic effect.

Since it was so visual and dynamic, YouTube was the perfect platform to make it globally famous. Before the existence of a social media site like YouTube, only a select few in the science community would have known about it. In the past, the Coca-Cola Company could possibly have handled this quietly behind closed doors; however, in today's world with the heightened social media exposure, Coke was forced to deal with the situation. Let's look at how they handled it.

In the past, Coke would have been alarmed by this discovery, and rightfully so. There was the potential that the public would jump to the incorrect assumption that Coke must be highly toxic and it would be undesirable to have this type of reaction going on in the stomach. *If shaking up a bottle of Diet Coke and Mentos can create a 20-foot geyser, imagine the havoc it would cause in my stomach!* The end result would have most likely been a long court battle by the Coca-Cola Company to discredit and shut these activities down.

The transparency and rapid distribution of information enabled by social media (Blogs, Twitter, YouTube, etc.) doesn't allow for events and news to be handled discreetly anymore. Equally important for Coke to consider was the reaction by the competition (e.g., Pepsi).

The scientists, Fritz Grobe (the short one) and Stephen Voltz (the tall one), through their testing, discovered that the best results came from using Diet Coke. Sprite, Diet Pepsi, Coke Classic, and Dr. Pepper didn't produce the same dramatic effect with Mentos. While it wasn't as dramatic an effect, these other sodas still produced a spectacular result.

Hence, a window was open for Pepsi to do something if Coke didn't (the mindset that if you don't do something, someone else will). Pepsi could have shown that their products didn't have the same explosive reaction and compared themselves side-by-side with Coke using a proactive question of "Which would you rather have in your kids' stomach?"

Weighing these factors, as well as other World of Mouth ramifications, Coke decided to embrace the exposure of this experiment and actually hired Grobe and Voltz as spokesmen. They, in turn, went on to do a much more elaborate video on YouTube that won Coke many marketing awards and has resulted to date in over 11 million views on YouTube. The transparency and exposure of social media is having the positive effect of companies starting to embrace items that they historically would have either ignored (in hopes they'd go away) or shunned for fear of legal liability or consumer backlash.

If a company or individual has something to brag about now or in the future, we will see that they are going to let the world know through every social media tool available. The great thing is that if someone or some company doesn't have anything to brag about, then they will presumably alter their behavior (e.g., watching TV) to something more interesting (e.g., writing a screenplay), which in turn has them contributing more and more to improving society as a whole.

Chapter Three Key Points

1. Social media allows individuals to take real-time inventories of their lives and helps answer the age-old question, "What am I doing with my life?" This benefits society because it encourages more people to engage in productive or charitable activities.
2. Reality TV has been replaced by reality social media—it's all about *my* friends and *my* reality.
3. Social media is the new inbox: Younger generations find e-mail antiquated and passé.
4. The interpersonal communication skills of Generations Y and Z have been retarded by reliance on social media tools that aren't face-to-face or verbal.
5. Generations Y and Z have a desire to contribute to the greater world around them and leverage social media for social and charitable causes.
6. Consumers want to take ownership of your brand and brag about your product; let them!

CHAPTER FOUR

Obama's Success Driven by Social Media

John F. Kennedy was helped into the White House by the increasing popularity of a new medium, television. The same can be said about Barack Obama. He was also greatly helped by a new medium, but rather than television, it was social media. Within minutes of Colin Powell's endorsement of Obama on October 19, 2008, it was posted on the Web. As mentioned throughout this book, this presidential election quickly forced traditional broadcasters on ABC, NBC, CBS, and so on to adjust how they covered election news; otherwise, people would find content elsewhere (YouTube, Wikipedia, blogs, podcasts, etc.). After Powell's endorsement on NBC's *Meet the Press,* NBC had the announcement ready to go on its sister property, msnbc.com.

NBC was also wise enough to post the video to the Web before the West Coast was able to see the interview on traditional television. It is essential that traditional broadcasters embrace Socialnomics; otherwise, they can quickly become less relevant. People use several media sources in combination to formulate an opinion—not just one source. Networks that recognize this and attempt to work effectively with the new forms of social media will survive.

"We should be careful of these zero-sum games where the new media drives out the old," said Andrew Heyward, a former president of CBS News who consults for the Monitor Group. "I think what we see is growing sophistication about making the channels work together effectively."[1]

Perhaps due to his widespread appeal to younger audiences, but more likely due to limited funding at the outset of his campaign, Obama embraced social media from the beginning—knowing that he had a chance to dominate this medium over his Democratic opponents. Attempting to dominate traditional media (newspapers, television, radio) would have been a tactical error against his well-known opponent, Hillary Clinton, and more important, the Clinton Political Machine. Because of the hard-fought battle with Hillary, Obama was well positioned from a social media perspective when he won the Democratic nomination and entered the presidential race.

His followers and supporters from a social media perspective, weren't going away, rather they were growing substantially and contributing in record sums—with $5 and $10 donations quickly adding up to a multimillion-dollar arsenal. Obama raised a record amount of money and 92 percent of his donations were in sums of less than $100.

By the time Obama was elected, he had over 3.1 million fans on his Facebook fan page. This number didn't include the various other fan pages and groups like "Students for Obama," "Pride for Obama," "Michelle Obama," "Florida for Obama," "Michigan for Obama," "Pennsylvania for Obama," "Women for Obama," and so on. If you added only the next top-20 groups, Obama would have an additional 2 million supporters. This is in stark contrast to John McCain who had 614,000 supporters for his fan page the day of the election and whose next largest fan page was for his wife Cindy with only 1,700 fans.

That's 5.1 million (Obama) to less than 1 million (McCain). On MySpace, Obama had 833,161 friends to McCain's 217,811, and this type of disparity held true on Twitter where Obama attracted 113,000 followers to McCain's 4,650.[2]

Obama Was Made for YouTube

Looking to YouTube, the disparity was even greater as the election neared. The BarackObamadotcom YouTube channel had over 20 million views, whereas the johnmccaindotcom channel had just over 2 million views.[3] A year and a half prior to the election, a young and attractive girl released the "I have a crush on Barack Obama video." This girl (Amber Lee Ettinger) would later be nicknamed "Obama Girl" and appear on many national television shows and be included in *Playboy* magazine.

This was prior to "Obamamania" sweeping the country; in fact, it was items like this that helped fuel it. This video was viewed 11.5 million times in the months leading up to the election.[4] In McCain's defense, his voting base skewed older, and they didn't use these types of tools so prevalently at the time, which meant a huge advantage for Obama. Obama used social media to his advantage in both the Democratic and National race to become the president of the United States.

This leveraging of peer-to-peer communication helped mitigate the violent swings that can be caused by traditional media and is one significant reason why Obama was able to overcome some controversial issues (e.g., Reverend Jeremiah Wright, William Ayers) during his campaign for the oval office.

"No one knows the impact of quasi-permanency on the Web yet, but it surely has changed the political world," said Allan Louden, a professor who teaches a course on digital politics at Wake Forest University. "The role of gatekeepers and archivists have been dispersed to everyone with Internet access."[5]

Obama Sings in the Shower—Behind-the-Scenes Content

Obama's team was also creative by providing their own original footage of events that the networks covet—behind-the-scenes moments. They were able to splice these together with decent, yet not too high-end, production quality. Even if they had the money, you wouldn't necessarily want top-level editing because that destroys the authenticity of the organic ambiance you are attempting to create and, more importantly, can increase the lag time to get the content in the hands of the socialmediorati (term for active social media users). Viewers are interested in timely information they can relate to—spending time and money on high-end production can often create distance between candidate and viewer. Viewers are interested in how a person acts when the lights of Hollywood aren't on—how does the candidate interact with his family and those closest to him on a day-to-day basis? That's why we see millions following Ashton Kutcher, Ellen DeGeneres, and Shaq on Twitter.

Social media user Lance Muller of Decatur, Georgia quipped, "I have been an Obama friend since his speech at the 2004 Democratic Convention. In social media, he actually virtually "pokes" me and sends memos and stuff. I don't know if it is really him, but it makes you feel more in touch with the process. His team is smart in utilizing social networks to reach people like me so that I feel connected personally."[6]

Knowing that social media users rely on the general freedom afforded by the Web, the Obama camp was smart in appealing to their base by introducing a Chief Technology Officer (CTO) position to the president's cabinet; which was dependent on an Obama victory. Aneesh Chopra became the first CTO of the United States on August 7, 2009. The main role of the CTO is to "ensure that our government and all its agencies have the right infrastructure, policies, and services for the twenty-first century."[7]

As we will discuss throughout this book, advertisers need to become providers of content. Obama's campaign did just that when they placed ads pushing an early voting message in EA video games, most prominently in a racing game called "Burnout Paradise." These games are socially interactive, with kids being able to compete with each other around the globe. Obama's objective for this particular campaign targeted players in ten battleground states. The key to this form of advertising is that it benefits the player of the game. The game appears more real-time with seamless and wireless updates to allow for such real-time product placement—in this case, the product placement was Obama with the specific message of early voting.

When you look at total views for Obama via YouTube, they accounted for 110 million views. This was estimated at 14.5 million hours of viewing on YouTube, according to Democratic political consultant Joe Trippi. He estimated that amount of time would have cost $47 million to purchase in commercial time.[8]

"If not for the Internet, Barack Obama would not be president or even the democratic nominee," claimed Arianna Huffington of the liberal Huffington Post website.[9] Overall blog mentions of "Obama" and "McCain" varied greatly during the election (and we can't delineate positive versus negative posts); close to 500 million blog postings mentioned Obama since the beginning of the conventions. During the same time period, only about 150 million blog posts mentioned McCain.[10]

Obama's almost micropayment style approach to raising funds allowed him to outspend McCain nearly three-to-one, which was a testament to the capabilities of social media. By engaging constituents directly, they were able to raise a staggering $660 million in campaign contributions.[11]

Close to 65 percent of the American population voted in the 2008 election, the highest turnout since the election of 1908.[12] These results are telling: a Democrat had not won Virginia and Indiana since then, either. Obama captured both.

Support came from everywhere for Obama during his historic and meteoric political run. Some help came from unexpected places. The famous Budweiser "Whassup" commercials, which debuted in 1999, immediately helped sell millions of Bud Lights. The ad became a part of U.S. pop culture following its exposure during the 2000 Super Bowl. Could this same whassup idea be resurrected to help Obama's cause for change? You bet.

The parody used the same characters from the original spots and opened in the exact same fashion, but instead of a guy comfortably relaxing on a couch, he was sitting on a foldout chair in a boxed-up apartment as a subtle hint at the housing crisis that was sweeping the country in 2008.

From there, the spoof segued into a series of whassup conversations in conference call fashion. The characters ranged from one friend stationed in Iraq, another fighting a hurricane, someone looking for help to pay for pain medication because of a broken arm, and the star of the original commercials, "Dookie," stealing the show again as he contemplates hanging himself after seeing his entire stock portfolio go essentially down to zero. Dookie, being overweight, pulls the entire ceiling fan down; hence, it keeps its original light tone while at the same time connects with the audience and sends a strong message. At the end of the video one of the characters asks again, "Whassup?" And the main character replies, "Change. Change, that's whassup," from his boxed-up apartment as he watches TV images of Senator Obama and his wife.

"It's a great juxtaposition of the original ads. It shows how the lives of these characters have dramatically changed in the past eight years—going from carefree and relaxed beer buddies to being confronted by a shift in global dynamics, an economic collapse, and all in all an unbelievable amount of personal challenge and difficulty. Being able to identify with the characters is what makes this video so strong, and they never once say or state Obama's name, rather it's a subtle glimpse of Barack and Michelle Obama on the television that the main character is watching at the end of the spot with a huge smile on this face. The short video ending with the word 'Change,' just like in the 1999 commercials that were followed by the word 'True,' was both powerful and brilliant," said author and political campaign expert Brian Reich.[13]

Reich was a key member of the Howard Dean interactive team largely recognized as the originators of many of the political Internet tactics that Obama successfully leveraged.

Charles Stone III, who was the idea man behind the original Budweiser ads, created this satire. The ad was posted on October 24, 2008, on YouTube a little over a week prior to the election, and received over 4.8 million views along with 14,891 user comments. Also, 21,746 viewers took the time to rate the video and it received the difficult-to-achieve 5-star rating.[14]

Stone was paid roughly $37,000 by Anheuser-Busch and Omnicom Group's DDB Chicago for the rights to license the concept for five years. Stone had originally created a "whassup" film that had caught Omnicom's attention. The fact that neither Anheuser-Busch nor their agency owned the rights to the concept is unusual in the advertising business, but in this instance, it allowed Stone to make his popular and effective parody. Stone appears in both the original and satire ads with his friends—who also happen to be African American. Stone felt that he could use the same concept to "make a difference" for a politician he believes in.[15]

In this instance, the brand is Obama. The Obama camp could have asked Stone to remove the video out of concern that the "hanging scene" and "soldier in Iraq" may have pushed the line too far. A traditional brand would have probably stopped this and diluted its viral power. Obama did not do this; instead, he allowed someone (Stone) outside of his camp to take ownership of the brand and promote it. As a result, he exposed his message to 4.8 million people right before the election without spending one penny or lifting one finger. That is the power of social media for brands.

However, it's important to not underestimate the potential bumps in the road when your supporters are a little too aggressive with your brand. This was the case with another video that was in support of Obama. This one was aptly named "Politics as Usual" and was produced by famous hip-hop artist Ludacris. One of the lines was "Obama would paint the White House black." This was tame in comparison to dismissing Hillary Clinton as a potential vice presidential running mate—"that bitch is irrelevant." Attacking the Republicans, Ludacris stated that John McCain should only be able to sit in the "big chair" if he is paralyzed. Prior to the election, this rap video received over a million views on YouTube.[16]

It was a tough spot for Obama to be in because he still wanted the support of the influential hip-hop community, but he also needed to avoid the controversy that these lyrics stirred. In the end he took corrective action, quickly and publicly denouncing it, calling the music video "outrageously offensive."

"While Ludacris is a talented individual, he should be ashamed of these lyrics," Obama campaign spokesman Bill Burton said in an e-mail statement.

"Of course, Obama and his people have to condemn the rap, because it does say some vulgar things. If you're running for president, you're supposed to be an upstanding individual," said John McWhorter, author of *All About the Beat: Why Hip-Hop Can't Save Black America.*[17] Many companies and politicians make the mistake of stopping there, but Obama went the extra mile to have a private meeting with the rap star. Rapper Ludacris said Barack Obama disapproved of the song he wrote because it insulted his rivals.

"The song was my artistic expression and was meant to get people who weren't involved in the political process involved. Being as though it was the first mix tape to reach the United States government, it was a bit overwhelming," said Ludacris. He indicated that when he met with Obama, they didn't just discuss the song. "What myself and the president spoke about is confidential, but I took it upon myself to not speak about the song."[18] By acting quickly and decisively, Obama was able to turn a negative into a positive, for he kept the support of Ludacris' fan base while distancing himself from the controversial content.

Can Google Predict the Next President or Flu Outbreak?

In the early part of this century, Yahoo! started to leverage the search data that was flowing into its data centers. At the time, Yahoo! was the world's preeminent search engine. They were noticing that they could predict some pop-culture trends, often six weeks in advance. They actually leveraged this data for one of their biggest advertising clients at the time, Pepsi-Cola. They identified through their buzz index that searches for an up-and-coming pop star by the name of Britney Spears were indexing high and rising rapidly. As a perk to their important client, Yahoo! disclosed this information, and Pepsi seized the opportunity. With little investment, Pepsi was able to sign Spears to a relatively cheap endorsement contract a few months before she became one of the music industry's biggest and brightest stars.

Fast forward to the present. Because of the transparency that social media demands, search engines don't hold this data hostage anymore. Much of the search data is open for public consumption. While the data is in aggregate (meaning privacy policies are upheld since you can't identify an individual) and the data isn't absolute (meaning there are indexes rather than the actual number of searches—otherwise financial analysts could extrapolate data to predict quarterly financial performance for the search engines), it is very helpful for many reasons.

Is the Flu a Virus or Just Simply Viral?

It appears that people make the habit of entering phrases like "flu symptoms" or "flu remedies" into search engines prior to actually going in for a doctor's visit. When you multiply this across millions of searches around the globe, you have something like a neighborhood watch for fast-spreading flu outbreaks.

Google flu trends is a service provided by the company's philanthropic arm (Google.org), released to do just exactly that. Historically, the Centers for Disease Control (CDC) based in Atlanta, Georgia, was the only source for tracking spikes in viruses like the flu. Comparing the CDC data to Google's data showed that Google's insight was roughly two weeks ahead of the CDC. The CDC data is inherently slow as a result of its dependence on data being supplied and analyzed from thousands of sources (e.g., doctors, labs, health insurance).

Search and social data is powerful stuff that can help stifle the spread of disease and ultimately save lives. Google is able to combine flu search data with their robust mapping tools to quickly showcase where the disease is spreading across the world. The potential doesn't stop at influenza, but can be used for all forms of disease and outbreak. The CDC data and other data can also be combined with search data to make it even more accurate. "Most forecasting is basically trend extrapolation," said Hal Varian, Google's chief economist. "This works remarkably well, but tends to miss turning points, times when the data changes direction. Our hope is that Google data might help with this problem."[19] The key is that the data has always existed and in some instances was being used (e.g., Pepsi and Britney

Spears), but Socialnomics has been a main driver behind it being shared for such beneficial causes.

In 2009, Prabhakar Raghavan, the head of Yahoo! Labs said search data could be valuable for forecasters and scientists, but privacy concerns had generally stopped Yahoo! Labs from sharing it with outside academics. "I think we are just scratching the surface of what's possible with collective intelligence,"[20] said Thomas W. Malone, a professor at the Sloan School of Management at MIT. For business and politics it is very intriguing: Do more people search: "cheap travel" or "travel"? "Coke" or "Pepsi"? "Obama" or "McCain"?

This last one was particularly intriguing. Could search data help predict the next president of the United States?

Indiana Goes Google Gaga for Obama

We compared U.S. search trends in April 2008 for the terms "Clinton," "McCain," and "Obama." Total searches for Obama far exceeded those of Clinton. For every Clinton search, there were 1.60 Obama searches. Yet, for every Clinton search, there were only 0.48 McCain searches.[21]

This makes sense, given the Democrats' heated primary. What's interesting is that Obama had so many more searches than Clinton. Keep in mind that Clinton is artificially inflated by the fact that it contains searches having nothing to do with Hillary (e.g., people looking for Bill, Clinton Township). Obama is a unique term, so it has less statistical noise. Also, the data doesn't factor in searches done for "Barack." So, Obama's 1.60:1 ratio was most likely even higher than the numbers indicated. It's important to note here that if you are launching a new product or brand, the more unique the name, the easier it is to crawl and collect data digitally. For example, Puma (shoes, jungle cat, purse, older female, etc.) has a much more difficult time crawling for data than adidas.

Google Insights data also pointed out that in April of 2008, searches for Obama in the state of Indiana greatly exceeded those of Clinton. It would've been easy to predict that Obama was closing the gap on Hillary in that state. After all, if the voters had already decided to vote for Hillary, there wouldn't be a need to search for information on Obama. Obama was supposed to lose handily in Indiana; but just as the data predicted, he closed the gap, narrowly lost the state, but was well on his way to achieving the nomination afterward.

Canada Cared the Most about the Next U.S. President

Data from Google Insights also gave a strong indication that Obama would defeat John McCain in the presidential election. Thirty days prior to the election, Obama searches outperformed McCain almost 3:1 even though McCain had gained 11 percent in search volume over the same time period. Predictably, U.S. allies (Canada, United Kingdom, etc.) seemed the most interested in the election, judging by their search behavior. Global searches indexed even higher for Obama over McCain by a 4:1 ratio, indicating that the world was also ready for a change. In the United States, not surprisingly, most searches for Obama and McCain came from those living in Washington, DC, and the same held true for college towns Austin, Texas, and Raleigh, North Carolina, which indexed within the top 10, primarily due to the younger voters being so involved in this election.[22]

McCain and Obama each tried to build up their respective *brands* in the eyes of voters. They used search data to answer questions such as: Is it better to print "Obama" or "Barack" on promotional posters. There were 3.5 more searches done on "Obama" than "Barack."[23] Pretty helpful information.

Just like in the political race, search data can also be used in the world of business to help guide companies in making strategic decisions. Should Coke use the term "soda pop" or "soda" to describe the products on its website? What regions in the world search for "Coke" more than "Pepsi"? In future decisions, such search data will be used more and more by all constituents.

Even more than search, social media tools like Twitter are becoming extremely instrumental in predicting trends from flu outbreaks to the spread of natural disasters like forest fires. In one celebrated case in March of 2010, celebrity Demi Moore's Twitter account played a vital role in stopping a teen from committing suicide. Moore's alias on Twitter is @mrskutcher and one man posted his intent to commit suicide. When Moore asked if he was serious and the reply was yes, another celebrity, Nia Vardalos (*My Big Fat Greek Wedding*) saw the post and called the Florida Police and the Suicide Prevention Hotline. Vardalos stayed on the phone with the police until she knew the man was okay and was taken to the hospital. Hundreds of others also tweeted their support.

Fireside Chats and Presidential Texts

In a text message sent to supporters on the eve of the election, Obama reaffirmed that they would be part of the presidency: "We have a lot of work to do to get our country back on track, and I'll be in touch soon about what comes next."

Obama was diligent in not abandoning social media once he took over as president. He realized that the people who elected him to office wanted to stay connected, and he also knew this would be key to success while in office. Just as users are willing to take ownership of brands when given the chance, if they believe it is their government and not Obama's, then there really is a true chance for change; change comes from within, not externally.

Social media allows for this two-way conversation. The U.S. president, for the first time, can cultivate grassroots communities directly, where people discover, create, and share information online. Obama has pledged to involve Americans in his decision-making, by giving them five days to comment online on any non-emergency legislation before he signs it. Whether he delivers on this promise remains to be seen.

To help with this conversation, Obama has resurrected the principles of FDR's fireside radio chats; only this time, the chats will be on YouTube or other online video format, which allows for commentary, posts, rebuttals, and ongoing dialog. His cabinet members are committed to having their own chats as well. The goal is to make the political process more transparent and give an identity to the White House. This is exactly the same strategy that good brands employ; transparency and having people connect and identify with the brand because the brand helps define them. Good companies put customers' needs first and foremost.

Whether you're a Republican, Democrat, Independent, or member of the Bull Moose Party, you can't deny the power of real-world community relations combined with the reach and engagement of online social communities and networks to change politics as usual. It's important to note that this isn't about using the latest shiny new toy out there. The key resides in the ability to identify and internalize issues that help precipitate change. Action earns support, not merely words.

As addressed in our preventative and braggadocian behavior sections of this book, it is important for the president to be transparent by showing the behind-the-scenes inner workings of the White House without sacrificing national security. It is irrelevant whether you like the transparent demands of social media or not; the fact is that society has drastically changed as a result of social media—this isn't just a nice perk for the president to use, it is something the public now demands.

This is an opportunity for government to meet demands by using new and influential channels to address voters' needs and win people over, one citizen at a time.

The office of the president will never be able to satisfy everyone, but if social media is utilized correctly, it will supply the ideas, insights, support, concerns, and satisfaction of the American public. It allows for a government to be more in tune with the country and to truly run as a democracy by stripping away the politics and getting to the core of what matters. Sometimes the best advisors are those who voted against the elected in the first place. Mr. Obama offered this message to his supporters during his closing arguments at a Democratic campaign rally in Canton, Ohio:

> *I ask you to believe—not just in my ability to bring about change, but in yours. I know this change is possible . . . because in this campaign, I have had the privilege to witness what is best in America. The story of the campaign and this historic moment has been your story. It is about the great things we can do when we come together around a common purpose. The story of bringing this country together as a healed and united nation will be led by President-Elect Obama, but written by you. The millions of you who built this campaign from the ground up, and echoed your call for the change you wanted to see implemented by the Obama Administration—this process of setting up that new government is about you.*[24]

In 2008, the Gartner Group hypothesized that social media would complement and even replace some functions of the government. For some people, this may seem laughable, but isn't that what the U.S. government is supposed to be about—a government of the people, for the people, and by the people? This will become even more prevalent with Obama's successors, whether they are Republican, Democrat, or Independent. As the 2008 presidential campaign's reliance on social media to persuade voters indicates, this will become an integral part of every candidate's campaign in the years to come, particularly considering that this election's online campaigns will be scrutinized more than any before. "There's going to be a lot of analysis of the campaign online this time around," Borrell's VP of Research Kip Cassino told ClickZ News. "This is absolutely a groundbreaking election for digital marketing and the candidates, and it's not just the money involved. It's the techniques that were developed and the knowledge that was gained."[25]

Is the White House More BlackBerry or Mayberry?

Of course, everything wasn't all roses for Obama and his pioneering ways. Days after the election, a decision had to be made on whether Obama could keep his BlackBerry, something that he, like many others, had become dependent on in his daily life. In fact, in one White House meeting, everyone was asked to put their BlackBerry in the middle of the table to ensure each person was paying attention. This was something new for Washington, but not for businesses where the device's addictive ways has earned an apt nickname—*crackberry*.

The reason for the discussion about whether Obama would need to relinquish his BlackBerry did not center on overuse. Rather, it revolved around the fact that his text messaging, tweets, status updates, and e-mails would be a part of public record. When George Bush entered the White House, he had to give up his AOL account (G94B@aol.com) for this exact reason. So, Obama's friendly joshing and side-kick conversations with his friends about the latest Bears playoff game would be public record. However, relating back to our discussion on preventative and braggadocian behavior, has Obama been around social media long enough to have established the correct behavior and fail-safes associated with it?

Perhaps so, which then allows for the use of such devices as a BlackBerry to transform information into an asset. Rick Sanchez of CNN used Twitter to grow his user base. He raised his CNN program to number three in the ratings, behind only Fox News's *O'Reilly Factor* and MSNBC's *Keith Olbermann's Countdown*. Because of Sanchez's success, viewers' microblog posts became a part of almost every CNN broadcast.

Does a president's transparency become an enormous asset? Can he go from one million followers on Twitter to 100 million? As president of the United States, his public record may be quite different from that of Joe the Plumber's, but the reasons for utilizing it are the same—to openly communicate with many. People are using these mechanisms as a public record. There are no secrets; we are living in a world of glass houses. That is why Obama is the first president to keep his BlackBerry or have the first presidential laptop computer. We know the positive impact of these tools, and one of the most powerful people in the world should still have the option to use them.

To Sarah Palin's credit, she seemed to be practicing correct preventative behavior. When her Yahoo! e-mail was hacked, there was not much *dirt* to be found, despite these being private conversations; it was *not* a social media forum. San Francisco Mayor Gavin Newsom agreed that for national politics, the Obama campaign used social media to an unprecedented level. "Now I'm more concerned with what it means when we can use this unfiltered conversation with people. How will it help construct public policy?" he asked.[26]

While Obama benefited enormously from the power of social media, there are still social media detractors. A Facebook group was formed prior to Obama even taking office with several hundred members called "Impeach Barack Obama." Social media has the good, the bad, and the ugly for everyone to see. When it comes to politics, isn't that the true beauty of social media? Its power speaks for itself; before social media, Obama would not have won his own party's nomination, let alone become the 44th president of the United States.

The 2010 oil spill crisis in the Gulf of Mexico also showcased how social media can provide political pressure as well as raise money for a good cause. Some creative minds took out the Twitter account BPGlobalPR and posted such snarky tweets as: "If you find any oil in the Gulf of Mexico please return it because it's ours" and "We don't forbid our workers from wearing respirators because it looks bad in photos, we just want to see their smiling faces." This parody account had over 120,000 followers only weeks after it launched. Greenpeace utilized the social sharing site Flickr to run a BP Parody Logo campaign. One of the better ones submitted by Russ A had an image of the Twitter Fail Wail being lifted out of the Gulf ensconced in oil with the tagline BP Fail. You could order these logos on T-shirts and the campaign helped raise thousands of dollars to aid the Gulf. Most importantly, these social outlets applied political pressure on BP and Obama's cabinet to increase efforts to resolve the issue.

Free Pancakes Anyone?

Starbucks, Ben & Jerry's, and others gave freebies on Election Day—did it work? Remember the free pancake breakfast you used to get as a kid down at the fire station? Of course it wasn't free; your parents would pay a donation to help out the firefighters, but it seemed like it was free, didn't it? Your parents likely donated more than they would have paid at the local Denny's for a Grand Slam breakfast, yet they too felt it was free—probably better than free.

This is the sense of community that human beings long for, and it is something that is strengthened with social media. In fact, it is part of the reason for social media's meteoric ascendancy in our lives. Face-to-face interaction still can't be beat on certain levels, but social media does help you feel as though you are part of a community. Social media can help a national or global item feel intimate. Once again, a good example of this was the 2008 U.S. presidential election; let's take a look

In year's past, there have been many campaigns that attempted to increase voter turnout (e.g., MTV's Rock the Vote) but few have seemed to work. In 2008, voter turnout was predicted to be strong for many reasons, but as a friendly reminder and incentive, several companies gave away freebies on Election Day. Generally, most marketers steer clear of anything political, but in this case the brand marketers wanted to be a part of a community, and the community in this instance, thanks to social media, was the American community.

Some of the more high-profile giveaways included a chicken sandwich from Chick-fil-A, a tall cup of coffee from Starbucks, a free scoop of ice cream from Ben & Jerry's, and a star-shaped doughnut with patriotic sprinkles (i.e., red, white, and blue) from Krispy Kreme. Along with many other factors, these freebies helped drive the highest voter turnout since 1908.[27]

For users to get their freebies they had to show their "I Voted" sticker, but in most cases they could simply say they voted. (After all, isn't community all about trust?) One entity that doesn't believe in trust was the government; it almost rained on this feel-good parade by highlighting a federal law that stipulates you can't give incentives to encourage people to vote. Fortunately, several companies didn't let this hurdle stop them and were able to work within it.

That is another example of the changes we are seeing with the advent of Socialnomics—it's a new way of thinking. In the past, large multi-nationals would have been *shrinking violets* and would have let their well-paid legal counsel pontificate on doomsday scenarios and suck the life out of the marketing and public relations departments until they gave up on the idea.

Today we are seeing less of this, partially due to the intense competition forcing companies to adopt the mantra: *If we don't do this, someone else will.* Part of competition is coming from foreign entities that don't have the same legal requirements as U.S.-based entities. Most of all, though, we are seeing companies and people within companies with the conviction to drive what they believe is best for the company even if it clashes with the opinion of legal counsel. If companies have confidence in what they are doing, then they will overcome the hurdles that formerly may have stopped them.

Contributing to this, in part, is the flexibility and real-time nature of social media. In the past, if Ben & Jerry's was going to promote a free giveaway via the expensive development of television, radio, and print advertising, they would have to think twice about the concerns of the law shutting down their good intentions, because it would be quite costly. However, given that the primary push for the Ben & Jerry's promotion was sending an alert to the followers on their Facebook fan page, there were few upfront costs, and the action of taking down the promotion was roughly only 20 to 30 minutes of work.

The variable cost of how many people actually show up for the freebies remains a factor, but it is the fixed costs of print and production of advertising that causes marketers to think twice about a promotion if there is a chance that it would be shut down for legal reasons. Social media helps mitigate these concerns because the upfront costs are so minimal that if a legal issue shuts down the program at the last minute, so be it. Also, social media allows things to be shut down in a few minutes, and for word to travel just as quickly. In this instance, if Ben & Jerry's needed to shut down, they would simply inform their 285,000 Facebook fans and let them spread the word virally.

As we will constantly reiterate within social media, it's not how cool Ben & Jerry's is that matters. Rather, the concern is whether they can give their loyal fans something to pass on that makes *them* (loyal fans) look cool. "I didn't know about the B&J free ice cream giveaway until my friend Stephen in Texas pushed it my way on Facebook. It was good to know he was thinking about me, and I felt like I owed him a scoop of ice cream," said Kim (Nashville, Tennessee).[28] During the promotion, Ben & Jerry's added over 100,000 fans to their Facebook fan page, resulting in a total of 385,000 fans.[29]

Starbucks promoted their coffee giveaway almost exclusively via social media mechanisms. They ran only one ad on *SNL*, which was primarily viral during the time because of the success of the Tina Fey-Sarah Palin spoofs (more than 50 percent of the views were within social media). They also ran 30 TV spots on Hulu and displayed placements on Facebook. The spots took advantage of the well-known Starbucks recycled paper brown coffee sleeve to animate and script a quick message helping to convey two salient points—we care about the environment and we care about the country. The message was: "What if we cared so much every day about these things?" In a rare instance, it covered off-branding (what Starbucks stands for) and also gave a call to action (come to our store). It is estimated that Starbucks spent less than $400,000 for this promotion, which Oprah quickly paid back by giving it some major coverage on her show, as did every other media outlet (including this book). On YouTube alone, the promotion received 386,000 views.

One measure that tracks this type of viral buzz (the amount of people that are talking or writing about your brand) indicated that Starbucks' buzz increased 26 percent as a result of this effort.[30] Starbucks would not disclose how much coffee was given away, but in some stores it was plenty: one Chicago franchise handed out 300 steaming cups of java and goodwill.[31] Facebook users also started downloading the application "Which Drink Is Meant for You?" resulting in almost 100,000 active monthly users, driving the Starbucks fan page to nearly 200,000 fans.[32] In order for companies to truly benefit from social media, they have to become part of the community. Is your company serving up fresh pancakes or stale messaging?

Social Media Creates and Solves the Problem of Long Voting Lines

To help assuage concerns about long lines due to record voter turnout, a Twitter Vote Report was established. Voters who were at the polls could use the microblogging tool to help supply real-time data on polling conditions. These messages and alerts were aggregated and applied to a Google Mapping tool so that people could see any voting issues in their area in the hopes of avoiding crowds and hassles. It was very simple to send in reports using your mobile device:

#wait:90 = Wait time is 90 minutes
#machine:30 = Wait time is 30 minutes due to machine issues

Users who didn't use Twitter could also send text messages to #voterreport, to 66, or could call an automated hotline. Hashtags or # are very convenient when using microblogging tools or text messaging, as they allow items to be easily tagged and categorized—which has been a dramatic part of the social media revolution. Convenient items like this contributed to the 2008 election having the highest voter turnout in 100 years.[33] Higher voter turnout is, therefore, one positive influence that social media has had on society. Moving forward, mobile geo-location tools like Foursquare, Gowalla, and Google Latitude will make it even easier to share this type of information.

Online Voting—The Future Is Now

If the political use of social media accelerates in the future, what new and exciting tactics can we expect? One thing that is surely inevitable is the introduction of online voting. Having the capability to easily cast votes via online mechanisms makes too much sense for it not to become a reality. For those who have always screamed that online voting is less secure than offline voting, you possibly do not understand the current offline process to obtain an absentee ballot. Let me explain.

For the 2008 presidential election, for the state of Florida, which one could argue should have the tightest system after the difficulties the state experienced in the 2000 election, the offline security was less than tight. For example, prospective voters were required to know their: (1) birth date and (2) address number—not the entire address, just the mailbox number! If you had these two relatively easy-to-access pieces of information, the state of Florida was happy to send you an absentee ballot to any address that you specified.

If you were a legitimate absentee voter and dutifully filled out your form, you proceeded to drop it in the mail. The outside of the envelope boldly proclaims ABSENTEE BALLOT, and it also bears your authorized signature. Anywhere along the way this ballot could be conveniently lost or stolen by numerous people. That doesn't sound nearly as secure as an online process that has point-to-point encryption, with only those two points having the proper access key.

This is analogous to when the Internet was first introduced to the masses as a place of commerce, aptly named e-commerce. It's hard to believe now, but at the time people were afraid to give out their credit card numbers online because of the false belief that it was unsafe to do so. Yet, these same people had no problem giving it to some random clerk along with their signature at the local convenience store. For now, let's assume that great minds are able to solve the major security holes in online voting (they will). Imagine the tremendous increase in voter participation when this occurs. In a SodaHead study, 79 percent of the respondents said they wouldn't wait an hour to vote during the 2008 presidential election.[34]

People can argue that not everyone has a computer or mobile device that can access the Web. While this is true, there are more people who have the ability to access the Web than have voting machines in their homes. Those who don't have access to the Web can go to their local library or voting station just as they have done in the past. The cost savings associated with no longer dealing with paper, staffing, parking, administration, voting machines, police protection, and so on would be significant. The increase in productivity would also be mind-boggling.

Assuming the U.S. population is approximately 310 million, and according to the latest U.S. census bureau data, 68 percent are of voting age, this equates to 210 million possible voters.[35] If the average hourly wage (factoring in white collar) is close to $16, and keeping in mind that the physical act of voting takes a rough estimate (very rough) of two hours (including drive time), the summation is startling. This is $6.7 billion in lost productivity (210 million × $16 per hour × 2 hours)! All that could be saved by a few simple clicks online.

The harder decisions aren't necessarily based on whether we introduce online voting or not, but rather on how it will function when it is introduced. There are several social behavioral pieces to keep in mind. Is early voting online a capability? It makes sense. In an online voting model, are the early results disclosed to the public so that everyone can see how the race is projecting? If someone has already cast his or her vote is that person allowed to go back and change it anytime before the election? In other words, how social would the government allow online voting to become? It would make sense to make it very social. For example—early voters could click on a radio button or have a form field for the main reason they selected or didn't select a certain candidate. Imagine, candidates could then address the concerns of the voting public during the election process itself. Sounds very democratic to me.

Even the Army Is Sharing Information

In an effort to relate with their desired target audience of 17- to 24-year-olds, the Army launched a tool called "Straight from Iraq." It was designed to allow potential recruits to get a better sense of what war is like from the people who know best. This is a long way from the days in Vietnam where television coverage was carefully screened. "Straight from Iraq" was historic because it was the first time candidates could ask direct questions of soldiers in combat.

"The goal is to provide those considering the Army—along with parents and others who influence their decisions—with verifiable information about what being a soldier is really like, what combat is really like," said Lt. Gen. Benjamin C. Freakley, commanding general of the Army Accessions Command in Fort Monroe, Virginia, overseeing recruitment at the time.[36]

"The campaign was successful in conveying the benefits of 'Army strong'—the physical, emotional, and mental benefits," said Ed Walters, chief marketing officer for the Army at the Pentagon.

"We wanted to more clearly articulate that," he added, "through efforts like sharing with civilians the video clips of 'real soldiers' stories."[37]

As we point out throughout the book, these types of open, social media conversations are much more effective than a unilateral communication to your audience. The best part, too, is that they are much more cost effective. In this example, while the Army couldn't disclose exact figures, it easily exceeded its recruiting goals for 2006 to 2008.[38]

For cost effectiveness comparison, the Army spent roughly $170 million per year on such high-profile items as NASCAR sponsorships and Rodeos. I'm sure it's fun for the Army's Director of Marketing to watch his NASCAR automobile go around the track every Sunday, but how effective is this, and how accurately can you track such a thing? The average sponsorship cost for a NASCAR car is in the $15 to $20 million range. In comparison, the social media campaign costs between $200,000 and $300,000.

While the Army embraced Facebook and other social media tools, they also understood that some items probably weren't best for public consumption. In October of 2009, they launched milBook, which is essentially Facebook, but restricted to only military personnel. Keep in mind that when Facebook originally launched, it was restricted to Harvard students, and then only to those with a college e-mail address. With 20,000 users, milBook may be a sign that for certain niche markets there will be "invite only" or "velvet rope" clearance to be part of a particular network. milSuite is a combination of social media tools that includes milBook, milBlog, and milWiki.

Chapter Four Key Points

1. Open, multilateral conversations are much more effective than unilateral communications to your audience, for politics and business. Social media enables these open conversations. Utilizing free social media tools and placements is more timely and cost effective than traditional advertising.
2. By engaging voters, social media has had a positive impact on voter turnout (the highest since 1908 and the highest youth participation).
3. The adoption of online voting in the future could save an estimated $6.7 billion in lost productivity (U.S. presidential election).
4. We are just scratching the surface of what's possible with collective intelligence in terms of being able to predict and control influenza outbreaks, predicting the United Kingdom's next prime minister, and so forth.
5. Fortune 500 companies should learn from Obama's faith in social media, allowing the public to take ownership of his brand and growing it to unexpected levels of success.
6. Just like businesses, politicians and governments need to keep up with advancements in social media; otherwise, they will be left behind. Successfully leveraging social media in politics pays big dividends—we need only look at Obama's 2008 victory. *Obama would not be president without the Internet.*
7. Social Media can help provide important political pressure and also raise money as evidenced by the Gulf of Mexico oil spill and earthquake rescue efforts in Haiti.

CHAPTER FIVE

I Care More about What My Neighbor Thinks than What Google Thinks

Social commerce is upon us. What is social commerce exactly? It is a term that encompasses the transactional, search, and marketing components of social media. Social commerce harnesses the simple idea that people value the opinion of other people. What this truly means is that in the future we will no longer seek products and services; rather, they will find us. Nielsen reports 78 percent of people trust their peers' opinions.[1] This is neither a new concept, nor new to the Web (e.g., epinions.com, complaints.com, angieslist.com).

What is new is that social media makes it so much easier to disseminate information. As the success of social media proves, people enjoy spreading information. This explains the popularity of Twitter, Foursquare, Gowalla, and so forth. These tools and products enable users to inform their friends what they are doing every minute of the day (I'm having an ice cream cone; check out this great article; listening to keynote speaker; etc.). Twitter is interesting from the standpoint that its popularity began with older generations, and time will tell how much Generation Y and Z embrace Twitter. This is the exact opposite trend of Facebook, which was originally popular with the younger generations and then Generation X and the Baby Boomers started to get engaged.

> *Social media is creating something that I think eventually is going to be very healthy for our economy, and that is institutional brand integrity.*
>
> —*John Gerzema, Chief Insights Officer, Young & Rubicam*[2]

The most popular feature of Facebook and LinkedIn is status updates. Status updates enable users to continuously brag, boast, inform, and vent to everyone in their network. This simple tool allows users to easily stay connected with their network. As a result, 60 million status updates per day![3] Let's take a look at a couple of examples of social commerce in action.

Buying the Right Baby Seat

Steve and his wife are expecting their first child. With this addition, they are in the market for a lightweight, but safe, child seat for their car. Steve doesn't know the first thing about child seats and is dreading the hours of researching and then searching on the Internet to find the appropriate one. Steve, like many fathers, is also fearful that he might, despite all of his diligent research, make a mistake. Making sure you provide the appropriate safety for your child can be stressful and at times overwhelming. The good news is that the majority of these purchase challenges, concerns, and unwanted stress will become things of the past with social media. Here's why.

On a search engine, if you entered "buying a baby seat" you are likely to receive a series of irrelevant search results and a bevy of sponsored ads. Not all of the search results are unrelated. Some will prove fruitful, but it may take some time-intensive trial and error before you wean the helpful results from the not so helpful results. Yet, as social commerce becomes more and more mainstream, when Steve performs a social search by entering the query—"buying a baby seat"—he will discover the following:

- 23 of Steve's 181 friends have purchased a baby seat in the last two years.
- 14 purchased the same make and model.
- The average price for the most popular model was $124.99 (10 of the 14 purchased online).
- 3 are looking to sell their used baby seats because their children have outgrown them.
- 7 different online videos showcasing this seat have been bookmarked—tagged by people in his network.
- 4 different reviews and articles have been bookmarked—tagged by his network.
- 11 of the 14 have posted positive reviews on the baby seat—two of which are video reviews.

Steve respects the opinions of the 14 people who purchased the same seat, so he clicks to find out more, and gets the following information:

We have three kids and have used this same baby seat model for all of them. My sister used Cheekie Brand's baby seat and it was clunky, awkward, and heavy. When she saw mine, she immediately went out and got one for her baby. I highly recommend these seats!

—Gab Fernandez

Steve can now confidently purchase the baby seat without the usual research, stress, and time required if he were starting his search from scratch. Once Steve starts to use the seat, he takes on a different role within the same social media conversation; he is actively using the product and can provide his own insight into features and benefits that the seat provides. Steve may notice that it's too easy for his child to undo one of the seat straps. Compelled, he may point this out to his network via a quick video example that may be relevant to his social network of friends. This then presents an opportunity for product improvement, which the manufacturer can act upon.

If the manufacturer's marketing team is listening and watching, then they will be able to quickly share this with the design and production team and hopefully get a quick resolution/improvement for future buyers. This is not only a benefit for the manufacturer, but a benefit to society as well, because future children will be much safer based on the quick advancements.

Correspondingly, just like his friends before him, if Steve finds features he really enjoys about the baby seat, he will feel compelled to write about them, since his friends with a similar purchase decision will benefit from his experience. When I worked at EarthLink, one of our key findings when working on referral incentives was that the main reason people recommended EarthLink was not for the incentive, but that they liked being viewed as the subject matter expert within their social graph. The same holds true in social media.

> *The popular belief that people only take the time to post something when they want to vent or discuss a bad experience is simply not true; at least in our experience. The majority of the over 20 million reviews and opinions we have received on TripAdvisor are positive ones. People are simply compelled to give back to a community that has given to them.*
>
> *—Steve Kaufer, CEO of TripAdvisor*

Minivan or Hybrid?

Steve and his wife eventually go on to have their second and third child, and their two sedans won't cut it anymore; he's in the market for a bigger vehicle. Having vowed to himself and his friends that he'd never own a minivan, he's considering an SUV or a crossover vehicle.

Steve is dreading the hours of searching on the Internet to find a vehicle that suits his needs. He's even dreading having to leave work early to visit the car dealerships to test-drive his selected vehicles and then the ensuing haggling process. Despite hours of research, Steve is also fearful that he may make a big purchase mistake when the moment comes. Again, most of these concerns are mitigated when we move to a social commerce model: Steve performs a search on his favorite social network—he types in "buying a car." Rather than receiving a series of irrelevant ads for car trader sites, he discovers the following:

- 23 of Steve's friends have purchased a car in the last year.
- 16 of his friends are married with two or more children.
- 14 purchased an SUV or crossover.
- 9 purchased the same vehicle.

Steve respects the opinions of the nine people who purchased the same vehicle, so he clicks to find out more, and gets the following information: "I test-drove Crossover X and Crossover Y. Crossover Y was the much better feel, and it was easier to get into the backseat. Coupled with the fact that it gets three more mph to the gallon, it was a no-brainer."

To further illustrate the importance of virulence today, a study conducted by online-market-research firm Marketing Evolution on marketing campaigns from adidas and video-game publisher Electronic Arts within MySpace found that 70 percent of the return on investment was the result of one consumer passing information to another virally. Social commerce is a referral program on steroids.

Blowing Out the Candles

Karen (age 48) just received a birthday check from her mum for 470 euros. She feels like treating herself by buying something, but doesn't have anything particular in mind. Karen quickly taps into her social network to see what other people she respects (friends/peers) are buying and whether they like or dislike their choices.

Within five minutes, she decides to purchase an Apple iPad because her friend Sally bought one and loves it. The fact that Sally has an iPad and likes it assuaged Karen's fear of technology because Sally is even more of a technical neophyte than Karen. Knowing this about Sally drove 95 percent of Karen's decision process within minutes. This intimate knowledge of people within your social network is key, and is one main reason why reviews via social media have gone to the "next level" compared to other online reviews in the past.

The big social networks (Facebook, LinkedIn, Twitter, QQ, etc.) will eventually dominate this portion of Social Commerce. Sites like ThisNext, Kaboodle, WeShop, and WishPot helped push the adoption of this market opportunity by enabling buyers to quickly share their purchases and reviews with friends. These sites were designed for people to go to for ideas about what products and services they should be purchasing and using.

Bon Voyage Online Travel Agents?

Suzy (age 34) has set aside a budget of £1400 to take a trip this year with her husband. The only thing she knows at this point: destination, South America. In the past, she would've performed a search on Google, which would have taken her to some helpful online travel agent sites (e.g., Travelzoo, TripAdvisor, GoAhead Tours, Lonely Planet, Orbitz, Priceline, Travelocity). She probably would've narrowed down her choices after hours of research. She would then begin the arduous task of finding the best deal for her flight, hotel, and so on.

As a result of social media, this process becomes much easier for Suzy. She simply goes to her social network of choice and searches for "South American Vacations." The results pop up: five of her friends have traveled to South America in the last year. Conveniently listed are their itineraries, hotels, and resorts, as well as prices and recommendations.

Suzy sees two of her friends both took a trip to Chile through GoAhead Tours and rated it highly. It's within her budget, and the same package is available. She quickly snatches it up before it's sold out. She saved hours of painstaking research and the fees of a travel agent.

If she only has 10 minutes before going to pick up the kids at day care, is her time better served scrolling through 400 reviews by people she doesn't know on a travel review site (some of which will be spam from the competing hotels), or is she better served looking at the recommendations from her friends? The time is much better spent with her friends' experience and recommendations. Social commerce gave her peace of mind and the anticipation of an enjoyable adventure. That is why TripAdvisor incorporated Facebook Connect into their site in 2010. Now you can see hotel reviews from your friends via TripAdvisor's connection with Facebook.

Listed alongside the qualitative reviews are certain data points for each friend: price, travel supplier, places recommended, day excursions, and so on.

We could continue with other examples, like trying to figure out what the trendiest online video game is for Christmas. This has several challenges; the first is trying to figure out what the *it* game is. The second is to determine if it is age appropriate for your child (e.g., sex, violence). Third, if it is the *it* game, the task of obtaining the game will be a challenge. Fortunately, social media lessens many of these worries, some of your early-adopter friends can show the way by providing insight into their purchase history and experiences. If a friend you trust bought the game for her child, that would be more insightful than trying to decipher the confusing game ratings for graphic and sexual content to determine if the product is age appropriate for your own child.

Social media has a much easier time tracking when the purchase is made online. It enables users to know where goods or services were purchased—which in turn may be a good indication that the item is in stock. This is done using cookie-based tracking that follows the user (if they opt in) as they traverse and transact on the Web. A *cookie* is a term used to describe a tiny piece of code that is placed in your Web browser.

What does this mean for brand marketing? Well, it means that companies and marketers better start spending more time listening to their customers and less time spending countless hours creating the next award-winning, but-no-customer-getting, 30-second television commercial. Consumers are taking ownership of brands, and their referral power is priceless.

Just as important as listening to the customer is acting on the information received. This entails all parts of the organization working more harmoniously than ever before—the speed of social media demands it. These certainly aren't new constructs, but in this new age, your brand will experience a quick death if these constructs aren't adhered to. The days of traditional brand marketing aren't necessarily dead; they're just taking on new forms.

Social Media increases efficiency by saving time as it eliminates multiple individual redundancies (MIR). This is obviously a tremendous benefit to the user, and it's mission critical for businesses to understand that this impacts almost everything they do from marketing to operations to manufacturing. As people increasingly look to social media for advice and recommendations, marketers need to make certain they are part of the consideration set. In order to accomplish this, companies need to create great products and services rather than rely on advertising campaigns to bail them out. When a transaction occurs, marketers need to encourage or give incentives for users to complete product and service reviews albeit good, bad, or indifferent. Companies that are able to encourage this information sharing from their consumers, via both online and offline, help water the seeds of viral success. Money to water these seeds will come from traditional advertising budgets (television, outdoor, radio) and will go directly into the consumers' pockets. This is another reason why consumers will take more ownership of the brands they associate with, and it makes the traditional referral model look like a dollhouse alongside the Taj Mahal.

Ken Robbins, founder of Digital Agency Response Mine Interactive, sums up the challenges and opportunities that individuals and companies face with social media:

> *Social media has evolved from a mere post it-answer it model (bulletin boards and blogs) to instantaneous publish-subscribe models (i.e., Twitter and Facebook updates). Combined with the portable surfing of today's phones, this pub-submodel has both fantastic and dire implications for businesses. It's fantastic from the standpoint that one can not only stand in front of a refrigerator in a store and check out reviews of that model, the consumer can Twitter his network to get advice on all models, this brand, and this store instantaneously. If the product and store have good reputations, buying hesitancy is removed and the purchase takes place. The dire side of this is that if the price, the model, or the store has poor reputations, the transaction will definitely not take place. We are moving to a world with total retail and product performance transparency for the consumer. The market will be much less tolerant of poor service and poor products and high margins with this social communications infrastructure.*[4]

Many may take umbrage with the two points or assumptions being made. One could make a good argument that people aren't going to want to share their purchase decisions. This is true; some will not. Others will share only certain purchase decisions and price points, while still others will share everything and anything. However, from an online buying perspective, the technology for this to occur is there, and as we have seen from the transparency of other social media usage, it's only a matter of time when purchases will be pushed to everyone who is willing. Not everyone will share, just like not everyone comments on TripAdvisor or edits on Wikipedia. However, as we've seen over the last few years, particularly with younger generations, people have an unbelievable willingness to share. That is why Facebook has over 400 million users.

The other piece that people will be concerned about is that buyers will be motivated to write a review. It's possible that a true tangible incentive may not be necessary, but what is certain is that more effort and marketing dollars will be used to implore customers to write a review of their product. This incentive model isn't anything new; when a hotel or airline asks you to fill out a suggestion card, it is usually with the hook of potentially winning a sweepstakes or free meal.

The hope is that incentives aren't necessary, but even if they are, that doesn't mean that the person will write a good review. This type of transparent review may not be for everyone, as some people like to remain anonymous, but that brings up another key point: All reviews don't necessarily need to be public to everyone—some may only feel comfortable posting reviews to their own network. All of this is a lot to digest for Generation X and beyond, but it's a way of life for the Generations born after 1980, as they have grown up in a transparent world.

We can see a dramatic shift in that 92 percent of consumers now cite Word of Mouth as the best source for product and brand information, up from 67 percent in 1977.[5] That is one reason why in this book we say we've moved from Word-of-Mouth to World-of-Mouth marketing.

Looking to Friends for Medical Advice

Other major societal benefits from social media will be made in the health care arena. 2008 survey results from online advertising agency iCrossing showed that 34 percent of Americans turn to social media for health research. While substantial, we are certain these numbers are even higher today. Twenty percent of the online health searchers went to Wikipedia for information. Other social networks were also used and the average age of people using social media for health-related questions was 37, whereas the average overall age for patients searching for health information was 44.[6] It is not surprising that it is younger, but it does again show that social media users aren't all teenagers; it will be mainstream sooner than people expect. When health consumers turn to social media they are in a decision-mode process. Needs range from finding out costs for certain operations or medical devices to the reputation of a certain provider or doctor.

When engaged in face-to-face or phone conversation, it can be awkward or even rude to discuss medical conditions. Social media eliminates this awkwardness. A simple post like: "Has anyone ever had their tonsils removed? I've had a sharp pain in my throat for the last day. Let me know"; or not even asking the question but simply stating: "Burned my finger with boiling hot water—top of the tea kettle fell off" will often elicit such responses as:

> *Sorry to hear that—the key is to run it under cold water for 10 minutes—don't use ice! After that, use Neosporin to disinfect and make sure to keep it covered and clean. I did this once, and it will heal in about a week, but it hurts like heck!*
>
> —*Sandy*

Don't use ice on it, only cold water. No need to go to the hospital even though I'm sure it looks red and awful.

—Logan

After their physician, nurse, or pharmacist, people look within their network from those they trust for good advice on medical treatments and medications. In the iCrossing study, more than 60 percent list "Consumer Opinion Leader" as "extremely important" or "very important." Some even list the advice from their friends above that of their physician.[7]

In the same study, 75 percent indicated that they use social media in health to "connect with other consumers to exchange information or obtain support"; 55 percent noted that the most important reason to use social media over other online sites is to get cost information for a procedure or medical equipment.[8] Consumer-generated health content is increasing in both supply and demand. Society is benefiting from this shift. Perhaps the largest benefit to this will be seen outside of the United States where in some small towns the local physician is revered as a demigod. This is fine if that physician is altruistic at heart, but that is not always the case. Social media allows for an inexpensive and relevant second, third, and four hundredth medical opinion, especially in underdeveloped regions of the world.

Jared and Subway's Almost Missed Opportunity

Marketers struggling with idea ownership are not doing so entirely because of advances in social media or technology. One of the most successful marketing campaigns of all time nearly didn't get off the ground. Jared and his Subway weight-loss story did not come from the top down; rather, it came from the bottom up. Jared actually started the now famous diet on his own accord, long before receiving royalty payments from Subway. Jared's unique diet story made its way from a college campus newspaper to a savvy executive at an advertising firm. Jared was attending the University of Indiana at the time and the advertising executive sent an intern to Bloomington, Indiana, to track Jared down on campus.

Once Jared was found, the advertising executive and his agency pitched the idea to Subway. The marketing executives at Subway originally rejected the idea, but the ad agency and this particular executive were so convinced of the idea that they sold it to local franchisees, and the agency paid to run the spots out of its own pocket! Only after proven success did the marketing executives at Subway's headquarters relent. This turned out to have a happy ending, but how many such ideas have never seen the light of day?

In the Subway campaign, recall that Jared was an avid user of a company's product and service—in this case, low-fat submarine sandwiches. This is another reminder that executives and companies who want to excel need to be comfortable in knowing that not everything related to the brand will be owned by them; their customers are beginning to take ownership. This is a good thing, because straightforward and true stories resonate well with consumers, and this particular story has helped Subway overtake McDonald's as having the most restaurants in the United States.

The beauty of social media is that fewer of these great stories will remain hidden, and as a result, companies will benefit. One of the top-10 viral videos in 2008 was "Christian the Lion."[9] This is a clip of two Australian men who raise a lion in the city of London. One year later they go to Africa to reunite in the wild with a giant hug (Remember, this is a lion!). This story was from 1969 and despite having a book published about it in 1971 (Broadway Books), prior to 2008 it was relatively unknown. Then along comes the social medium of YouTube and the story spreads globally in little time at all by using the film footage from 1969. Imagine, this incredible story would have only been known by a few until the advent of social media—what a shame! Ironically, it has come full circle, and a second book has been published on this story: *A Lion Called Christian: The True Story of the Remarkable Bond between Two Friends and a Lion* by Anthony Bourke, John Rendall, and George Adamson (March 10, 2009), and it is on Borders' Best Seller's Shelf! This is also an example of how social media can drive offline revenue in new forms as well.

Not All Applications Are Created Equal

Businesses, both large and small, have to realize that they no longer own relationships. Yet, when it comes to social media, many companies haven't shaken their old tried-and-true marketing models. Other companies quickly figured it out. Next, we discuss three companies that all had the same goal when they set out, but wound up experiencing different levels of success based on their strategies.

In 2007, Facebook introduced the ability for developers to make applications (tools/widgets that allow users to do everything from tracking a favorite sports team's scores to playing a game of tic-tac-toe against a friend in another city) to enhance the Facebook experience. When the application platform was originally introduced, three separate travel companies correctly surmised that people would want to input and track all the places in the world they had visited. Each company set out with different strategies resulting in various levels of success. The three companies were:

1. Where I've Been (a new company)
2. TripAdvisor (a popular online travel agent)
3. ACME Travel (a large, traditional, publicly traded tour operator)

One of the top executives at ACME Travel had a relationship with someone at Facebook and was aware that Facebook was planning to open its application program interface (API) allowing any company to develop useful widgets within Facebook. For example, Delta Airlines could develop an application in which users could view upcoming flights on Facebook, or Crayola could have you fill out some simple questions and tell you what color crayon you most represent.

ACME Travel thought it would be helpful for the users to be able to easily track where they had traveled. The idea sprang from an employee who had invented an Excel spreadsheet that allowed you to check off boxes next to countries traveled. This spreadsheet was based on other people using maps tacked to a wall with a push pin for every place traveled.

The idea for the application was a good one because within the first few days, hundreds of thousands of Facebook users downloaded the application. Understanding also the braggadocian behavior of social media, ACME Travel set up the application so that people could send an alert to their friends whenever they traveled to a new city. So, if Kim went to Auckland, it would alert everyone in her network "Kim indicated she has traveled to Auckland within ACME's travel application."

ACME Travel was ecstatic at the success of their application; they estimated that the internal cost to build the application was $15,000, and they were receiving 50,000 downloads per day, which means they were capturing 50,000 names to put into their prospect database.[10] To go into this particular aspect a bit further, the download process for Facebook applications doesn't require users to forfeit their e-mail addresses—yet ACME Travel made the decision to place an extra page in the middle of the download process indicating it was mandatory for users to supply name, mailing address, and e-mail address in order to use the application. About a week into the process, ACME received word from 20-something Craig Ulliott. Craig's belief was that the additional page during the application download process was cumbersome and would discourage many users who didn't want to disclose personal information to get the application, ultimately hurting the overall success of the application. ACME Travel pondered the suggestion from Ulliott and conceded that there probably were people they were turning off, but then again, they were getting 50,000 names on some good days, so things were going very nicely. Besides, they thought, this was the entire reason they were doing social media marketing: it was a *carrot* to get names for the database. Why should they fix something that wasn't broken?

Things continued successfully for ACME Travel for a few weeks. Meanwhile, Craig Ulliott wasn't your typical user; rather, he was a very established programmer. He liked the idea of the *mousetrap* that ACME Travel was offering, but he thought he could build a better one. So, he continued with his own vision; a very similar application called *Where I've Been*. *Where I've Been* was graphically more appealing and also contained some sexier pieces of flash programming that made it easier to click on a particular part of a map to indicate you'd traveled to a certain place. However, the key difference was that Craig didn't add the additional page during the download process that required users to enter their personal information. He simply used Facebook's standard two-step process. Here's what happened next.

Where I've Been quickly became one of the must-have applications and also the top-downloaded travel application. It was so successful that Craig was able to help form a seven-person company under the same name. With 800,000 active monthly users, Craig was attracting the attention of the big online travel agents like TripAdvisor, Priceline, and Travelzoo.

TripAdvisor was savvy enough to realize that an application like this would be an unbelievable marketing tool for their business. TripAdvisor began behind-the-scenes negotiations with *Where I've Been*. By this time, Craig had joined forces with an experienced and dynamic Internet Travel guru named Brian Harniman to head up his strategy. The asking price for *Where I've Been* was a little steeper than TripAdvisor had originally hoped. They had hoped that they would be dealing with some wet-behind-the-ears kid and get the application for a bargain.

They came within a whisker of buying the application for $3 million. So close, in fact, that a story was released. Then they did something very smart—they begged, borrowed, and made better. TripAdvisor pulled back, took a deep assessment, and calmly said we think we can do this better. Instead of investing $3 million, they decided to build their own application for a fraction of the cost. Now it's important to point out that TripAdvisor used two very good tactics. The first one was a prudent attempt to leverage an already proven and successful product application in *Where I've Been*.

On discovering the expensive asking price, TripAdvisor re-assessed the situation and correctly decided there was enough opportunity for more than one company to succeed. With Facebook counting user growth in millions, TripAdvisor was hopeful that this type of travel application had not "jumped the shark." Jumping the shark is an Internet term for something that is past its prime or no longer *in*. According to Wikipedia the specific definition is as follows:

> Jumping the shark *is a colloquialism used by TV critics and fans to denote that point in a TV show or movie series history where the plot veers off into absurd story lines or out-of-the-ordinary characterizations. In the process of undergoing these changes, the TV or movie series loses its original appeal. Shows that have "jumped the shark" are typically deemed to have passed their peak. According to the theory, once a show has "jumped the shark" fans can designate the point of the show's perceived decline in overall quality with the "jump the shark" moment.*[11]

The term was taken from one of the later *Happy Days* episodes where Fonzie, leather jacket and all, attempts to jump a shark on water skis. It was *not* one of broadcast television's finer moments. The tech community eagerly snapped up this television term, and today it is more recognized in the Internet community for the moment that something goes past its prime. For instance, most MP3 players had a jump the shark moment when the iPod was first released.

Anyway, TripAdvisor moved forward with building a bigger, better version of *Where I've Been*. Within a month they released *Cities I've Visited*. They were smart to name it something very tangible and stick with cities. TripAdvisor leveraged Google Maps so travelers could place pins on the digital map just like many people do in their home or office on paper maps. Using Google Maps was smart in four ways:

1. People were familiar with Google Maps.
2. Google Maps was free.
3. No development was needed.
4. It worked.

That old adage that you can only have two out of the following—cheap, quick, or quality—doesn't hold true within social media because you can often leverage preexisting human capital or preexisting products and solutions. In this instance, TripAdvisor was doing both—they were leveraging the idea (human capital) that *Where I've Been* and ACME Travel had produced before them, and they were leveraging Google Maps (preexisting product). So, their cost investment was approximately $20,000. What they received in return is somewhat staggering. In April of 2009, TripAdvisor's application had 1,779,246 monthly active users, while *Where I've Been* had 885,577 monthly active users.[12] In June of 2010 TripAdvisor's application had grown to 5,187,366 monthly active users, while

Where I've Been was up to 1,031,902 monthly active users. Both were very successful—that's over 5 million people who actively interact with TripAdvisor's brand every month! Craig was able to help start a company due to the success of this one application as well. That is truly the power of social media.

> *A key thing to note is that for every successful Cities I've Visited or Traveler IQ application we had just as many, if not more, not achieve wild success. The importance in a social media age is to be nimble and not afraid to make mistakes. The more things you can test or try, the more chances you have for success. I have a sign outside my door that simply says Speed Wins. We have adopted this as our motto and it serves us well. If our development team says something will take four months, we challenge ourselves to do it in four days, and more often than not we succeed. It may not be perfect for that initial beta launch, but that is okay, because with the help of our users we will make small, rapid changes to constantly improve. If you aren't constantly evolving along with your customers you will be doomed to fail.*
>
> —*Steve Kaufer, CEO, TripAdvisor*

Marketing to Zombies

We introduced the term *active monthly users*. This term was coined by Facebook in 2007 and is an important one. Historically, most tracking just dealt with pure volume. How many hits did you get on your website? Then it was determined that hits weren't really relevant since hits were tracking the number of times certain elements on a page were served up. If your website home page had several images and form fields and one person visited this site, the unique visit could equal 13 hits; this type of count is not too helpful. So, tracking progressed to visits; this wasn't very good either because it could be the same person coming back several times. The next logical step was to measure unique visitors.

Social media has changed the paradigm of tracking again. Originally, Facebook rated top applications by how many times they were downloaded, but downloads aren't necessarily relevant; what truly matters is how active the users are. If a user downloads the application and never returns, that's not very valuable to the creator of the application. If a million people download something but never use it, then in a sense it is worthless to both the user and to the creator. Or, if 500,000 people "like" your brand on Facebook, but never return to the page, comment, share, or post anything they may not be particularly valuable. This is why Facebook tracks most items by active users, which changes everything.

Having 12 million e-mail addresses in your database doesn't mean much if only 1,000 open and click on your e-mails. It's much more important to have 10,000 e-mails with 9,000 people opening and clicking. With social media, marketers are able to measure user activity and capture helpful information such as age, sex, education, hobbies, interests, and so on. This assists marketers in one-to-one conversations between companies and consumers.

Going one step further is just how powerful the social graph is. Take, for example, the 9,000 active people mentioned above. E-mail is generally a one-to-one conversation. If you have an e-mail that contains something particularly entertaining, then you could be lucky and those 9,000 people forward it on, and so forth. This is powerful, but not quite as effective as social media. The main reason is that the viralness of e-mail is really related to that one particular e-mail, whereas in social media people are constantly pushing content to their network. In e-mail it's an anomaly, whereas in social media it is inherent.

To showcase this point, in April 2009 EF Educational Tours had roughly 800 Twitter followers—people who actively want to know the latest news from EF Educational Tours. If you looked at the number of followers these 800 people had, then the social graph influence was 8.5 million people (based on results from a query on http://twinfluence.com/).

Leveraging Success

The TripAdvisor story doesn't end with the brand value derived from the application; that was only the beginning. The beauty is that 1.8 million users are feeding TripAdvisor information. These augment their 30 million user base—talk about a large focus group! The days of advertising executives sitting behind two-way mirrors munching on stale chips and M&Ms will become a distant memory. More important than healthier marketers is the opportunity this vast amount of data presents. First of all, companies can provide this data to reporters as part of their public relations efforts. For example: "Top-five cities that people want to travel to in the coming year"—"35- to 45-year-olds more likely to travel to Australia—teenagers to Europe."

Reporters and bloggers are always looking for this type of hard data that is of interest to consumers. What they learn real time can also help shape their product and services. The level of demographic information passed within social media is unprecedented. If TripAdvisor sees in October that 80 percent of males 55 to 65 are putting Machu Picchu as a place they desire to visit when historically only 20 percent select that destination, then it would make intuitive sense to change the TripAdvisor home page to have a callout for a Machu Picchu Senior's special. This is where marketers' jobs are changing drastically. This data is being collected from the website, as well as all the social media touchpoints.

Marketers need to be joined at the hip with their production team to ensure they are getting this real-time information. They also need to recognize that they are no longer sending a one-way message but are serving more as a conduit. "Those who will succeed need to act more like publishers, entertainment companies, or even party planners, than advertisers,"[13] says Garrick Schmitt, Group Vice President of Experience Planning for leading digital agency Razorfish.

The process TripAdvisor employed while building the *Cities I've Visited* application presents a new way of thinking in that TripAdvisor didn't know for certain what they would be able to monetize. "Users are challenging publishers, advertisers, and marketers to meet their needs in new, distributed, and largely uncharted territories—many of which have no analog touch points—and to provide services that have no immediate monetization models,"[14] indicated Schmitt.

It's also a communication cycle. In this case, if someone within the *Cities I've Visited* application selects Athens under the category "I'd like to visit," then TripAdvisor has the ability to serve up its top-five most popular tours of Athens (which of course are clickable) and take the user directly into a booking process at the appropriate point in time. It's easy to see why this isn't interruption marketing like in days gone past; but it is a value-added part of a useful tool for the user. TripAdvisor is offering value to the user in providing a tool to track and brag about where he's gone as well as where he'd like to go, and at the same time, the user is receiving valuable information from TripAdvisor that is directly tied to his particular travel interests. There is no marketing guesswork or marketing laboratory—the user is informing marketers implicitly through his actions.

Companion Credit Union: New Logo

One Australian company, Companion Credit Union, actually turned over the decision on its brand logo to the social community. "The credit union is really owned by the members, and therefore, we decided we should invite them to actively participate in helping us decide,"[15] said Ray O'Brien,

CEO/Companion. Of the 12,000 members, 1,000 of them voted. "Many of our current members founded Companion Credit Union, so it only seemed fitting that they would be a part of our new journey and direction," said Companion's Marketing Manager Cas Scott.[16]

eReaders/Tables

Mobile devices acting as e-book readers (Amazon Kindle, Sony eReader, Apple iPad, etc.) are wildly popular (Kindle is the #1 selling product on Amazon), and the fact is that online books offer many of the same advantages as digitized music, newspapers, and magazines. The *New York Times* is available via eReader for a monthly subscription fee that is drastically less than the traditional paper edition.

It is only a matter of time before we will see advertising and marketing efforts creep into both fiction and nonfiction materials. This is virgin territory for marketers. This is a good thing because as the traditional channels of marketing like television, radio, and magazines diminish in effectiveness, marketers need these new marketing outlets to continue to thrive. One way in which marketers, publishers, and authors will come together as it relates to e-books is within the content itself. How is this possible without compromising the story? On some levels, this is very simple. Let's say that within a scene of a novel the author describes a hot, dusty day where the main character refreshes himself with an ice cold Coca-Cola. Authors generally like to describe items specifically so the reader can really visualize them. That is why more often than not they use branded items in their descriptions—they don't write "soda," they write "Coca-Cola"; they don't write "listening to an MP3 player," they write "listening to an iPod"; and last but not least, they don't write "a stylish Swedish over-the-shoulder baby carrying device," they keep it short with "Baby Bjorn." Because of this, there is tremendous potential for advertisers and authors as e-books continue their rise in popularity.

In the previous example, if there is a mention of Baby Bjorn, the company can pay to have that mention become a hyperlink within the e-book's digital format. The benefits of this are that it makes the brand term more pronounced, and if the reader is inclined, he or she can click on the term and either be given more description, branding, an image, or be taken directly to babybjorn.com. Another benefit to Baby Bjorn is that the search engine spiders will read its hyperlink, which will help Baby Bjorn come up high in the search rankings.

Where in the World Is Bangladesh?

Thinking outside of brands entirely—books often mention a geographic location. With traditional books, curious readers will look up places like Transylvania with maps or mapping tools to learn where it is. With e-books, this is made simple because it is only one click away, taking you straight to the location on a digital map, providing a benefit to the reader. Think of a particular word in a novel that you may not know the meaning of—say *panoply*. Rather than having to look up panoply in the dictionary, the definition would be one click away or you may even be able to mouse over it with the cursor to see a pop-up definition. Both of these can be monetized by the publisher and author. Google currently generates revenue from its mapping application, so it makes sense that a business development could be struck whereby Google would be the preferred provider of mapping information within books; in return, the publisher or author receives a portion of the revenue that Google generates.

This paragraph was written in 2008, and my, have we already come a long way. All eReaders and iPads have this functionality. Today Kindle sales already top hardcover book sales and Amazon predicts digital book sales will outpace paperback sales in 2011.

Going back to the brand-product-placement-within-a-book scenario, you could argue that if the author is already placing brand terms into the book (e.g., Coke), then why would a company like Coke pay for something that is already there? Coke would want to do this for two reasons: (1) the competition (Pepsi) could swoop in and take this placement, or (2) the placement isn't currently a hyperlink in the e-book. By paying a small sponsorship fee, the company could make it a hyperlink, thus driving traffic and helping improve organic search engine rankings (because search engines reward hyperlinks).

If all of this makes so much sense, why haven't they had this type of product placement in books before now? It wasn't feasible primarily because of tracking. An advertiser wouldn't be able to track the effectiveness of this form of product placement in a hardbound or paperback book. Now, with product placements in e-books you will be able to see how many people viewed (millions of impressions) along with how many people clicked or *moused* over the word with their cursor. This is great for advertisers and even better for the authors and publishers who now have an additional revenue stream without compromising their content, but rather enhancing it for their readers. It will be interesting to see how advertisers will be charged for these types of placements; the most logical would probably be a cost-per-thousand-impressions model.

While the transition from both hardcover and paperback to electronic versions will occur, we are at the beginning of this movement. It will not be as rapid or absolute a succession as other industries (e.g., music, movies). Rather, e-books will be complements or alternatives. Part of this is because there is something more genuine and romantic about curling up with a good book. It's not quite the same if you are curling up with your electronic reading device. Another factor is that books are one of the most viral offline items that exist today. Books, especially paperbacks, are disposable—passed from friend to friend; owners don't really plan to ever see the book again. Also, with today's technology, it is still 10 to 30 percent faster to read something on a piece of paper than it is to read from a computer screen, or a smaller handheld e-book reader.[17] It will be interesting to see if advances in technology for eReaders, tablets, iPads, slates, and so forth, eventually help make it faster to read. My guess is they will, and they will soon.

Unlike music and news content, the information within books is not as time sensitive, especially for fiction. The shelf life for a book is much longer than news content or the popularity of a song. A salient example of this is the fact that today, middle-school kids are still reading *Huckleberry Finn* and *The Catcher in the Rye.* In the foreseeable future, while e-books will be exceedingly popular, they will not be an absolute replacement in the short term like the music, newspaper, and magazine industries have experienced. However, the popularity will be huge; in particular for books like the one you are reading right now. Most likely you are reading this on an eReader and you are sitting in your robe drinking coffee (okay, hopefully not that second part).

For publishers, there are both pros and cons to the book-publishing model being influenced by the rise of e-books. On one hand, publishers potentially save millions of dollars on the physical printing and shipping of inventory, and they would have an additional revenue stream in terms of the advertising via hyperlink placements within the e-books. On the other hand, they are middlemen, which may not be as crucial a role when an author can get his or her content directly to the reading audience easily. (A good example of this is Google Books allowing authors and publishers to upload their content in PDF format. Google was sued and did lose a court battle because more than one proprietary owner didn't want their content placed on Google Books.) However, look for Apple's iBooks to help fill this void. Expect Apple to make a strong play to put a stranglehold on the publishing industry just like they did on the music industry; their next frontier are TV shows.

Unlike the music and movie industry, the book industry has thrived, even though for hundreds of years there has been a free alternative to purchasing a book—public libraries. It will be interesting to see how the public library model morphs to address e-books. The book industry still thrives in spite of the free availability of the same content at the public library for many reasons: (1) people like to own books; (2) it takes an effort to go to the library, check out a book, and then remember to return it on time; (3) library books have return dates; and (4) there are often long waiting lists for new books. With e-book technology, it is possible that hurdles 2, 3, and 4 from the previous list will go away entirely. Specifically, there is no need to go to the library because the content can be wirelessly pushed or downloaded to the e-book device direct from the library. Also, once you have the e-book, you don't have a time limit in which to return it. As for the waiting list for the more popular books, because there is no physical item or inventory (i.e., the book itself), it is limitless; theoretically, everyone in the world can read the book at the same time.

Libraries will need to set up some sort of licensing agreement in the short term with publishers when it comes to e-books. So, there may not be limitless inventories and time lines for library e-books. For example, if you want to read *The Girl with the Dragon Tattoo* as an e-book from the library, the library may only have the rights to five e-book copies at a time, and the content may automatically expire from your e-book reader in 30 days. The good news is that inventory will be easier to track (no more lost books), saving the taxpayer some money; libraries will be less costly to maintain. In the long run, the best model would be limitless, eliminating restrictions. The more information that is free and available, the more society benefits. The industry will also need to figure out how an e-book purchase can be passed from one friend to another. This is additional revenue for those in the publishing world, who historically haven't made money from this passing-on tradition. Many reading this right now may be doing so on an eReader, iPad, Tablet, phone, and so forth. Books are strangely social, so there could be new revenue streams for digitally passing a book from one device to the next.

Chapter Five Key Points

1. Consumers are looking to peers for recommendations on products, services, health issues, and more via social media. Only companies that produce great products and services will be part of these conversations; mediocrity will quickly be eliminated. Today, 78 percent rely on what others say, while 14 percent rely on advertising.[18] Social commerce is coming and it is going to be huge.
2. Social media's ability to share information helps eliminate different people performing the same tasks (multiple individual redundancies), resulting in a more efficient society.
3. The old adage that you can only have two of the following—cheap, quick, or quality—doesn't hold true within social media. It's possible to have all three.
4. Successful companies in social media will function more like entertainment companies, publishers, or party planners rather than as traditional advertisers.
5. With the increasing popularity of e-books, there will be new digital media placement opportunities for brands. This is very similar to product placement in movies, only this is for books, and the placements are clickable and trackable.
6. The most successful social media and mobile applications are those that allow users to brag, compete, or look cool by passing it on.
7. The main threat to Google in the search wars is not another search engine, but the rise of search queries within social media. More and more, products and services will find us (as opposed to us finding them).

CHAPTER SIX

Death of Social Schizophrenia

If you are Generation X or older you have most likely spent most of your life in a schizophrenic[1] world. You took on a different role or character depending on where you were and whom you were with. Most of us had at least two personas: a work persona and a non-work persona. And many of us had several personas: social, work, family, coach, charity, and so on.

Your behavior at an event like Woodstock, Mardi Gras, or Burning Man was very different from your behavior at the office. "Al the Accountant" may only be known by his coworkers as "Meticulous Accountant Al"; while his bowling pals would know him only as "Al-Valanche," because you better get out of the way when he is partying, otherwise you could be the next victim of the "Al-Valanche."

Even if you believe that life with social media is worse, you cannot argue that social media has forever changed the *way* in which we live.

In 2008, North Carolina's All-American basketball player Tyler Hansbrough found himself in the middle of a media whirlwind. Hansbrough was a hard-nosed player and the poster child of all that is good about college basketball. Because of his intensity, he was nicknamed Psycho T.

One sunny day in Chapel Hill, Hansbrough was hanging out with some friends at a fraternity house off campus. With some encouragement, Hansbrough thought it would be a thrill to launch his 6′10″, 260-pound body into the fraternity swimming pool. The thrill part being that he was jumping off the roof of the three-story house. Now, this type of behavior has been going on for decades from college students. However, on this particular day, one of the observers captured a video of Hansbrough's skydiving act on his smartphone.

Once this video became known to the general media, North Carolina's head basketball coach (Roy Williams) had a difficult decision to make. Should he suspend Hansbrough or not? Because drinking wasn't involved and Hansbrough was a model student athlete, he made the tough decision not to suspend Hansbrough. Helping Hansbrough's cause was his modus operandi of being intense—after all, Psycho T was just being Psycho T. If this had taken place five years ago, Coach Williams and Hansbrough would not have found themselves in such a predicament. Boys would be boys, no one would have known about it, and life would have continued.

Psycho T being Psycho T is a good example of the new world not having as many casual schizophrenics. People are best off being comfortable in their own skin and not pretending to be anything that they aren't. Well-known author Marcus Buckingham's (*Now Discover Your Strengths*) philosophy of playing to your strengths is further reinforced in a social media world. Transparency demands it, and with so much information flow, it is extremely difficult for a person who is well rounded to stand out in this new world.

Without a doubt, it is somewhat daunting to always be on one's best behavior. It is mentally taxing to have fewer avenues to blow off steam or to always maintain a perfect persona. Perhaps Al the Accountant is more effective at work and dogmatic on the details because outside of work he can let it all go and doesn't have to burden himself with the details.

As a result of preventative and braggadocian behavior, extra-curricular activities like music, theatre, and organized sports will become even more popular and important because they provide mechanisms of release for people.

There seems to be a place for interactive and virtual worlds, while the names and popularity change over time (Second Life, Sims, Webkinz, FarmVille, etc.). These social games allow users to create fictional personas (often in the form of what is called an avatar—from which the James Cameron movie may have derived inspiration) in computerized virtual worlds.

Farmville is a good example of how quickly these things can sprout up (forgive the pun). At the writing of this book, Farmville had 85 million users.

Like many successes, it is simple in nature. You start with a plot of land and your goal is to grow a very successful farm. You meet other farmers (real people playing the game) who can help you on your mission. There is even currency in the game where you can acquire items and use real currency (hard earned dollars, euros, etc.). FarmVille is most likely not here to stay, but after it has its run, something similar will come along to replace it. People simply enjoy meeting and competing against others online through these easy-to-use gaming mechanisms.

On the other hand, these simulation games may experience a rapid decline because people may find it difficult to brag about playing a simulated game that replicates life instead of just leading their own lives. Also, these games may be too transparent. A high school teacher can't simply take on the persona of a hooker specializing in sadomasochism without realizing long-term ramifications when this eventually becomes known. In fact, schools have terminated several teachers for this type of social media behavior. After all, there is a high degree of probability that the teacher could run into one of his or her students within the virtual world as well.

A happy medium may be social video games, which are already wildly popular. If I'm going to spend 60 minutes on the bike at the gym, it's much more exciting if I'm competing against digital avatars of people I know and don't know at other gyms, and even more exciting if there is a celebrity rider like Lance Armstrong who also happens to be on a stationary bike in Austin, Texas, while I'm on one in Cambridge, Massachusetts. Social gaming on the social networks themselves is going to be massive business. In fact in China, most people join networks in order to game first and meet people second.

While there are downsides to such 24/7 personal openness, overall, it's easier to argue that appropriate transparency is a good thing for individuals and society. It is, without question, much cooler to say you are bungee jumping off a remote mountain pass overhang in New Mexico than to update your status with "I'm watching the latest adventure reality series." Imagine a world that reintroduces people to living their own realities, rather than watching someone else's. Maybe this is why simulation games like Second Life haven't been as wildly successful as many pundits predicted; perhaps people have come to the realization that in reality (pun intended), it is much cooler to lead their own lives. Or perhaps there will always be a place for these types of games and networks when you think about Farmville and Webkinz.

One of the more overt examples of the downside of not *being yourself* within social media is the tragic case of Lori Drew. Lori was concerned that her daughter's friend, a 13-year-old named Megan Meier, was mistreating her daughter, Sara. So, Lori decided to set up a MySpace account pretending to be an attractive teenage boy named Josh Evans. Josh flirted with Megan and eventually they became social media friends and developed an online relationship. Once the hook was set, the persona of Josh then started berating Megan through a series of unfriendly comments and nasty remarks. These remarks proved too much for Megan, who had a history of battling depression, and one day she decided to take her life. At the time, Lori Drew (a 49-year-old Missouri mom) faced three years in prison and a $300,000 fine for an online harassment campaign that resulted in the suicide of a teenage girl. More laws are being enacted to curtail cyberbullies like Lori Drew.

Even Football Players Need to Calm Down

A University of Texas Longhorn offensive lineman found out the hard way the importance of preventative behavior in social media. The lineman posted a racist update on his Facebook profile just after Barack Obama was elected president of the United States: "all the hunters gather up, we have a #$%& in the whitehouse."[2]

Soon after that was posted, Coach Mack Brown kicked the lineman off the team. The lineman was unable to participate in Texas' 2009 bowl game. The lineman posted an apology to anyone his comment had offended, but the damage had already been done:

> *Clearly I have made a mistake and apologized for it and will pay for it. I received it as a text message from an acquaintance and immaturely put it up on Facebook in the light of the election. I'm not racist and apologize for offending you. I grew up on a ranch in a small town where that was a real thing and I need to grow up. I sincerely am sorry for being ignorant in thinking that it would be okay to write that publicly and apologize to you in particular. I have to be more mature than to put the reputation of my team at stake and to spread that kind of hate which I don't even believe in. Once again, I sincerely apologize.*[3]

Meanwhile, on another football team, University of Colorado Head Coach Dan Hawkins instituted the following rule for his players:

> *If I request to see your page, you'd better let me in and let me see it. Everybody's kind of got their own standards. I tell them if your mom can see it, and neither you nor she is embarrassed, then it's okay. But if your mom can't look at it, then it's probably not right.*[4]

Even the cheerleaders need to learn how to behave correctly in this newly opened society. A New England Patriots Professional Cheerleader was kicked off the cheer squad for inappropriate photo postings on her Facebook page. She and her friends went out on a wild drinking binge. When one of her friends passed out, they decided to write all over her half-naked body. They drew penises and other lewd symbols along with phrases like "I'm a Jew" and swastika symbols. They posted and shared these images of their crazy night with their friends.[5]

As a result of these examples and more, NFL teams started engaging in a controversial practice for the 2009 draft. Player personnel from respective NFL teams (Packers, Lions, etc.) started creating fake Facebook accounts. Most of these profiles were designed to look like they were those of young, energetic, and attractive females. The purpose was to become friends with potential draft picks so that the teams could conduct further research. Historically, NFL companies would spend hundreds of thousands of dollars on background investigations prior to paying a young college kid millions of dollars. This progression into social media subterfuge only makes sense for them. Similar to regular employers, hiring agents are looking for anything that could be viewed as detrimental. In some instances, they have seen drug posts and gambling items on the college player's profile.

The ethical nature of these NFL football teams creating fake profiles to bait 20-year-old athletes can certainly be questioned, but the key message is don't put anything on social media that you don't want the whole world to know about, because eventually, one way or another, the world will know about it.

Just like athletic programs, governments around the world are struggling to determine how to handle some social media issues. Twenty-two-year-old Croatian Niksa Klecak was picked up by police and interrogated after starting a Facebook group critical of Prime Minister Ivo Sanader. The group was dubbed "I bet I can find 5,000 people who dislike Sanader."[6] The interrogation drew sharp criticism from Croatia's opposition Social Democrat Party and has inspired a host of copycat Facebook groups.

Just as companies have discovered, perhaps the best tactic is not censorship, but rather to address the problem and/or have enough good karma produced that it overwhelms and drowns out the negative. Obama's 2008 election campaign is a good example of an overwhelming amount of good social media vibes drowning out the negativity of the various opposition groups.

Be the Best at Something, Not Everything

As previously discussed, the transparency and speed of information flow via social media mitigates casual schizophrenic behavior. This is generally a positive result because maintaining different personas is stressful, exhausting, and disingenuous.

The same holds true for corporate behavior in social media. For corporations, trying to be too many things to too many people is costly. Historically, we have seen the "we are the best at everything" messaging come out of many marketing departments. The marketers always start off with high hopes of simply highlighting one message in a 30-second commercial; but by the end of production, they have flooded the spot with numerous messages. The original intent of an advertiser may be to convey the message: "We have been in the business for 45 years." However, the end product is often something similar to: "We have been in the business for 45 years, we have the lowest prices, and we have the largest selection. Our brand name *Perfect* is the most trusted, and you can find us at great retailers like Sam's, Costco, and BJ's."

In a 140-character world, if you want to have a chance at helping the consumer retain a key message and eventually pass it on, it is imperative that you focus on your strengths or particular niche. There is also a need for the continuous flow of information across the entire organization; in particular, it is mission critical for production and marketing to be feeding information back and forth. It's one thing for marketing to respond to consumer complaints; it's an entirely different thing to respond to the customer's complaint, look for trends in product deficiencies, and work closely with production to develop solutions.

The role of a marketer today, and even more so in the future, has less to do with creating 30-second television commercials and guessing what jingle will resonate with prospects, and more to do with having ongoing external conversations with the customer or prospects—while at the same time having internal conversations with operations, customer care, and product development.

In turn, production and development will be less about being behind closed doors in a laboratory and more to do with being connected with marketing; they, too, will have an ongoing dialogue with the customer. Two prime examples of production personnel in 2008 that have the dual role of product vision and being a public face to the organization are Dave Morin of Facebook and Matt Cutts of Google. At developer conferences, Dave and Matt are almost at the level of rock stars, and they have become the faces of their respective organizations in the development community. They aren't behind closed doors trying to figure out the next best thing for their target audience, they are in constant contact with their target audience, and a large part of their role is also marketing. These are two great examples of what marketers will look like in this Socialnomic era.

One Message

Companies that engage in brand marketing have always known it is best to keep the message simple and convey one salient point. Some companies were able to adhere to this principle, including 7UP's "Uncola" campaign or FedEx's "When it absolutely positively has to get there overnight" campaign. However, many companies have struggled with this concept. Most often, they get myopic—this product/service is so great we need to get it out there—or they get internal pressure from too many executives trying to get their particular interests across. Companies are lucky if the advertising they create gets remembered at all by the customer, let alone gets the key message across.

So, when a car company crams in that they have the best miles per gallon, horsepower, and stereo, and they list all the special promotional lease offers with an accompanying disclaimer and then add all the local dealer names at the end of a 30-second commercial, all they are doing is causing mass confusion for the viewing audience. Even when marketing teams know they are supposed to stick to one message, companies often fail to do so because of the pressure of all these different elements and parties involved; too many cooks in the kitchen spoil the broth.

The beauty and curse of a 140-character world is that there is no longer a choice. Tony Blair indicated at the 2008 World Business Forum in New York, "Because of the proliferation and speed of information, people and the press want everything in succinct and easy to digest packages. However, some very complex problems can't be put that way. It is quite an extraordinary challenge."[7] Whether we like it or not, right or wrong, we have to adapt to communication in succinct and salient sound bites.

From production and strategic positioning standpoints, the beauty is that it forces companies to improve. If your company or product can't definitively state what it stands for and how it differs from the competition in a few short words, then it is time to reevaluate exactly what you are doing. If you don't have a niche position in a marketplace that you are attempting to defend from your competition, and you are trying to be all things to all people, then you are doomed to failure.

This destructive behavior may have taken longer to figure out in the past because marketing mediums allowed advertisers to cram in many different benefits in the hope that so many great things would entice consumers to buy. This was also during a time when customers were more willing to be *spoken to* rather than have a *conversation with*. They may have bought your product based solely on the glitz and glamour of your marketing. This possibility is very limited now that we are living in a world with social media.

The good news is that in this new world order, once you have determined your initial messaging strategy you have the ability to reevaluate and tweak it for relevancy based on feedback from the marketplace. Because you will be engaging in a conversation with your customer, you will be able to identify and adapt to changing needs much quicker. That's why it's important to ensure your marketers and production teams are on the same page.

Past Marketer's Philosophy

- It's all about the sex and sizzle of the message and brand imagery.
- It's all about the message; good marketers can sell anything.
- We know what is right for the customer—we are doing the customer a service because they really don't know what they want.
- We develop products and messaging "inhouse" and then disperse them to the public.

Present/Future Marketer's Philosophy: It's important to listen and respond to customer needs.

- It's all about the product; it's necessary to be in constant communication with all other departments.
- We never know what is exactly right for the customer; that is why we are constantly asking and making adjustments, because we usually don't get it right the first time.
- Take up the motto: Fail forward, fail fast, fail better.
- Often our customers will market the product better than we can; if we can leverage one of their ideas, then it is beneficial to everyone.

Referral Program on Steroids

If you were to ask chief marketing officers (CMOs) of varying businesses, ranging in size from Fortune 500 companies to small business owners, what their top performing channels or programs are, the majority would indicate that their referred customers are the most valuable. *Top performers* being defined in terms of return on investment (cost to acquire said customer) as well as the quality of the customer acquired.

The logical follow-up question for the CMOs—what is the greatest challenge you face? The response would again focus on referrals, only it would be fixated on the difficulty in obtaining mass volume from this lucrative channel—"how can we get more?"

For the first time, social media enables corporations and marketers to generate this desired mass scale from the existing customer base. It is truly Word of Mouth on Steroids. Or Word of Mouth goes to World of Mouth.

In the 1990s and continuing into the twenty-first century, Jeff Bezos and Amazon have done a stellar job of introducing the concept of affinity marketing to millions worldwide. For example, when you purchase a DVD or book from Amazon, Amazon gives real-time suggestions of what you might like based on your own prior purchases.

Millions have found this feature to be very helpful, and it has taken us into an appropriate progression in marketing. However, as many have also learned, there are a few pieces to this program that are suboptimal—such as, if you purchase a gift for your four-year-old niece under your own Amazon account. While your niece may enjoy suggestions to buy My Little Pony or American Doll, you as an adult aren't often in the market for such items.

Much more helpful and useful was Amazon's introduction of the ability to showcase to users: "People who purchased this book also purchased these other ones." Here's where social media comes in and takes this one giant step forward. In the Amazon model just described, you don't know the other people that are referenced. They are an aggregation of thousands of others who happen to have the same purchasing patterns. In other words, there is no personal connection between you and them. The only shared connection is that you *might* share similar buying habits.

In social media, you still have this same aggregate data made available to you by the Amazons and RedEnvelopes of the world: "Here's what the total universe enjoys." But, in social media, it goes significantly deeper to show: "Here's what your specific network enjoys." Within your network, you will begin to identify a handful of friends, possibly more, who seem to have similar tastes and opinions that you can trust. The circle you trust for recommending movies may be entirely different from the circle you trust for restaurant recommendations.

For example, when you see on your favorite social media tool that your friend Angie—who normally purchases and reads romance novels—purchased and begun reading a science-fiction novel (there are social media applications and widgets that do exactly this), you might scratch your head and think it quite odd that Angie would be reading such a thing. However, Angie's recommendation and write-up on the science-fiction book pops up a few days later on your updates, and you are quickly enlightened regarding this oddity:

> *For those who know me well, you may be surprised to see that I just completed a science-fiction piece. This was quite a diversion from my usual romance novel obsession—but let me tell you it was a refreshing one. Thanks goes to my husband who is an avid sci-fi fan; when he came across this book and read it, he thought I would like it too—and right he was! I loved it. I highly recommend this book and can say it's one of the best I've read in the past three years.*

Now, as Angie's good friend who shares very similar tastes when it comes to reading, how likely is it that you are going to want to read this book? My guess is pretty likely. You are definitely more apt to give it a try than if you had seen the *exact same* write-up on Amazon.com by someone you didn't know; someone who you didn't identify with or trust immediately.

Then there is Angie; she has a reputation to uphold within her network. If it were a blind review process—like Amazon or Yahoo! movies, she would be less likely to put as much thought into it as she will for her own network. Spelling a word incorrectly isn't quite as taboo for Angie if it's not going to be knowingly shared with those who know her and are close to her. If users are debating between giving a particular movie three or four stars and the user has "identity immunity," studies have shown that he/she is more likely to give four stars. Conversely, if the user's review is going to their friends, they are more likely to be conservative and give it three stars. This is somewhat intuitive because you would never want to be the cause of a friend's bad evening at the show; instead, you would rather under promise and over deliver.

Of course, this concept of sharing and reviewing among friends isn't new—book clubs have been around for years. The difference is that book clubs meet once per month and will continue to do so. The need for book clubs doesn't go away. However, with social media, information is shared daily and is about much more than just the single book that was assigned. It also allows others to be involved who can't make it to traditional book clubs for a myriad of reasons, geographical limitations, family commitments, job demands, and so on.

So, what does this change mean for companies exactly? It means that many of their dreams have become realities—"If only we could get more referrals." Well, the referral floodgates have been opened, my friends. However, companies should be careful what they wish for. Great companies that already produce great content, products, or services welcome the frontier of Socialnomics with open arms. While they are not guaranteed continued success, they are certainly positioned for it. Meanwhile, those companies that have survived to date by being great at middleman games—whether distribution-related, direct mail, brand marketing, lobbying, public relations, or legal rights—will have a greater challenge in front of them. This challenge must be taken on immediately to secure survival.

Middlemen are becoming less important than they've been in the past, and the rise in power is shifting rapidly to the social graph. This was no more evident than in the 2008 race for the Democratic Party presidential candidate (more in Chapter 4) where a little-known senator from Illinois was able to defeat one of history's great political machines—Hillary Clinton. This type of historic victory would have been extremely difficult to architect without the Obama camp having the ability to understand and to leverage the power and advantage that Socialnomics brings. In this instance, the Clinton Political Machine was the item that had lost some of its power, and that power was transferred to the social graph.

Chapter Six Key Points

1. The transparency and speed of information exchanged within social media mitigates casual schizophrenic behavior. Having a work personality *and* a party personality will soon become extinct. People and companies will need to have one essence and be true to that essence.
2. Being well rounded as a company or individual is less beneficial. It's more productive to play to your core strength. This differentiates you from the competition. You need to stand out in order to be outstanding.
3. Companies that produce great products and services rather than companies that simply rely on great messaging will be winners in a Socialnomic world. The social graph is the world's largest and most powerful referral program.
4. Marketers' jobs have changed from creating and pushing to one that requires listening, engaging, and reacting to potential and current customer needs.
5. Fail forward, fail fast, fail better.

CHAPTER SEVEN

Winners and Losers in a 140-Character World

Today there are websites that reduce or make URLs tiny so that people can fit them within their social media postings, which often have character limits. These tools take a URL string of roughly 100 characters and condense it down to 15, making the URL tiny. This is necessary in today's soundbite world and is a reflection of a societal shift from the languid days of sipping lemonade on front porches to multi-tasking in WiFi-enabled Starbucks. In a world where everything is condensed and hyper-accelerated, who wins and who loses? In this section, we will explore several case studies that shed light on what it takes to succeed in the world of Socialnomics.

Does ESPN Have ESP?

Some savvy entrepreneurs at ESPN were ahead of the curve in recognizing the different fundamentals of Socialnomics. Their success was the result of innovation and necessity. Fantasy

Football's popularity has grown rapidly since its beginnings in the 1980's. As a result, in 2008, ESPN started to dedicate more of its television programming to discuss pertinent events related to Fantasy Football; but this increased coverage still wasn't enough. Fantasy Football experts Matthew Berry and Nate Ravitz knew that the public hungered for more and approached the ABC/ESPN brass. Their plea for more Fantasy Football airtime proved successful.

Although they were not granted airtime or support, they were given the green light to produce their own podcast, *Fantasy Football Today,* which quickly became one of the top-20 most downloaded podcasts within the Apple iTunes store. This was a great achievement, but they were still moonlighting and hadn't produced any revenue that would spark ESPN's attention for more support. This is when they embarked on two very innovative facets and, whether knowingly or not, they were engaging in Socialnomic activity. These two facets were actually making the sponsors part of the show's content and also allowing listeners to help produce some of the content as well.

As a result of their rapid ascent in the iTunes download rankings, *Fantasy Football Today* drew the attention of some savvy, big-time marketers. Their first sponsor included the feature film *Eagle Eye.* This movie featured Shia LaBeouf and was produced by Steven Spielberg. Aside from covering the latest in Fantasy Football, Berry and Ravitz often touch on pop culture, including commenting on the popular 1990s' television show *Beverly Hills 90210* as well as the *New 90210.*

The podcast varies in length from 15 to 30 minutes depending on how much news they have to cover. The varying lengths of the podcasts are an important item to note and a reflection of how our world is changing. Radio and television broadcasts historically attempt to fill an allotted slot of time. That isn't the case with podcasts. If a podcast only has 16 minutes of newsworthy items to cover, then why waste the commentators' and viewers' time trying to fill the slot with subpar content?

The fact that *Fantasy Football Today* was able to secure a sponsor for the podcast wasn't innovative—this was inevitable once they began to attract a vast audience of listeners. We have seen this type of sponsorship in various podcasts. Another good example is the technology podcast, CNET's *Buzz Out Loud (BOL)*. Recognized as one of the most popular podcasts in 2008[1] covering Internet and Technology news, it too plays up the fact that its segments are of "indeterminate length." Its popularity is well deserved because the information is delivered in a concise, but humorous fashion and all angles are covered.

Although BOL was successful in securing big-name sponsors including Best Buy, they originally adopted an old paradigm format when it came to their advertising model. They played a commercial in the beginning, middle, and end of the podcast. Just like in the television world, it was not integrated but rather interruptive; this is disruptive to the listening audience. Worse, for seven months straight, Best Buy played the same exact commercial! Please keep in mind that the podcast listening audience is not made up of casual listeners. People don't simply flip through channels and land on something of interest. This podcast is downloaded daily, so many of their loyal listeners are the same from podcast to podcast.

What a wasted opportunity for Best Buy! They could have taken advantage of the glowing personalities of the hosts (at the time Molly Wood, Tom Merritt, and Jason Howell) and adjusted the messaging daily by having the hosts read or incorporate the messaging into the show as they saw appropriate. Instead, Best Buy took its terrestrial radio spot and plopped it right in the middle of the show. However, the good news is that CNET was able to learn from this and in 2010 started taking advantage of the colorful personalities and insights of Wood, Merritt, Needleman, and Howell. Hence, these guys were able to seamlessly work the sponsors in as part of the show, often with tongue-in-cheek references about how the products are used. This helps showcase something else: "the talent" of these shows getting actively involved with every facet of the production of the show, which ultimately makes it better for the listening audience and sponsors.

In fact, the hosts made so much fun of one sponsor's voice over sounding like a mafia hit man that the company made all new spots making the entire spot sound like a scene out of *The Godfather*. This makes advertising fun, and this is a far cry from playing the same commercial for 7 months straight.

Stop the Charade—Nobody Is Perfect

Let's stay on that thought for a moment and review what ESPN did with their sponsor, *Eagle Eye*. As we mentioned, getting a sponsor for the podcast wasn't innovative; rather, it was the way in which they seamlessly incorporated the advertisements into the show, often in a tongue-in-cheek fashion. Host Matthew Berry was single at the time, and the running joke was that he couldn't get a date.

Occasionally, Berry would even chide himself about his want for female attention. Around the release date of the *Eagle Eye* movie, Berry kept with this shtick and dropped comments like "even if this movie is terrible, you should go see it to pay homage to Michelle Monaghan's hotness." A comment like that would often lead into a few other comments about what movies she was in and so on. This was all done without disrupting the flow of the football-themed show. Often, these tangents by Berry were about various female celebrities' attractiveness quotient—which wasn't a stretch because the listening audience is 90 percent beer-swilling males. The hosts would even give candid feedback and comments after watching the movie and discussing what they liked and didn't like about the film.

The sponsor, the producers of *Eagle Eye,* were also engaging in some basic principles of Socialnomics by allowing the hosts to say what they thought about the movie even if it included negative phrases like "even if this movie is terrible." This was a very smart move by the advertisers. By pointing out flaws, people will give more credence when you point out your strengths. If you try to present yourself or your company as always being perfect, then the listening audience will suspect what you have to say isn't completely true. In fact Bazaarvoice, a leading provider of ratings systems, has studies showing that if a website has two similar products side by side the consumer is more likely to purchase the product with a 4.5-star rating than the product with a 5-star rating. This doesn't make intuitive sense; so the consumers were questioned about their decision. The responses were similar in the sense that they thought the product with the 4.5-star rating was more credible. They also liked the fact that they were able to see what other people didn't like about it and discovered the complaints weren't important or relevant to them. A 5-star rating didn't seem credible to them, because they felt no product can be perfect.

Southwest Airlines realizes they are better off stating: "We only give you peanuts so that our fares cost peanuts." Rather than trying to claim that they have great food and great low airfares.

Certainly a movie is a simple product to incorporate into a show without it being too intrusive. However, the Fantasy Football podcast followed up the movie trailer success with an even greater success—their subsequent sponsor, Charles Schwab. It's difficult to find anything invigorating to say about a financial company, especially during the 2008 financial meltdown, but this podcast was able to deliver the Charles Schwab message brilliantly. The whipping boy on the show was the producer, aptly nicknamed "Pod Vader" (a takeoff on Darth Vader), who was constantly hazed by the hosts for killing the show by virtue of his incompetence. In one of the early podcasts, while they played a robotic-sounding device that answered yes or no questions, they dubbed the robotic voice "Chuck" because the advertising slogan at the time for Charles Schwab was "Talk to Chuck."

They even had a running joke that Pod Vader was Chuck and that Chuck was Pod Vader.

A typical show during this time went something like this:

Nate: Willie Parker is listed as questionable for this week's game and the *Pittsburgh Gazette* reports that his backup, Maurice Moore, is most likely to start. So if you have Parker, you may want to pick up his backup Moore, because Parker will most likely not be able to play.

Berry: Yes, but the Steelers are going against the Ravens and the top-rated run defense. So, you may be better off picking up Dominic Rhodes of the Colts instead of Parker.

Nate: I disagree; **let's ask Chuck. Chuck**, don't you feel that Moore is a better choice than Rhodes?

Synthesized voice: No.

Nate: Okay, **Chuck** has spoken. Now it's time to read some e-mail from our listeners. This one comes from Fred in St. Louis, and he asks, "Should I trade Roy Williams for Larry Johnson? If it helps my chances of you reading this e-mail on air, I went and signed up for a **Charles Schwab** checking account after hearing you guys say I can earn **3 percent interest."**

Berry: It does help because **Chuck** knows when to **buy low** and **sell high** just like the stock market, and in this case, you should sell Roy Williams high because he isn't going to have any more value than he does right now.

Nate: Great job in working in the sponsor.

Berry: Well, I am a company man.

Synthesized voice: **Chuck** says yes. [Laughter]

Berry: That was Pod Vader not **Chuck** because Pod Vader is **Chuck.**

Pod Vader: No I am not Chuck! [Laughter in the studio . . .][2]

This was brilliant and far different from a traditional 30-second radio advertisement because the sponsor and *Fantasy Football Today* realized their format (daily podcast) differs from regular radio advertising—they weren't going to make the same mistake that Best Buy did by running the same spot for seven months straight to the same audience. Instead, creatively incorporating Charles Schwab placement became an integral part of the show without it being intrusive; in fact, you could argue that it enhanced the show by adding a witty element to it. In this case, through creative thinking, the advertiser's involvement actually added content rather than interruption. While we point out a mistake made by Best Buy, they quickly learned from their mistake and enabled by a CMO with a strong love of social media, have pioneered some great social media programs (e.g., Best Buy Blue Shirt employees empowered to answer customer needs on Twitter).

Consumers today, in particular Millennials and Generation Zers, don't want advertisers to shout; they'd rather have conversations and steady ongoing relationships with companies. The callers and e-mailers on the *Fantasy Football Today* show were having fun with the sponsorships by writing them into the show and referencing the sponsors in their e-mails. For example: "I have my **Eagle Eye** on the Packers game this week" and "**Chuck** may know finances, but he was wrong about running back Dominic Rhodes—that chump didn't score a touchdown this week so I am going to **Chuck** him off my fantasy football team this week."

The most Socialnomic piece of all in regards to this *Fantasy Football Today* podcast example is that the advertising wasn't wrapped around the content, but rather was an integral part of it. This is important because when items are passed virally between individuals using social media tools, if the advertisements are on the front or back end of the valuable content or they are banners or display advertisements that float on the periphery of the content, they are too easily stripped or removed when the content is passed from one person to the next. For example, in a company-sponsored video on YouTube, where banners are to the left and right of the video, when the video is shared among a social network—since the ads aren't in the video itself—only the video will be passed on. The advertising placement will be eliminated from the string, and the potential viral activity will be lost.

In Chapter 3, we discussed a Diet Coke and Mentos example, in which you can see that the Diet Coke items and product placement are the actual content itself. It's important to note the dramatic shift that is being propelled by social media. The world around us is shifting from a model where marketers historically have supported content to a world in which marketers and companies need to create their own content or seamlessly integrate with existing content. Ironically, this harkens back to the advent of television, when sponsors helped produce the content; soap operas are aptly named because soap powder companies used to write shows around the use of their products.

Free Labor

In the *Fantasy Football Today* podcast, it would be painfully difficult to try to find every iteration or mention of "Charles Schwab" or "Chuck" because it is actually part of the show—it's not nearly as simple as removing an advertisement that was placed at the front, middle, and end of a broadcast. The second major Socialnomic piece that the football podcasts at ESPN employed was leveraging the audience base to assist with content. As mentioned, these podcasts needed to be produced inexpensively. They weren't getting large financial backing from corporate headquarters; rather, it was "sink or swim."

One segment during the week was to report on the various teams across the league. If they had employed the principles of the past, they would have started by using and leveraging existing field reporters (e.g., Sal Paolantonio, Adam Shefter, and John Clayton) who would be sent to the various cities and team camps to learn and report back on the particular happenings of those teams. In this scenario, the shows' producers would receive high-level reporting from experts on a few teams during the week. This is an outrageously expensive model because it includes incurring costs for flights, hotels, and transportation, per diem, as well as paying top talent with celebrity-esque salaries easily in the six-figure range. These are costs that the *Fantasy Football Today* podcast could not afford to sustain. As a result, the producers of these podcasts decided to travel down a different path that has resulted in a brilliant revolution in news reporting. Because of its success, we are seeing a shift toward this type of news reporting today.

The producers had people write the show requesting to be the "Super Fan" for their particular team. Many companies attempt to get this level of engagement by giving away a costly contest prize for people who submit their photos with a product, create a video, or write an essay about why they deserve to be a contest winner.

This historically popular giveaway or sweepstakes approach can have the opposite effect on people submitting entries because it devalues what you are attempting to do and a typical response from a potential contestant may be "oh this company needs to bribe us to submit something and since that prize is of no value to me, I will *not* submit anything for it."

The Tom Sawyer Approach

ESPN decided to engage in a different practice rather than employ a typical sweepstakes model. ESPN didn't give anything away, and they had hundreds of applications from fans expressing heartfelt reasons and arguments about why they should be the Super Fan of their particular NFL team. Keep in mind that if these applicants were selected as a Super Fan, then their responsibilities would include weekly check-ins reporting the current status of their particular team—they would need to know everything about them. Rather than a sweepstakes prize, the winners would actually be put to work!

This is a monumental step toward leveraging the audience base. ESPN's loyal podcast listeners were begging to do free work! This is analogous to when Tom Sawyer was painting the fence white and made it appear so appealing to those around him that they were hoodwinked into begging Tom to have a chance to paint the fence. Tom Sawyer knew that if his approach was "ah come on, if you help me paint this, there is a chance I will buy you some red licorice," it wouldn't be nearly as effective as giving the illusion that painting the fence was fun.

In this ESPN instance, the audience has become Jane the Blogger (Chapter 1). These are people who have a pressing desire to be heard. They are people who want to be a part of something bigger than themselves. They are also fanatical about their teams, and their teams say something about who they are (similar to brands). A fan of the San Francisco 49ers is more "wine and cheese with a flair for the dramatic" whereas a fan of the Pittsburgh Steelers is more "meat & potatoes, Jerome Bettis, and no nonsense."

ESPN leveraged its worldwide platform to ensure that these Super Fans didn't make competing platforms at the local level. It is a proactive way to look at the old saying, "if you can't beat 'em, join 'em." They reversed this old axiom with an approach of "join 'em before they beat you." Every person today is a competitive media outlet.

During the Super Fan selection process, they even allowed for the audience to help determine the criteria for selection. If your suggestion was taken, then you were automatically named a Super Fan. One of the winning suggestions was that each applicant should have to donate a minimum of $25 to the Jimmy V Foundation for the Fight Against Cancer. So, as part of the application process, submitters were showing receipts to prove that they had in fact donated at least $25.

They picked the best and brightest of the bunch to be the delegated Super Fan for each team. There was a San Diego Chargers Super Fan, Detroit Lions Super Fan (bless their heart), and so on. Whether ESPN knew it or not, they were practicing Socialnomics and utilizing a brilliant strategy that can be summarized by the following:

1. The show garnered hundreds of fans who demonstrated their engagement with the show by sending in applications detailing why they should be a Super Fan. Some of the more humorous entries were read on the air even if they weren't selected as the winner.
2. They asked their audience what the selection criteria should be and received a recommendation that was better than anything they would have conjured up behind a closed studio door. Specifically, requiring donations to the Jimmy V Foundation for the fight against cancer as part of the application process was a great contribution for a great cause.
3. They avoided paying reporters and associated travel costs.
4. They are able to report on all 32 teams during the same week.
5. The Super Fans became expert reporters. As team fanatics, they were able to give a fan perspective on what people cared about. They digested all pieces of media just like Jane the Blogger about their particular team. They were a little unpolished in delivery, but since it was a podcast and not live, they could edit it accordingly to glean the appropriate sound bites.

6. ESPN was proactively helping to avoid competition in the future. These individual Super Fans had more than enough knowledge to do their own podcasts on their particular teams. By proactively asking them to join ESPN, ESPN proactively eliminated some potential competition down the road. Every individual today is a media outlet.
7. These 32 Super Fans also have tremendous reach within the communities and social media tools in which they engage. "Hey Mom, I know you don't know anything about football, but download this podcast because I'm on it today!"

Point 7 isn't a new construct, but it is very powerful with social media. Local newspapers have used this principle for years. The content of the local newspaper story wasn't half as important as ensuring that it was as crammed with local names—the closer it was to a yellow pages listing, the better. This is a testament to Dale Carnegie's statement that everyone's favorite word in the English language is his or her own name. ESPN realized, just like Dale Carnegie, that if they took on 32 new helpers, those 32 new helpers would be excited to spread the word to their respective social graphs.

While ESPN gets an A, they don't get an A+. One thing they will learn in time is that it's difficult for a host like Berry to perform double duty in the Socialnomic age. At the time of this writing, Berry was doing both Fantasy Baseball and Fantasy Football podcasts. Since the respective seasons have crossover, it is virtually impossible for him to be as knowledgeable as the users demand for either baseball or football. Some of these fantasy fans are fanatics of just one sport. If you can't convey to listeners that you are more expert than them, then they will tune out or may even decide that they could do a better podcast! In our new niche world, Berry should focus on just one sport, because his audience and future competition will.

Everybody Wants His or Her 15 Minutes of Fame

Another good example of a company effectively using the Tom Sawyer Approach is CNN (iStory and Twitter). CNN anchor Rick Sanchez was an early adopter of harnessing the power of the social graph. Recognizing the huge potential of microblogging, Sanchez became an avid user of Twitter early on. Twitter's main function allows users, in 140 characters or less, to update people who are following them about what they are doing by using various interfaces (Twitter website, TweetDeck, Hootsuite, Twitter modules for iGoogle, Facebook, Yahoo!, etc.). Usage ranges from business, "Great article on Southwestern Airlines earnings release can be found here www.abc.com" to the inane, "Just had my fifth Starbucks Pumpkin Spice Venti!"

Obviously, some of Sanchez's activities, "Briefing about Prime Minister David Cameron interview tonight; just learned that he may disclose some new and interesting information about Barack Obama and the BP Oil Spill," are much more interesting than a friend informing you that he is hopped up on pumpkin-flavored Starbucks. Rick was probably pleasantly surprised when within a few weeks over 75,000 people were following what he was tweeting. He then discovered it was more important to talk less about himself and more about his upcoming interviews. From there, he started to leverage the Twitter platform to ask thought-provoking questions like: "I'm interviewing Colin Powell tonight. What would you like to know most about Iraq or Iran?" Here is a string of tweets from the 2008 Presidential Debate between McCain and Obama:

> ... if they twittered they'd know how to make the words fit right? (8:17 *PM* Oct 15 from Web)
>
> ... like this ... put it on joe the plummer, personalize it. way to go mccain (8:11 *PM* Oct 15 from Web)

. . . mccain plan, do you rescue everybody, even guy who paid for house he couldn't afford. even . . . flippers? (8:10 *PM* Oct 15 from Web)

. . . Okay, i can't dance. my mother is so ashamed, she can. (3:05 *PM* Oct 15 from Web)

. . . many blaming palin for Mc-palin slide in polls? is that fair? what u think? (12:43 *PM* Oct 15 from Web)

. . . mccain: "doesn't think i have guts to bring up bill ayers" should he? how should obama respond? this could be fun, showdown okay corral. (10:47 *AM* Oct 15 from Web)[3]

These examples illustrate why social media is so revolutionary. Rick is able to have a relationship with 75,000 people—they feel more connected with him than they had before he started to leverage the Twitter platform. By responding to Rick's questions, they think they are helping to produce the show, which in many ways they are.

Become a Modern Day Pied Piper

Rick also started following a large percentage (roughly 32,000) of the people following him. "How can he follow so many people?" you astutely ask. He isn't actually keeping tabs on their tweets unless they relate directly to his questions. He is following these people as a courtesy. The etiquette on Twitter is debatable, but many believe that if people follow you, then you should probably follow them. They will never know if you didn't read one of their tweets! If you don't re-follow someone, then you are saying that you have something more important to say than they do, which might not be the impression you wish to convey. The counter argument to this is, if I am a known celebrity or company, am I openly endorsing someone by following him? What happens if that person performs nefarious or lewd actions? Does it reflect poorly on me since I'm following him? This etiquette will flush itself out in time. If you want to be conservative, then limit who you follow; if you want to follow everyone who follows you with the hope of developing a fan base—go for it. Many of these decisions boil down to your appetite for risk versus reward.

Getting back to CNN, the next logical progression was to get them on the show. Obviously, you can't get 75,000 firemen, carpenters, tech nerds, teachers, and the like on the show. Or can you?

So, Rick and his producers started asking the 75,000 followers about their thoughts on various subjects and they put the responses/tweets up on TV during the show on the scrolling byline at the bottom of the screen. This was brilliant because it added content to the show and also encouraged Rick's 75,000 followers to watch just so that they could see if their comment made the show! Remember the local newspaper philosophy: The closer it is to a phone book full of names, the more possible readers you will attract. The same can be said for 75,000 tweets scrolling on CNN.

In a Socialnomic world, companies need to relinquish the total control they have had over the last few centuries and allow users, consumers, viewers, and so on to take their rightful ownership. Rick Sanchez's experiment, which turned into an overnight success, can be summed up in the following tweet from Rick's producers:

> *just finished editorial meeting with my group, may have great new video today. will share more shortly. like i say, it's your show. (9:31 AM Oct 21 from Web)*[4]

The key line in this tweet (message sent on Twitter) being "like i say, it's your show." Credit should go to CNN for allowing Rick to express himself on Twitter. Rick didn't go through any formal training on Twitter, nor did he sit through public relations and brand courses at CNN on what could be said. Rather, CNN let Rick and his producers run with it. Rick was representing CNN, but because of the nature of the technology, the brand chiefs and executives couldn't approve every sentence that Rick was issuing. They had to know that Rick was going to make some mistakes but that he would quickly adjust and move forward. CNN learned from Rick and replicated his success across all their shows and anchors.

Everybody Is Twittering, But Is Anyone Listening?

Whether Rick Sanchez, Britney Spears, or Lance Armstrong has 75,000 or 1,750,000 followers, they're all "A-Listers." People want to hear what they have to say. It's not because of Twitter; it's because these celebrities previously had a fan base.

Now, there will be a few new A-Listers that result simply from Twitter or microblogging. However, these will be few and far between.

So, what about the rest of us? If we have 1,500 followers, are any of them really listening? I'd argue that most are not. However, it's still a huge marketing tool, and the nobodies are now the new somebodies for the following reasons.

Twitter and other means of microblogging are free. If a local plumber has 1,500 followers, even if most of them aren't likely to be listening at any given moment, as long as at least one person is, that's all that matters. If that one person has a plumbing issue, the plumber now has a shot at new business, especially if the plumber acquired these followers simply by limiting his search.twitter.com query to people within a 25-mile radius. For that plumber, that one listener goes from a nobody to a somebody in a hurry. Twitter has enabled geo-location tools so that if a user has it enabled, you are able to see where that tweet came from—this is a huge help for local businesses.

Some salient uses of microblogging:

- Businesses following what is being said about them or their industry—Zappos, JetBlue, Best Buy, Comcast, and so on.
- Celebrity updates—Lance Armstrong tweets about his collarbone. Actor Ashton Kutcher has close to five million followers on Twitter and often his tweets are cause related.
- Real-time updates of news events, especially natural disasters.
- Niche topics, like #MSU, #Kansas, or #Duke basketball during March Madness.
- Tweets for causes, charities, organizations, churches, fundraising, etc.
- You name it, you can probably make it happen on Twitter.
- Individuals or companies promoting themselves.

And it's the last point—individuals or companies promoting themselves—that may eventually cause Twitter to become tiresome. Is Dale Carnegie rolling over in his grave because everyone on Twitter is trying to be heard, when the key to winning friends and influencing people is actually listening? Some of Twitter's popularity in the beginning was the fact that not everyone was on it, giving it effectiveness and a cool factor. When it becomes flooded with marketing messages, it loses both effectiveness and uniqueness, which may lead many users to abandon Twitter and move on. In fact, a majority of users who sign up for Twitter quickly abandon it. That being said, Twitter and other forms of microblogging will be popular for quite some time. Facebook will definitely make a large play in the near future to have their status updates attempt to replace Twitter by increasing their functionality. There is just too much business being generated.

Smithsonian Student Travel sent more than 6,000 students to Washington, DC, for the presidential inauguration. In the past, it would have been difficult to get major media outlets' attention. However, Twitter made it easy. NPR, MSNBC, and PBS immediately replied to Smithsonian Student Travel's tweets, expressing interest in hearing from middle-school students and teachers.

However, two months after that, I typed in #JetBlue, expressing my concern that their in-flight televisions may not work on my particular flight. This was important to me because I selected JetBlue solely for the purpose of watching March Madness on DirectTV. Instead of hearing tweets, I heard crickets chirping. It's cool when companies and even CEOs respond in real time. This was not the case, however, in this particular instance.

In JetBlue's defense, they're somewhat victims of their own success on Twitter (Morgan Johnston does a fantastic job). People expect the best from them because they've been one of the pioneers. As a result, more people tweet and follow them and it's difficult for them to keep pace. In another instance with JetBlue, there were some massive storms in the Northeast beyond JetBlue's control and their call center was flooded. The average hold time was over an hour. Hence, I turned to Twitter to see what my options were. Unfortunately, they weren't able to respond to these tweets either, but guess who was: some other people who were in the same situation! My flight was scheduled for Sunday out of the SXSW conference before it was abruptly cancelled. Here are some of the helpful tweets I received:

@equalman: Don't bother waiting on hold, the first flight out of Austin Thursday—suggest Houston on Continental

@equalman All flights out Austin and Dallas are booked, you need to buy new ticket via Houston or San Antonio

While these tweets were not what I wanted to hear, nor did I hear back from JetBlue, they were very helpful! I was able to stop waiting on hold and take appropriate action. There were 15 other tweets like this since so many people were in a similar situation and had already done the vetting process. This helped eliminate redundancy on my part as well as many others. It also helped free up the phone lines and customer service for JetBlue, as there were other fliers like me who hung up once they were informed via other travelers on Twitter.

In another example, I tweeted an interesting article about Travelocity along with #travelocity and indicated that Travelocity was in deep trouble. Here are the responses I received:

@Travelocity: How deep of trouble?

@equalman: Pretty deep as it appears Priceline has the lead and only one or two online travel agents will survive. I love the gnome, so good luck!

@Travelocity: We like Gloria Gaynor;)

It took me a second to get it, but then I was laughing at this witty retort. Gloria Gaynor's famous disco song is "I Will Survive."

As more people join Twitter, this type of one-to-one relationship will be difficult to maintain. Many celebrities like Britney Spears and Kayne West have "ghost tweeters."

In the future, instead of getting a witty and salient reply from a CEO or well-informed employee, you'll most likely get an uninspired reply from a call center (tweet center?) in New Delhi—if you're lucky enough to get a response at all. Remember, I received no response to my #JetBlue tweet, where I was surprised and delighted by the Travelocity response. Again, to be fair to JetBlue, they are a shining example of a company that is taking social media head on and they are being rewarded. It's not a fluke that they have over 1.7 million followers on

Twitter while most of the other airlines, as of the writing of this book, have less than 60,000 followers.

Companies should still microblog, because the upside is still greater than the downside and it's similar to building a robust prospect and user database that you can message when appropriate. It's the modern age database.

TV Repeats Mistakes of the Music Industry

During the heyday of Napster, the music industry filed lawsuit after lawsuit about these new file-sharing technologies. While copyrights are important, energy and efforts should have been placed elsewhere. Instead of actions that disenfranchised their customer base (some of the largest numbers of downloaders and sharers were made up of music fanatics), the music industry should have been rejoicing that their distribution, production, and packaging expenses became almost nonexistent!

Music labels could sell direct to customers without the need to pay for packaging, shipping, compact discs, and so on. Some would argue that they didn't embrace the model because of copyright infringement, but the real reason they didn't embrace the model is that they didn't understand it.

By the time they understood the implications of such a runaway hit, it was too late. Apple deftly took a stranglehold of the industry with iTunes. Ironically, the music producers had been giving away free promotional records since the 1950s to radio stations. The music houses understood back then that the more their records got played, the more their sales would increase. Also, think about juke boxes, a very similar concept. Somehow the music labels lost sight of this construct in the digital era. Television executives could also make the same errors as the record labels and find themselves similarly standing on the outside looking in. Let's take a quick look at some developments.

NBC Earns Fool's Gold in the Olympics

The 2008 Beijing Summer Olympics were the most watched games in Olympic history. The opening ceremony was the biggest television event next to the Super Bowl, reaching 34.2 million American viewers, according to Nielsen Ratings.[5] Michael Phelps' historic swimming captured the nation. The recognition and use of online tools and video by NBC is commendable for that time.

So, did NBC deserve a gold medal for their coverage? On the surface, using old measures, they reached the podium, but they were awarded only fool's gold. Here's why.

There's This Thing Called the Internet

For one of Phelps' gold medals, NBC showed the action live in every time zone except on the West Coast, which was delayed three hours. Is NBC President Dick Ebersol not aware of a thing called the Internet? NBC failed to do what others had learned long ago: beg, borrow, and make better is the way of the Web.

Too many companies—in this instance, NBC—believe their problems are unique when it comes to the Web. However, plenty of other companies have already wrestled with similar issues.

Back in June of the same year, ABC made the right decision by streaming live on the Web the Tiger Woods and Rocco Mediate 18-hole playoff to decide the U.S. Open Championship. This was in addition to their television coverage. Company Web servers cringed, and America's productivity declined in March Madness-like fashion on that Monday, June 16, but ABC and the PGA were the big winners because they captivated millions of viewers on the Web that otherwise would have been lost.

The beauty is that ABC learned from their serendipitous situation in 2008 and leveraged social media fully in the following year (2009). Not only did they stream live action of the event online, but they also allowed seamless and easy commenting via Twitter, Facebook, and MySpace.

Why didn't NBC do the same thing with their Olympics coverage? Most likely because. . . .

Old Metrics Are Deceiving

They were fooling themselves with old metrics. Sure, NBC was happy to show less popular events online, but not precious events like swimming and gymnastics.

Why? Most likely, NBC and their advertisers (adidas, Samsung, Volkswagen, McDonald's, Coca-Cola, etc.) were judging themselves using old metrics, and that earned them nothing but fool's gold. They're judging success on some archaic Nielsen Television Rating system. They have the irrational fear that online viewership will cannibalize their normal ratings. However, eyeballs are eyeballs. They would have been better served opening up their online viewership because:

- It's more measurable.
- It has a younger audience.
- Users can't TiVo through commercials.
- Users are willing to give you valuable demographic information like name, age, gender, and so on in return for live online video.
- It increases—not decreases—your total viewership, which means more eyes on advertisements.

Don't Lie to Your Audience

NBC treated viewers with little regard, indicating that swimmer Dara Torres would be up in 14 minutes; 35 minutes later she finally swam her race. Worse, one night they indicated Phelps would be on in 32 minutes, and then when the time came, it was four minutes about his eating habits—he wasn't even swimming! Not to mention the whole computer-generated-enhancement-of-the-opening-ceremony debacle. As a quick refresher, they used animation on top of what was occurring at the actual ceremony so that the viewer at home had an enhanced version of what was actually occurring live.

Dead Air Equals Missed Opportunity

They got it right showing basketball in the early morning hours (8 and 10 EST) online; however, they missed two golden opportunities.

First, there was no option to hear announcers.

Second, and much worse for their advertisers, there weren't any advertisements during downtime. So, during basketball timeouts, there was just a wide shot of the court for awkward, three-minute intervals. Why didn't they use this opportunity to give their advertisers free placement during this dead air or even have additional Web-only advertisers? The technology to pull this off has been around for almost a decade—remember how Mark Cuban became a billionaire when Yahoo! purchased his broadcast.com?

Worse, for the 2010 Winter Olympic Games in Vancouver, NBC didn't learn from their mistakes. Instead, they took a giant step backwards, at least in the United States. In the United States, in order to watch anything online, you needed to prove that you were a paying subscriber of some form of cable, satellite TV, and the like. In countries like Canada, you could watch any event live online. The Canadians are smart; they realize that eyeballs are eyeballs and that an advertising model always works better for the paying client when more people can potentially *see* the advertisements.

For people who are traveling abroad, or people at work, sometimes the only way they can watch a particular show or an event is via the Internet. Denying potential viewership doesn't make much long-term business sense.

If a tidal wave is coming, it's better to start swimming with the current. Just like many people today no longer have landline phones in their homes; this medium has been replaced by the mobile phone. Likewise, more and more households are getting rid of their expensive cable or satellite televison subscription fees and relying on Web content for their entertainment.

Google Failed

It's potentially understandable that an old-school company like NBC may get some things wrong, but Google didn't exactly turn in a world record Olympics performance either.

When lesser-known athletes burst on the scene, the search engines had a difficult time serving up relevant search results. When the United States' David Neville dove for the finish line in a gallant effort to capture the bronze in the 400-meters, the search results on Google showed an actor/model by the same name, along with a company that could help you find people's phone numbers.

These poor search results were consistent for many of the athletes, so much so that Yahoo! and MSN attempted to manipulate the results by hand. Google finally threw in the towel and manually pushed news feeds and Wikipedia results to the top of the listings for many of the athletes. More and more people started going straight to Wikipedia; Jamaican runner Usain Bolt's page was updated within seconds of him breaking the record in the 200 meters.

Also, the last-minute nature of the YouTube/NBC deal was laughable. They signed the deal only days before the 2008 Olympics started. This should have been done weeks before; it's not like YouTube was new. They were the established player in the online video market. Since Google owns YouTube, Google and NBC should've placed a sponsored listing within the Google Search results for "watch Olympics on YouTube" explaining how the deal didn't cover the United States but was only for those people living outside of the United States. There were many frustrated Americans who thought they could watch Michael Phelps on YouTube and only discovered after several minutes of frustration that this option was only available in select countries.

That being said, NBC did show some improvements since 2004 (for instance, the Microsoft Silverlight picture quality online was a big advancement in the right direction). However, they don't deserve a gold medal for their incorporation of online tools. NBC failed to leverage best practices in regards to combining offline and online content. A bronze, or perhaps even a silver medal, was in order.

TV Shows Viewed through the Internet

It's inevitable that all of our broadcasts will eventually be pushed through the Internet and a majority will be viewed on tablets and iPads. Brand budgets that historically went to television, magazine ads, and outdoor boards are moving to digital channels for three main reasons: (1) the audience has moved there, (2) it's more cost effective, and (3) it's easier to track. What will happen?

In the short term, there will be companies that are able to take advantage of this transition. Just as online travel agent sites like Priceline, Orbitz, Expedia, and Travelocity were able to take advantage of suppliers (hotels, airlines, cruise lines, rental cars) and make a slow progression to Web bookings, aggressive conduit companies will be able to deliver what the audience wants. The same holds true for Napster, Limewire, and iTunes jumping on the opportunity made available by the ineptness of the music industry to embrace digital music.

At the beginning of 2008, Jeff Zucker, the boss of NBC Universal, told an audience of TV executives that their biggest challenge was to ensure "that we do not end up trading analog dollars for digital pennies."[6] Zucker understood that the audience was moving online faster than advertisers were, thus leaving media companies in a position of possibly losing advertising revenue and having their inventory devalued if and when they moved online with their television content. In the fourth quarter of 2008, online advertisements in video grew 10.6 percent and went from 2 percent of advertising to 3 percent.[7]

A good example of the use of this medium was also presented during the 2008 presidential election. Candidates don't care about distribution rights or upsetting their offline sponsors. They only care about getting the word out and making it as easy on their users (in this case, potential voters) to access and consume the information. Through their respective websites, each party streamed high-definition convention coverage around the clock. This forced CNN, MSNBC, FoxNews, and the like to do the same. The major networks didn't have time to decide if they would allow the public access—they were losing their audience to these other new distribution channels. This type of intense competition from unexpected places is a harbinger of the future. Who could have ever guessed that our political parties would be more advanced in terms of online video than our television networks?

The way in which we view broadcasts is also changing. In the political convention example, you had the ability to select various cameras to choose how you wanted to view the process. Specifically for the Democratic National Convention, you could have selected: (1) national broadcast angle, (2) side camera, (3) backstage, (4) camera focused on Barack Obama, (5) camera focused on Joe Biden, or (6) camera focused on Michelle Obama.

This ties back to braggadocian and preventative behaviors from Chapters 1 and 2. For example, if you are Michelle Obama, and you are being filmed throughout the entire convention, it's imperative you make certain that you aren't chatting away with your mom during the Speaker of the House's presentation. The upside for the viewer is that it allows for a more intimate relationship with the candidates and their families because viewers can see what they are like off camera.

NBC's *Sunday Night Football* was one of the first to introduce the idea of these various camera angles. They smartly viewed it as a way to capture online viewers, but also as a way to capture their regular television viewers who had laptops open for an enhanced viewing experience. NBC allowed the users to select various angles on the field as well as select cameras that were only following star players (like Tom Brady or Peyton Manning). The irony is that while NBC didn't excel for the Olympics, they were extremely progressive when it came to their NFL coverage online.

Applying this concept to content-focused shows like ABC's *The View* could prove to be a further success. Marketers would serve up different product offerings to someone who was viewing via the camera and was fixated on Elisabeth Hasslebeck, versus the viewer who was focused on Whoopi Goldberg.

Adjust Shows Based on Fast-Forward Behavior

Real-time data helps dictate content: With devices like TiVo and other digital video recorders (DVRs) in the offline world and YouTube analytics, producers of content are able to get real-time feedback about the content of their shows. If ESPN captures the TiVo/DVR information from their *SportsCenter* telecasts, and they see that fast-forward or skip rates increase 35 percent during hockey segments, it would behoove them to possibly cut this segment down or eliminate it altogether. They can make these adjustments in real time.

One entity rose quickly based on its ability to recognize the consumer's demand for online video of traditional programs and movies. The site hulu.com formally moved from private beta to product launch in March of 2008. Analysts, reporters, and bloggers panned the effort as Johnny-come-lately because there were several similar options in the marketplace (e.g., Veoh, Joost) and gave Hulu a limited chance at success because it would be weighed down with its commercially supported advertising model.

By September of 2008, Hulu was the sixth most-watched video-content provider on the Web with NielsenOnline reporting 142 million streams and 6.3 million unique monthly visitors.[8] They were able to surpass such television giants as Disney, MTV, ESPN, and CNN. Much of their success can be attributed to identifying the need for high-production-quality television shows and movies aggregated in one place on the Internet. They were so successful that in October of 2008, YouTube announced that they would start offering more full-length content and original production.In July of 2010 YouTube increased the upload capability for users to 15 minutes, the equivalent to 1/2 a sitcom.

An important part of Hulu's original success was the direct result of their understanding of Socialnomics. They understood that the 8 minutes of advertising that was generally included in a 30-minute sitcom would not be optimal for the user or for the advertiser. So, they went out of their way to ensure their 30-minute programs averaged 2 minutes worth of commercials. How can 2 minutes be better than 8 minutes worth of commercials for the advertiser? It was worth more because the recall was much higher.

"The notion that less is more is absolutely playing out on Hulu," Jason Kilar, the chief executive of the site, said. "This is benefiting advertisers as much as it is benefiting users."[9]

According to the Insight Express survey, advertisers saw a 22 percent increase in ad recall and a 28 percent increase in intent to purchase. This caused their advertising base to grow from 10 to 110, and clients ranged from McDonald's to BlackBerry.[10] "I've been waiting for this for 10 years," said Greg Smith, the chief operating officer of Neo@Ogilvy, an interactive agency of the Ogilvy Group.[11]

In some instances, Hulu users had the ability to select the format in which they receive the advertising. They elect to receive it all in one big chunk—usually movie trailers—or have it spread out in the typical format. The typical format for a 30-minute TV spot starts with a 30-second upfront "brought to you by," a 30-second commercial at the midway point, and then a closing commercial. Another social piece that was pure genius was that Hulu would indicate how long the commercial would be. Users don't have the ability to fast forward through commercials, but if they know it's only a 30-second commercial break, what are the odds of them getting up from where they are watching—not likely. The user likes this sense of control, and it echoes avid Internet video-fan Mary:

> *I was watching* Mike and Mike *on television at the gym, and they went to commercial break for six minutes, then came back and said they would be right back, well that was another eight minutes later. A 14-minute commercial break! Also it's maddening not knowing how long the break will be. At home, I TiVo through all the commercials, but when I watch online, I don't mind the commercials on Hulu because they are so short and they tell me when the show will be back on. In fact, my husband and I play a game trying to guess who will be the sponsor of* The Daily Show.[12]

Mr. Kilar of Hulu couldn't agree more: "We think that a modest amount of advertising is the right thing because that's going to drive atypical results for marketers."[13] A survey conducted by ABC also supported this notion—seeing that only running one advertisement during a 30-minute program generated an astounding 54 percent recall rate.[14]

The format was well conceived for the user and for the advertiser. Users are appreciative that sponsors are helping to provide them with *free* television in these types of new formats. In a survey conducted by Hulu and Insight Express, 80 percent of the viewers rated their experiences on hulu.com as good to excellent.[15] Users are less tolerant of commercials on cable and satellite services because they are already paying over $100/£60 for the service. Whereas on sites like Hulu, users are most appreciative of the sponsor, because when they hear that the program was brought to them by McDonald's, they know they owe McDonald's some gratitude for making it available online for free. This same message sounds hollow to the viewer via traditional broadcast television.

This is the same concept that television embraced back in the 1950s. However, over time they kept putting the advertiser ahead of the real client—the viewer. This marginalized the viewer experience, which in turn impaired the advertiser and eventually the broadcaster. Alarm bells should ring when the technology product winner of the year (TiVo) is a direct attempt to circumvent your service offering. Instead of fighting legal battles to stop such technology, advertisers should take the Socialnomic approach of understanding that something in the chain is broken and must be addressed.

Contrast this with a site like Hulu, where 93 percent of respondents to the Insight Express survey (18,000 surveyed) said they felt they were receiving the right amount of advertising for the free content they were enjoying. A large percentage of the sample even expressed that there could be more advertising. An estimated 14.3 million viewed the first Tina Fey "Palin Skit" on Hulu, while only 10.2 million viewed the September 13, 2008, episode on television. Of course, Hulu's numbers usually benefited from the same user viewing it more than once. The September 27, 2008, skit attracted 10.1 million views on Hulu and 7.9 million views on television.[16]

Due to the popularity, Hulu actually needed more advertising, not to compensate for lost revenue but to enhance the user experience. Similar to CNET's *Buzz Out Loud* podcast example with Best Buy, it's important for the advertising to stay as fresh as the content. You can't serve up the same ad to the same viewer 20 times. The beauty of it being pumped through the Internet is that sites and broadcasters have insight into how many times a viewer saw an ad, while historically this has been something of a guessing game at best for the television ad community.

The executives of Hulu understand that sites like theirs are just as social as a Wikipedia, MySpace, or Facebook. That is why they have allowed users to give commercials thumbs-up or thumbs-down ratings.

Hulu's initial success is probably not sustainable, and there were indications in mid-2010 that content providers were losing favor and wanted to take back control of their content. However, Hulu and other sites like it contribute to moving us toward a more Socialnomic way of viewing our favorite video content from anywhere. It's analogous to Napster and Apple pushing the music industry and Priceline, Orbitz, and Expedia doing the same in the travel industry. Disruptive technology may not be sustainable in the short-term but it pushes everyone in the proper direction for the long-term. Do you own a landline? When's the last time you purchased a full music album? The television industry is on its way to massive change.

SlingCatcher is a product that allows users to access their home-cable-fed programming from anywhere in the world. This complements their popular Slingbox device that allows travelers to set up a small box in their hotel rooms (or anywhere outside their homes) to be able to watch their regular programs and DVR from what is being delivered to their homes. This is very convenient for the international traveler who doesn't want to watch a Spanish Novela or a French cooking show when traveling abroad.

Hulu's success may be short-lived; only time will tell. But at a minimum, they understood the customer needs of their space and forced the industry to move in a new direction. As Kevin McGurn, Hulu's Vice President of National Sales pointed out at an OMMA panel:

> *Hulu starts mostly with professionally produced content that already has an audience. But for other content, we use what our editors think is cool, and also what is popular on the site. They aren't always the same. We want to make video as viral as possible. If you think your friends would like a video, we want you to be able to share it. Things on the Web don't have to be an instant success. In fact, they generally aren't, unless they were popular somewhere else first.*[17]

Another item to consider in understanding why TV will quickly move to Internet pipes is the sociability. If you are watching a particular game, you will be able to easily inform your social network and invite other fans to join you. You will then have the ability to comment and chat real time, thereby allowing you to be connected to the tailgate in Columbus, Ohio, even though you are sitting in San Diego, California.

The end winner here will be the consumer because these innovative tools and companies, no matter if they last or not, will bring new ideas to the table and change the way that we as consumers have been trained to accept broadcast media.

We started to see a glimpse of this in April of 2010 during CBS's broadcast of the Masters. They had online streaming of the event in high definition. It was full coverage for the first two days and then for the last two days you had your choice of four holes to watch. You also had the choice to follow only the lead group.

Again, it wasn't quite all the way there, because why wouldn't you show the entire thing? It's all about distributing your product. The more people see your product, the more people see your client's advertising. As technology becomes cheaper and cheaper, it's conceivable that you could follow only the player in whom you are interested. This could have dramatic effects on the ratings. Today, if the player you like is in 15th place, unless his name is Tiger Woods, he most likely will get zero airtime. However, if you are given the choice to follow any player you like, then it truly changes the game.

In many instances, when people are at work the only option they have for watching an event is via the Internet. Also, more and more people are choosing to forgo an expensive monthly cable bill and they make do with simply their Internet connection. This should sound oddly reminiscent of a trend that happened about 10 years ago—people started to not have a landline in their house or apartment; rather they got by with their mobile phone. The same could happen in the television industry.

Most likely we can anticipate some intense legal battles in Washington, because the foreseen problem is that many of the suppliers of cable television are also the suppliers of the Internet connection! If Time Warner or Comcast starts to see more and more people cut their $100 monthly cable television bill, they could react by increasing the fee for the Internet connection or set up pricing models to charge per stream—they have attempted this before in some markets. The consumer can only hope that competitors and alternatives for high-speed Internet emerge or that policies are put in place to obstruct cable companies from implementing such policies. This is part of what the net neutrality discussions are all about.

Circling back to the 2009 Masters: On the final two days, CBS showed only four holes. A few years from now we will be in a much better place. I would predict that not only will there be full coverage over the Internet, but that the viewer will be able to select which hole, or which player, they would like to watch. The power will be in the user's hands, which is where it should be.

Scrabulous—A Fabulous Example

A great example of a situation companies want to try and avoid involves Hasbro and two entrepreneurs from India. Quickly identifying the potential of the Facebook application platform, two young programmers in India, Rajat and Jayant Agarwalla, thought there might be interest from people playing Scrabble against each other across the globe. They couldn't find an acceptable version of Scrabble to play online so they decided to create their own. They named it "Scrabulous" as a direct reflection of the game (Scrabble) that they were adapting. Scrabulous co-creator Jayant Agarwalla indicated he sent a letter to Hasbro in January 2008 asking for permission to use the trademarked Scrabble template. He never heard back, and took that as permission to go ahead with his program.

There was more than enough interest with over 500,000 daily users at its peak. The application became one of the top-10 most-used applications on Facebook,[18] and during a 2008 interview on CBS's *60 Minutes,* Facebook founder Mark Zuckerberg even mentioned that he enjoyed playing against his grandparents. Speaking of grandparents, it was estimated that 40 percent of the players were over 50 years old, which proves what we've been saying throughout this book—social media is for everyone. Who knew that such an old game would be so enormously popular in this digital age?

When the Agarwalla brothers eventually heard back from Hasbro, they were issued a cease-and-desist letter and a lawsuit was filed against them for copyright violation. At first glance, you could argue that Hasbro/Mattel took the logical route in protecting what they rightfully own by suing Scrabulous for copyright infringement. However, it is apparent that they may have missed the bigger picture and, better yet, the opportunity to capitalize on the existing user base who likely associated Scrabulous with the makers of Scrabble anyway. We can't help but wonder if the legal cost and negative publicity have simply washed away the potential profits that Scrabulous was *freely* providing Hasbro/Mattel. So it would seem that rather than suing the online game's creators, Hasbro could have formed a partnership with them or bought them out.

"But in today's fast-changing social networking environment, Hasbro's lawsuit and its attempt to control its online image may not be the right move," said Peter Fader, co-director of the Wharton Interactive Media Initiative. He believes Hasbro's action is an "incredibly bad business decision." There is no evidence that the Agarwalla brothers were doing "something absolutely disparaging" to the Scrabble brand. In fact, Scrabulous has been such a fabulously good thing for the Scrabble franchise [that] Hasbro should have been celebrating."[19]

"It is not clear if Hasbro did the right thing by going after Scrabulous," chimed Kevin Werbach, Wharton professor of legal studies and business ethics. "Many copyright owners today are over-inclusive as they try to assert their rights. The question for Hasbro is whether the benefit they get in terms of direct and indirect revenue from their own Scrabble game exceeds the cost of negative publicity from this action. But it certainly got them a black eye in the online community, although most people who play Scrabble have no idea this has happened."[20]

In the dismantling process, on the morning of July 29, users were abruptly denied access to the Scrabulous application on Facebook. If positioned correctly, Hasbro could have capitalized and made a strategic move with an introduction of their own Online Scrabble. Had Hasbro been ready to launch their internal electronic Scrabble application, the transition would have been almost seamless to the user, and Hasbro would have continued to profit from the free Scrabulous publicity. Instead, users found that the Hasbro Scrabble application was jammed with glitches, extremely slow to load, and the variety of word selection (the basis of Scrabble) was poor compared to any *Webster's* dictionary.

You could argue that those who really lost out from this ugly episode are both the end users, who were left a little in limbo during the transition, and Hasbro, who had some upset fans as a result of the transition:

> *You didn't have the smarts or initiative to come up with as good a product as the boys did, so your alternative is to mess with the superior product? Do you think that the thousands of folks who were enjoying this superior application will now come running to your inferior product?*[21]

The numbers also took an immediate hit. At the launch of Hasbro's official version of online Scrabble, the game attracted fewer than 2,000 daily Facebook users compared to the more than half a million players a day worldwide on Scrabulous. Another issue with the new application was that there were various groups holding the rights from country to country. So, for the main Scrabble game, it was no longer a global game, but only for U.S. and Canadian citizens. Mattel owned the rights to many of the other countries. What a great benefit for society, millions of people connecting with others across the globe to play an educational game like Scrabble. The Agarwalla brothers may well have been on their way to a Nobel Peace Prize (admittedly a stretch) before Hasbro spoiled the fun. To be fair, the Agarwalla brothers were pocketing an estimated $25,000 a month from Scrabulous.[22]

According to Fader, many companies sue "just because they think they have the right to, instead of pursuing what's in their shareholders' best interests." It is "irrelevant if Hasbro was right or not" in its copyright claims against the backdrop of how Scrabble benefited from Scrabulous, he says. "The downside they have created for themselves and others is a lack of an upside."[23]

Companies "need to move aside from knee-jerk tendencies to bring in legal action," he adds, noting that Hasbro had other options besides suing. "It would have been smart to pay (the Agarwalla brothers) millions of dollars. That would have been minuscule compared to legal fees and their own application development expenses. . . . Hasbro may have won the battle but it has surely lost the war."[24]

If there is a lesson to be learned from all this, it would be that it is best to weigh your options (like TripAdvisor did with *Cities I've Visited*) before jumping in to claim what is rightfully yours. Take advantage of others who have already done the legwork to help you position your brand throughout the social media space. Think strategically before exposing your brand. Hasbro failed to anticipate the speed at which users would react to the abolition of Scrabulous and the introduction of Online Scrabble. They could have favorably capitalized on the work done by the Agarwalla brothers, but instead chose to fight the battle uphill. Behind the scenes they may have tried this, and to be fair to Hasbro, perhaps the path they chose was the only viable one legally. Whatever the case, all of this translated into the Scrabble name being dragged into unflattering associations: lawsuit, popular application banned, and so forth.

However, Hasbro and Scrabble did eventually make their way through and kudos to them—and Scrabble on Facebook today has over 900,000 monthly users. A question that we may never know the answer to is, could this whole ugly situation have been avoided?

Advertising within Social Networks Is Actually Effective

Because social media lends itself to unobtrusive advertising, that advertising is effective. In a 2008 survey done by Razorfish—"The

Razorfish Consumer Experience Report"—76 percent of the 1,006 people surveyed said they didn't mind seeing ads when they logged-in to Facebook, MySpace, or other social media sites. Razorfish also found that 40 percent of the respondents said they made purchases after seeing those ads.[25]

Intuitively this makes sense because social media can accomplish things that we weren't necessarily able to do in the past. For example, when my friend changed her status from "In a Relationship" to engaged, she started getting ads for wedding photographers, DJs, and so on. This was information that she didn't necessarily view as advertising, but rather part of the experience—and a helpful part at that.

Smart companies like TripAdvisor understand this technique and approach the market from an outside-in viewpoint rather than from the old inside-out paradigm. ACME Travel was using inside-out thinking and old metrics. They approached the opportunity of Facebook from the perspective of "How can we grow our database so that we can mail potential customers brochures and send them e-mail?" Actually, the question that companies should ask first is "What do we have to offer that is unique and valuable to our customers and potential customer base?" Also, engaging in role-playing in which you put yourself in the shoes of your users is always extremely beneficial. As a user would I take the extra step of giving you my personal information? Only if what the company is offering is valuable enough to me that I choose to forfeit my personal information.

Users generally want to be communicated with through the medium in which you met to begin with. In this example, TripAdvisor knows that they will be communicating through the user's Facebook inbox or Facebook news feed, not via traditional e-mail or brochures. At some point during the relationship, if the user wants to sign up for an e-mail distribution, then TripAdvisor will be more than happy to accommodate them.

A few months after the travel application battle, ACME Travel was discussing a different Facebook tactic, establishing a fan page. A fan page is usually for your company or product home page within Facebook. Facebook users can select a simple "+" symbol, and they are added as fans so that they can receive updates in their news feeds for anything going on with that product or service. There was a heated debate about what adjustments they should make to the fan page prior to a large e-mail drop that was going to deploy later that week. For several weeks, ACME showcased two products on their fan page. The various product managers were arguing about which product should be placed higher on the page and how many outbound links they should have driving to lead forms. This is a classic example of a traditional marketing pitfall; people arguing for months over the color of a car to be featured in an upcoming commercial, or disputing if a URL should be printed as www.company.com or http://www.company.com in the next edition of a magazine ad. Sound familiar? This type of behavior is nonstrategic and wastes energy because the decisions are not being driven by consumers of the product or service.

Fortunately for ACME, the marketing director sat patiently quiet while the quarreling continued and finally intervened with the following:

> *We already know what needs to go on top. Italy Vacation Packages has always been on the bottom, which is harder to see and historically this position gets less clicks. However, what we have seen is that Italy Vacation Packages has outperformed France Vacation Packages. Our data shows that more people have clicked on Italy Vacation Packages and there are 90 percent more comments and pictures posted about these packages versus the France Vacation Package. It's not for us to decide; the users have already decided for us. Italy should go to the top of the fan page. Also, we will not have any outbound links to our lead-capture forms on this main page. We don't want to make the same mistake again that we made with the application.*

The meeting room went silent when this was expressed. The meeting was over shortly thereafter. In the past, employees alluded to the fact that meetings had gone on for hours resulting in a poor decision or even a compromise. With the advent of social media, this type of discussion ceases to exist. Business decisions become more about letting the user decide what's important. As discussed at the beginning of this section, this is commonly referred to as outside-looking-in thinking versus the traditional inside-looking-out thinking, and it is becoming necessary with regard to social media.

Content and Conversation Will Drive Awareness—Not Advertising

More and more companies will be developing content in the form of Webisodes (five-minute episodes that could be a series), applications, and widgets. Money historically spent on media will be spent to develop and promote this varying content.

Sometimes, this content will be developed from the ground up by the companies themselves—think soap operas on steroids. A good example of this is EF Educational Tours 2009 Web series "Life On Tour." It's a story of six students who go on a tour abroad. It's produced by Bunim/Murray Productions, best known for their MTV "Real World" series. There is no overt marketing placement in the show itself except at the end with a small EF logo. While on the tour abroad, teenagers can chat with the cast members on their Facebook page.

Advertising will be less about social media *campaigns* and more about an ongoing conversation.

Other times, the idea or content will already have been produced, and companies will join forces, often with individuals who may go from being a nobody to a somebody overnight because of the power of the social graph.

Don't Put All Your Eggs in One Basket

How do companies know what the next great thing is? How do they avoid missing out on a great opportunity without over-exposing themselves? Some argue that given the speed of technology, companies should try everything; they should throw a bunch of small tests out against the proverbial wall and see what sticks. If budgets and resources were not at the forefront of profitability, this would make sense. But with the importance of watching every dollar and companies trying to increase their return on investments, a more strategic approach should be taken. For example, if your company is about to plunge into social media, it's best to understand fundamentals as they relate to:

- **What** you are doing
- **Where** you are doing it
- **Why** you are doing it
- What **success** looks like
- What **potential pitfalls** you may encounter

The best way to look at these five pillars is through an example: Summer Cheerleading Camp.

What

Betsy knew that there was a need for a community centered around the summer cheerleading camps so that the kids could interact, and Betsy decided that they needed two things in the short term: (1) A group or fan page to attract the kids, and (2) a tool or application that would allow the kids to easily connect and interact. The first few months would be a beta release. This was a smart idea that took minimal time to set up. Companies sometimes fall into the trap of trying to make everything perfect before releasing it into the wild.

This harkens back to old Procter & Gamble schooling—a model that doesn't work well in social media space because it moves too slowly; the world would pass you by before you got anything out the door. If the initial setup costs make sense, it's better to get an idea out the door and run the risk of it failing than not doing anything at all.

The old paradigm of spending 14 months to produce a 30-second television commercial is counterproductive. Customers appreciate the speed at which you deliver innovative products to market and are forgiving with beta sites. Users will go out of their way to help you accelerate the release from beta to full release if they feel the product or service is worthy of the investment (in this case the investment being users' time to provide feedback/insight). Moreover, if users aren't helping you with the beta, you should be appreciative of this silent feedback and understand that they are signaling to you that there is probably not a need for your idea in the marketplace. As a company, you profit not only from releasing those ideas that your consumers have beta tested, but you also avoid costly upfront fees and development time on ideas that generate a negative return.

This summer cheerleading project could have easily swelled into a six-month project by having the application pull information from a database to determine where the campers would be assigned at the start of the year. Instead, Betsy's Socialnomic idea pulled the information from the campers themselves to determine where they should be assigned. The campers input data, and the application showed who was in each location based on the input rather than having it pulled from a database. This is an important part of Socialnomics—*companies don't have to do everything*—users/customers are willing to help connect the dots!

Where

Betsy wasn't going to have her campers come to her, rather she would go to them. She did some quick research on where most of her campers spent their time. Because they were in mostly rural areas and younger (14 to 16 years old), they used several social media tools, but seemed to spend a majority of their time on Facebook with some campers using MySpace. She didn't know if they would be interested in a community, but knew that her greatest chance for success would be on Facebook. If successful, she would then roll it out to other social media sites. She avoided a mistake that many companies fall into, trying to build every possible iteration from the get go. Betsy knew that an approach of this nature would get her nowhere. She wasn't about to "boil the ocean"; rather, she was going to "eat the elephant" one bite at a time.

Why

The reasons for taking this project on were to: (1) keep the kids excited and engaged leading up to camp, (2) have them develop new relationships prior to the camp in an effort to reduce cancellation rates, (3) gain some potential viral exposure by having campers tell their friends about the idea, (4) establish a continued conversation with the campers to gain valuable real-time feedback, and (5) allow past campers the ability to stay connected and provide advice to first-time campers.

Success

So many times companies fail to ask themselves, *"What does success look like?"* It's important for companies to show a united front when it comes to their definition of success, otherwise the team responsible for implementation may be striving for something that is different from what the executives deem as important. In this example, success was going to be measured by (1) how many people joined the group and (2) determining if those who added the "meet other campers" application had a lower cancellation rate than those campers that didn't interact with the group or download the application.

Notice that success wasn't judged by how many of the campers continued their interactions or comments/postings within the application. Betsy knew that a lot of the kids would meet via the application but would then extend their relationship to other places (e-mail, phone, text, social media mail, etc.). She knew that it was analogous to introducing people at a house party and expecting that every time these people interacted it had to be at the same house where the original party was hosted.

By aggregating all of these campers into one area, the organization knew they had to watch for two key elements: (1) the competition would find it easier to pick off their high schools, and (2) potential pedophiles who might descend on this collection of high school campers. The camp programmers made sure to put in the necessary safeguards to help thwart such activity without strangling growth from legitimate campers.

Pitfalls

Companies that believe in Socialnomics must understand and be willing to unleash control over their brands. Companies that wish to produce a 100 percent fail-safe program in terms of brand and user security are doomed to paralysis. These companies will forever remain in a development phase and miss the opportunity for execution. Companies must exercise social responsibility, and users must also engage in best-practice behavior to ensure user security. Companies should leverage existing platforms such as Digg, Delicious, Vkontakte, Facebook, Twitter, and so on, which have already vetted some of the security and privacy gaps. This also shifts any potential liability to reside with the platform, not the advertiser.

In a major socioeconomic shift, individuals are taking responsibility for their own cyberactivity. This started with spam e-mails and viruses, where people quickly learned that they probably don't have an Uncle in Nigeria who has willed them $1 million. Then came the savvy and complex phisher sites. These are sites and e-mails that look like an established brand such as FedEx, eBay, or Bank of America. However, users learned to look closely at the URLs and misspellings. If the URL wasn't www.fedex.com, but something unusual like 345262.freshexample.com/fedex, then something definitely appeared *phishy.* In these examples, the major brands take painstaking steps to flush these types of scams out of the system, and in large part are reliant on their online community to alert them of such scams. However, the companies aren't responsible or liable for any loss resulting from these scams.

This isn't new to the world. If a burglar was dressed up like a Maytag repairman, Maytag is not held responsible. It is up to the person at the house to question why the Maytag repairman would be there if no repair service was ordered. Neighborhood watch programs are analogous to today's online safeguarding communities.

So when it comes to pitfalls, companies should be aware of them and attempt to mitigate them, but they shouldn't be paralyzed by them or throttle good users' abilities to get what they need from the program.

Second Life Equals Idle Life for Coca-Cola

> *As worldwide head of interactive marketing at Coca-Cola, [Michael] Donnelly was fascinated by its commercial potential, the way its users could wander through a computer-generated 3-D environment that mimics the mundane world of the flesh. So one day last fall, he downloaded the Second Life software, created an avatar, and set off in search of other brands like his own. American Apparel, Reebok, Scion—the big ones were*

easy to find, yet something felt wrong: "There was nobody else around." He teleported over to the Aloft Hotel, a virtual prototype for a real-world chain being developed by the owners of the W. It was deserted, almost creepy. "I felt like I was in The Shining.*"*[26]

Donnelly and Coke went ahead and invested some serious dollars into hiring a consulting company to help them get up and running on Second Life. If it didn't feel right, then why would you go ahead and invest in it?

According to Joseph Plummer, chief research officer at the Advertising Research Foundation:

The simple model they all grew up with—the 30-second spot, delivered through the mass reach of television—is no longer working. And there are two types of people out there: a small group that's experimenting thoughtfully, and a large group that's trying the next thing to come through the door.[27]

Another important piece in this Second Life example is to take a step back and truly assess the potential upside. It's easy to have your vision blurred by hype and propaganda. In this Second Life instance, *Wired* magazine points out what the opportunity really was:

Second Life partisans claim meteoric growth, with the number of "residents," or avatars created, surpassing 7 million in June. There's no question that more and more people are trying Second Life, but that figure turns out to be wildly misleading. For starters, many people make more than one avatar. According to Linden Lab, the company behind Second Life, the number of avatars created by distinct individuals was closer to 4 million. Of those, only about 1 million had logged on in the previous 30 days (the standard measure of Internet traffic), and barely a third of that total had bothered to drop by in the previous week.

Most of those who did were from Europe or Asia, leaving a little more than 100,000 Americans per week to be targeted by U.S. marketers.[28]

How do companies find the right balance between launching every possible idea through the door and ensuring they are not missing out on a great opportunity? If you have been paying attention, for success as a company in today's world it is critical to:

1. *Leverage the success that is out there.* It doesn't necessarily have to be built from within—swallow the pride pill.
2. *Leverage your loyal customers.* Understand that they will help you build and adjust real time.
3. *Don't overinvest.* Build light betas that can quickly be tested and adjusted.
4. *Take the time to decide where you will be.* Don't try to be everywhere. Once you decide, move quickly and with a purpose.

Worse than making a Second Life mistake is doing nothing. As Irish poet George Bernard Shaw once said, "A life spent making mistakes is not only more honorable, but more useful than a life spent doing nothing." Even so, there are still a large number of companies that have been slow to embrace and benefit from social media.

As a company, you don't necessarily need to be the *first* to move, so don't feel like you've completely missed the boat if your company hasn't done anything to address social media. Sometimes it's prudent to sit back, and watch and learn from some of the more nimble players in the space. In social media, small businesses are sometimes the best to watch and imitate. Many of them have already waded in and learned some valuable lessons from their successes and their mistakes.

Search Engine Optimization for Facebook

Imagine if you were a mortgage lender and could go back in time to 1999 and optimize your home page for the query "Low Finance Rate." Would you do it? Of course you would. Well, the same opportunity exists today with social networks. Let's assume that the owner of Cathy's Creative Mugs (a fictitious small business) wants to post a fan page on Facebook, essentially a company promotional flyer. When prompted by the Facebook interface to name her fan page, she begins to type "Cathy's Creative Mugs," but then realizes she can probably leverage search engine optimization (SEO) best practices here. So instead, she names this page "Coffee Mugs," which is a rich keyword for her industry.

This will help Cathy return searches on "coffee mugs" within Facebook, as well as boost her rankings in the traditional search engines like Google, Yahoo!, and MSN.

In many of the social media pieces, the first few years will be a "land grab of opportunity." Just like in the search world, if you were a savvy website back in the late 1990s and ranked high for major keywords like "mortgage loans," "cheap travel," "wedding favors," and the like, you made out like a bandit. If you are one of the savvy first movers, in the first few years in social media you could set yourself up for some hefty revenue streams down the road. A good case in point is for fan pages on Facebook. There is a fan page for chocolate milk that as of April of 2010 had over 1.9 million fans! This type of passion should peak the interests of companies like Nestle, Hershey's, and Ghirardelli. As of the writing of this book, Facebook was attempting to make "communities" rather than "fan pages" for items such as this in an effort to help major brands stand out a little more from the clutter. Case in point being that Coke has over 5 million fans, but there are also 500 other Facebook Fan Pages for Coke. Facebook also made the decision to change "become a fan" to "like" a particular brand.

While as a company you can sit back and learn, you better not take too long to do it—you need to launch and learn. Companies that still think they control whether they "do" social media or not are terribly mistaken. Companies don't have a choice on *whether* they do social media; they have a choice in how *well* they do it. If you're a large brand, you can rest assured that there are conversations, pages, and applications constantly being developed around your brand and by the community at large. The community is "doing" social media even if you choose not to.

This is very different from e-mail, search, banner ads, television ads, radio ads, outdoor signs, and so forth. In all those instances, companies had a choice regarding whether or not to engage. If they didn't want to buy paid search ads or a television spot, that choice was up to the company. With social media, they don't have a choice, because consumers and others will do something around your brand without you.

John Deere Mows Over Facebook

Want proof? Let's take a look at a Web 2.0 product like a lawnmower. If you performed a search within Facebook in August of 2008 for "John Deere," you'd see:

- More than 500 groups dedicated to John Deere.
- More than 10,000 users in the top-10 groups.
- All groups were developed by the John Deere community, not John Deere corporate headquarters.
- Their chief competitor, Caterpillar, had a page in the top-10 listings.
- A group called "John Deere Sucks!!!!" is ranked in the top 10.

This is a great example, because:

- Your users will take ownership in your brand and will *do something* in social networks (both positive and negative) even if your company chooses not to.
- This has huge potential—10,000 users in the first 10 groups alone—kudos to the power of the John Deere brand.
- Your competition and your users can leverage a recognized trademark to their advantage—unless you hired a few new staff to dedicate their time to cease and desist letters.
- Malicious postings (*"John Deere Sucks!!!!"*) can show up high in the rankings if you don't have more favorable listings to push it down to insignificance.

Who has the power now: John Deere or the kid who posted the *"I love John Deere"* group? Just like the person who started the chocolate milk page, in this instance, the kid has the power. After all, what's to stop this kid from posting a nice static image of a special offer for a competitor like Caterpillar on his site? Money talks, and this could be a cheap purchase for Caterpillar to a highly specialized target audience.

As of June 2009, John Deere wised up and started a fan page, and they now have 65,000 fans, which Facebook in 2010 changed from fan pages to simply pages and changed fans to "likes."

Many of these constructs are similar to SEO best practices. The company that puts in the time will see the payoff.

Sheep without a Shepherd

Another reason a company may decide to do nothing? They don't want to aggregate their hard-earned customers in a public forum because they're afraid the competition will come in and pick them off.

This might be a valid concern, as many companies crawl and scrape the Internet looking for client names of their competitors so they can poach them through various sales methods. If your fans and enemies in the social networks weren't doing anything without you, then maybe it could be a valid strategy to be safe and not aggregate your clients or fans all in one place. But, as evidenced by the John Deere example, they're out there, mobilizing around your brand. They are far from doing nothing, so you need to join the conversation. Also, if your customers are that easy to pick off, you have likely failed to build brand equity or produce a great product or service and thus probably have much bigger issues to address than your social media efforts being easily viewed by the competition. The beauty of social media is that it will point out your company's flaws; the key question is "how quickly will you address these flaws?"

Some of these concepts are difficult to grasp, but when you choose to do nothing, it's analogous to a shepherd (company) watching over his flock of sheep (customers/users). In this analogy, a fence breaks, and the sheep suddenly have access to a new pasture (social media). More than a few wander into this new pasture because it has a lot to offer. The shepherd (company) is uncertain about what to do and decides not to go into this new pasture to find his sheep. What's most likely to occur? Sheep may get eaten by a wolf (competition), or they may get lost (customers frustrated that they can't find what they're looking for). There is no doubt that if the shepherd herds the sheep into a flock, the wolf (competition) has a better idea of where the sheep are.

However, in a flock, even though the sheep are all in one easy-to-find place, the sheep are less vulnerable because there is safety in numbers and the wolf is less likely to attack. Also, if an attack were to occur, the shepherd will be well aware of what occurred and can better prevent it in the future. If the shepherd were to have done nothing, when the fence broke his sheep would be getting eaten by wolves, getting lost, and falling off cliffs, and he wouldn't have a clue until he went out to find them—and by then it would have been too late. Even if you decide not to herd your sheep, you should be in the new pasture helping to guide your sheep away from dangerous cliffs and waterfalls.

As a company, you need to be aware of the wolf and proactive to any reaction the wolf may have. There is no question that your competition will be out culling the Web for information that will help give them an advantage (looking for potential customer names, pricing, etc.). Transparency is definitely a two-way street. While it is great for the customer, it is also great for your competition.

As a company, you should also be out culling for information to give you an advantage. While it may win you new customers, it should also alert you to how the competition is grabbing your information. This will give you ideas on how to safeguard where you can divulge information and where the downside outweighs the benefit. As discussed in another section in this book, if your customers are that easy to pick off, then you don't have a problem with your social media or online strategy, you have a problem with your product.

1. Making multiple mistakes within social media is far better than doing nothing at all.
2. If you're a large brand, you can rest assured that there are conversations, pages, and applications constantly being developed around your brand and by the community at large. The social community is "doing" social media even if your company chooses not to.

Chapter Seven Key Points

1. No person or company is perfect, so it is best to admit your faults and the public will respect you for it.
2. Advertising historically has been wrapped around the outside of content (i.e., shows, articles); it now needs to be integrated with the content to take advantage of viral opportunities.
3. Companies should leverage the "Tom Sawyer Approach" like CNN and ESPN have and let fanatics contribute to your product, show, or service.
4. Your customers and fans of today are the potential competition of tomorrow. Understand this and proactively avoid letting it happen.
5. Be more like Dale Carnegie and less like David Ogilvy; listen first, sell second.
6. It's better to live a social media life making mistakes than living a social media life doing nothing.
7. Don't forget that Search Engine Optimization (SEO) and social media go hand-in-hand.
8. Companies don't have a choice in *whether* they do social media; they have a choice in how *well* they do it.
9. Businesses concerned with exposing their clients to competition don't have a social media problem, they have a business/product problem. Why do your customers want to switch?

CHAPTER EIGHT

Next Steps for Companies and The "Glass House Generation"

> I didn't have time to write you a short letter, so I wrote you a long one instead.
>
> —Mark Twain

People have always found extreme value in the brevity of messages. As a result of our ability to have constant connectivity, people believe that immediate, simple, and constant communication matters. These interactions can be one-to-one or open to a broader audience.

The shelf life of conversations has been dramatically shortened. In 2000, when there were only a handful of blogs, a post or article would be commented about for a full week; its half-life would be around three to four days. Today, given the myriad of blogs and the expansion of tools like Twitter and Foursquare, the half-life of conversations has been reduced from days to minutes.

At the simplest of levels, this brevity has been caused by the massive amount of information readily available.

This technology isn't always about the personal and the frivolous; it can be highly leveraged in a time of crisis like a national disaster. The wildfires of San Diego in 2007 offer a good example of this. Nate Ritter, local to San Diego at the time of the fires, began twittering about what was happening from "Smoke has completely blocked out the sun" to "300,000 evacuated, to relief areas which can be found here." Realizing that it would be most effective to have as many people twittering about the fires with constant updates, Nate set up the hashtag #sandiegofire that many others quickly picked up. This helped all thoughts and news on Twitter to be organized under #sandiegofire. These tweets worked in concert with other social media tools, from users uploading videos and photos to YouTube and Flickr to Google Maps showing some of the danger zones.

Another example was when two cellular cables were vandalized in San Francisco, knocking out all forms of mobile telecommunication for AT&T users. Many customers kept abreast of updates from AT&T via Twitter #AT&T updates.

Tony Blair, the former prime minister of the United Kingdom, was asked what he found most challenging about his job throughout the span of his tenure as prime minister. He responded:

> *The way in which information is exchanged so quickly has forever changed the way in which people want to consume information. They demand that things be condensed into 20-second sound bites. With complex problems, this is exceedingly difficult, but to be an effective communicator and leader you need to be able to condense complex items down to the core and be able to do this quickly.*[1]

IBM ran some popular television advertisements starting in 2005 highlighting their business services division and juxtaposing long messaging versus short. The ads generally spent the first 25 seconds showing a bombastic and often pompous consultant using big and long buzzwords in long sentences to discuss what a company should deploy as its strategy. The last five seconds usually pulled the rug out from under these suggestions with an intelligent quip, "Can we implement it?" or "How does this make us money?" to which the pompous consultant usually returned a vapid stare or scratched his head.

Karl James Buck, a graduate student at the University of California-Berkeley, found out just how powerful one word can be in April of 2008. Karl was in Mahalla, covering the political unrest in Egypt. One day, things got extremely heated and some of the protestors began throwing Molotov cocktails at government buildings. Afraid they would be arrested, Buck and his translator began to retreat from the area. The police quickly halted their progress. Thinking quickly on his feet, Buck sent out a text to his Twitter network with one word "arrested." One of his colleagues was an Egyptian student studying abroad at Berkeley. She, along with several others who received the text immediately became worried and set themselves in action, contacting local Egyptian authorities and having UC-Berkeley hire local legal counsel.

"The most important thing on my mind was to let someone know where we were so that there would be some record of it . . . so we couldn't [disappear]," Buck said. "As long as someone knew where we were, I felt like they couldn't do their worst [to us] because someone, at some point, would be checking in on them."[2] Twitter co-founder Biz Stone knew that this type of platform could be used for larger-purpose items because they had previously tested the technology during earthquakes in the San Francisco area. "James' case is particularly compelling to us because of the simplicity of his message—one word, 'arrested'—and the speed with which the whole scene played out," Stone said. "It highlights the simplicity and value of a real-time communication network that follows you wherever you go."[3]

Power to the People

If power is being transferred more and more to the people via social media mechanisms, what other forms does this take and look like? First, anytime there is a macro-shift, a small window of opportunity is unlocked where companies and people can benefit. Most evident are the neophyte companies of the dot-com boom who received good money from venture capitalists. You saw companies go from a garage to multimillion-dollar corporations overnight. You also saw people win. At one point, a company called All-Advantage was paying people by the hour so that a bar beneath their browser could scroll ads. And working like the Amway model, if you were able to get more people to use the advertising scroll bar, you received a commission for their viewing as well.

Some people were making thousands of dollars per month just to surf the Web. Others were ordering their groceries online and having them delivered by a company called Web Van. In the grocery store and at gas stations, some people were paying one-fourth of the normal price because the price was set on Priceline. Yes, at one point in time you could use Priceline to get a great rate on gasoline and groceries.

Eventually many of these ideas failed or were modified. Priceline adjusted their technology to give the user more control when it came to booking hotels, and their stock has skyrocketed the last few years. It's not likely we will see such an overt shift with the explosion of social media. In fact, this evolution of the Internet will probably mirror the shift we saw with the preeminence of search. Not quite as flashy and obvious, but certainly more powerful in shaping how we behave, live, and work.

In theory, the idea that All-Advantage embraced was noteworthy—paying consumers for the placement space rather than going through a middleman (buying outdoor boards, interactive banner placement on highly visited sites, etc.). However, All-Advantage failed miserably at execution. All-Advantage was serving ads based on what users selected they were interested in, but they neglected to understand that a user's mere interest does not translate into purchases and so the placement of the advertising alone was not sufficient to justify the spend.

The construct was sound, but the world and technology available just weren't ready for it. The world will be more than ready in the next few years. We will see more than a few business models constructed to take advantage of this fundamental shift caused by social media, and only time will tell what the best model is, but it's interesting to see some models already taking shape.

Customers Get Paid for Their Search Efforts

One shift we will see is that the money previously dispersed to middlemen is now being redistributed to the companies themselves and to the consumers. A good example of what some programs will resemble is Microsoft's Bing cashback program. Microsoft announced it would be giving cash back to people who use Bing and subsequently click-through and make a purchase. This program was rolled back in May of 2010, but the idea is still sound.

This program is vaguely analogous to the credit card cashback programs (e.g., Discover Card); search engines that give cash back.

What we want to highlight is that these are the types of programs that we will see in a socially driven world.

For Those Who Think This Will Never Work . . . Surprise, It Already Does

People often mistake anything on the Web as new, when in fact the construct is often not new at all. It is only the delivery mechanism that's new and innovative. Microsoft giving cash back for searches is very similar to a frequent flier/hotel stay program. Let's look at an example:

Starwood has many hotel properties (W, Sheraton, Westin, etc.) = Microsoft's 700 merchants
Users call Starwood reservations = Users search on Bing
Starwood gives points for bookings = Microsoft gives cash back for purchases/bookings made via searches on Bing

What Model Does This Hope to Replace?

This type of model is geared toward augmenting and ultimately replacing the existing paid-search model. The historic paid-search model consisted of:

- Advertiser spends money based on an anticipated return on investment
- Search agency is typically paid a percentage of the buy
- Search engine is paid a cost per click based on an auction, resulting in the searcher receiving no payment, even though they are driving all the revenue stream

As you can see from this model, there are two points where the majority of the money is flowing to middlemen. A percent is going to the search agency and a percent is going to the search engine. Now let's take a look at a new model. Keep in mind that this is a similar model to *MSN*'s Bing cashback program:

- Advertiser spends money based on actual return—a sale is completed
- Search engine receives a percentage of revenue derived
- Searcher receives a discount or cash back

The winners and losers in this new model can be strikingly obvious. The consumer is the big winner because he or she is now getting a cheaper product as a result of less wasted money in the middle. Another winner is the advertiser who is spending less to acquire a consumer or purchase, and there is less risk associated with the transaction. In the historic model, the advertisers were paying based on a cost per click in the hope that the click would lead to an action (i.e., purchase of a good or service, subscription, lead). In the new model, advertisers are only paying per action (cost per action).

Another winner of this model is the search engine that deploys it most effectively in an effort to gain market share. Coincidently, the search engine incumbent (e.g., Google) would be the least likely to introduce such a model. By endorsing such a shift, Google could see itself as a potential loser because it currently generates a fair amount of money from the inefficiency of the old model.

Because the search engines are paid on a per-click basis, if a customer found exactly what he or she wanted on the first try and were ready to purchase, this would diminish the revenue because the transaction would be completed with just one click. Whereas if it takes 20 clicks to get that one purchase, the search engines' revenues are 20 times greater.

The most obvious loser in this potential model is the search engine agency. If search engines are able to handle the entire transaction, and they have a vested interest to produce a sale versus a click thru, and this is performed efficiently, then the middleman (agency) ceases to add value in the chain, and so ceases to exist. The key and critical piece here is the ability for the search engine to optimize both its best interest and the advertiser's—which should be the same.

Let's take a quick look at this example using vacuum cleaner manufacturer Hoover. (Note: this is just an example, this isn't something Hoover actually does or endorses, nor are these numbers real):

Historic Search Model

- *Advertiser:* Hoover is willing to pay $50 to produce a sale for their $200 vacuum cleaner.
- *Search engine:* Hoover has determined that it takes roughly 15 clicks to produce a sale and therefore is willing to pay the search engine $3 per click (3 × $15) = $45.
- *Search agency:* The search engine agency charges 11 percent commission, resulting in $5 for this buy going to the search engine.
- *Searcher:* Must pay $200 to purchase the vacuum cleaner.

New Model

- *Advertiser:* Hoover is willing to pay $50 to produce a sale for their $200 vacuum cleaner. In the historic model, they paid $50, but in the new model, they will pay a net of $40.
- *Search engine:* Hoover has agreed to pay the search engine 10 percent commission of total revenue produced. So in this instance, the search engine will receive $20 for the sale.
- *Search agency:* Receives $0 because they are no longer part of the process.
- *Searcher:* Receives $20 cash back if they purchase the vacuum cleaner; net cost ($200 – $20) = $180.

Once the new model is multiplied by a larger revenue stream, the gains are enormous.

So you ask, why on earth would a search engine do this? The minority search engine (e.g., *MSN* Bing cashback) would do so to help differentiate themselves by perfecting this model in the hopes of capturing more marketing share and in turn more revenue. Competition in the market space breeds innovative ideas that ultimately benefit the end user. In the search engine space, the "it's an auction model" argument doesn't fly as this example clearly points out. If there is a monopoly in the search engines, the consumer and manufacturer both lose. However, in the previous new model example, Hoover paid less ($40 instead of $50) and the consumer paid less ($180 instead of $200). The reason this is possible is because it eliminates inefficiencies.

Join Them Before They Beat You

Media giant Viacom offers a good example of a company realizing it is better to embrace social media rather than fight it (as the music industry did with music sharing). Viacom was aggressively trying to impose a "no" strategy from the beginning. They were suing YouTube for upwards of $1 billion for allowing users to post copyrighted content through its service. Originally Viacom's strategy was "Let's sue YouTube and block this." However, they quickly realized that would not work. Instead, a better solution is "Let's create a system where content can derive some benefit,"[4] said Forrester Research analyst James McQuivey.

The courts determined that YouTube wasn't responsible for proactively policing content; rather, they were responsible for removing content if the appropriate paperwork or complaint was filed by the copyright owner (e.g., Viacom). This was obviously a laborious process for YouTube to constantly sift through these complaints and rid the site of any violators. Also, it wasn't good for the user, because it meant there was less of the content that the user desired. At the same time, it wasn't good for the copyright owner of the material either because they had to go through the tedious process of finding the violation and then submitting the request through the proper channels to have the content taken down.

YouTube at this point in time had yet to produce a profitable return for its parent company Google. Realizing that the current "fighting" model wasn't working well for anybody, YouTube came up with a progressive solution. When they received a takedown notice, they gave the copyright owner two options: (1) remove the content or (2) keep the content up but allow YouTube to serve advertising and share in the revenue. YouTube foresaw that if they continued down the path they were on, they'd collectively be beaten. As a result, they employed the strategy of joining them (copyright owners) to their cause. You have probably seen this in action when you are viewing a YouTube video with music. A sleek pop-up message appears that denotes the name of the song and the artist along with a clickable link to purchase the song. This is great for the user, as well, since they can easily make the purchase if they enjoy the song.

After this creative idea from YouTube, Viacom, the owner of Paramount Pictures and MTV networks, decided to take a similar approach with MySpace. One of the more popular activities that MySpace users engage in is passing around video content—often copyrighted video content. MySpace was more than happy to engage in a win-win relationship with Viacom. "Consumers get to share some of the content they want without having it blocked or removed," said Jeff Berman, MySpace's president of sales and marketing at the time. "This is a game changer. It takes us from a world of 'no' to a world of 'yes,' where the audience gets to curate content, express and share it as they choose, while copyright holders are not only respected, they get to make money."[5]

Contrasting this, Warner pulled all of its royalty content off of YouTube in a disagreement about how much revenue it should receive from YouTube. Time will tell if this is a poor decision. The odds are it will result in failure because the philosophy of "this is my ball so only I'm going to play with it" has failed time and time again on the Internet.

History repeats itself because no one listens the first time. This can truly be said about the strategy the Associated Press (AP) employed in April 2009. If you recall in our Jane the Blogger example in Chapter 1, some newspapers and traditional writers have had to adapt to these rapidly changing times. Some succeed, while others fail. The AP became fixated on others failing around them and panic is the appropriate word to describe what they did next. They went with a "these are my toys and you can't play with them" strategy. This only works if you are the only game in town, which is a rare position to be in. From our Jane the Blogger story and supporting documentation, you can see that the AP is not the only game in town. But what did they do? They requested that Google remove their stories from the Google News feed. Now, legally, Google would have been fine saying your request is unreasonable, but they didn't. Google did say your request is unreasonable, but we will remove it if you desire. Sometimes, it's best to take technology out of the question.

This is analogous to a record label in the 1950s asking the world's largest provider of jukeboxes to not put their songs on the jukebox. A hypothetical conversation would go like this:

Jukebox Company: We could remove your songs, but then people will not be able to find them and listen to them.

Record Label: That's okay—we don't really see any direct revenue from the quarters they put into your machine, so why should users be able to listen to our music?

Jukebox Company: At that moment in time, it's the only place they can listen to the song. Even if they own the record, they aren't going to carry their stereo into the bar or dance club. Don't you want people to be exposed to your music? If they like it, don't you think they will come in and buy the record?

Record Label: No, these are my toys and you can't play with them.

This is precisely what the AP is doing by asking Google and YouTube to remove its content. While companies that get it are paying millions in pay-per-click and search engine optimization to rank high in Google, the AP doesn't want this free traffic and exposure. The even bigger kicker is that there was a deal in place where Google was providing some revenue share to the AP. One story in particular went something like this:

AP: You need to pull down that YouTube AP video from your site.

AP Affiliate/Partner: No, we are an affiliate, a partner of the AP.

AP: It doesn't matter, affiliate, partner, or not, you need to remove that video from your website.

AP Affiliate/Partner: But we actually got this video from YouTube—someone must have posted it.

AP: Even more reason to pull it down.

AP Affiliate/Partner: Yes, but you, the AP, are the ones that posted this to YouTube and supplied the embed code that allows others to copy and play it on their respective sites. That is what we did. If you, the AP, didn't want to share this video, then why did you post it to YouTube and supply the embed code?

AP: Let me get back to you on this, but in the meantime take the video down from your site.

Panic, panic, panic is happening all around us. Companies that keep a level head will be fine and in some instances better off as their competition self-implodes. Don't fall victim to FEAR (False Evidence Appearing Real). FEAR is an acronym borrowed from SCUBA diving. When things change under 100 feet of water, it's not the most technical diver that is the best off in that situation. It's the diver that doesn't panic and create FEAR (False Evidence Appearing Real). Who in business can remain calm and keep their heads when the environment around them changes rapidly?

Despite the controversial bailouts of 2009, on the technology front government and politicians are not likely to bail out companies that do not implement swift strategies to survive, nor are they willing to step into this sticky mess. President Obama's stance on this was intentionally vague. Following his election, he stated, "We need to update and reform our copyright and patent systems to promote civic discourse, innovation, and investment while ensuring that intellectual property owners are fairly treated."[6]

This is a big step for companies like Viacom; they recognize that they need to embrace social media rather than fight it. One important step to understanding this is realizing that for many companies, revenue streams will be reduced, but at the same time, so will costs. A prime example is on the music side; instead of $5 for a 45 vinyl record (remember those?) you receive $0.99. However, there is also an enormous cost reduction: no costs to produce, ship, store, stock, and so forth.

If you resist embracing the change, you could quickly find yourself in the same declining mode currently being experienced by newspapers, broadcast news, and the music industry, all of whom to date have failed to embrace and understand this new way of doing business. Isn't it better to have a smaller piece of the pie than no pie at all?

Role of Search

Google product guru Marissa Mayer told the *New York Times* that social search will be a key component in the future of search. Social Commerce deserves Google's unbridled attention.

Why are Google, Yahoo!, Baidu, and Bing interested in social networks? Because social media could eventually dominate the search landscape. This is already evidenced by the social media site YouTube.

YouTube, which for years had been struggling to turn a profit, despite being acquired by Google, eventually decided to take a play out of its parent company's playbook, and in mid-November of 2008, deployed its own pay-per-click search program. This was launched only a few days after it became the second-most-searched site on the Web, dethroning Yahoo! from that perch. Yes, YouTube in 2008 became the world's second-most-searched site.

It seems logical for YouTube to introduce a Google AdWords (brand name for Google's Sponsored Ad Listings)-like model so that amateur and professional videographers can easily monetize their creative materials. The model is simple: a person who uploads a video has the ability to easily place advertising that complements or is entrenched in the video. The difficulty is pairing up the advertisers to appropriate video content. For example, companies like Lexus or Puma would not want to damage their respective brands by being associated with less than top-notch creative videos. This is less of a concern in the Google AdWords model, which is text based; however, they too were able to work out the kinks several years ago when they ran into issues like an ad being served for Aflac Insurance next to an article discussing a major lawsuit against Aflac. Google worked out the kinks there, and they will work out the kinks here as well.

The truly great companies in this model are those that go beyond simply appending advertisements to existing videos. The truly great and innovative marketing minds will roll up their sleeves and get "on the ground" by being nimble and identifying quick wins and reacting adroitly when it comes to developing original content that can be further incorporated into the video.

For example, during the 2008 U.S. presidential election, when the Tina Fey "Palin" spots were popular, a brand like Budweiser could have placed an ad and said, "If there was a Joe Sixpack drinking game for every time the word *maverick* was mentioned, you better believe the people playing it would be drinking a Bud." This played off the fact that Tina Fey was spoofing Palin for always saying Joe Sixpack and Maverick. Again, this is all about becoming part of the content and enhancing the user experience rather than an interruption model. Dodge did this well in the popular NBC show *The Office* when they asked the audience during the commercial break what the bumper sticker on Dwight's desk said. This is the type of real-time stuff that engages the audience; it's part of the content rather than an interruption to it. Green Mountain coffee also ran a clever outdoor advertising campaign that was along the lines of "Complete this sentence and your response could soon appear here: I'd rather be drinking a coffee. . . ." and they supplied the number to which you should text your response. In Chicago, Mini-Cooper billboards were reading chips in Mini-Cooper cars and welcoming the driver by name. *Hello Cindy, welcome to downtown Chicago.*

Originally designed for the visually impaired, the new system of tagging videos (using text to define what's in the video) makes things easy because there are tools that convert Web pages into audio descriptions of the page content. These tags make it simple to categorize the Web by efficiently determining what the video content contains. Tagging is a huge driver of transparency. If someone is tagged in a video, everyone in their network is instantly alerted. The old saying is "Those who live in glass houses shouldn't throw stones." Well guess what? With social media, the world is one gigantic glass house. That's why kids growing up today could appropriately be labeled the "Glass House" generation.

Also, an enabler for success is for companies to be more open and comfortable in letting go of the ownership and control of their brand. It's not going to be perfect every time, and the end user is smart—they understand that user-generated content is beyond a brand's control. If 90 percent is good and only 10 percent is negative, the positive will overwhelm the negative, and the 10 percent will not cripple your brand reputation. In fact, negative comments help add credibility. Numerous studies have shown that products with zero negative comments are consistently outsold by products that have a few negative comments.

This will be a new approach for some established brands who in the past have often played "not to lose" more so than to "win." Heck, if there isn't 5 to 10 percent negative noise around your brand, then your brand is either irrelevant or not being aggressive enough in the space. TripAdvisor CEO Steve Kaufer states "The quickest death in this new world is deliberating rather than doing." Fear of failure is crippling to a company or individual. One needs to fail forward, fail fast, and fail better. It's no coincidence that TripAdvisor has been one of the first companies to embrace social commerce. In June 2010 they launched the ability for a visitor to their site to not only see the ratings on a certain hotel, but to also see who in their Facebook network had stayed at that hotel! This is the game changer, this is what Socialnomics is all about. The ability for me to see what my friends and peers think about anything and everything.

This is a monumental difference in mindset compared to when well-established brands had to be almost 100 percent on message all the time—and rightfully so because it would damage the brand if something was off (e.g., Rolex sponsoring NASCAR). This could still damage a brand today, and steps should be taken to quickly resolve issues when they occur, but if you are producing a ton of noise, or more important, your consumers are producing a ton of noise around your brand, then the few blips along the way will often be drowned out by the rest.

What Happens When the Internet Advertising Structure Collapses?

The foundation and historical model for Internet advertising revenue as we know it today is inherently flawed from a sustainability standpoint. Just as TiVo and digital video recorders were invented to help users avoid having to view advertising on television, tools such as pop-up blockers, spam filters, and banner blockers perform similar functions for Internet users. These Internet tools aren't limited to simply blocking only nefarious advertising activity. People also have a desire to be shielded from legitimate, but highly intrusive Fortune 500 marketing. Why? For the simple reason that these advertisers still use "push" messaging rather than develop conversations with their users.

In the late 1990s, the hot dot-com start-ups weren't based on advertising revenue models; rather, they were based primarily on e-commerce models, developing steady revenue via transactions. These types of start-ups were the darlings of venture capitalists, and they shied away from start-ups that based their revenue solely on advertising models. Then during the Web 2.0 era, advertising revenue models became all the rage thanks largely to the success of Google.

If you had the eyeballs (people visiting your site)—even if you couldn't develop direct advertising relationships (e.g., advertisers pay you to have their marketing materials on your site), you could always have a fail-safe fallback by putting Google search results on your page. This was accomplished via Google's successful AdWords program. The program allows a Website owner to place contextual search results from Google on any page, resulting in instant revenue creation. Google serves up ads on a website for example, www.american-novel.com. The ads are related to the site's content. So, for this example to work, the contextual search ads placed on the pages of www.american-novel.com would be related to American authors and American novels. The owners of www.american-novel.com would be paid by Google every time someone clicked on the text ads. For example, if the cost per click for the ad was $4, Google generally would give $2 of this revenue to the owners of www.american-novel.com and put $2 into their own pocket.

This is obviously great for small websites. It also works well for paying advertisers, since they are able to generate more reach outside of just being on www.google.com. This is also good for Google as it increases their revenue stream (as of January 2009, the AdWords program accounted for roughly 10 percent of Google's revenue).[7]

However, what has been seen over time with sophisticated advertisers and robust tracking tools is that the quality of clicks coming from the AdWords network is much lower than those coming from www.google.com. The clicks weren't resulting in leads or sales.

The AdWords program is still a valuable one, but it will continue on a much smaller scale, and Google has already developed tools to allow advertisers to have more control over which sites the ads are placed on rather than placing the ads on every site in the network. For example, Nike may see that their ads don't perform well on www.american-novel.com and can remove the ads from being served there. While this type of targeting and new tools are good for the advertisers, if Google's revenue from this program dips from 10 percent (current) to 5 percent, that would be significant as it would equate to over $1 billion in revenue being removed from the Internet advertising market. Many companies are dependent on Google's sustained success. For example, the open-source Firefox browser revenues in 2007 were $75 million, with search-related royalties from Google accounting for 88 percent of the total, or $66 million.[8]

Where Have All the Banners Gone?

Does online banner or display advertising get a bad rap? Yes and no. Is banner advertising going away any time soon? No. Will traditional banner advertising be reduced? Yes. Just like a quarterback on a football team, banner advertising historically was getting too much credit when things were good and too much blame when things went bad. Online banners have better tracking than offline marketing methods like television, radio, outdoor, and the like. Because of this, banners were getting too much of the credit simply from the fact that they could track something. The biggest ruse was the "view-through" sale. Tracking is available to place a *cookie* (small piece of text) on people's Web browser when they surf the Internet. If a user went to the home page of CNN.com, tracking tools would be able to see that this occurred.

When an advertiser, say 1-800-Flowers, was running a banner ad on the home page of cnn.com, they'd be able to see that a certain amount of users had that banner on their screen when they were at CNN. Advertisers did, and sometimes still do, make the assumption that the user saw that banner ad—which, in some cases they probably did, and in others, they probably did not. The second assumption that advertisers make is that if that same user takes a positive action (buys flowers or gives 1-800-Flowers his information), then the advertiser gives credit to the banner for driving that action. In some cases, the banner should be credited for that sale, but in many cases, it should not be. If the banner ads are the only marketing that 1-800-Flowers is running at the time, they can safely assume that the action is most likely a result of the banner campaign.

Since large companies are often running multiple advertising programs, this ultra clean scenario is not too common. In reality, what occurred was that online marketers took credit for sales that may have been driven by other marketing efforts like television, radio, magazines, and so on because the online marketer had the power of robust tracking. Also, this tracking cookie was set for 30 days, so if a user (Will) was on CNN.com and potentially *viewed* the 1-800-Flowers banner—again, there was no confirmation that Will actually saw the ad, just that it was on the page when he visited CNN. If Will were to buy flowers in the next 30 days, then that banner marketing would get credit for the sale when, in fact, it was a magazine ad that ultimately drove Will to make the flower purchase.

Marketers became addicted to this perceived success, which led to them buying banners on millions of low-quality pages at very cheap prices and having banners served to millions and millions of people. The odds of someone running across a site in 30 days that didn't place a 1-800-Flowers banner cookie "on them" was very unlikely.

The primary culprits of this were the advertisers and advertising agencies. Essentially three things were occurring:

1. It never dawned on the people managing the campaign that they may be overinflating the effectiveness of their online banner marketing efforts.
2. The managing advertising agency wanted to show the best return to the client and essentially "snowballed" the client with this type of measurement.
3. The client wanted to show the best return to his executives and "snowballed" the executives with this type of tracking to garner more budget for his or her fiefdom.

We point out these items because too many companies believe that they can have a profitable and healthy online business by simply using the old advertising revenue model. This is not the case anymore. New forms of advertising online need to emerge to offset the ones that are currently broken. America Online (AOL) is a great example of this. When they decided to get out of the business of supplying dial-up and high-speed Internet connections, they figured they could merely survive with an ad revenue model—this hasn't worked out so well. Banners and display advertising will still have its place and serve a purpose, but it will be in a much smaller capacity.

Banners and display advertising will also have a place in social media, but it will be much different from the traditional banner approach. One of the huge advantages of social media for advertisers is that social networks can give them insight into a user's demographic (age, geography, occupation, etc.) and psychographic information (hobbies, clubs, networks, desires). In the past, advertisers often had to guess at this type of data. With social media, the user tells you exactly what they have been trying to determine for years.

As people change, the message can change to match their lifestyle. For example, in Facebook if you change your relationship status from "in a relationship" to "engaged," you will start to see relevant advertisements showing photographers, stationery options, and music providers.

A few weeks later, if you make an online purchase of stationery, then these types of advertisements to you would be greatly reduced, if not completely removed. Also, some banners reflect "social actions" of those in your network. So a company placing a banner to sell lipstick can elect to have a social network to create an ad based on people's behavior around their product. So if Kelly is friends with Beth and Beth purchases the lipstick, Kelly will be served a banner with Beth's picture stating "Beth has just purchased this cherry lipstick" and probably has a picture of Beth. This banner reflecting "social actions" will be more effective than a generic banner and is one of the powers and progressive nature of social media. Many companies, both large and small, are doing this very effectively through Facebook's Paid Ads. It has even been proven that if you know what you are doing within the Facbook Interface that you can actually target a single individual.

However, in the general Internet, we have already seen a rapid decrease in the percentage of revenue derived from display and banner advertising. In 2008, the Interactive Advertising Bureau (IAB) reported that search had overtaken display advertising, accounting for 41 percent of the market, whereas display accounted for 34 percent.[9] This is radically different from 2001 when banner advertising dominated the advertising revenue landscape. Could we see the same type of shift from search to social media? Most likely; in Q4 2008, PubMatic indicated that the effective price that advertisers were willing to pay for display/banner ads fell 21 percent on average from the second to the third quarter, with the biggest declines coming at small and medium sites.[10]

A shift or other form of change needs to occur in order to replace such lost advertising revenue at the macro level. If it is not filled, the user will suffer because content companies will vanish and the free content that users have grown accustomed to will be limited or cease to exist. If a new or revised online revenue model is not found to fill this hole, it could have a dramatic effect on the online community and on our economy as a whole. The good news is that there is a ready willingness and desire by companies to advertise on social media. We are at the start of a digital decade, and the advertising components will be largely shaped by mobile and social media. For example, 75 of the country's top 100 advertisers placed ads on Facebook in 2008, according to the company.[11] Mobile items such as applications and iAds are going to produce huge new revenue streams. For example, today Google Maps is free. However, if Google Maps can't survive on an advertising based model, most smart phone users would be more than willing to pay $4.99 for a one-time download of an application. The new subscription-based model in terms of magazines/newspapers may more closely reflect one-time application downloads.

Search Engine Results Are Still Prehistoric

Users and advertisers collectively crave more real-time relevancy from search engines. Unfortunately, due to the complexity of crawling the Web, this is inherently difficult to achieve in organic results. Why, though, has it taken so long to correct this problem on sponsored search sections?

Why can't an advertiser easily alert users of a winter sale? Search engines are racing furiously to address this shortfall. The first search engine that does so will have a distinct advantage with users and advertisers. Let's look at an example.

Paid Search Relevancy Dilemma

An online travel agency sells hotels, airfare, car rentals, cruises, and so on. Because their business is centered on fulfilling demand, they're spending millions annually on search.

It's tough enough for consumers to differentiate the brands of Priceline (William Shatner), Travelocity (Roaming Gnome), and Expedia (Suitcase) in the marketplace. It's even tougher within search engines. A good example: perform a search for "Chicago Hotels." There will be 10 sponsored results showing at the top of the page and on the right rail. All the ads are almost identical. They all say "cheap hotels," "best rates," "Chicago Hotels," and so on. None of them stand out for the user. Wouldn't it be better for the user and the advertiser if the results were more specific? For example, here's a better ad:

Boutique 5-Star Hotel

- $89: Normally $299
- Next to Wrigley Building

The results are infinitely more relevant for the user. In turn, it would produce a greater return for the advertiser. So it's a win-win strategy.

How much greater is the return on investment? We tested this exact scenario within a top-10 travel company that spends around $15 million annually on search. When specific travel deals were dynamically inserted, the click-thru rate was *five times greater* than the campaign average. And, conversions were a whopping 413 percent higher.

If the returns are so great, why isn't everyone doing this? That's where it gets complex.

Tedious, Manual Feeds

Despite what Google will tell you, there isn't a simple way to set up a feed from your database that updates product pricing, specials, sales, and so on. Even if you did, you'd run into the problem of automatically generating copy that makes sense. Imagine the opportunity for a search engine that could solve this issue for Target, Foot Locker, Expedia, Home Depot, and so on.

There Must Be New Keywords

Even if you decide to hire cheap labor to upload your sales, travel deals, and so on into the search engines weekly, you'll run into an issue.

Example: Orbitz has a travel deal that is only good for the next week—50 percent off a hotel in Paris. Let's say Orbitz is buying over 100,000 keywords in their campaign. The odds of Orbitz not already buying a relevant travel keyword (e.g., Paris Hotel, Cheap Hotel in Paris) are slim.

Their campaign keywords are relevant and have built up a history over time. Due to Google's quality score, which essentially gives keywords in a campaign a good reputation over time, you can't quickly infuse new copy into Google's AdWords program. Your incumbent or generic copy that's been running the past several months will almost always win in the short term. Your new copy will have a tough time even being served in the coming week, and if it is, the cost per click is much greater.

Not giving up, Orbitz decides they'll pause all the other copy iterations for "Paris Hotel" and serve the new sale copy announcing 50 percent off. The problem here: no beneficial quality score. Orbitz would be paying more per click and would lose all the efficiencies gained. There is no easy way for them to quickly get a sale for a major city listed in search engines that makes sense from a return-on-investment standpoint.

Integration with Third-Party Optimization Tools

We haven't mentioned the complexity of an optimization/bidding tool (most likely via a third-party search agency) that Orbitz is probably employing. Many of the most popular tools in the marketplace today can't react effectively when given a short window of opportunity (less than a week) to make adjustments to existing terms within a current campaign.

Everybody loses: the user (results don't show the sale), search engines (lost potential click revenue), agency (disgruntled client and lost commission), and advertiser (lost leads/sales revenue).

All of these needs seem relatively basic, at least conceptually. Will someone seize the opportunity to fill this obvious void?

Just think, we haven't even mentioned branded images and video within the search results. So, as you can see, we'll soon be looking back at search shaking our heads asking, "How did we ever survive with such a basic model?"

This is where social media will force the acceleration of better search results. One size doesn't fit all. One person who searches for "Paris" may want to know about the capital of France, while another person wants to see photos of the hotel chain heiress. Also, people want to quickly type in semantic queries like "best pizza parlors in downtown Manhattan Beach, California" to get quick results from a Zagats, as well as qualitative results from their social network—this is where things are progressing rapidly.

Oral Communication Skills Decline

If you still don't believe that some traditional interpersonal communication skills may be suffering, then maybe this example will make you a believer. Second Life is a virtual reality application in which many users engage. It's a digitized life that allows you to do anything that you could do in normal life. People develop avatars (digital graphic representations of themselves), sometimes reflecting who they are in real life and other times taking on different personas (a librarian may become a dominatrix). In 2008, a couple got divorced over Second Life, and here is how their story goes: Amy Taylor (28) met David Pollard (40) in Second Life, or their avatars met each other in Second Life, rather.

Things went swimmingly, but Amy, being cautious, hired a Second Life Private Investigator (yes, they exist!). This investigator posed as a voluptuous virtual prostitute and tempted David inside Second Life. David resisted the temptation and passed the test with flying colors (a test he was unaware of at the time). Their courtship continued until their marriage. Because they had met in Second Life, they had their marriage ceremony on Second Life (hey, if nothing else, it saved a bunch of money).

Offline they signed the legal documents, and they were officially married. Things were going fine until Amy discovered that David was chatting with another female avatar (not her) and showing genuine affection. Amy was so disgusted with this that she filed for divorce both in Second Life and in the real world.

Is the Journalistic Interview Dead?

More and more interviews will be conducted on video because the cost to entry is much lower. iPods, phones, and flip cameras are cheap and have the ability to post video clips on social media sites within minutes. The ability to use video Skype over smartphones has changed things as well.

Traditional paper and pencil journalism is dying. For articles that will appear in newspapers, magazines, blogs, or online media, the way in which these interviews are conducted has radically changed. In the past, interviews were mostly conducted in person or occasionally on the phone. Now, they are generally conducted by the reporter or writer sending a list of questions to the interviewee. The interviewee texts, tweets, e-mails (social network or web mail), or instant messages back their responses. This may seem inherently lazy on the part of the interviewers, but it makes sense on many fronts. It (1) allows the reporter or interviewee to save travel time, (2) saves on the hassle of scheduling a physical time, (3) saves the interviewee prep time, (4) gives the reporter a written record, (5) allows the interviewee to not be misquoted, and (6) offers less chance for the reporter to misreport. Another big advance is video Skype interviews—so not just the big networks with the studios have this capability. Everyone has this capability and you can even do it from your phone.

The three major downsides to this style are: (1) there is no face-to-face interaction, another highlight on why people's interpersonal communication skills are diminishing, (2) the reporter may miss out on some good information that the interviewee may divulge, and (3) there is no chance for the reporter to read body language cues to determine where they've hit a spot and where they can probe further—although with hi-definition Skype it does get closer and closer to an in-person conversation.

Mobile Me

According to a study by e-mail marketing firm ExactTarget and the Ball State University Center for Media Design, 77 percent of Internet and mobile phone users ages 15 to 17 use instant messaging, 76 percent use social networking sites, and 70 percent communicate via text messaging.[12]

One of the more popular Apple iPhone applications is called "Tracker," but it could have just as easily been called Stalker. This works on the GPS in the phone to locate your friends and tell you exactly where they are. This is similar to Harry Potter's marauder's map. I guess you just need to make sure that this isn't enabled if you are trying to throw a surprise birthday party for someone. This application is also very practical for parents of teenagers—keeping track of where their kids are. Twitter also has the same functionality.

Mobile social media applications like Foursquare and Gowalla have taken this geotargeting even further by allowing you to "check-in" to popular destinations. The way this works is that if you go to a restaurant, you can virtually check-in. This alerts all of your friends in Foursquare, as well as your other social media tools (Facebook, Twitter, etc.), about your whereabouts. This is infinitely helpful when you are at a major conference or at an event like the Super Bowl cheering on your team (many of your other friends will probably have flown in for the game). When you check-in to the restaurant, you can also provide tips for other future visitors to the restaurant. For example: "There is no street parking, only $10 valet" or "If you are a healthy eater get the oriental chicken salad not the Santa Fe, as that is served on iceberg lettuce." If you frequent a restaurant more than anyone else on Foursquare, then you receive the title of mayor, and the owner of the restaurant may give you discounts or preferential treatment.

These applications are also very helpful if you are in an unfamiliar airport terminal as it quickly pulls up all the restaurants in the terminal and what other travelers think about them.

Opera Software shows mobile phone Internet access exploding, indicating that during 2008 use of its Min Browser on mobile phones more than tripled—reaching 5 billion page views in October. Opera said, "In many of the Southeast Asian countries the mobile Web exists not because it complements existing means of access, but rather because it replaces them."[13] In the United States, research conducted by The Kelsey Group and ConStat showed that 9.6 percent of mobile users were connecting to a social network as of October 2008, compared to 3.4 percent in September 2007.[14] By 2012, eMarketer projects that more than 800 million users worldwide will participate in social networks via their mobile device, up from 82 million in 2007.[15] Of Apple's projected sales in 2010, only 4 percent were desktop computers and 6 percent were laptops. The remaining 90 percent were mobile devices; this is where the world is heading.

In 2010, Facebook indicated that 25 percent of their users accessed Facebook via a mobile device, and they see this trend continuing to increase. Facebook introduced Facebook Zero for mobile users who didn't have robust connections. Facebook Zero strips out some of the "heavy" files like photos and video so that the experience is quicker on a handheld device.

Field of Nightmares: Lufthansa and American Airlines

Lufthansa's statement about genflylounge.com: "GenFlyLounge is a social networking site for Generation Fly and allows you to connect with like-minded travelers. Get the inside information from other travelers you can trust and who share your interests and travel preferences. Explore destinations before your go there. Review, add and rate trips. Join now for free!"[16]

While you can applaud Lufthansa for attempting to reach out to the next generation, you could argue that we already have too many social networks, and that we don't need another one. Lufthansa and others would be better served developing applications that work with the various forms of social media. It's that age-old cliché: "Fish where the fish are." That is why I affectionately refer to it as the "Field of Nightmares." This is taking creative liberty with the line delivered by a celestial voice postulating in the movie *Field of Dreams*: "If you build it [the baseball field], he will come." In this instance, *Field of Nightmares*, you may build it and they *won't* come. When companies like Lufthansa decide to build an application/tool/widget that complements social media, the first question they should ask themselves is: "What do we have the ability to develop that is not a poor replication of an existing tool, but is actually useful and places us in the best position to provide relevancy to our audience?" Let's look at a few examples for Lufthansa:

Poor idea: Let's focus on allowing other Lufthansa users to share their thoughts on the best places to travel. This is relevant to Lufthansa's travel base; however, it is a poor idea because there are many companies that already do this better than Lufthansa (Lonely Planet, TripAdvisor, Frommers, etc.). One airline that understood there was already enough good general marketing out in the marketplace attacked this same concept, but from a unique (at least unique at the time) angle. Scandinavian Airlines (SAS) desired to establish close ties with their high-profile, high-income demographic group. They dedicated social media tools to the gay, lesbian, bisexual, and transgender/transsexual community. Gay staff members of SAS provided recommendations and tips on the best venues, night-life, and eateries in Sweden and Denmark. SAS also partnered with several organizations and publishers so the site can offer gay maps, gay guides, and an events calendar that is updated daily.

The potential for SAS to be able to market directly to the community of people with the highest propensity to travel is very clear because they found a niche that wasn't being addressed in the general marketplace. Hence, they could truly add value rather than producing a watered down version of something already existing. Seems pretty logical, yet company after company continues to miss this important concept—always wanting to build inward-out rather than outward-in. Build something from the user's viewpoint, not the company's viewpoint.

Good idea: Implement a functionality (wiki) that allows users to see every seat on every plane and allows users to input the pros and cons about each seat. Sites like seatguru.com do exactly this, so that is why it is categorized only a *good* idea, not a *great* one. But unlike seatguru, this makes it easier on the user because it would be specific to Lufthansa's planes, which may configure the same plane differently than other airlines.

Great idea: Why with today's technology do travelers often run into a situation where they run out of the popular meals? For example, the two choices may be beef or chicken and halfway down the aisle the exasperated stewardesses (excuse me, flight attendants) are out of chicken. Why couldn't it work like a wedding when you make your reservation? Or worse, when airlines sell boxed food and you as a flyer are counting on buying one of these delicious (tongue in cheek) boxes on your five-hour flight, but they run out, and the only thing you have to eat is a pack of gum.

This type of social functionality still will not be 100 percent accurate, but it's much better than the system we have in place today. Also, airlines could employ the same concept as trains. Trains have no "no speaking" or "no cellular phone" sections. Travelers on planes vary by whether they want to talk or whether they want tranquility. The unsophisticated way to do this is to divide the plane into a predetermined number of seats for each flight. This would not work so well. However, if you develop the right social media application, the work would be done by your travelers who wouldn't feel it was work at all, and the process would be fluid and variable from flight to flight.

Love connections could occur on flights more often because more single "talkers" would be aggregated and people who don't want to be annoyed by an incessantly boring "talker" need not worry. This could potentially give Lufthansa a competitive advantage in the short term—obviously if this was successful, it would be replicated by the competition. However, the ultimate success, although it might be difficult to replicate, would be if through social media you were able to attract a particular crowd (e.g., intelligent, professional, singles, attractive) and that helped define your brand—people would actually choose to fly your airline because of the types of people they would encounter on that airline. Airlines have been fighting to distinguish themselves for years, and this could become a reality. This may be taking things a step too far, but you could have the preppy airline, the grunge airline, middle-class airline, blue collar, and so on.

The executives at Budweiser said that they learned some valuable lessons from their failed YouTube rip-off initiative of Bud TV. Let's hope so. They spent $15 million over the first two years alone, and for their efforts, Compete Inc. indicates they don't have enough traffic data to give an accurate reading.[17] They aren't alone though. We are already seeing such popular sites as Dell.com, AT&T.com, Xbox.com, and Apple.com losing site traffic, but they aren't necessarily losing users! Their customers are just spending more time on social media and getting what they need from the companies there. Although it is cliché, it's vitally important to fish where the fish are.

Skittles took this to the extreme to showcase a point. For some time during 2009 if you visited www.skittles.com you wouldn't see their regular website. Instead there was a nice beautiful landing page with an interactive flash navigation box in the upper left. On this box were items like connect, video, photos, info, chat, news, etc. The beautiful thing was that when you click on these links, they didn't take you somewhere on the Skittles site, rather they took you off the site to social media.

Connect = Skittles Facebook Page

Video = Skittles YouTube Channel

Photos = Skittles Flickr Account

Info = Skittles Wikipedia Entry

News = Skittles Blog

Skittles was acting as an integration point or hub to great authentic content that existed elsewhere about them.

The funny thing is that in terms of the *Field of Nightmares* scenario, this same flawed replication methodology has repeated itself several times (no pun intended) in this relatively short Internet age. Whether it was e-mail, browsers, portals, search, video, and now social media, many companies believe they will be the starting point rather than an integration point. The example of BellSouth thinking that their users would have a My BellSouth start page (portal) that included weather, sports scores, and stocks is just one example (for the record, people just wanted their phone bill from BellSouth integrated into their established portals, MyYahoo!, iGoogle, etc.) of companies recreating a poorer version of the wheel.

To help avoid making the same mistakes or our clients making the same mistakes, we do a very simple exercise. For the social network example, we have them write down all the features and functionalities they desire on their 'site' or 'social network' onto a transparent piece of acetate. Unbeknownst to them we have all the features and functionality of the technology industry leader (in this case leading social network) on a white piece of paper. We take that acetate and lay it over the white incumbent listing and it is pretty powerful. It usually goes quiet for a few moments, and then we begin discussions on how to appropriately integrate with the leading technology.

Don't build your own Field of Nightmares.

A Truly Interconnected Web?

A key question that remains to be answered (at least at the writing of this book) is about the interconnectivity of the various social media tools. Just like a carmaker doesn't use the same supplier for all of its various parts; rather, they select the best manufacturer for each specialty (e.g., headlights, sun roof, seats). Social media providers can't be the best at every functionality (social network, social bookmarks, wikis, video sharing, photo sharing, etc.). Users like the simplicity of one-stop shopping. Corporations do like these walled gardens—these are my toys and nobody else can play! A *walled garden (technology),* with regards to media content, refers to a closed set or exclusive set of information services provided for users (a method of creating a monopoly or securing an information system). This is in contrast to providing consumers access to the open Internet for content and e-commerce.[18] This is primarily due to greed. Some easy to grasp examples of "walled gardens" are the following:

1. AOL's original strategy of containing all of its content exclusively for its Internet subscribers.
2. The ability to only get the NFL Game Day Package if you have DirectTV versus regular cable.
3. Apple iTunes store—originally having set pricing at $0.99 even though the music industry would prefer they have

variable pricing (some songs at $0.69, others at $1.26). They finally went to this model in 2009, so at least some companies are listening and learning.

"It's a race to see who will work better and faster with everyone else," said Charlene Li, founder of consulting company Altimeter Group. "It's recognition that you can't be an island of yourself."[19]

Microsoft Outlook's tied in contacts, calendar, and e-mail is a good model for how someone will tie up the loose ends of Web services.

We've seen this constantly over time, whether it was VHS versus Beta Max, Blue Ray versus High-Definition DVDs, having to fill out the same three forms at the doctor's office with the same information every time you visit a different doctor, and so on. The hope is, due to the open reliance and nature of social media, that this boils down to one seamless connectivity platform. We have already seen companies' willingness to be more open than ever before by Facebook, Google Android, and even Apple allowing programmers access to their systems (via Application Program Interface) to make cool widgets and tools that consumers can enjoy (e.g., Google Maps on the iPhone, Music I like Widgets on MySpace).

If this type of cooperation were to occur, it would further propel the adoption of social media by the mainstream (Moms and Grandmoms) because there would be more relevant offerings for more people and it would also simplify things. The power user would love it as well because they would have easier access to the best of each type of tool rather than having to wade through various watered down versions (analogous to having all of your clothes, shoes, and glasses from one brand versus getting your sunglasses from Oakley, watch from Rolex, and your jacket from L.L. Bean).

Imagine the ability to only have one login! How nice would that be, along with only a few places to visit when we finally reach an uberstate of truly everything being pushed on us rather than us hunting and gathering and putting things into one basket—we would have the basket being constantly filled with suggested information or products from friends we trust! With tools like Facebook Connect and Open ID, we are getting close, as these tools allow you to use your existing Facebook IDs to easily access other sites as well as to have your information follow you.

> *I have stated all along that I truly feel that in the end game, Facebook and the like will be less of a destination and more of a tool that you use wherever you may happen to be and that it will connect you to other portions of the Web.*
>
> —*Natalie Del Conte, CNET TV*

You can already see this with the new thinking that has been put forth by Facebook. In particular, the Facebook Connect product is all about openness. The thought behind Facebook Connect and other such platforms is to allow you to take your friends with you; it's what will result in the emergence of the social Web. Instead of trying to hoard all of a user's data, it will be shared on the Discovery Channel site, *San Francisco Chronicle*, Hulu.com, Digg, and so on.

"Everyone is looking for ways to make their Websites more social," said Sheryl Sandberg, Facebook's chief operating officer. "They can build their own social capabilities, but what will be more useful for them is building on top of a social system that people are already wedded to."[20]

This type of open thinking is one of the building blocks of the social commerce items that we discussed previously. Specifically, this allows people to post a restaurant review on opentable.com and easily share it with Facebook, Foursquare,

Zagats, etc. Before we crown Facebook as saints, their ultimate goal is to monetize this information for billions of dollars. The proliferation of Facebook Like buttons on various websites is so that Facebook has the ability to aggregate this data for social commerce revenue. Now, if only hospitals and dentists could help me out by only having one form to complete.

You Don't Find a Job, It Finds You

Another huge shift in the way we do things, both as individuals and as businesses, is the process of job recruitment. To better understand this shift, we should review the historical practice of job recruiting and job hunting.

For the past 10 years, if you were attempting to recruit talent, you would pay money to post on job boards like Monster, CareerBuilder, Hot Jobs, and so on. Or you could hire a recruiting firm or headhunter to assist in the recruitment effort. As you will read throughout this book, middlemen are removed in most instances as a result of the social Web. In the job recruitment market, middlemen are job boards, job fairs, classified advertisements, and job search firms. For the near future, these traditional recruiting avenues will remain but their influence will be greatly reduced, and not too far down the line they will probably vanish altogether, except for very specialized or C-Level recruiting. Social networks like Craigslist, LinkedIn, and Plaxo will ultimately take over the recruitment role because they provide more direct and insightful connections between the employer and potential employee.

The newfound transparency from social business networks is a godsend for employers. They no longer have to employ a large internal human resource or recruitment staff to perform this type of research, or hire an expensive headhunter. Instead, the potential workforce is already doing this for you (the employer), and they are doing it at much greater depths. Reviewing a résumé in the past was part art and part science; it was necessary to read between the lines on a static piece of paper to formulate whether the person deserved a screening call or interview. Now, social business networks supply photos, videos, links showing a person's actual work, 15 to 20 snapshot references, links to blogs or articles the person may be included in, and so on. If a picture can say a thousand words, then a video résumé must be in the millions, because there is nothing more helpful than this for a recruiter. Recruiters can quickly screen through potential hires in minutes versus all the guesswork associated with traditional paper résumés (paper résumés will still be a nice complement to video résumés).

LinkedIn is a good place to start because they are a powerful pseudo-monopoly. As of the writing of this book, LinkedIn has almost cornered the market on the social business network. This will be tough to supplant because users already have their recommendations on the site. Unless there is an easy way to port these recommendations to a new business network, it would be a somewhat uncomfortable task for people to solicit their previous references to rewrite what had already been posted for a new social business network (this book covers the importance for all social media tools to be interconnected). Imagine having to call your reference and say, *"Morning, Carol, this is Ted. I know I haven't spoken to you in three years, but about that nice comment and thumbs-up you gave me on LinkedIn about four years ago, I was wondering if you wouldn't mind signing up for this new job site, after you get your account, which will take six minutes. Can you then write the exact same thing you did for me previously?"* That would obviously be no small order. That being said, the hope is that, as previously stated, LinkedIn also figures out how to make the Web more open by allowing your LinkedIn data and recommendations to easily flow and follow you accordingly.

For job seekers, the "always keep your résumé updated" paradigm is gone because now it doesn't even scratch the surface of the importance of maintaining updated information, and more important, updated connections. It is essential to constantly update your career progress on social business networks as well as other social media, websites, blogs, and so on. It is also much more than simply updating your paper résumés on these sites. It behooves you to have an updated and professional photograph; also, a list of articles that mention you is helpful.

A link to your own personal and professional website with additional information about you will put you a step ahead of the competition. Any radio or video interviews of you should be easily accessible to augment your video résumé. Most important of all is to capture positive feedback and postings from your bosses, peers, partners, and subordinates. In the past, you really only needed one or two solid references from your supervisors.

Previously, once recruiters were able to get potential hires in through the doors, the screening process was difficult at best. It was generally based on a few interviews, a possible call to a reference or two (most likely not), and then your standard background check (this step was also sometimes skipped).

However, that didn't really tell employers the entire story, did it? You could be a superstar adored by your boss, but a recruiter may miss the fact that you are a terrible team player, that you treat your peers and subordinates with little respect, and that as a whole, you'd be a detriment to add to an organization that already has good team chemistry. That is why as an individual it is important that you have well-rounded feedback from various divisions and peer groups in and outside the organization. If you skew too heavily one way or another, it may quickly reveal a weakness to your potential employer.

One of the most important things employers look at today is the person's network itself! If the employer is hiring a bunch of new talent and brings on someone who has a polished network, then the new hire instantly becomes a recruiting asset. It was never possible before to have this type of insight into someone's network. You could assume they were connected with people at their current place of work, but you could never confirm it. Bringing on someone who has 300 well-respected professionals in her network is a tremendous asset to any company because after she is hired, the recruited quickly becomes the recruiter. In other words, as you hire job candidates, look at their potential reach; how many friends and connections do they have? That person's extended digital network is a favorable asset for the hiring company.

What really makes a network like LinkedIn helpful is that it allows users to share their online Rolodexes. Shally Steckerl uses social network LinkedIn (industry leader) to more easily recruit talent for Microsoft and other online companies. Steckerl says:

> *With my Rolodex, I had to call any one of these thousand people and say, "Hey, Bob, I'm looking for someone that does this, or I'm looking for someone in this industry, or I'm looking for a job, who do you know? With social networking, I don't need to go to Bob directly to find out who Bob's friends are. Or Bob's friends' friends. So, effectively, I have a thousand contacts that could potentially lead me to 100,000, now I have 8,500 contacts that could potentially lead me to 4.5 million.*[21]

Echoes Maureen Crawford-Hentz of global lighting company Osram Sylvania, "Social networking technology is absolutely the best thing to happen to recruiting—ever. It's important to load your profile with the right keywords so people like me can find you easily."

It's also important within these social business networks to be constantly building equity. This can be obtained by connecting two people that you have in your network to posting jobs that you are aware of, to giving your peers a thumbs-up and adding written recommendations next to these approval ratings.

Aside from building equity that can be drawn on later, it's imperative that workers proactively manage their brand, whether they are currently in the job market or not. Employers will perform Google and YouTube searches on a potential recruit's name as well as filter through MySpace, Facebook, and Foursquare networks to see what is posted out there. Employers are always looking to mitigate risk. So, even though you may have a 3.9 grade point average and a 1300 SAT score (which would equate to a much higher number on the new version of the SAT) on your résumé, this information is immaterial if your Foursquare profile picture is of you holding a beer bong while wearing a jockstrap on your head; good luck in landing that dream job!

While I hope you aren't that stupid, you most likely have some friends who are. So it's important to spot-check what is out there and aggressively ferret out potential job career landmines. Job seekers should act like a potential employer and go to the search engines to investigate what shows up when searching for their name. Unflattering items should proactively be removed from the public eye. Part of this search includes confirmation that there aren't any egregious videos out there. Also, if job seekers share a common name with an individual that is less than scrupulous, then the job seeker needs to make certain the employer knows that that person is not them, but rather someone else with the same name. This due diligence and research can take time, so even if you aren't currently in the job market, it's imperative to keep items inside and outside of your business social networks as buttoned up as possible.

It's also important for individuals to build out their digital business network before they actually need the network. If you haven't communicated with someone in three years, it's much harder to ask them a favor than if you had been maintaining your network and been in consistent contact with your social graph. Once you do find yourself in the interview room or via video Skype it's imperative to show your story rather than simply tell the story. In an old job interview you would tell your story as the candidate. However, today you can literally walk them through your items digitally—showing them versus merely telling them why you are the right person for the job.

Thirteen Virgin Airline employees should have heeded this advice before they were let go from the U.K.-based airline for inappropriate behavior on Facebook. The 13 employees formed a group on Facebook and thought it would be a fun joke to insinuate that there were plenty of cockroaches on the Virgin Airline's planes and that the passengers were generally *chavas*. Chava is the British equivalent to calling someone a redneck, or more specifically:

> *Chav, Chava or Charva, or Charver is a derogatory term applied to certain young people in Great Britain. The stereotypical view of a chava is an aggressive teen or young adult, of working class background, who wears branded sports and casual clothing (baseball caps are also common). Often fights and engages in petty criminality and are often assumed to be unemployed or in a low paid job.*[22]

Obviously, the competition among airlines is fierce, so Virgin didn't hesitate to quickly fire these employees for what they deemed insubordination. The world has shifted, and whether we like it or not, we are always representing who we are, whether we are *on the clock* or not.

Hunters Become the Hunted

The good news for job seekers is that they too also have new and similar powers to check up on a potential employer, thanks in large part to social media. Within these social networks, they have review boards about various employers. And just like in the Kevin Bacon game that uses the famous *Six Degrees of Separation* concept, there is potential that a friend of a friend will have worked for a particular company if a job seeker wants to get the scoop firsthand.

Along those lines, you can readily see if anyone in your social business network is interlinked to the person who may ultimately be your boss in the new job. The ability to check on your potential future boss's background along with what other people are saying about that person is very comforting and useful.

This is also great preparation for the interview. If you know your interviewee is a member of Big Brothers and Big Sisters, you may steer the conversation in that direction. But, even more important, if you are selected for the job, examining the profile of the person who may become your boss will help you decide if you want to work for this person. Do you think you can learn from this new boss? Do you have the same theories, aspirations, and approach to work and life?

Other social media tools that are popping up are companies like glassdoor.com. Glassdoor was started by Rich Barton, who was also very successful with Expedia and Zillow, both of which opened up information previously not available to end users for travel and real estate. Zillow in particular allowed users to go in and change items listed about their house in wiki format (if there were two bathrooms instead of one, the owner could go in and adjust the data). Glassdoor was started using the concept of "What would happen if someone left the unedited employee survey for the whole company on the printer and it got posted to the Web?"

The site mentions what they do: "Glassdoor.com provides a complete, real-time, inside look at what it's really like to work at a company—ratings, reviews, confidence in senior leadership, and salaries—for free." Well it is free in terms of cash outlay, but the site does require users to share salaries of their current or past positions before they can see salaries that others have posted. The site encourages and demands sharing for the social product to work. Networks like this give the interviewee some power, especially when it comes to salary negotiation, because they can see what others in the same position are currently making.

In the past, information on the ins and outs of companies as well as background on potential bosses was limited, if not nonexistent. In a very short time, social media has eliminated this information deficiency. There are even some Web-based recruitment companies sprouting up that are looking at a social commerce model where instead of headhunters getting paid, they actually pay the interviewee money for the opportunity to interview—one such site is called paidinterviews.com. It will be interesting to see if this represents a wave of the future.

A Better Workplace for Employees and Employers

Generally, this makes for a better work environment for employers and employees. It also can greatly increase productivity in companies because the wrong person is less likely to be put into the wrong job. The number of employees leaving within a year will also be reduced because new recruits will have a better sense of what they are getting into (job, boss, company). Also, once employees are in place, now more than ever before, it's essential that they work well with their peers, subordinates, partners, and bosses because their ability to land their next job will depend on it. Skeletons are no longer in the closet; rather, they are available for everyone to see in social business networks.

Hiring the Internet Generation

Just as the one-way messaging strategy of advertisers is no longer viable in this new age, it no longer works for employers, either.

Millennials are used to and want collaboration, but they will not necessarily acknowledge or adhere to traditional lines of authority or chains of command. Soon, many baby boomers in executive level positions will retire, and there will be an intense talent fight between companies. Companies can give themselves an advantage by understanding that this new talent has different attitudes, expectations, and skills than the previous generations.

Some people paint members of this under-30 crowd as spoiled or lazy. That is far from the truth. They are just different, and in a lot of positive ways. Work and life balance is much more important to them than it was to their parents, and they desire positions that are able to conform to their lifestyles (e.g., work from home or at odd hours). Company beliefs and values need to align with those of employees. A company mission of simply making as much money as possible turns many of this generation off. Companies need to contribute to the greater good of society, and to be part of the social community and causes.

Ironically, though, if another firm offers Millennials more money or a better opportunity, they will go. There is less loyalty; on average, a person will have 14 different jobs by the time they are 40 years old. Members of this generation have seen that companies in general aren't loyal to their employees, so why should they in turn be loyal to their employers? They desire to stay at the same company and grow, but they understand this probably isn't going to be a reality. They've also seen that companies may only have a strong robust lifespan of 10 to 20 years (e.g., Lycos, Prodigy, Atari, Enron, Circuit City). Fun at work isn't a *nice-to-have*, it is a *need-to-have*.

Employers need to throw away the old human resources playbook that consisted of hire, train, manage, and retain. This generation wants collaboration in all aspects of their lives, in part because of the social media tools they grew up with and are accustomed to, but especially because work is where they spend the most time.

Showing up at a college campus for a career fair isn't going to get the job done, because it's a whole new world. Online sites now hold 110 million jobs and 20 million unique résumés. Traditional advertising to attract young talent is as good as burning money. As a company, you need to use everything in your arsenal—blogs, podcasts, social media sites, and so on. However, your current staff members are your best recruiters because they are the ones with the networks and referral power. Just as marketing will be more focused on referral programs, the same holds true for recruiting.

Retaining Talent

By using social media tools during the recruitment process, companies have a better chance of maintaining talent because it's more likely to help put the right person in the right position. However, an employer's work is just beginning when they hire someone. Generation Y desires constant feedback, and they also evaluate the company from day one. They will not wait around in hopes that things will get better or things will change. There is too much opportunity for them to go to a competitor or even for them to start their own businesses.

Employers are best off exposing new hires to various departments, leaders, and projects. Often the best thing that managers can do is simply get out of the way, because the young talent may be vastly more talented than them in certain areas (great hire!). So, instead of traditional management and micromanagement, bosses may be more focused on fostering an environment for success.

Just as employees shouldn't burn bridges, employers shouldn't either. When an employee leaves, it can be bittersweet.

But it's important to focus on the sweet versus the bitter because today, talent may boomerang back once they see it's not so great out there. It's imperative that employers not take a smug "we told you so" attitude, but rather, take pride in knowing that they must be doing something right if this talent is coming back. Often within social networks, people stay engaged with their previous company through specific groups. That's why Yahoo! Alumni and Microsoft Alumni groups on Facebook have 2,300 and 1,600 members respectively. In a study done in Canada of 18- to 34-year-olds, it showed that the average person held five full-time jobs by age 27. Rehiring saves money. *Harvard Business Review* indicated it costs roughly half as much to rehire and that person is also 40 percent more efficient in their first 90 days[23]—which intuitively makes sense. Plus, they are also less likely to leave again. The key is for companies to embrace this change in the workforce and to learn as much from Generation Y and beyond as they do from your company.

Tony Tweets

Tony Hawk is the Michael Jordan of skateboarding. Tony owns more skateboarding titles than anyone in history and he literally put the sport on the map. After retiring from competitive skateboarding, Tony continued his success in the business world, becoming a global icon from the sale of his video games, clothes, skateboards, etc.

When Twitter started to grow in popularity, Tony saw an opportunity and seized it. His first foray was to leave a skateboard randomly in a hedge on a street. He sent this note out on Twitter that somewhere along said street was a free skateboard for whomever found it first. This was so successful that he continued doing this and he saw his followers on Twitter grow to over 2 million. More importantly he started to see sales grow.

Then, Tony started to use Twitter to announce impromptu town events. Tony and some other professional skateboarders would show up at a skateboarding park and ride with the locals. This was so successful that in time Tony realized he couldn't send out the tweet more than an hour in advance, otherwise there would be so many people that he couldn't physically get through the sea of humanity to actually skate.

Keep in mind that Twitter's initial popularity wasn't with Tony's normal customer base (young adults), rather it indexed high for business usage for people 35–50 years old.

Tony is a great example showcasing that no matter what you do or what you sell, if you are creative, passionate, and use common sense you can use social media tools to succeed.

Southwest Is No Ding-a-Ling

As we mentioned previously, we have grown accustomed to the news finding us. We have also grown accustomed to other pieces of information finding us rather than searching for them. Brands and companies that understand this have benefited and will benefit in the future. Southwest Airlines recognized this early on with its Ding Widget. This widget allows users to place it somewhere convenient (desktop, social network, etc.). For a user who lives in Nashville (Tennessee) and whose Mom lives in Birmingham (Alabama), the widget will alert them with a "ding" whenever an appropriate airline ticket sale is available. After the first year, the widget hit the 2 million download mark and then went on to generate $150 million in sales.[24] It is estimated that the widget receives upwards of 40 million clicks per year. The cost to develop and maintain such a widget is so low that it is almost at the point of insignificance.

The key with successful widgets like this is for the companies to show restraint in their push messages. Some smart companies have almost adopted a publisher's model. Historically, newspapers and magazines kept their writers in a distinctly different silo than their advertising sales team to ensure that their articles or content were not compromised by pressure from their largest clients.

With successful widgets and applications, some companies go to great lengths and in some extreme cases even turn over how these widgets are messaged to the product team versus the marketing team. In the past, many companies have seen with cost-efficient delivery channels (think e-mail) that marketing will spam the user. With these widgets, if you spam the user (in this example, that would be Southwest sending a general reduced-fare message for 20 cities of which neither Nashville nor Birmingham is included), they will be gone.

Speaking of being gone, that is exactly what is happening to some business and personal behaviors. This book highlights that some traditional behaviors, constructs, and principles will continue in this new world, while others will not be suitable. Individuals and businesses face new challenges if they are to stay relevant and viable in this new Socialnomic world. Are you up to the challenge?

Chapter Eight Key Points

1. Don't build your own *Field of Nightmares* by creating or replicating a social network for your company. If you build it, they most likely will not come. You are better connecting to the best in class social media tools that exist. You aren't a social media company, so don't attempt to parade as one.
2. Social media is helping to drive the transformation of mobile devices to being the dominant Internet access point instead of computers.
3. The information exchanged in social media in relation to job searching and recruiting has rendered it unrecognizable from the information exchanged 10 years ago. Appropriate matches between employer and employee have increased as a result of this increased information flow.
4. Just as marketing will become more referral based as a result of rapid information exchanges enabled by social media tools, job seeking and recruitment will be more referral based than ever before.
5. The younger generation's interpersonal communication skills are starting to suffer as a result of overdependence on nonverbal and non-face-to-face interactions.
6. Search engine results and the traditional Internet advertising model are antiquated—social media will push both of these to revolutionize, otherwise they will see a dramatic decrease in market share.
7. The overall achievement of individuals and companies will be largely dependent on their social media success.
8. Fail forward, fail fast, fail better.
9. Advances in mobile are making for an always connected society. Social consumption will only increase as the mobile consumption devices continue to advance.
10. Proactively build your digital business network before you need it.

CHAPTER NINE

Social Media Rolodex and Resources

As you near the end of this book, I want to ensure you continue your digital education. By all means, I'd be flattered if you continue to follow my writings, videos, and other exploits. I thought it would also be helpful if I supplied a list of people and resources whom I draw inspiration from and look to for ideas, advice, and the opportunity to collaborate with. I hope you find these resources helpful as you continue your digital education. Admittedly the downside to this section is that I'm certain to leave off some very talented people! Feel free to contact me with any that I have missed or that you have discovered and I'll augment on www.socialnomics.com. This list is in reverse alphabetical order.

The social media space is constantly changing, so it's important to continue to have the lastest news and changes pushed your way. Feel free to revert back to *Socialnomics* often while staying abreast of new findings and trends from the following people and resources.

Dan Zarrella, often called a social media scientist, Dan does a great job of collecting tons of data and making sense of it all by spotting trends. He has insightful findings on which types of tweets have the best chance to be re-tweeted. He is a product owner at HubSpot and the author of *The Social Media Marketing Book*. @danzarrella

Larry Webber founded one of the world's largest and most successful PR companies. He has written five books in the PR/Social Media space with his latest being *Sticks & Stones*. @TheLarryWebber

Gary Vaynerchuk, a social media sommelier who has proven that passion + effort + social media = a healthy return. He has helped grow his family wine business from $4 million to $50 million through the use of social media. He is best known for his "Wine Library TV"—a series of videos giving insights on wine. He is also the author of *Crush It!*, a best seller detailing how he uses social media and how anyone can do this. @garyvee

Liz Strauss is an influential non-celebrity blogger helping people to learn. She's been called an idea machine and is the CEO and founder of SOBCon and author of the popular Successful-Blog.com. She likes to provide the human touch. @lizstrauss

Scott Stratton is the President of Un-Marketing.com. He is an expert in Viral, Social, and Authentic Marketing which he calls Un-Marketing. His book is also titled by the same name @unmarketing

Biz Stone is the cofounder of Twitter. @biz

Brian Solis is principal of FutureWorks, an award-winning PR and news media agency in Silicon Valley. His book *Engage* has a foreword from Ashton Kutcher. Solis is cofounder of the Social Media Club and is an original member of the Media 2.0 Workgroup. @briansolis

Mari Smith is a social media business coach. *Fast Company* magazine called her the "Pied Piper of Online." She has intimate insight on social media strategies for small business and is an expert on Facebook. Her smile, Scottish-Canadian accent, and ebullient personality have attracted many fans and followers—she is a great case study in developing one's own brand. Smith combines a good mix of energy and honesty. She is the co-author of *Facebook An Hour Per Day*. @MariSmith

Shiv Singh is Avenue A/Razorfish VP and global social media lead. He is also the author of *Social Media Marketing for Dummies*. He is a regular author and contributor to numerous Avenue A/Razorfish white papers and studies on social media. @shivsingh

Clay Shirky is an NYU graduate professor of the Interactive Telecommunications Program (ITP) and one of the world's most requested speakers on social media. @cshirky

Peter Shankman is perhaps best known for founding Help a Reporter Out (HARO). In addition to HARO, he is the founder and CEO of The Geek Factory, Inc., a boutique marketing and PR strategy firm in New York City, with clients worldwide. @skydiver

Dharmesh Shah, cofounder of HubSpot, is a very entertaining and informative social media speaker. He is coauthor of the bestselling book *Inbound Marketing*. @dharmesh

David Meerman Scott, marketing strategist and author. He was well ahead of the curve in 2007 with his bestselling book, *The New Rules of Marketing & PR*. He appears to have another winner in the book *Inbound Marketing: Get Found Using Google, Social Media, and Blogs* as a contributing author and editor. Scott is very generous with his time and is an active contributor across the Web and on the speaking circuit. @dmscott

Jeremiah Owyang is Partner, customer strategy, at Altimeter Group and columnist for *Forbes* CMO Network. He is also a great complement to Charlene Li at the Altimeter Group and excels at interpreting news. As an industry analyst he tells us "what it means" and is a great reference for the market. @jowyang

Lee Odden is one of 25 online marketing experts featured in *Online Marketing Heroes*, published by Wiley, and has been cited for his search and social media marketing expertise by the *Economist*, *U.S. News & World Report*, and *Fortune* magazine. Odden is the CEO of TopRank Online Marketing. @LeeOdden

Amber Naslund is director of the community for Radian6. She loves to dissect the collision of community and business within social media. @AmberCadabra

Dave Morin is a former senior platform manager at Facebook. Morin was named one of the "100 Most Creative People in Business" by *Fast Company* in 2009. Rumor is he is doing some collaborative work with Shawn Fanning. @davemorin

Scott Monty is the digital and multimedia communications manager at Ford Motor Company. He practices what he preaches by having ongoing conversations with car buyers and influencers. While he is a marketer rather than an engineer, his new type of thinking and passion has changed the way Ford thinks and is ultimately the reason why Ford is looking more like a Macintosh computer and less like a Model T. Much can be learned from Monty's intelligence, foresight, and fortitude. @scottmonty

Amy Jo Martin has over 1.3 million followers on Twitter. She works with Shaquille O'Neal and other professional athletes and franchises. She has hosted a few NFL teams at the Social Media Clubhouse during SXSW. @digitalroyalty

Valeria Maltoni writes a blog, Conversation Agent, that is recognized among the world's top online marketing blogs (among the top 25 on *Advertising Age's* Power 150, as well as three categories in Guy Kawasaki's Alltop). Maltoni was handpicked by *Fast Company* as an expert blogger to write about creating conversations between the marketer and customer. She built one of the first online communities affiliated with the magazine. @ConversationAge

Charlene Li is the founder of Altimeter Group, coauthor of *Groundswell* (along with Josh Bernoff), and author of *Open Leadership*. She is also a great public speaker and has presented frequently at top technology conferences such as Web 2.0 Expo,

SXSW, Search Engine Strategies, and the American Society of Association Executives. @charleneli

Ashton Kutcher is an actor gone social. Kutcher has more Twitter followers than the president. Kutcher understands that in the future all of his stories/productions can be efficiently broadcasted via social media. He is also the cofounder of Katalyst, a studio for social media. @aplusk

Guy Kawasaki is a founding partner at Garage and co-founder of Alltop. Kawasaki describes Alltop as an "online magazine rack." He has written nine books and is always one step ahead of the curve. If you have a chance to read Kawasaki's bio, it is well worth it—a very interesting background (Apple disciple) and an avid hockey fan. @GuyKawasaki

Mitch Joel has been dubbed by *Marketing Magazine* as the "Rock Star of Digital Marketing" and "one of North America's leading digital visionaries." Joel is the author of the book, *Six Pixels of Separation* and former board member of the Interactive Advertising Bureau of Canada. @MitchJoel

Brian Halligan is cofounder and CEO of HubSpot. He is also coauthor of *Inbound Marketing*. He is a Sloan Fellow at MIT. @bhalligan

Scott Galloway is a clinical associate professor at NYU's Stern School of Business where he teaches brand and digital strategy to 2nd year MBA students. He is also the pioneer of the Digital IQ Measurement. Scott founded Red Envelope (Nasdaq: REDE) in 1997 and has served on the board of Gateway Computer (sold to Acer). He is currently on the board of directors of The New York Times Company. @profgalloway

Paul Gillin was editor-in-chief and executive editor of the technology weekly "Computerworld" for 15 years. His 2007 book *The New Influencers* was awarded a silver medal in the business category by *ForeWord* magazine. @pgillin

Seth Godin is an award-winning author of too many books to mention. He is always a few years ahead of the curve and is a wonderful story teller who is able to break down complex issues into very digestible constructs. Seth is the Godfather of permission-based marketing.

Maggie Fox is founder and CEO of Social Media Group.com, one of the world's largest independent social media agencies. It has been Ford's social media agency since 2007. @maggiefox

Sarah Evans, a self-described "social media freak," initiated and moderates #journchat, the weekly live chat between PR professionals, journalists, and bloggers on Twitter. She is also a guest writer for Mashable. @prsarahevans

Frank Eliason put customer service on the social media map by his pioneering on Twitter with Comcast. @comcastcares

Sam Decker has been a thought leader in the space since his days at Dell. As the CMO of Austin-based Bazaarvoice, he is helping to lead the charge on social commerce and truly helping Socialnomics become a reality by, among other things, combining social data with rating data (what do my friends buy and like?). @samdecker

Pete Cashmore is founder of Mashable and one of the most followed on Twitter. He is also a contributing editor to CNN. @mashable

Chris Brogan is president at New Marketing Labs. He is recognized as one of the "World's Top Bloggers" (Advertising Age Power 150 Top 10 Blog) and his book *Trust Agents* (coauthor is Julien Smith) reached the *New York Times* Best Seller's list. He is the author of *Social Media 101* and the cofounder of the PodCamp new media conference series. He takes time to respond to almost everyone who reaches out to him. @chrisbrogan

Josh Bernoff is coauthor of the *BusinessWeek* best-selling book, *Groundswell: Winning in a World Transformed by Social Technologies*, and senior vice president, idea development, at Forrester Research. @jbernoff

Jay Baer has founded five companies and spent 15 years running digital marketing agencies. He has worked with the biggest of the big brands. He is the founder of Convince and Convert. @jaybaer

Additional Digital Thought Leaders

Dan Schawbel, Brian Reich, Corey Perlman, Louis Gray, Richard Binhammer, Robert Scoble, Lee Aase, Eric Bradlow, Sally Falkow, Don Steele, Julien Smith, Michael Lazerow, Sarah Hofstetter, Mike Lewis, Mack Collier, Mike Barbeau, Todd Defren, Tom Gerace, Elizabeth Pigg, Richard MacManus, Jon Gibs, Chris Cunningham, Paul Beck, Matt Goddard, Chris Heuer, CC Chapman, Chris Penn, Shel Israel, Tamar Weinberg, Morgan Johnston, Tim Washer, David Armano, Mark Cattini, Nick O'Neil, Mike Stelzner, Jason Falls, Dave Kerpen, Sonia Simone, Adam Singer, Jessica Smith, Michael Brito, Geoff Livingston, Mike Volpe, and Wayne Sutton.

Others Who Inspire

Additional luminaries who aren't specific to the "digital" space, but have helped me and millions of others include: Dan and Chip Heath, Malcolm Gladwell, Tom Izzo, and Dale Carnegie. Their insights can be applied across any walk of life.

Resources

CNET's *Buzz Out Loud* daily podcast
IAB's Social Media *SmartBrief*
Social Media Today
Mashable
TechCrunch
Silicon Alley Insider
DMNews
BoomTown

CHAPTER TEN

Other Insights and FAQs

Some reading this book are social media geniuses, while others are just starting. The interesting part is that no matter where you are in this cycle, there are four easy steps that should always be adhered to and revisited.

Even if your company is a social media trailblazer, it's important to always take a step back and make certain you are following the basics. This is similar to when two college football teams are preparing for the National Championship. In 2010, as Alabama and Texas prepared for the game, Alabama's philosophy was as follows:

> *"The focus will be on fundamentals and execution, rather than scouting Texas . . . It's going to be important for us that we get back to where we're physical and aggressive in what we're doing," Alabama Coach Nick Saban said, "That we play with the mental and physical toughness that kind of trademarks our team."* [1]

Which was very similar to how Texas was striving to achieve excellence:

> *"It's like starting over and having a one-game season," Texas coach Mack Brown said. "So you really have to go back and work on fundamentals."* [2]

Both of these teams were the best in the country; both had perfect records. Yet, they still both felt it was necessary to go back to the fundamentals.

Now, if we are going to replicate a championship caliber team and practice revisiting the fundamentals, it's important to examine the necessary paths and building blocks an individual or business needs to undertake within social media to have success.

One must wrestle with many complex social media issues. These can be overwhelming. Where to even begin?

Rather than be paralyzed, it's often best to understand that there are four simple, yet critical, steps to social media (see Figure 10.1).

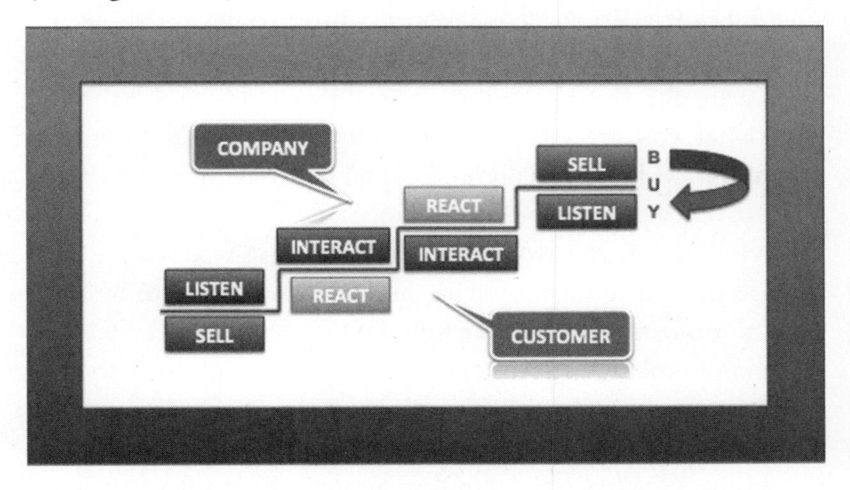

Figure 10.1 Diagram = Socialnomics. Social media escalator.

It's easiest to think of it as a stairway (see diagram). If you learn anything, it's that you need to constantly practice this first step: listening. It's the most important step. As showcased in the diagram, the four steps are:

1. Listen—To your customer and conversations around your brand.
2. Interact—Join the conversation.
3. React—Adjust your product or service based on feedback.
4. Sell—If you Listen, Interact, React, this will happen with less effort.

Companies often enter the social media fray and jump straight to step four, selling. This is the worst thing you can do, and it won't be effective.

You need to start with step one, which is listening. Without listening, the other three steps won't achieve any degree of success. As many have said before me, there's a reason we have two ears and one mouth.

After listening, then you have the appropriate baseline and credibility to join the conversation. Imagine if you were at a housewarming party and walked up to a group of four people who were already engaged in a conversation and said, "I'm not sure what you are talking about, but here is what I want to talk about." This is socially unacceptable behavior in the offline world. Yet, we also need to remember it's socially unacceptable behavior in a digital world as well. You don't want to be "that girl" at the housewarming party and you don't want to be "that girl or company" in the socialsphere.

Many embrace the listening and interacting correctly, but then they commit a terrible crime. They don't do anything (react) based on the suggestions and information gathered. If 90 percent of the people complain about a certain aspect of your product or service, it's imperative that this issue is resolved, and resolved promptly. If 90 percent of the conversation is centered around certain aspects of the product or service that people love, then it's imperative that this information is placed in the appropriate hands (PR, production, sales, customer service, etc.)—*let's make sure we do more of this! Everyone loves it.*

We won't touch on selling too much, because if you do the first three steps well (Listen, Interact, React), then the selling will happen with a proper push here and a prod there.

Notice in the diagram that the steps for the customer then happen in the reverse order of the company. This is *huge*. It's these steps that the customer takes within social media that give an exponential return (good or bad). Please note that we use company in the diagram but this could easily be charitable organization, political party, small business, or something else.

If it makes it easier to grasp, you can consider the following as steps 5, 6, 7, 8. This is where the magic can really happen.

- **Listen:** The customer buys the product or service from the selling company. The customer's first step is to *listen* for what to expect from the product or service (important expectation setting here). What is the value that will be delivered? This also may involve reading instructions or a manual.
- **Interact**: The customer will then *interact* with the new product or service (e.g., use the product or service).
- **React:** During or after this interaction, the customer will *react* according to his or her experience (good/neutral/bad).
- **Sell:** The consumer's reaction to the product or service will determine if they *sell* for or against (the company/product). Keep in mind if it's a negative reaction, you still have a chance to correct the situation by *interacting* and *reacting*.

That's the beauty of social media. As a company, if you appropriately engage in the four steps, the stairs in the diagram act more like an escalator (pun intended) rather than a traditional stairway (i.e., Social Media Escalator). It will create a positive circular motion, which, with the appropriate greasing (effort), will continue to take your product or service to the top. And that is the true beauty of Socialnomics.

The best strategy in social media is a simple one; in life and social media speed and simplicity win. Always remind yourself of the fundamentals.

What We Can Learn from *Footloose*

As of the writing of this book, it is common practice for companies and organizations to ban social media in the workplace or office. It reminds me of the 1984 movie *Footloose*, where a town banned rock music until Kevin Bacon's character helped save the day.

In today's version, instead of starring Kevin Bacon, perhaps either Biz Stone (co-founder of Twitter) or Mark Zuckerberg (founder of Facebook) could star in the lead role. Just as we now look back on *Footloose* as being rather silly, the same will likely apply to these social media bans that companies and organizations now employ.

On October 22, 2009, *USA Today* reported that 54 percent of companies completely block Facebook, whereas another 35 percent apply some limitation. That leaves only 11 percent that don't put restrictions on Facebook in the workplace.

Why does this feel like déjà vu? It is. When Web mail first came out, many banned it (Yahoo!, Hotmail, AOL, etc.) in the workplace. A few years before that, companies banned the Internet or eCommerce sites at the workplace.

And it's not just companies that placed these types of bans; teachers often ban mobile phones in the classroom as well. Is this the right thing to do?

Banning social media at work is:

- Analogous to banning the Internet.
- Analogous to banning the phone because you might make a personal phone call.
- Analogous to banning paper and pens because an employee might take a note that isn't related to work.
- Could potentially signal workers and future recruits that your company just doesn't "get it."

Wasting Time on Facebook Actually Makes You More Productive

"People who do surf the Internet for fun at work—within a reasonable limit of less than 20 percent of their total time in the office—are more productive by about 9 percent than those who don't," according to Dr. Brent Coker, from the Department of Management and Marketing at the University of Melbourne.

Before we dive back into the workplace, the teacher example is an interesting dilemma to review. Some phones have such a high-pitch ringer that teachers can't hear them while the students' younger ears can hear them. But, is this really a technology issue, question, or problem? Or is it a historic problem that teachers have been wrestling with since the first school opened?

Whether a student is whispering, day dreaming, sleeping, passing a note, doodling, or sending a text, it's all the same thing. The teacher isn't reaching them. Recently, Lee Scott, Wal-Mart's chairman, said for his first four years on the job he was looking for new critics, when all along he should have been looking to produce a better product or store experience.

Capturing students' attention has been historically difficult. The teacher's task isn't an envious one. However, the really good teachers have been able to overcome the hurdles presented before them.

If you ban today's technology, does it solve the problem? Probably not. Also, texting is probably less intrusive than whispering, or passing notes, as it doesn't affect the others in the room as much.

Also, a good student might suffer as they may be potentially looking up something on their mobile browser that the teacher is covering to either fact check or see if something visual clicks with their brain in a way that's better for them than how the teacher is attempting to explain it. Or, if they have already grasped the concept, why shouldn't they be able to learn something else new and exciting at their fingertips?

Some teachers may benefit by leveraging this technology in the classroom; students have grown up with technology. Rather than being lectured at, they're used to dynamic interaction with various technologies and sources to provide possible answers.

It also depends on the age of the student. This is applied more easily to college students than, say, middle-school students, where anything that could possibly distract attention from the teacher isn't good. (It's also another reason why our teachers should be paid more as it's one of the most difficult jobs around, and now teachers have the added challenge of keeping abreast of new technology.)

Company Restrictions on Social Media

Banning social media could send the wrong message to employees and potential recruits as a company that "doesn't get it." Also, how can companies learn what to do in social media if they aren't allowing their employees to even use the tools?

All new tools have a learning curve. When people started using phones in the workplace, they had to be educated not to make 30 minutes worth of personal calls, call internationally, or speak too loud.

More recently, when e-mail was introduced, classes were held in the workplace on tonality of e-mails, not replying to all, not wasting much of the workday on e-mail, and so forth. With social media, similar instruction and guidance should be given to the workforce. For example, Facebook IM chatting with your friends may not be the best use of your time, and it will make it difficult for you to achieve your goals, nor is it wise to status update "glad I'm out of the jail I call work for today."

An employee either produces desired results or doesn't. If one employee reads Wikipedia during her break time but produces 40 sales per week and another employee reads books outside during his break but only produces 15 sales per week, which employee would you keep? If you're in the business of making money, you'd keep the one producing 40 sales per week and let her read Wikipedia.

"Short and unobtrusive breaks, such as a quick surf of the Internet, enables the mind to rest itself, leading to a higher total net concentration for a day's work, and as a result, increased productivity," Coker said.

Some employees might benefit from having social media in the workplace. If you're in outbound sales for home insurance, it would be helpful to receive a tweet from a friend in California indicating that the wildfires have taken a sharp turn toward Orange County or that the telephone lines are out in Minneapolis. Or to see a user-generated picture or video of the fires taking place that includes a geo locator on them.

Or think about sales in general. What are two of the top rules of sales? *Listen* and *know the customer*.

Google isn't so great at supplying real-time results, but social media certainly is (there's a reason why deals in 2009 were cut between Bing, Twitter, Google, and Facebook). So, if I'm a salesperson about to make a phone call, tools like technorati, search.twitter.com, and Wikipedia are helpful for figuring out what is being said about this prospect or prospect's company. Why would you ban tools that are valuable to your workforce?

One possible answer: management doesn't trust workers not to abuse the sites for other reasons. Is that a social media issue? I'd argue it's a workforce issue.

Also, whether you're at work or in the classroom, when you treat people like kids by not trusting them, expect them to behave like kids. Is that what you want?

Do you think Apple or Google bans people from these sites? Their stocks were up 140 percent and 79 percent respectively early in 2010. They must be laughing out in Silicon Valley.

Occasionally, some bans make sense. For example, a university that bans downloading music on their network because of bandwidth issues is reasonable. Other bans (like those in *Footloose*) are just silly.

Don't ban social media. In the near future we'll look back and say, "Remember when we used to ban social media? What were we thinking?" Don't be a dinosaur; they became extinct.

Social Media ROI (Return on Investment)

A big question out there these days is: What is the ROI of social media? Or the ever popular: How do I measure the ROI of social media? Often an appropriate retort to this question is: *"What's the ROI of your phone?"* Other times it's not appropriate to respond with this answer, which, if done in the wrong tone, or place, can win you a free punch in the face. Often the simplest response to this question is: *"The ROI of social media is that in five years your company will still exist."* Then there are the naysayers who adamantly proclaim: *"We aren't doing social media because there isn't any ROI."* Again, it's important to stress for companies, organizations, churches, and the like: There is not a choice in *whether* to do social media; the choice is how *well* you do it. Some companies and marketers are becoming paralyzed with attempting to determine the ROI of social media by incorrectly using inappropriate tools and measurements.

To borrow from the conductor of the Boston Philharmonic Orchestra, Benjamin Zander,

> *There are those in life who sit in the back row with their arms folded, judging, and complaining. Then there are those who sit in the front row with a vision, and they are spending their energy on making that vision a reality.*

When Google exploded onto the scene, what did the good companies do? The good companies immediately started buying pay-per-click advertisements to help drive sales.

What did the great companies do? They also jumped in with both feet into the pay-per-click arena, but they further realized that 70 percent of the clicks happened outside of the paid listings. The majority of the clicks (roughly 70 percent depending on what data you use) happen in the free, organic, and natural listings rather than the sponsored listings. In order to rank high organically, the great companies realized that some search engine optimization principles needed to be applied. SEO has come a long way, but even today a CEO may view it as black magic and it's often tough to calculate a *hard* ROI for it; it can take years, not weeks to see the fruits of the labor. However, great companies didn't sit back with their arms folded saying we aren't doing SEO until you prove an ROI. Great companies went on the attack, since they recognized that these major shifts present opportunities that don't come along often. Great companies went full speed ahead attacking keywords like "home mortgages," "cheap travel," and "black dress," and they derived tremendous revenue. Some even adjusted their business models entirely. They had a vision.

To borrow a line from NYU Professor Scott Galloway, social media is not checkers; it's chess (I believe he credits the line to Denzel Washington in the movie *Training Day*).

Social media is something the likes of which we haven't seen (just like SEO before it, but with greater impact). As a result, I prefer to ask "What does or will success look like?" rather than "What's the ROI?"

After all, why are we trying to measure social media like a traditional channel? Social media touches every facet of business and it should be viewed more as an extension of good business ethics—which, if done properly, will harvest sales down the line. Co-Chairman Alex Bogusky of Crispin Porter & Bogusky puts it best when he states:

> *You can't buy attention anymore. Having a huge budget doesn't mean anything in social media . . . The old media paradigm was PAY to play. Now you get back what you authentically put in. You've got to be willing to PLAY to play.*

If your executives are stubbornly set on tracking like a traditional ROI, you can do it. Below are some points to ponder. However, I would caution you that even though you can measure certain aspects of social media this way, I strongly argue that you are *greatly* undeserving your current and future efforts by not understanding that social media touches every aspect of your company and isn't a simple ROI formula for your marketing department. Before going into a list of ROI examples, one that I love is from General Mills. General Mills owns Green Giant and they placed codes on packs of their frozen vegetables that consumers could redeem for Farm Cash on FarmVille. FarmVille is a social gaming tool produced by Zynga that had close to 100 million users in 2010. Green Giant is actually able to track if their sales indexed higher for the packages containing the Farm Cash codes. 7-Eleven did a similar thing with some of their products. For example, if you purchased certain flavors of ice cream the buyer was rewarded a Neapolitan cow (quite difficult to get) in FarmVille. "People are asking, 'How do I know what the ROI is on these social media programs?' and in this case, we can definitely track directly to sales on our registers," said 7-Eleven Marketing Manager Evan Brody.* These are two quick and creative examples on how you can track a hard ROI using social media. Here are a few more quick statistics relevant to ROI:

1. Over 300,000 businesses have a presence on Facebook and roughly one-third of these are small businesses.
2. Gary Vaynerchuk grew his family business from $4 million to $50 million using social media. Gary's eccentric personality and offbeat oenophile knowledge have proven a natural path to success with his Wine TV Library.
3. Vaynerchuk found firsthand that $15,000 in Direct Mail = 200 new customers; $7,500 Billboard = 300 new customers; $0 Twitter = 1,800 new customers.

4-5. Wetpaint/Altimeter Study found companies that are both deeply and widely engaged in social media significantly surpass their peers in both revenue $ and profit $. The study also found company sales with the highest levels of social media activity grew on average by 18 percent, while those companies with the least amount of social activity saw their sales decline 6 percent.

6. Lenovo was able to achieve cost savings by a 20 percent reduction in call center activity as customers go to community websites for answers.

7-8. Burger King's Whopper Sacrifice Facebook program incented users to give up 10 of their Facebook friends in return for a free Whopper. The estimated investment for this program was less than $50,000, yet they received 32 million media impressions, which roughly estimated equals greater than $400,000 in press/media value. To put this in context, this is somewhat like

*_DMNews_, "Marketers pull products into online perks," by Nathan Golia, June 7, 2010.

reaching the entire populations of 19 states (understanding this doesn't account for unique versus repeat visitors, etc.).

9. BlendTec increased its sales five times by running the often humorous "Will it Blend" videos on YouTube, blending everything from an iPhone to a sneaker.
10. Dell sold $3,000,000 worth of computers on Twitter.
11. To put things into perspective, only 18 percent of traditional TV campaigns generate a positive return on investment. This is where the majority of media dollars reside today. I don't believe the majority of media dollars will reside here for much longer.

12–14. "You can't just say it. You have to get the people to say it to each other," says James Farley, CMO Ford. Ford seems to know what they are doing, especially with Scott Monty leading the social media charge. By giving away 100 Ford Fiestas to influential bloggers, 37 percent of Generation Y were aware of the Ford Fiesta before its launch in the United States. Is it any wonder why 25 percent of Ford's marketing Ford Fiesta social media spend has been shifted to digital or social media initiatives? Ford is the only U.S. auto company that didn't take a government loan.

15. Naked Pizza, a New Orleans Pizzeria that specializes in healthy pizzas, set a one day sales record using social media. In fact, 68 percent of their sales came from people "calling in from Twitter." On top of that (no pun intended), 85 percent of their new customers were from Twitter. So, yes, social media does work for small businesses. Feel free to have a bottle of Vaynerchuk wine with your pizza.
16. Volkswagen goes 100 percent mobile for launch of GTI. The reason I mention this is that mobile drives social media usage and social media usage drives mobile. More

and more, we will see most social media usage on mobile devices, tablets, and iPads.

17. *Tweets for a Cause* sent out a tweet from Atlanta to encourage support of Susan G. Komen for the Cure. As a result of retweets from such notables as @mashable, @G_man, @zaibatsu and others, the Atlanta Chapter site received 11,000 visitors in 24 hours as a result of this initiative by ResponseMine Interactive.
18. Intuit introduced "Live Community" into their TurboTax® products two years ago. Due in part to the resulting Word-of-Mouth, they have seen unit sales increase 30 percent each year and have now integrated "Live Community" into other products like QuickBooks, Quicken, and so forth. "Live Community" allows customers to ask other customers questions, which has proved both beneficial to the customer and to Intuit. In some instances, the customer can answer questions that Intuit isn't allowed to answer because of regulatory restrictions.
19. Software company Genius.com reports that 24 percent of its social media leads convert to sales opportunities.

20-23 During Barack Obama's rise to the White House, he garnered 5 million fans on social media and 5.4 million clicked on an "I voted for Obama" Facebook button. Most importantly, this resulted in 3 million online Shepard Fairey Obama hope image donors contributing $500 million in fundraising. An astounding 92 percent of the donations were in increments of less than $100.

24. The University of Texas MD Anderson Cancer Center witnessed a 9.5 percent increase in registrations by using social media.

25-28 Web host provider Moonfruit more than recouped its $15,000 social media investment as their website traffic soared 300 percent while correspondingly sales increased

20 percent. They also saw a huge lift in their organic search engine rankings, getting on the first page for the term *free website builder*.

29. eBay found that participants in online communities spend 54 percent more money.
30. Co-Chairman Alex Bogusky of Crispin Porter & Bogusky puts it best when he states: "You can't buy attention anymore. Having a huge budget doesn't mean anything in social media . . . The old media paradigm was PAY to play. Now you get back what you authentically put in. You've got to be willing to PLAY to play."
31. "Think of Twitter as the canary in the coal mine."—Morgan Johnston, JetBlue.
32. Seventy-one percent of companies plan to increase investments in social media by an average of 40 percent because of: (1) Low Cost Marketing, (2) Getting Traction, and (3) We Have To Do It.
33. "Our head of social media is the customer"—Quote from unknown source at McDonald's.
34. Old Spice Guy social media campaign increased sales 107 percent over one month and 55 percent over 3 months in 2010.

To points 12–14 above: "Have You Driven a Ford Lately?" Ford may want to rekindle this old slogan. With Alan Mulally spearheading the way, Ford has made great strides in changing its image as a "truck only" company in the United States. It's hard not to like Mulally's passion and enthusiasm. I was fortunate to be a keynote speaker along with him at a private non-tech event. In fact, it was a room full of CEO's; I was floored by how much he discussed social media and technology. Then he was on stage as a keynote speaker at the 2010 Consumer Electronics Show (CES) in Las Vegas. This in itself is a tremendous step in the right direction for an automaker—these CES speaking slots are generally reserved for the Steve Jobs of the world. While at Boeing, Mulally helped design the digital cockpit and now he is doing the same with Ford. Some of the more exciting features:

- Ability to stream Pandora Radio
- MyFord Touch is an iPhone-like customizable touch screen that replaces your typical "radio dials"
- Ability to have text and tweets read aloud to you via Ford's Sync technology
- Ability to send text or tweets via voice command

Mulally also has a vision of changing dealer Showrooms into an experience more akin to an Apple store. Rather than having giant lots filled with hundreds of cars/weeds, the vision is a clean, open dealership with showcase cars where users can interact via technology and order cars suited to their needs.

What is striking about Ford is that many ask about the ROI of social media. With the great work of Alan Mulally, James Farley, and Scott Monty at Ford, there is something that can't be measured: a cultural change. Progressive thinking from the top down causes this cultural change to happen both internally and externally. The revitalization of Ford is much more than social media and technology; social media and technology are playing a huge part not only in the bottom line, but also in the perception and culture of Ford, which is often the bottom line of tomorrow. So, perhaps a more important question is: What is the ROI on a positive cultural change?

Eye Opening Statistics

1. Over 50 percent of the world's population is under 30 years old
2. 96 percent of them have joined a social network

3. Facebook tops Google for weekly traffic in the U.S.
4. Social media has overtaken porn as the #1 activity on the Web
5. 1 out of 8 couples married in the U.S. last year met via social media
6. Years to reach 50 million users: Radio (38 Years), TV (13 Years), Internet (4 Years), iPod (3 Years) . . .
7. Facebook added over 200 million users in less than a year
8. iPhone applications hit 1 billion in 9 months
9. We don't have a choice on whether we DO social media, the question is how well we DO it"
10. If Facebook were a country, it would be the world's 3rd largest ahead of the United States and only behind China and India
11. Yet, QQ and RenRen dominate China
12. 2009 U.S. Department of Education study revealed that on average, online students out performed those receiving face-to-face instruction
13. 80 percent of companies use social media for recruitment; percent of these using LinkedIn; 95 percent
14. The fastest growing segment on Facebook is 55-65 year-old females
15. Ashton Kutcher and Britney Spears (combined) have more Twitter followers than the populations of Ireland, Sweden, Israel, Norway, or Panama.
16. 50 percent of the mobile Internet traffic in the UK is for Facebook. . .people update anywhere, anytime. . . imagine what that means for bad customer experiences?
17. Generation Y and Z consider e-mail passé—some universities have stopped distributing e-mail accounts
18. Instead universities are distributing: eReaders + iPads + Tablets
19. What happens in Vegas stays on YouTube, Flickr, Twitter, Facebook . . .

20. The #2 largest search engine in the world is YouTube
21. Every minute 24 hours of video are uploaded to YouTube
22. Wikipedia has over 15 million articles . . . studies show it's as accurate as *Encyclopedia Britannica* . . . 78 percent of these articles are non-English
23. There are over 200,000,000 blogs
24. Because of the speed in which social media enables communication, Word of Mouth now becomes World of Mouth
25. If you were paid $1 for every time an article was posted on Wikipedia you would earn $1,712.32 per hour
26. 25 percent of search results for the world's top 20 largest brands are links to user-generated content
27. 34 percent of bloggers post opinions about products and brands
28. Do you like what they are saying about your brand? You better
29. People care more about how their social graph ranks products and services than how Google ranks them
30. 78 percent of consumers trust peer recommendations
31. Only 14 percent trust advertisements
32. Only 18 percent of traditional TV campaigns generate a positive ROI
33. 90 percent of people that can TiVo ads do
34. Kindle eBooks now outsell hardcover books
35. 24 of the 25 largest newspapers are experiencing record declines in circulation
36. 60 millions status updates happen on Facebook daily
37. We no longer search for the news, the news finds us
38. We will no longer search for products and services, they will find us via social media
39. Social media isn't a fad, it's a fundamental shift in the way we communicate

40. Successful companies in social media act more like Dale Carnegie and less like *Mad Men*; listening first, selling second
41. The ROI of social media is that your business will still exist in 5 years
42. comScore indicates that Russia has the most engaged social media audience, with visitors spending 6.6 hours and viewing 1,307 pages per visitor per month—Vkontakte.ru is the #1 social network

The above statistics tell the story; social media isn't a fad, it's a fundamental shift in the way we communicate. Please feel free to share with any non-believers!

All sources for this data can be found at: http://socialnomics.net/2010/05/05/social-media-revolution-2-refresh/

FAQs

The following questions are some of the more common that I have received from reporters, readers, and fans over the years.

Do most companies seem to have clear strategies and direction with social media or does it seem like people are still trying to figure out what to do with it and how it can help them?

Some of the good companies have a clear strategy, while others are just dipping their toes in the water. The key with social media is to fail fast, fail forward, and fail better. You aren't going to get it right the first time, but you aren't going to learn anything if you don't take that first step. The beauty of social media is that your customers are very forgiving and, at the same time, helpful at expressing exactly what they need from you as a company. It is the world's largest focus group on steroids. It's imperative that companies incorporate their social media strategy into their overall business strategy. A big mistake is making it a one-off strategy.

Debate between Content Curators and Creators:

Today, everyone is a potential media outlet. A curator understands their audience and is able to package created content in a digestible manner for them. Creators need to view curators as distribution points for their content rather than as pirates. Content creators and curators that will thrive in this new world understand the importance of this symbiotic relationship. But is it symbiotic? In the end, almost every person is a little of both (creator and curator). After all, there is no such thing as a new idea and imitation is the sincerest form of flattery. These cliches symbolize the irony of the topic being discussed.

What is the disadvantage for companies using social media?

Great companies embrace social media because they have nothing to hide and welcome everyone to discuss their products, services, etc. Social media is a big disadvantage for companies that have had mediocre products/service/offerings and have hidden behind big marketing budgets, distribution advantages, etc. There is nowhere to hide with social media.

Do you think most companies will go in-house with their social media, or will there still be a place to hire the freelance person who gets paid to tweet, or the consulting firm?

Since social media touches every facet of the business, it inherently lends itself to the majority being taken in-house. Also, the conversations need to be genuine and it's easier to establish that trust if it's coming from you, not a surrogate. Social media is not an *or*, it's an *and* in your business. Dell indicated that they originally had 40 people focused on social media. They soon realized it's not just the 40 people who need to own social media; it's the entire company. Every person, whether it's someone on the phone answering customer service, or any other employee, might have a Facebook and/or Twitter account, and they are representing Dell, whether it is working hours or not.

While a majority of social media activity will reside in-house for certain components, it still makes a world of sense to bring in help from an external agency or consultant for certain aspects of the strategy and execution. If you look at the successful Old Spice Guy campaign this was produced externally by Weiden & Kennedy.

How should marketers be measuring the success of their social media efforts?

Some items can be measured directly, similar to PPC Search or Direct response. For example, if you run Facebook Ads with a direct action you can measure the ROI similar to how you do for PPC Search—it has its own nuances, but it's pretty close.

A majority of other social media activity affects your entire business, so it's really measured by the overall health of your business. It's hard for us to understand this right now, but in the future we will. Social media is that big and that important. In fact the Altimeter Group did a study that showed Companies actively engaged in social media increased revenues by 18 percent while those least engaged saw a decrease in revenues by 6 percent.

Does social media mean more content, less advertising, better results and Why?

Historically Word of Mouth has been the most beneficial marketing effort for businesses. Social media takes Word of

Mouth and puts it on digital steroids and essentially turns it into World of Mouth.

What actions should BP have taken digitally within the first 24 hours of the Gulf Coast oil spill?

BP should have immediately posted the HD video images and indicated how they were deriving their flow estimates. We live in a fully transparent world and it's always better to point the finger at yourself rather than wait a few days to have someone else point the finger at you (e.g., Bill Clinton, Tiger Woods, Enron, Lehman Brothers, Eliot Spitzer). This is counterintuitive to how we've done business for the past centuries with the legal mindset of trying to keep the bodies buried. However, with social media you have to assume the bodies will be exhumed quickly.

What should BP have done in the days after the oil spill?

First, and foremost, attempt to humanize BP. They should have put cameras with their employees down on the Gulf showing what they were doing to help the region. People that work for BP are human; try to humanize BP rather than continuing to be simply a logo hated by so many. Not everyone who works for BP is evil. They should have showcased, via video, real people accessing claims to give a sense for the process. Also, ask for feedback, listen, and react accordingly.

Rate BP's online strategy on a scale of 1 (worst) to 10 (best)

[Score: 4] One good thing BP did was to not overreact and go hard after parody accounts like BPGlobalPR on Twitter that posted tweets like "*50 percent off blackened shrimp today*" and "*Hey, if you see any oil in the Gulf it's ours, please return it.*" Going hard after parody accounts right away would have been adding fuel to the fire as people would have been upset that BP wasn't focusing on the important task of capping the well.

Another positive is they have many resources posted on www.bp.com and you can also drill down (no pun intended) to specific regions (e.g., Alabama, Florida).

They needed to do a better job of listening to how "big" politically this was becoming and adjusted their PR and spokesmen accordingly. It also wasn't easy to find their social presence (Facebook, YouTube, etc.) on www.bp.com.

How has social media changed the attitude and usage of media, consumer behavior, and enterprises?

We no longer search for the news, the news finds us. A good example of this was in the U.S. during the 2008 elections. Tina Fey of SNL did some wildly popular Sarah Palin skits. More people watched the 5 minute clip online than via regular television. This is a good example of the massive shift in how we consume media. We don't sit in front of the television to watch 90 minutes of SNL, nor do we walk down to the end of the sidewalk to grab the morning paper. News, information, products, and services are pushed to us.

What does social media mean for publishers? How could they integrate it into new business models?

The beautiful thing about digital publishing is that it eliminates so many costs (shipping, printing, paper, etc.). In fact many of you may be reading this digitally right now. There are also possibilities to make money off pass-alongs. Books are social by nature. Historically when a paperback gets passed along, there is no additional revenue derived. With digital distribution you can charge $1 for this pass along. Also, product placement is now plausible with items in a digital format. We can also track what is being read the most so that we produce more of that and less of the items being ignored. We can track how many people read a particular book, or even page. The education front is even more exciting.

Many business travelers love the convenience of their favorite eReader (Nook, Kindle, Sony eReader, iPad, etc.). This is very similar to when we turned in our bulky music CD cases (sorry Case Logic) for lighter and more elegant iPods. As we peer into the future, the thing that excites me the most about eReaders, iPads, etc. is the social component. One quick example is:

When I went to college and purchased a used book, I'd spend a few minutes sifting through the various copies in the student bookstore before placing one into my shopping basket. After selection, I hoped and prayed that the person who took the notes in the margins and highlighted certain passages was smart. Sure, I had my own system—a tattered book was better than a fresher looking one as I assumed it was read more. I also equated neat handwriting and color coded highlighting as a sign of aptitude. Not a perfect system by any means, but it got me through college.

With the sharing capability of eReaders though, buying used books will quickly become a thing of the past. How great will it be to have one tiny eReader or iPad to tote around campus rather than straining the straps of a backpack loaded with books? Also, students will be able to perform quick digital searches and sorts for all the notes from the A+ students. Imagine the improved knowledge transfer from student to student. This is what excites many about the future world of education being enabled by social components of eReaders/iPads.

How will Generation Y and Z's media consumption change?

There will be more mobile consumption as technologies like smart phones, netbooks, and tablets improve. Wireless broadband penetration will make for an always "on" world.

How long will it take for online marketing budgets to match traditional marketing budgets?

Not long. In 2009 Ford moved their digital spend from 10 percent to 25 percent. My guess is that it's possible that in 3 years digital budgets will match and surpass those of traditional media. Keep in mind that most television as we know it today may be fed through an IP in the future.

Do you feel that it is imperative for non-profits to have a blog?

If you have something of relevance to say, and you enjoy saying it, then yes you should have a blog. Blogs are one of the best ways to create inbound traffic. However, they are a lot of work to maintain. Make sure you are willing to put in the time and commitment before launching a blog. They are free from a tangible "hard" cost, but they are far from free. Blogs are free like puppies, not free like beer.

You wrote about how Generation Y and Z is more creative and collaborative and young adults are more willing to promote brands online. Should marketers be focusing on this group in their social media campaigns?

Companies should only focus on this group if they provide a product or service that is of value to these Generations, or if they are influencers. If you are selling denture cleaner, targeting this group isn't going to do you much good.

How do you think the marketer's role in the non-profit sector differs in comparison to the for-profit world?

The same constructs apply. Sometimes non-profits have less resources, but that is the beauty of social media; it helps mitigate these disadvantages. It rewards those willing to work hard to develop relationships, not necessarily those with the most money.

What, in your view, are the most common ways that corporations have embraced social media? Is it making a Facebook page, sending official tweets, or maybe a mix of things?

The good companies know a solid social media strategy is much more than a Facebook page or setting up a Twitter account. The good companies know that social media has to be integrated into everything that they do—it's a part of their overall strategy since it touches every facet of the business. They also understand you get out what you put in; it's hard work. Just like offline relationships it takes time and commitment.

My students tend to get sloppy with their grammar online. What do you think about the importance of using good grammar on digital posts?

Language is a living and breathing item and will constantly evolve. Hence, this is why we see Twitter as the most used word in 2009, beating out Michael Jackson, Barack Obama, H1N1, etc. Some SM tools have character limitations that require people to use shorthand like u instead of you or 4 instead of four. I wouldn't view this as sloppy. That being said, some people are sloppy with the written word and online posts live online forever, so it's always prudent to put your best foot forward as you are representing the brand that is you.

I am in the process of expanding eLearning (online) classes here at my college. Which of the many social media products would you say is the best to select for online projects, communication, chats, etc.?

Fish where the fish are. If they are college students, most likely they are on Facebook and YouTube. It would be tough to go wrong here. But it depends on your goals and what you are teaching.

What do you say to small biz owners who want immediate results? What are realistic results?

It depends on what you define as success and also what you are selling. Immediate results are possible—Naked Pizza in New Orleans had record pizza sales for a day by effectively utilizing Twitter. However, this is the exception, for the most part you need to think strategically and long term with social media. It's not a magic pill and if your client thinks that going in, it's going to make it difficult to succeed.

What do you see about using podcasts?

There is still a strong market for podcasts, especially in commuting cities and cities heavily dependent on public transportation. Podcasts take commitment, which many aren't able to maintain. Hence, you can stand out if you produce a timely and consistent podcast.

What's the difference between "bleeding" vs "cutting" edge?

Bleeding edge is when you are too far ahead of the market—cutting edge is where you are ahead of your competition, but not too far ahead of the market/consumers. When Google Wave launched it was too bleeding edge, the general market couldn't grasp it. When the iPhone originally launched it was cutting edge; ahead of the competition but still easy for consumers to understand and use.

What is the worst thing about social media?

Some people start to hide behind social media and their interpersonal communication skills diminish.

What objectives are realistic for a small business owner who is only now just starting to practice social media?

Take the proper steps: (1) listen, (2) interact, (3) react, (4) soft sell. If you only do step one you will at a minimum have a much better understanding about your business and also your customer, and their needs—this is invaluable. Take the next progressive steps from there. Define what success looks like before you start.

I've heard that participation in social media increases your vulnerability to viruses and identify theft. Is this a myth or a valid concern?

If you leave your house you are more vulnerable to catch the flu or get hit by a bus. Yet, living your life confined to your house can cause other problems. The same holds true here. Yes you are more susceptible, yet common sense goes a long way! The nefarious tactics in social media are very similar to those used on e-mail and other parts of the Web.

Do you believe social media is a threat to online newspapers?

Yes I do feel it is a threat. All of us have the ability to report the news now. We are all media outlets. Imagine if you were walking the dog and saw what happened between Tiger Woods and his wife and took pictures or video with your smart phone?

Can "traditional" online news in some way take advantage of social media?

One thought is that "traditional" online news could set up services that (a) pay these onsite reporters/bloggers/experts per story, (b) they provide the vetting process, and (c) provide the distribution platform as well as a reputable source since they are doing (b) (the vetting process).

Do you believe social media could become a threat to democracy because the news doesn't reach the broad layers of the population?

I would say the opposite is true. Social media allows for Democracy to flourish since there is more transparency and it allows for more ownership and input from the people. In the U.S., Obama would not have been able to win without the Internet—and social media played an enormous part.

Some classified information is easy to leak, which isn't necessarily good. Wikileaks posted some confidential intelligence around the war in Afghanistan which may have put allied troops and Afghan citizens in harms way. This type of activity is not good.

Who is going to lead this new marketing? Big agencies? Specialized agencies? Media agencies? Brands themselves?

It's a people-driven economy stupid—people will lead the charge. People that shepherd brands (e.g. Tony Hsieh, Morgan Johnston) will also play leading roles. Technology development (application development, etc.) will continue to be outsourced to specialists.

How will we avoid ad saturation on social media?

Only advertising that delivers value to users will be tolerated. The days of shouting are over. Many of these sites have thumbs up and thumbs down ratings for advertisements. What people care about is what their friends are buying/using and what they like/don't like.

Which one do you think is the best business model for social networks? Is advertising the only way?

That is already proving to be one effective revenue stream for social networks, but there are many more. Think about people exchanging gifts in social media, small businesses setting up their businesses and using PayPal type functionality (many are already doing this), social search, social commerce, social gaming, Craig's List functionality, etc.

Do you know an agency that is doing it right in social media? Or a brand?

Zappos, Comcast, Ford, JetBlue, Skittles, Starbucks, Oreo, Nike, Lady Gaga, Ashton Kutcher, Ben & Jerry's, Best Buy, Bazaarvoice, Dell, and Virgin are leaders in the space. Crispin Porter & Bogusky, Weiden & Kennedy, and Razorfish have been progressive agencies in this area as well.

One of Google's Vice Presidents for engineering, Udi Manber, said his job is to do rocket science that will be taken for granted. How do you suppose social media fits into that rocket science?

A lot of success is dependent on execution rather than idea. Think of how much "High School Reunion" activity Facebook has captured. Why didn't this all go to classmates.com a decade ago? I agree with Manber in the sense that you want to be "cutting edge" rather than "bleeding edge." The end user doesn't care how things work; they just want them to work.

Marshall McLuhan once famously observed that "The future of the book is the blurb." Is social media eroding our collective attention span and ability to concentrate?

Seems like our mind has been conditioned to absorb information the same way Twitter distributes it: in a rapidly flowing stream of bite-sized updates.

Often people believe that evolution is a negative thing. On the contrary, it's just a different thing. People today are used to contributing, collaborating, and multi-tasking; not necessarily a bad thing. It reminds me of an old saying that was attributed to Mark Twain . . . "I didn't have time to write you a short letter, so I wrote you a long one." The fact that we are getting better as a society at getting to the "essence" of things quickly should be celebrated rather than frowned upon. However, there has been some erosion in terms of interpersonal communication skills and that's a trend I hope stops. 80–90 percent of all communication, is non-verbal, hence social media should be used as an "and" rather than an "or" when it comes to communication. I still fly around the world to give presentations. There is still nothing like face-to-face communication.

How does social media impact the process of job recruitment?

If there are 10 people on your team and your collective networks are stronger for your specific area of expertise (e.g., SQL database programmer) than any recruiter/headhunter you could hire, then odds are you will probably leverage a tool like LinkedIn. Many recruiters/headhunters' first stop is to do advanced searches in LinkedIn. LinkedIn wouldn't be able to charge for "In" accounts (ability to send e-mail to people you aren't connected with) if recruiters didn't find it helpful. So, if your team already has a network of trusted individuals, there is no reason to seek help, unless you simply don't have the time to reach out to your network. Great recruiters will survive and thrive, but I do see there being less of a market for recruiters as a whole.

How important to the future of political discourse is social networking?

Very important. It helps break down all types of social and cultural barriers created by distance. We all can't afford to travel internationally, but we can all hop on a social network to better understand our friends globally.

Impersonation on social networking sites has been described as both fraud and satire, how do you see them?

As long as you are upfront that you aren't the real person, I have no issue with this. If there is an audience for it then let Perez Hilton provide entertainment or @BPGlobalPR bring environmental concerns to life. I find it similar to *Saturday Night Live*, David Letterman, etc. making satire of political figures.

What about people sending friend requests to their kids, nieces, nephews, etc.—when and why would that be a good or bad idea?

If minors are on social media, I highly recommend parents are connected with their children on social media—this is just good parenting.

Should people use sites like Facebook or Twitter for dating, or is that best left to dating-specific sites (like Match.com)?

I believe it makes more sense to go on a date with someone that a good friend of yours knows rather than a complete stranger, so by all means some of the social media players like Facebook can be used in this manner.

Where do you see the future of social media?

Much will be around data aggregation and the sharing of this information with the social graph. What have my friends purchased? What services or restaurants have they rated highly? You will see search and social media begin to merge with the end result being we will no longer search for products and services via a search engine. Rather they will find us via social media. This is one of the true powers of social media! I care more what my friends and peers link to than about what an algorithm or opaque rating system spits out. A large part of Socialnomics is Social Commerce. Think Word of Mouth on steroids. Mobile and geolocation will be other major factors that will help both advertisers and consumers.

Consumers will also demand to have more control of their privacy. In a simplified example, there are some photos a consumer doesn't mind sending to the universe, while others they only want to send to five select people.

Oh, and 30 other things we haven't even dreamed up—that's what *is* exciting.

These questions are only scratching the surface; feel free to send me your questions by commenting at www.socialnomics.com or send a tweet to @equalman.

SOCIALNOMICS SUMMARY

It's about the economy, stupid. No, it's about a *people-driven* economy, stupid. Whether you are a businessperson or a high school student, social media transforms the way you live and do business.

As an individual, you need to live your life as if your mother is watching, because she probably is via social media. Individuals behaving appropriately is a good thing for society. But is it beneficial for the individual? If we can no longer have split personalities (*Work William* versus *Weekend Warrior William*) providing necessary stress relief, will more and more individuals experience nervous breakdowns? On the other hand, individuals being able to constantly update their status and micro-blogs allows them to take real-time inventory of their collective lives. It also allows us to be connected with the ones we love like never before.

Because of this, there may be no looking back on a wasted youth. Social media is not a waste of time; it actually makes people more productive. We no longer look for the news or things of interest—they find us. If a person is updating his status or micro-blogs with "watching reruns of *Saved by the Bell*," that certainly isn't quite as cool as "learning how to kayak white-water rapids." Reality TV has been replaced by reality social media—it's all about my friends and my own reality.

And that is what social media does—it rewards first-class behavior and punishes improper behavior (what happens in Vegas stays on YouTube). Time will tell if our newly transparent world cuts down on crime, infidelity, and so on.

And it's not just criminals and unfaithful spouses who can't hide; inferior companies and products can no longer hide behind massive marketing budgets. The days of shouting and imposing your message on the masses are gone. Successful companies in social media will function more like entertainment companies, publishers, or party planners than as traditional advertisers.

The 30-second commercial is being replaced by the 30-second review, tweet, post, status update, and so on. Not all great viral marketing ideas need to originate in the marketing department—businesses need to be comfortable with consumers taking ownership of their brands. The marketers' job has changed from creating and pushing messages to one that requires listening, engaging, and reacting to potential and current customer needs. And it's not just marketing that changes; business models need to shift. Simply digitizing old business models doesn't work; businesses need to fully transform to properly address the impact and demands of social media.

But who is the winner in this new world? Customers and good companies win—which, as a society, we have been trying to achieve since the industrial revolution. Social media enables this utopia-like state. Good companies view negative feedback as an opportunity to act on and adjust their products or services accordingly; bad companies view it as a nuisance or something they need to put an effort toward hiding.

Social media is helping enable a truly connected world. This results in tremendous time savings for individuals. It eliminates millions and millions of people performing the same tasks—multiple individual redundancies. Now only a few people need to research and test the best vacation spot or baby seat.

Others in your network can leverage your experiences and learn, creating the world's largest referral program.

People care more about what their friends and peers believe is the best Italian restaurant in Manhattan than what Google thinks. That is why it is no surprise that Google shows an interest toward social media technologies like Facebook and Twitter. Google understands that its future competition isn't other search engines, but rather its social media.

We need to look no further than Barack Obama's historic Democratic primary and U.S. presidential victories to understand the true power of social media. This is a whole new world that is best for individuals and businesses alike to embrace social media before they are squashed by it. Making multiple mistakes within social media is far better than sitting back and doing nothing at all. Companies don't have a choice on *whether* or not they do social media; the choices is how *well* they do it. This is the world of Socialnomics.

Socialnomics Winners and Losers

Winners

- Good companies that deliver products of great value
- Team players (employees)
- Society
- Democracy
- Referral programs
- Good talent
- Entrepreneurial talent (including musicians, comedians, etc.)
- Consumers: As consumers, good products will be easier to find and decisions will be easier to make because recommendations from people you trust and conversations with companies you develop a relationship with will replace the traditional one-way marketing messages

Losers

- Companies solely reliant on great marketing: all sizzle and no steak is a recipe for failure
- Undisciplined individuals: individuals exhibiting schizophrenic behavior
- Companies that *deliberate* rather than *do* will quickly die in a Socialnomic world
- Middlemen
- Search engines—if they fail to properly integrate social components
- Traditional advertising agencies
- Established talent (celebrities, singers, reporters, writers, etc.) that lacks talent
- Traditional media
- Businesses that don't listen or react

NOTES

Introduction

1. James Carville, "It's the economy, stupid." Wikipedia, accessed April 23, 2009, http://en.wikipedia.org/wiki/It%27s_the_economy,_stupid.
2. Barack Obama, Election Night Speech, Chicago, November 4, 2008.

Chapter 1 Word of Mouth Goes World of Mouth

1. Hitwise, June, 2008.
2. Chris Anderson, *The Long Tail* (New York: Hyperion, 2006), Chapter 2.
3. Christoph Marcour, personal interview.
4. Business Analysis and Research, Newspaper Association of America. October 2008, http://www.naa.org/TrendsandNumbers/Advertising-Expenditures.aspx.
5. Daisy Whitney, "SNL Palin Skits: Seen More on Web Than TV," *TVWeek*, October 1, 2008, http://www.tvweek.com/news/2008/10/snl_palin_skits_seen_more_on_w.php.
6. Alan D. Mutter, "$7.5B Sales Plunge Forecast for Newspapers," *Reflections of a Newsosaur,* October 12, 2008, http://newsosaur.blogspot.com/2008/10/75b-sales-plunge-forecast-for.html.
7. Nicholas Carlson, "PC Magazine Goes Out of Print," *Silicon Alley Insider*, November 19, 2008, http://www.businessinsider.com/2008/11/pc-magazine-goes-out-of-print.
8. Julie Johnson, "Playboy Considers Radical Changes to Flagship Magazine," *Chicago Tribune*, May 11, 2009. http://www.chicagotrib.com/business/chi-biz-playboy-magazine pla,o,12113400.story
9. Alan D. Mutter, "Print Drives Online Ad Sales at Newspapers," *Reflections of a Newsosaur,* February 3, 2009, http://newsosaur.blogspot.com.
10. Jupiter Survey, 2009.
11. Jim Giles, "Internet Encyclopaedias Go Head to Head," *Nature,* December 15, 2005.

12. Brian Morrissey, "Small Brands Teach Big Lessons," *AdWeek*, October 27, 2008, http://www.adweek.com/aw/content_display/news/digital/e3ia353f77f11f28ab959172cf3f7595abb.
13. Jose Antonio Vargas, "Obama Raised Half a Billion Online," *Washington Post* http://voices.washingtonpost.com/44/2008/11/20/obama_raised_half_a_billion_on.html.
14. Mary Schenk, "YouTube Co-Founder Tells Grads to Be Persistent, Take Risks," Department of Computer Science, University of Illinois at Urbana-Champaign, www.cs.uiuc.edu/news/articles.php?id=2007May15-266/.
15. YouTube, April 2009.
16. David Wilson, "American Airlines Crisis Management and Response," *Social Media Optimization,* April 2008, http://social-media-optimization.com/2008/04/american-airlines-crisis-management-and-flyers-response/.
17. Hitwise, 2008.
18. Hitwise, 2008.

Chapter 2 Social Media = Preventative Behavior

1. C. C. Chapman, "Managing the Gray," May 23, 2008, www.managingthegray.com/2008/05/23/comcast-wins-with-twitter/.
2. "JetBlue Engages in Real Conversation on Twitter," *Socialized*, March 17, 2008, http://www.socializedpr.com/jetblue-engages-in-real-conversation-on-twitter/.
3. Jeff Jarvis, "Dell Hell," *BuzzMachine*, June 21, 2005, http://www.buzzmachine.com/archives/cat_dell.html.
4. Michael Michelson Jr. (2003) writing for *The American Salesman Journal*.

Chapter 3 Social Media = Braggadocian Behavior

1. "CMOs Not Ready to Embrace Social Networking Sites, Survey Shows," survey conducted by Epsilon, November 24, 2008, http://www.corporatelogo.com/hotnews/cmo-marketing-social-networking-sites.html.
2. Bill Tily, personal interview.
3. Heather Endreas, personal interview.
4. Melissa Dahl, "Youth Vote May Have Been Key in Obama's Win," msnbc.com, November 5, 2008, http://www.msnbc .msn.com/id/27525497.
5. Facebook Application Statistics.
6. Jerry Seinfeld, http://www.wittcom.com/fear_of_public_ speaking.htm.
7. Anick Jesdanun, "OMG! :(It Ain't Write," AP–*New York Post*, National Commission on Writing at the College Board, April 27, 2008, http://www.nypost.com/seven/04252008/news/nationalnews/omg_it_aint_write_108037.htm?CMP=EMC-email_edition&DATE=04252008
8. "Young Adults Eager to Engage with Brands Online, Global Research from Microsoft and Synovate Reveals," November 11, 2008, http://www.synovate.com/

news/article/2008/11/young-adults-eager-to-engage-with-brands-online-global-research-from-microsoft-and-synovate-reveals.html.
9. "Young Adults Eager to Engage with Brands Online, Global Research from Microsoft and Synovate Reveals."
10. "Young Adults Eager to Engage with Brands Online, Global Research from Microsoft and Synovate Reveals."
11. "Advertising Nielsen Online: Kids Encounter Ads Less than Adults," E&P Staff and The Associated Press. October 13, 2008, https://listserv.temple.edu/cgi-bin/wa?A2=ind0810&L=net-gold&D=0&I=-3&T=0&P=58988&F=P.

Chapter 4 Obama's Success Driven by Social Media

1. David Carr and Brian Stelter, "Campaign in a Web 2.0 World," the *New York Times*—Media and Advertising, November 2, 2008, http://www.nytimes.com/2008/11/03/ business/media/03media.html?_r=1&ei=5070&emc=eta1.
2. Facebook Fan Data, October 2008.
3. YouTube View Data, October 2008.
4. YouTube View Data, October 2008.
5. Carr and Stelter, "Campaign in a Web 2.0 World."
6. Lance Muller, personal interview, June 2008.
7. Barack Obama, *Barack Obama: Connecting and Empowering All Americans Through Technology and Innovation,* November 2007, http://www.barackobama.com/pdf/issues/ technology/Fact_Sheet_Innovation_and_Technology.pdf.
8. David Needle, "Huffington: 'Obama Not Elected Without Internet,'" Internetnews.com, November 7, 2008, http://www.internetnews.com/webcontent/article.php/3783741/Huffington+Obama+Not+Elected+Without+Internet.htm.
9. "Web 2.0 and the Internet Delivered the Vote for Obama," *Huliq News*, November 10, 2008, http://www.huliq.com/ 2623/72572/web-20-and-internet-delivered-vote.
10. "Web 2.0 and the Internet Delivered the Vote for Obama."
11. Brian Solis, "Is Obama Ready to Be a Two-Way President?," *Tech Crunch*, November 15, 2008, http://www.techcrunch.com/2008/11/15/is-obama-ready-to-be-a-two-way-president/.
12. Solis, "Is Obama Ready to Be a Two-Way President?"
13. Brain Reich, personal interview, November 2008.
14. YouTube, October 2008.
15. Burt Helm, "Who's Behind the 'Wassup 2008' Obama Ad? Not Budweiser," *BusinessWeek*—Innovation, October 27, 2008, http://www.businessweek.com/the_thread/ brandnewday/archives/2008/10/whos_behind_the.html.
16. YouTube, October 2008.
17. John McWhorter, *All About the Beat: Why Hip-Hop Can't Save Black America* (New York: Gotham Books, 2008).
18. Ismael AbduSalaam, "Ludacris Explains Controversial Obama Song," *All Hip Hop*, November 6, 2008, http:// www.allhiphop.com/stories/news/archive/2008/11/06/ 20666656.aspx.

19. Miguel Helft, "Google Uses Searches to Track Flu's Spread," the *New York Times*—Technology, November 11, 2008, http://www.nytimes.com/2008/11/12/technology/ internet/12flu.html?8au&emc=au.
20. Helft, "Google Uses Searches to Track Flu's Spread."
21. Google Trends, April 2008.
22. Google Trends, April 2008.
23. Google Trends, April 2008.
24. Federal News Service, "Campaign Rally with Senator Barack Obama (D–IL), Democratic Nominee for President," *Chicago Sun-Times,* October 27, 2008, http://blogs.suntimes.com/sweet/2008/10/obama_closing_argument_speech_1.html.
25. Kate Kay, "Web Ads Mattered More than Ever in 2008 Election," *ClickZ,* November 4, 2008, www.clickz.com/showPage.html?page=clickz_print&id=3631395/.
26. Needle, "Huffington: 'Obama Not Elected without Internet.'"
27. "America Goes to the Polls," *A Report on Voter Turnout in the 2008 Election*, Nonprofit Voter Engagement Network, November 2008, www.nonprofitvote.org/Download-document/America-Goes-to-the-Polls-A-Report-on-Voter-Turnout-in-the-2008-Election.html.
28. Kim Estes, personal interview, November 2008.
29. Facebook Fan Data.
30. "Free Pancakes Anyone?," December 1, 2008, http:// socialnomics.net/page/2/.
31. "Free Pancakes Anyone?"
32. Facebook Fan Data.
33. "America Goes to the Polls."
34. "2008 Election Polls: How Long Would You Wait in Line to Vote?" *SodaHead,* November 4, 2008, www.sodahead.com/ question/184094/2008-election-polls-how-long-would-you-wait-in-line-to-vote/.
35. "Population Division," U.S. Census Bureau, July 1, 2007, http://www.census.gov/popest/states/asrh/SC-EST200701.html.
36. Stuart Elliott, "Army to Use Webcasts from Iraq for Recruiting," the *New York Times*, November 11, 2008, http:// www.nytimes.com/2008/11/11/business/media/11adco .html?pagewanted=print.
37. Elliott, "Army to Use Webcasts from Iraq for Recruiting."
38. "Army Exceed Recruiting Goal for Fiscal Year 2008," Army.mil/news release, October 10, 2008, http://www.army.mil/-newsreleases/2008/10/10/13228-army-exceed-recruiting-goal-for-fiscal-year-2008/.

Chapter 5 I Care More about What My Neighbor Thinks than What Google Thinks

1. "Nielsen Online Global Consumer Survey," Nielsen, April 2007.
2. Stewart Quealy, "Interview: John Gerzema," *SES Magazine*, March 2009, 57.
3. Facebook Statistics, retrieved April 2010, http://www.facebook.com/press/info.php?statistics.
4. Ken Robbins, personal interview, December 1, 2008.

5. Quealy, "Interview: John Gerzema."
6. iCrossing, "How America Searches: Health and Wellness," January 14, 2008, http://news.icrossing.com/press_releases.php?press_release=icrossing-study-finds-internet-top-resource-for-health-information.
7. iCrossing, "How America Searches."
8. iCrossing, "How America Searches."
9. YouTube View Data, 2008.
10. ACME Travel, in-house data.
11. "Jumping the Shark," Wikipedia, April 2009, http:// en.wikipedia.org/wiki/Jumping_the_shark.
12. Facebook Application Active User Data, April 2008.
13. Razorfish, "The Razorfish Consumer Experience Report 2008," http://feed.razorfish.com/publication/ ?m=2587&l=1.
14. Razorfish, "The Razorfish Consumer Experience Report 2008."
15. "Credit Union Members Vote on Logo Makeover," *The FinancialBrand.com,* November 21, 2008, http:// thefinancialbrand.com/2008/11/21/companion-logo-contest/.
16. "Credit Union Members Vote on Logo Makeover."
17. "Reading Online or On Paper: Which is Faster?" Sri H. Kurniawan and Panyiotis Zahiris, Insititue of Gerontology and Dept. of Industrial & Manufacturing Engineering, http://users.soe.ucsc.edu/~strikur/files/HCII_reading.pdf.
18. Quealy, "Interview: John Gerzema."

Chapter 6 Death of Social Schizophrenia

1. Schizophrenia is a very serious illness and our intent by the use of this term is not to make light of its serious conditions or those who suffer from this illness.
2. "Texas Lineman Facebook Status Gets Him Booted Off Team," The World of Issac.com, November 6, 2008, http://www.theworldofisaac.com/2008/11/texas-linemans-facebook-status-gets-him.html.
3. "Texas Lineman Facebook Status Gets Him Booted Off Team."
4. B. G. Brooks, "Coaches Deal with Athlete's Social Network," *Rocky Mountain News,* October 12, 2008, www.rockymountainnews.com/news/2008/oct/12/coaches-deal-athletes-social-networking/.
5. "Patriots Cheerleader Fired After Facebook Swastika Photo," Foxnews.com, November 6, 2008, http://www.foxnews.com/story/0,2933,448044,00.html.
6. Facebook.com, 2008.
7. Tony Blair, "Challenge of Change" (speech, 2008 World Business Forum, New York, September 2008).

Chapter 7 Winners and Losers in a 140-Character World

1. Apple iTunes Podcast Download Data, 2009.
2. *Fantasy Football Today* Podcast, ESPN, November 2008.

3. Twitter Postings, October 15, 2008.
4. Twitter Posting, October 21, 2008.
5. "News from the Olympics," Nascar Licensedathletics.com, September 3, 2008, http://nascar.licensedathletics.com/news.php.
6. "Not Ye Old Banners," *The Economist*, November 27, 2008, http://www.economist.com/business/PrinterFriendly.cfm? story_id=12684861.
7. "Online Ad Spending Grows 10%; Video Ads Strong (Just Not at Google)," *Marketing Pilgrim*, March 31, 2009, http://www.marketingpilgrim.com/2009/03/online-ad-spending-grows-20-video-ads-strong-just-not-at-google.html.
8. "March Video Streaming Soars Nearly 40% Compared to Last Year," *Nielsen Wire*, April 13, 2009, http://blog.nielsen.com/nielsenwire/tag/youtube/.
9. Brian Stelter, "Website's Formula for Success: TV Content with Fewer Ads," *New York Times,* October 29, 2008, www.nytimes.com/2008/10/29/business/media/29adco.html.
10. Stelter, "Website's Formula for Success."
11. Stelter, "Website's Formula for Success."
12. Mary Alison Wilshire, personal interview, December 5, 2008.
13. Stelter, "Website's Formula for Success."
14. Out of Home Advertising Bureau PDF, www.ovab.org/OVAB_ANA_Guide_2008-09.pdf.
15. "Hulu Celebrates First Anniversary, Gains Popularity by Serving Fewer Ads," blog.wired.com, October 29, 2008, http://blog.wired.com/business/2008/10/hulu-turns- one.html.
16. Stelter, "Website's Formula for Success."
17. "OMMA Panel: David vs. Goliath," *Online Video Watch*, http://www.onlinevideowatch.com/omma-panel-david-vs-goliath/.
18. Facebook Active User Data, 2008.
19. "War of the Words: Scrabulous Is Off Facebook, but Did Hasbro Win the Game?" Knowledge@Wharton, August 6, 2008, http://knowledge.wharton.upenn.edu/article.cfm?articleid=2029.
20. "War of the Words."
21. Facebook, 2008.
22. http://www.businessweek.com/debateroom/archives/2008/08/scrabulous_face.html
23. "War of the Words."
24. "War of the Words."
25. Razorfish, "The Razorfish Consumer Experience Report," http://feed.razorfish.com/publication/?m=2587&l=1.
26. Frank Rose, "How Madison Avenue Is Wasting Millions on a Deserted Life," *Wired*, July 24, 2007, www.wired.com/techbiz/media/magazine/15-08/ff_sheep/.
27. Newt Barrett, "Millions for a Virtual Coke on Second Life," *Succeeding Today,* June 25, 2007, http://succeedingtoday.com/2007/07/25/millions-for-a-virtual-coke-on-second-life/.
28. Rose, "How Madison Avenue Is Wasting Millions."

Chapter 8 Next Steps for Companies and The "Glass House Generation"

1. World Business Forum, Radio City Music Hall, New York, October, 2008.
2. "Student 'Twitters' His Way Out of Egyptian Jail," CNN.com, April 25, 2008, http://edition.cnn.com/2008/TECH/04/25/twitter.buck/.
3. "Student 'Twitters' His Way Out of Egyptian Jail."
4. Jessica Guynn, "MTV Networks in Deal to Monetize Uploaded Videos," *Los Angeles Times,* November 3, 2008, www.latimes.com/business/la-fi-myspace3-2008nov03,0, 6256914.story.
5. Steve O'Hear, "MTV and MySpace Partner to Monetize Pirated Content," ZDNET, November 3, 2008, http://blogs.zdnet.com/social/?p=602.
6. Organizing for America, http://www.barackobama.com/issues/technology/.
7. Author's estimate.
8. Erik Schonfeld, "Google Makes Up 88 Percent of Mozilla's Revenues, Threatens Its Non-Profit Status," *TechCrunch*, http://www.techcrunch.com/2008/11/19/google-makes-up-88-percent-of-mozillas-revenues-threatens-its-non-profit-status/.
9. 2008 Interactive Advertising Bureau Online Marketing Report.
10. Pubmatic AdPrice Index Q4 2008, http://www.pubmatic.com/adpriceindex/AdPriceIndex_Quarterly_Q4_08.pdf.
11. Patrick Smith, "Digital Media: Facebook, Yahoo!, Microsoft Profit From Open Networks In Europe," March 9, 2009, http://www.paidcontent.co.uk/entry/419-ft-digital-media-facebook-yahoo-microsoft-profit-from-open-networks-in-/.
12. "College Student and Teen Web Tastes," *eMarketer*, November 19, 2008, www.emarketer.com/Article.aspx? id=1006736/.
13. "Is the Mobile Web Replacing the Wired Web in Southeast Asia?," *Fierce Wireless*, November 20, 2008, http://www.fiercewireless.com/press-releases/mobile-web-replacing-wired-web-southeast-asia.
14. Sidhaarthaa Bezboraa, "Mobile Social Networking Use Grows 182% over 2007 in US, March 17, 2009," http://www.wirelessduniya.com/?p=1062.
15. Mark Walsh, "Buzzwire Unveils Mobile Social Site," *MediaPostNews*, http://www.mediapost.com/publications/?fa=Articles.showArticle&art_aid=100709.
16. https://generationfly.com/lounge.
17. Bob Garfield, "Widgets Are Made for Marketing, So Why Aren't More Advertisers Using Them?" December 2008, https://heartbeatofnewmediablogspot.com/2008/12/widgets-are-made-for-marketing-so-why.html.
18. Wikipedia, s.v. "walled garden (technology)," http://en.wikipedia.org/wiki/Walled_garden_(technology) (accessed December 21, 2008).
19. Microsoft's New Windows Live Aims to Be Hub for Web, InfoTech.TMCnet.com, November 13, 2008, http://it.tmcnet.com/news/2008/11/13/3783709.htm.
20. "Facebook Aims to Extend Its Reach Across the Web," SM2, http://www.sm2.com.au/content/view/777/76/.

21. NPR Radio, *Weekend Edition Saturday,* November 22, http://www.npr.org/templates/archives/rundown_archive_hub.php?date=11-22-20082006.
22. Wikipedia, s.v. "chava," http://en.wikipedia.org/wiki/Chav (accessed 11/25/2008).
23. *Harvard Business Review.*
24. http://www.videoactivereport.com/southwest_airlines_ding_widget_racks_up_150_million_in_ticket_sales

Chapter 10 Other Insights and FAQs

1. Gentry Estes, "Alabama Gets Back to Work in Preparation for BCS Championship Game," December 20, 2009, http://blog.al.com/press-register-sports/2009/12/alabama_gets_back_to_work_in_p.html.
2. *Austin American Statesman*, "Title Game Rarely Meets Month-Long 1 vs. 2 Hype," by John Maher January 2, 2010. http://www.statesman.com/sports/longhorns/title-game-rarely-meets-monthlong-1-vs-2-159734.html.

ROI Examples:

1. Jon Swartz, "More Marketers Use Social Networking to Reach Customers," *USA Today*, August 28, 2009.
2. Lee Odden, "Book Review: *Crush It*, by Gary Vaynerchuk," Online Marketing Blog.
3. Jan M. Rosen, "Be It Twittering or Blogging, It's All About Marketing," *New York Times*, March 11, 2009.

4-5. Wetpaint/Altimeter Group Engagement db study, 2009, http://www.marketingcharts.com/interactive/social-media-engagement-directly-linked-to-financial-success-9858/&http://www.altimetergroup.com/2009/07/engagementdb.html.

6. Jon Swartz, "More Marketers Use Social Networking to Reach Customers," *USA Today*, August 28, 2009.
7. http://www.advertolog.com/burger-king/print-outdoor/whopper-sacrifice-316211/. Estimate based on taking 32 million impressions at an average CPM of $13 based on eMarketer estimate found here. http://www.emarketer.com/Article.aspx?R=1007053. Less than $50,000 is a very conservative estimate (probably cost much less) to actually build the application plus the cost to Burger King to give out less than 20,000 coupons/whoppers. Please note these are estimates, but they fall on the conservative side.
8. Based on state populations of Arkansas, Kansas, Utah, Nevada, West Virginia, Nebraska, Idaho, Mississippi, Maine, New Hampshire, New Mexico, Hawaii, Rhode Island, Montana, Delaware, South Dakota, Alaska, North Dakota, Vermont, http://en.wikipedia.org/wiki/List_of_U.S._states_and_territories_by_population.

9. Kristen Nicole, "Will It Blend Videos Boost Sales 5x," *Mashable*, September 27, 2007.
10. Claire Baldwin, "Twitter Helps Dell Rake in Sales," Reuters, June 12, 2009.
11. "Marketing to the Social Web," Larry Webber, Wiley Publishing, 2007.
12-14. David Kiley, "Ford Spending 25% of Marketing on Digital and Social Media," *BusinessWeek*, October 16, 2009, http://www.businessweek.com/autos/autobeat/archives/2009/10/ford_spending_2.html.
15. Jacob Morgan, "Two Examples of Companies Measuring Social Media ROI," *Social Media Globetrotter*, 10/12/2009 http://www.jmorganmarketing.com/two-examples-of-companies-measuring-social-media-roi/.
16. Karl Greenber, "VW Goes All Mobile For Launch Of GTI," *MarketingDaily*, October 22, 2009, http://www.mediapost.com/publications/?fa=Articles.showArticle&art_aid=115919.
17. ResponseMine Interactive Agency (Atlanta, GA).
18. Intuit Inc. (Mountain View, CA).
19. "Increase B2B Lead Generation Using Social Media," *Social Media B2B*, July 14, 2009, http://socialmediab2b.com/2009/07/b2b-lead-generation-social-media/.
20-23. Jose Antonio Vargas, "Obama Raised Half a Billion Online," *Washington Post*, http://voices.washingtonpost.com/44/2008/11/20/obama_raised_half_a_billion_on.html.
24. Ed Bennett, "Hospitals and Social Media," SlideShare, http://www.slideshare.net/edbennett/hospitals-social-media.
25-28. Daniel Adler, "Twenty-One Top Twitter Tips," *Forbes*, 7/31/2009 http://www.forbes.com/2009/07/31/top-twitter-tips-entrepreneurs-technology-twitter.html.
29. Marshall Kirkpatrick, "Social Media ROI: Dell's $3m on Twitter and Four Better Examples," *ReadWriteWeb*, June 12, 2009, http://www.readwriteweb.com/archives/social_media_roi_dells_3m_on_twitter_and_four_bett.php.
30. Alex Bogusky, Co-Chairman, Crispin Porter & Bogusky.
31. Daniel Adler, "Twenty-One Top Twitter Tips," *Forbes*, 7/31/2009 http://www.forbes.com/2009/07/31/top-twitter-tips-entrepreneurs-technology-twitter.html.
32. *Social Media in the Enterprise*, White Paper, Vignette Software, February 2009, http://www.vignette.com/dafiles/docs/Downloads/Social-Media-in-the-Enterprise.pdf.
33. Quote from unknown source at McDonald's.
34. Samuel Axon, "Old Spice Sales Double with YouTube Campaign," *Mashable*, 7/26/2010.

ABOUT THE AUTHOR

Erik Qualman is the author of *Socialnomics: How Social Media Transforms the Way We Live and Do Business. Socialnomics* made Amazon's #1 Best Selling List in the U.S. and U.K after only three weeks of publication and later went on to be #1 in Korea, Germany, Japan, and Canada. Qualman is a frequently requested International speaker of the Fortune 500 and has been highlighted in numerous media outlets including: *BusinessWeek, The New York Times, CNET, San Francisco Chronicle, Mashable, USA Today, Forbes, CBS Nightly News,* and *The Huffington Post.*

He has been fortunate to share the stage with Alan Mulally (Ford CEO), Lee Scott (CEO/Chairman Walmart), José Socrates (Prime Minister of Portugal), Olli-Pekka Kallasvuo (Nokia CEO), Julie Andrews (Actress), Al Gore (former Vice President), Tony Hawk, and Sarah Palin. He also has one of 2010's most viral videos on YouTube "Social Media Revolution" [http://bit.ly/RTzPe]. Qualman is a MBA Professor of Digital Marketing at the Hult International Business School. For the past 16 years Qualman has helped grow the online marketing and eBusiness capabilities of many companies including Education First, Cadillac, EarthLink, Yahoo!, Travelzoo and AT&T. He is a columnist for *ClickZ*, while also owning the social media blog socialnomics.com.

Qualman holds a BA from Michigan State University and an MBA from The University of Texas. He is currently the Global Vice President of Online Marketing for EF Education. EF Education is headquartered in Lucerne, Switzerland, and Qualman works out of the 850-person Boston office. He was Academic All-Big Ten in basketball at Michigan State University and still finds time to follow his beloved Spartans.

twitter@equalman
equalman@gmail.com
www.socialnomics.com

In his spare time he enjoys SCUBA diving, golfing, tennis, and MSU hoops, and he has been fortunate to travel to 38 countries. He lives in Boston with his wife Ana Maria and daughter Sofia.

He is also founder of the charitable organization Paperback Robin Hood.

INDEX

CRITICAL [illegible] FOR
DANIELLE STEEL

"STEEL IS ONE OF THE BEST!"

—*Los Angeles Times*

"THE PLOTS OF DANIELLE STEEL'S NOVELS TWIST AND WEAVE AS INCREDIBLE STORIES UNFOLD TO THE DELIGHT OF HER ENORMOUS READING PUBLIC!" —United Press International

"Ms. Steel's fans won't be disappointed!"

—*The New York Times Book Review*

"Steel writes convincingly about universal human emotions." —*Publishers Weekly*

"One of the world's most popular authors."

—*The Baton Rouge Sun*

A LITERARY GUILD DUAL MAIN SELECTION
A DOUBLEDAY BOOK CLUB MAIN SELECTION

"ENTIRELY PLAUSIBLE . . . VERY MUCH ABOUT 'REAL' PEOPLE . . . DADDY HAS MORE MALE TEARS THAN YOU FIND IN YOUR AVERAGE NOVEL—BUT THEN, OLIVER'S IS A FOUR-HANDKERCHIEF SITUATION." —*Daily News* (New York)

"A REFRESHING NEW TANGENT . . . A WELL-DONE, OFFBEAT STORY." —*Los Angeles Times*

"A BITTERSWEET STORY . . . IT'S DIFFICULT TO TURN THE PAGES FAST ENOUGH."—*US* magazine

"CAPTIVATING . . . A GREAT STORY, A REAL PAGE-TURNER, FULL OF INSIGHT AND COMPASSION AND CHARACTERS THAT WILL TUG AT YOUR HEART AS THEY STRUGGLE WITH THE CHANGES IN THEIR LIVES. YOU'LL WANT TO CHEER THEM ON AS THEY LEARN TO COPE . . . STEEL IS AT THE TOP OF HER BEST-SELLING FORM." —*Houston Chronicle*

"MAY EVEN BE THE BEST OF THE TWO DOZEN NOVELS STEEL HAS MINED IN 17 YEARS."
—*Fort Worth Morning Star-Telegram*

"THERE AREN'T ANY SLOW MOMENTS, AND THE THREE GENERATIONS GIVE THE AUTHOR A LARGE CANVAS ON WHICH TO SKETCH IN DETAILS OF SINGLE PARENTHOOD, ROMANCE, AND MODERN SEX IN AN EVER-CHANGING WORLD."
—*Richmond Times-Dispatch*

"FAST-PACED PLOTTING."
—*The Plain Dealer* (Cleveland)

"ONE COUNTS ON DANIELLE STEEL FOR A STORY THAT ENTERTAINS AND INFORMS . . . IT WOULD BE HARD TO FIND A BETTER BIT OF POPULAR FICTION FOR READING ON A COLD NIGHT."
—*The Chattanooga Times*

"A PAGE-TURNER . . . [WE] GROW TO CARE ABOUT HER CHARACTERS . . . FRESH, NEW . . . HER MOST INTERESTING AND UNIQUE NOVEL IN MANY YEARS."
—*Rave Reviews*

"STEEL CONTINUES TO DO WHAT SHE DOES VERY, VERY WELL."
—*Kirkus Reviews*

Also by Danielle Steel

HEARTBEAT
MESSAGE FROM NAM
STAR
ZOYA
KALEIDOSCOPE
FINE THINGS
WANDERLUST
SECRETS
FAMILY ALBUM
FULL CIRCLE
CHANGES
THURSTON HOUSE
CROSSINGS
ONCE IN A LIFETIME
A PERFECT STRANGER
REMEMBRANCE
PALOMINO
LOVE: POEMS
THE RING
LOVING
TO LOVE AGAIN
SUMMER'S END
SEASON OF PASSION
THE PROMISE
NOW AND FOREVER
PASSION'S PROMISE

DANIELLE STEEL

DADDY

A DELL BOOK

Published by
Dell Publishing
a division of
Bantam Doubleday Dell Publishing Group, Inc.
666 Fifth Avenue
New York, New York 10103

ISBN: 0-440-20762-2

Reprinted by arrangement with Delacorte Press

Printed in the United States of America

Published simultaneously in Canada

November 1990

10 9 8 7 6 5

RAD

DADDY

To the Very Best Daddy
I know . . . times nine!
Daddy theirs. . . .
  Daddy ours. . . .
    Daddy mine!!
With all my heart,
With all my love,
To Popeye again,
but this time from
All of us,
        with all my heart
          and soul,
            my love,
              from
                Olive.

Daddy

First love,
first son,
or perhaps
a precious
daughter,
their laughter
swift
and sweet,
his hand so sure,
his love so pure,
his loyalty
to them
amazing,
his patience
vast,
and his heart
wider
than the heavens,
the leaven
for their
lives,
the bright sun
in their skies,
the one to
whom they
turn,
the man for whom
they burn,
the flame
of love
so bright,

his wisdom
always right,
his hand
so strong,
so seldom
wrong,
so sweet,
so near,
so dear,
so much the hub
of all,
and once upon a time
so tall,
his love for them
never waning,
always entertaining,
handsome,
dashing,
teaching,
reaching
for the stars,
driving funny cars,
a loving hand and heart
for every lass
and laddy,
beloved man,
eternal friend,
how lucky
you are,
sweet children,
to have him
for
your
daddy.

Chapter 1

The snowflakes fell in big white clusters, clinging together like a drawing in a fairy tale, just like in the books Sarah used to read to the children. She sat at the typewriter, looking out the window, watching snow cover the lawn, hanging from the trees like lace, and she completely forgot the story she'd been chasing around in her head since early that morning. It was so damn picturesque. So pretty. Everything was pretty here. It was a storybook life in a storybook town, and the people around her seemed like storybook people. They were exactly what she had never wanted to become, and now she was one of them, and had been for years. And probably always would be. Sarah MacCormick, the rebel, the assistant editor of the *Crimson,* the girl who had graduated from Radcliffe in 1969 at the top of her class and knew she was different, had become one of them. Overnight. Or almost. In truth, it had taken almost twenty years. And now she was Sarah Watson. Mrs. Oliver Wendell Watson. She lived in Purchase, New York, in a beautiful house they almost owned, after fourteen years of struggling with the mortgage. She had three children, one dog, the last hamster had finally died the year before. And she had a husband she loved. Dear sweet Ollie. He graduated from Harvard Business School when she finished Radcliffe, and they'd been in love since her sophomore year. But he was everything that she wasn't. He was conservative when she was wild, he had believed in what they had tried to do in Vietnam, and for a while she had hated him for it. She had even stopped seeing him for a time after graduation, because she insisted that they were too different. She had gone to live in SoHo, in New York, and tried to write, and she'd actually done pretty well. She'd been published twice in *The Atlantic Monthly,* and once . . . holy of holies . . . in *The New Yorker.* She was good and she knew it. And Oliver lived uptown, in an apartment he shared with two friends on East 79th Street, and with his MBA, he got a pretty good job in an ad agency on Madison Avenue. She wanted to hate him for it, wanted to hate him for conforming, but she didn't. Even then, she knew how much she loved him.

He talked about things like living in the country, having Irish setters, wanting four kids, and a wife who didn't work, and she made fun of him for it. But he just grinned that incredible boyish grin that made her heart pound even then . . . even when she pretended to herself that what she really wanted was a man with hair longer than her own . . . an artist . . .

a sculptor . . . a writer . . . someone "creative." Oliver was creative, and he was smart. He had graduated magna from Harvard, and the trends of the sixties had never touched him. When she marched, he fished her out of jail, when she argued with him, even calling him names, he explained quietly and rationally what he believed in. And he was so damn decent, so good-hearted, he was her best friend, even when he made her angry. They would meet in the Village sometimes, or uptown for coffee, or drinks, or lunch, and he would tell her what he was doing and ask her about the latest piece she was writing. He knew she was good, too, but he didn't see why she couldn't be "creative" and married.

". . . Marriage is for women who are looking for someone to support them. I want to take care of myself, Oliver Watson." And she was capable of it, or she had been then, after a fashion. She had worked as a part-time gallery sitter in SoHo, and a free-lance writer. And she'd made money at it. Sometimes. But now, sometimes, she wondered if she would still be able to take care of herself, to support herself, to fill out her own tax forms, and make sure her health insurance hadn't lapsed. In the eighteen years they'd been married, she'd become so dependent on him. He took care of all the little problems in her life, and most of the big ones. It was like living in a hermetically sealed world, with Ollie always there to protect her.

She counted on him for everything, and more often than not, it scared her. What if something happened to him? Could she manage? Would she be able to keep the house, to support herself, or the kids? She tried to talk to him about it sometimes, and he only laughed, and told her she'd never have to worry. He hadn't made a fortune, but he had done well and he was responsible. He had lots of life insurance. Madison Avenue had been good to him, and at forty-four, he was the number three man at Hinkley, Burrows, and Dawson, one of the biggest ad agencies in the country. He had brought in their four biggest accounts himself and he was valuable to the firm, and respected among his peers. He had been one of the youngest vice-presidents in the business, and she was proud of him. But it still scared her. What was she doing out here, in pretty little Purchase, watching the snow fall, and waiting for the kids to come home, while she pretended to write a story . . . a story that would never be written, that would never end, that would never go anywhere, just like the others she had tried to write in the last two years. She had decided to go back to writing on the eve of her thirty-ninth birthday. It had been an important decision for her. Thirty-nine had actually been worse than turning forty. By forty, she was resigned to "impending doom," as she woefully called it. Oliver took her to Europe alone for a month for her fortieth birthday. The kids were away at camp, two of them anyway, and her mother-in-law had kept Sam. He had only been seven then, and it was the first time she'd left him. It had been like opening the gates to heaven when she got to Paris . . . no car pools . . . no children . . . no pets . . . no PTA . . . no benefit dinners to run for the school or the local hospitals . . . no one . . . nothing . . . except the two of them, and four unforgettable weeks in Europe. Paris . . . Rome . . . driving through Tuscany, a brief stop on the Italian Riviera, and then a few days on a boat he rented, drifting between Cannes and St. Tropez . . . driving up to Eze and Saint-Paul-de-Vence, and dinner at the Colombe d'Or, and then a few final whirlwind days in London. She had scribbled constantly during the trip, and filled seven notebooks. But when she got home . . . nothing. None of it wanted to be woven into stories, or tales, or articles, or even poems. She just sat there, staring at her notebooks, and a blank page in her typewriter that she never seemed to fill. And she was still doing it a year and a half later. At forty-one, she felt as though her entire life were behind her. And Oliver always laughed at her when she said it.

"Christ, Sarrie . . . you haven't changed a bit since I met you." And he meant it. It was almost true. But not quite. She, and those who wanted to be critical, could tell the difference. The shining dark red hair that used to hang down her back in sheets of coppery brilliance had faded to a reddish brown now. She wore it to her shoulders and there were more than a few threads of silver, which bothered the children more than they did Sarah. The bright blue eyes were the same, they were a dark, vibrant blue, and the creamy skin was still fine and for the most part unlined, but there were tiny traces of time here and there, but Oliver only said that they gave her face more expression. She was a pretty woman, and she had been a pretty girl, long and lean, with a good figure and graceful hands, and a sense of humor that danced in her eyes. It was that that he had loved about her from the first. Her laughter and her fire, and her courage, and her rabid determination to stick by what she believed in. There were those who thought her difficult when she was young, but not Ollie. Never Ollie. He liked the way she thought, and the things she said, and the way she said them. They had a relationship built on mutual respect and caring, and they had a very good time in bed. They always had, and they still did. Sometimes he even thought that after twenty years it was better. And it was, in some ways. They knew each other perfectly, like satin-smooth wood that had been touched and caressed and traveled a thousand times by loving hands and the tenderness of true belonging.

It had taken him exactly two years to convince her to marry him after her SoHo days, and at twenty-three she had become Mrs. Oliver Watson. Balking all the way, and in typical fashion, she had refused to have a traditional wedding. They had been married in the garden of his parents' Pound Ridge home, and her parents and her younger sister had come from Chicago. Sarah had worn a bright red dress and a big picture hat, and she looked more like a young girl in a painting than a bride, but they had both been happy. They had gone to Bermuda for their honeymoon, and the weather had been lousy, but they never noticed. They laughed and played, and stayed in bed until the late afternoon, emerging only for an early foray in the staid dining room of the hotel, and then they would hurry back to their room again, giggling and laughing, like two children.

It was three weeks after that that Sarah was less amused. They were living in a small apartment on Second Avenue, in a building filled with stewardesses and young executives, and "singles" who seemed to turn the entire building into a constant party.

He had come home from work to find her looking as though her best friend had died. But it was no friend, it was only "the rabbit." She had been puzzled by the absence of her period once they got home, but she had been religious about using her diaphragm, and knew she couldn't be pregnant. She had worn it practically night and day from the altar till they got home from their honeymoon, but somehow, some way, something had gone wrong, and she was pregnant. And she wanted to have an abortion. Oliver was horrified that she would even think of it. But Sarah was even more so at the thought of having children so quickly.

"We don't want a family yet . . . I want to get a job again . . . to do something . . ." She'd been thinking of getting a job this time as an editor at a literary magazine, her stories hadn't been selling quite as well, and she had applied to Columbia Graduate School to do some work toward her master's. She had quit the gallery-sitting job as soon as she married Ollie, because commuting to SoHo every day wouldn't have been convenient.

"You can always get a job later!" He reasoned with her. He comforted, he cajoled, he did everything he could to try to make her feel better. But she was inconsolable, and every evening on the way home, he was suddenly overwhelmed by a wave of terror . . . what if she did it . . . if she went to someone while he was at work, and had an abortion. But she didn't. Somehow, she was too sick, and too exhausted, and too depressed to even attempt it, and the next thing she knew she was waddling around their apartment, wondering how she could have let it happen. But Oliver was thrilled. He wanted four kids, he had always said so, and even if it stretched their budget just then, he was willing to face it. He was doing well, advancing rapidly in the firm, and even if they had been starving, he wouldn't have let her get an abortion. He just wouldn't. It was their baby. Theirs. And long before the baby came, he loved it.

Benjamin Watson arrived with a shock of bright red hair, and a look of astonishment in his bright eyes, exactly nine months and three days after his parents' wedding. He looked anxious to discover the world, cried a lot, and looked almost exactly like his mother, much to Oliver's delight, who was thrilled to have a son, and particularly one who looked like Sarah. Benjamin grew like a weed, and had more than Sarah's looks. He had her determination, her stubbornness, and her fiery temper. And there were days when she thought she would strangle the child before Oliver got home to soothe them. Within minutes of his arrival on the scene, he had the baby cooing happily, laughing, playing peekaboo, and he walked around the house, carrying him in his arms, while Sarah collapsed in a chair with a sigh and a glass of wine, wondering how she was going to survive it. Motherhood was definitely not her strong suit, and the apartment was so small, it was driving her crazy. When the weather was bad, as it often was that year, they couldn't get out at all, and the baby's screams seemed to echo off the walls until she thought she would go crazy. Oliver wanted to move them out of town somewhere to a home of their own, but that dream was still a long way off, they couldn't afford it. Sarah offered to get a job, but whenever they tried to figure it out, it seemed pointless, whatever she might have earned would have gone to pay a sitter, leaving them with no more money than they had before. The only purpose it would serve would be to get her out of the house, and although it appealed to Sarah, Oliver thought that it was important for her to be with the baby.

"Talk about chauvinistic, Ol. What do you expect me to do, sit here all day and talk to myself while he screams?" There were days when she really thought she couldn't take it. And the prospect of having the four children he still wanted made her suicidal.

Her own parents were no help because they were in Chicago, and for all their good intentions, his weren't much better. His mother had had one child, and the memory of how to cope with it seemed to have escaped her. Being around Benjamin only seemed to make her nervous. But not nearly as nervous as it was making Sarah.

Eventually the baby settled down, and Benjamin seemed a lot less terrifying to her by the time he was walking. They were finally out of the woods. They rented a house on Long Island for the summer, and in another year she could send him to nursery school . . . one more year . . . she was almost home free . . . and then she could go back to writing. She had given up the idea of a job. She wanted to write a novel. Everything was starting to look up, and then she got the flu. It was the flu to end all flus, and after a month of it, she was convinced she was dying. She had never been so sick in her life. She had a cold that simply would not go away, a cough that sounded like TB, and she was nauseated from morning till night from coughing. In the end, after four weeks of battling it, she decided to go to the expense and see the doctor. She had the flu, but she had more than that. She was expecting another baby. This time there was no anger, no rages, no outrage or fury, there was simply despair, and what seemed to Oliver like hours and hours and hours of crying. She couldn't face it, she couldn't do it again. She couldn't handle another child, and Benjamin wasn't even out of diapers, and now there would be two of them. It was the only time she had actually seen Oliver down too. He didn't know what to do to turn her around. And just like the first time, he was thrilled about the baby, but telling her that only made her cry harder.

"I can't . . . I just can't, Ollie . . . please . . . don't make me. . . ." They argued about an abortion again, and once she almost swayed him, for fear that if he didn't agree, she might go crazy. But he talked her out of it, and he got a raise when she was halfway through the pregnancy, and spent every penny of it hiring a woman to come in and help her with Benjamin three afternoons a week. She was an Irish girl from a family of thirteen children, and she was just what Sarah needed. Suddenly she could go out, to libraries, to meet friends, to art galleries and museums, and her disposition improved immeasurably. She even started to enjoy Benjamin, and once or twice she took him to the museum with her. And Oliver knew that although she wouldn't admit it to him, she was beginning to look forward to their second baby.

Melissa was born when Benjamin was two, and Oliver started thinking seriously about moving his family to the country. They looked at houses in Connecticut almost every weekend, and finally decided they just couldn't afford them. They tried Long Island, Westchester, and it seemed as though every weekend they were riding to look at houses. Pound Ridge, Rye,

Bronxville, Katonah, and then finally, after a year, they found just what they wanted in Purchase. It was an old farmhouse that hadn't been lived in in twenty years, and it needed an enormous amount of work. It was part of an estate, and they got it for a song in probate. A song that still cost them dearly to sing, but scraping and saving and doing most of the work themselves, they turned it into a remarkably pretty place within a year, and they were both proud of it. "But this does not mean I'm going to have more children, Oliver Watson!" As far as she was concerned, it was enough of a sacrifice that she was living in the suburbs. She had sworn that she would never do that when they were dating. But even she had to admit that it made more sense. The apartment on Second Avenue had been impossible to manage, and everything else they'd looked at in town seemed tiny and was ridiculously expensive. Here the children had their own rooms.

There was a huge but cozy living room with a fireplace, a library they lovingly filled with books, a cozy kitchen with two brick walls, heavy wooden beams overhead, and an old-fashioned stove that Sarah insisted on restoring and keeping. It had huge bay windows that looked over what she magically turned into a garden, and she could watch the children playing outside when she was cooking. With their move to the country, she had lost the Irish girl, and it was just as well, because for the moment they couldn't afford her.

Benjamin was three by then anyway, and he was in school every morning, and two years later Melissa was in school too, and Sarah told herself she would go back to writing. But somehow there was no time anymore.

She always had things to do. She was doing volunteer work at the local hospital, working one day a week at the children's school, running errands, doing car pools, keeping the house clean, ironing Ollie's shirts, and working in the garden. It was a hell of a switch for the once assistant editor of the *Crimson.* But the funny thing was, she didn't mind it.

Once they left New York, it was as though a part of her got left behind there, the part of her that had still been fighting marriage and motherhood. Suddenly, she seemed a part of the peaceful little world around her. She met other women with children the same age, there were couples they played tennis and bridge with on the weekends, her volunteer work seemed to be constantly more demanding, and the thrashing and fighting she had done was all but forgotten. And along with all of that went her writing. She didn't even miss it anymore. All she wanted was what she had, a happy, busy little life with her husband and children.

Benjamin's screaming babyhood began to fade into distant memory and he turned into a sweet sunny child, who not only had her looks but seemed to share all her interests and passions and values. He was like a little sponge, soaking up everything she was, and in many ways, he was like a mirror of Sarah. Oliver saw it and laughed, and although Sarah seldom admitted it to anyone, in some ways it flattered and amused her. He was so much like her. Melissa was a sweet child too, she was easier than Benjamin had been, and in some ways she was more like her father. She had an easy smile, and a happy attitude about life. And she didn't seem to want much from either of them. She was happy following Sarah everywhere with a book or a doll or a puzzle. Sometimes, Sarah even forgot she was in the next room. She was an undemanding little girl, and she had Oliver's blond hair and green eyes, yet she didn't really look like him. She looked more like his mother actually, which when commented on by her in-laws never failed to annoy Sarah.

She and Oliver's mother had never really become friends. Mrs. Watson had been outspoken early on and had told her only son what she thought of Sarah before they were married. She thought her a headstrong, difficult girl, who wanted her own way at any price, and she always feared that one day she might hurt Oliver badly. But so far Sarah had been a good wife to him, she admitted to her husband begrudgingly when he stood up for the girl, but Sarah always felt that the older woman was watching her, as though waiting for some slip, some faux pas, some terrible failing that would prove her right in the end. The only joy the two women shared was the two children, who delighted Mrs. Watson, and whom Sarah loved now as though she had wanted them from the first, which Mrs. Watson still remembered she hadn't. Oliver had never told her anything, but she had sensed what was going on, without being told. She was an intelligent woman with a quick eye, and she knew perfectly well that Sarah hadn't been happy to be pregnant, nor had she enjoyed Benjamin's early days, but on the other hand, she had to admit that he hadn't been an easy baby. He had unnerved her, too, with his constant colicky screaming. But all of that was forgotten now, as the children grew, and Sarah and Oliver thrived, both of them busy and happy, and doing well. And Sarah finally seemed to have given up her literary aspirations, which had always seemed a little excessive to Mrs. Watson.

"She's a good girl, Phyllis. Don't be so hard on her. She was young when they got married. And she makes Oliver very happy." Her husband had always been more philosophical than she was.

"I know . . . but I always get the feeling that she wants something more, something just out of reach . . . something that will cost Oliver dearly." It was an astute remark, more so than she knew. But George Watson shook his head with an indulgent smile.

"Ollie can handle her."

"I'm not sure he wants to. I think he'd let her have anything she wants, whatever the cost to him. He's that kind of man." She smiled gently up at the husband she had loved for almost forty years, years that were too precious to even count now. They had become bonded like one body, one soul, long since. She couldn't even remember a time without him. "He's just like his father. Too good. Sometimes that can be dangerous in the hands of the wrong woman." She was always concerned about her son, and even after all these years, always faintly distrustful of Sarah.

But the compliment had not gone unnoticed by her husband, as he smiled down at his bride with the look that still made her tingle. "Give the girl a little credit, Phyllis. She hasn't hurt our boy, and she's given him, and us, two beautiful children." Indeed they were, and although neither of them looked exactly like their father, they both had some of his classic good looks. Oliver was tall and graceful and athletic-looking, with thick, straight blond hair that had been the envy of every mother when he was a child, and every girl when he was in college. And although Sarah seldom acknowledged it to him, because she didn't want to bloat his ego beyond something she could cope with, more than once she had heard it said that Oliver Watson was the best-looking man in Purchase. For six months of the year, he had a deep tan, and his green eyes seemed to dance with mischief and laughter. And yet he was unaware of his good looks, which made him all the more attractive.

"Do you think they'll have more children, George?" Phyllis often wondered but would never have dared to ask her son, much less Sarah.

"I don't know, darling. I think they have a full life as it is. And these days, you can never be too sure of what's going to happen. Oliver is in an insecure business. Advertising is nothing like banking when I was a young man. You can't count on anything anymore. It's probably wiser for them not to." George Watson had been talking that way for the past year. He had lived long enough to watch many of his investments, once so sound, begin to shrink and dwindle. The cost of living was astonishingly high, and he and Phyllis had to be careful. They had a pretty little house in Westchester they had bought fifteen years before, around the time when Oliver was in college. They knew that he'd never be coming home again for any great length of time, and it seemed foolish to continue hanging on to their rambling old house in New London. But George worried about their finances constantly now. It wasn't that they were destitute by any means, but if they both lived another twenty-five years, which at fifty-nine and sixty-two they still could, and he hoped they did, it could stretch their savings beyond their limit. He had just retired from the bank and was getting a decent pension. And he had made numerous wise investments over the years, but still . . . you could never be too careful. It was what he told Oliver every time he saw him. He had seen a lot in his lifetime, one big war and several small ones. He had fought in Guadalcanal, and been lucky enough to survive it. He had been twelve in the crash of '29, he knew just how brutal the Depression had been, and he had seen the economy go up and down over the years. He wanted his son to be careful. "I don't see why they'd want any more children."

And Sarah completely agreed with him. It was one of the few subjects on which she and George Watson were in total agreement. Whenever the subject came up with Oliver, once in a while in bed late at night, or on a quiet walk in the woods in a remote corner of Purchase, she always told him she thought it was silly to even consider it. "Why would we want more kids now, Ollie? Melissa and Benjamin are growing up. They're easy, they have their own lives. In a few years we'll be able to do anything we want. Why tie ourselves down with all those headaches again?" Even the thought of it made her shudder.

"It wouldn't be the same this time. We could afford someone to help us. I don't know . . . I just think it would be nice. One day we might regret not having more children." He looked at her tenderly with the eyes that almost made women swoon at the PTA, but Sarah pretended not to notice.

"The kids wouldn't even like the idea by now. Benjamin's seven, and Melissa's five. A baby would seem like an intrusion to them. You have to think of that. We owe something to them too." She sounded so definite, so sure, and he smiled and took her hand as they walked back to where they had parked the car. He had just bought his first Mercedes. And she didn't know it yet, but he was going to give her a fur coat for Christmas. He had just picked it out at Bergdorf Goodman, and it was being monogrammed with her initials.

"You certainly sound sure." As always, he sounded disappointed.

"I am sure." And she was. There was no way he was going to talk her into having another baby. She was thirty-one years old, and she liked her life just fine the way it was. She was swamped with committee work all day long, she spent half her life running car pools, and the rest of it going to Cub Scouts and Melissa's ballet class. Enough was enough. He had tamed her as far as she was willing to be tamed. They had the picket fence, and the two kids, and the house in the country, and they had even bought an Irish setter the year before. More than that she could not give, even for Ollie.

"What do you say we take the kids skiing after Christmas?" he asked as they got in the car. He liked to stay close to home for the actual holidays, because he thought it was more fun to be at home, and he thought it was nicer for his parents. Sarah's parents had her sister and her kids, and they went to Chicago every Christmas from Grosse Pointe, but his parents had only him. And Sarah had no burning desire to go home for the holidays anyway. They had done it once, and she had complained about it for three years. Her sister annoyed her, and Sarah and her mother had never gotten along either, so the arrangement they had was perfect.

"That would be fun. Where? Vermont?"

"What about something a little racier this year? What about Aspen?"

"Are you serious? That must have been one hell of a bonus you got last week." He had brought in the agency's biggest client ever. He still hadn't told her how big the bonus was, and they had both been so busy in the last week, she hadn't pressed him.

"Big enough to splurge a little if you'd like to. Or we could stay around here, and then go away just the two of us after the kids are back in school, if you want to. My mom would come and stay with them." She had before, and now that they were a little older, it worked better. "What do you think?"

"I think it sounds terrific!" She gave him a hug, and they ended up necking in the new car, which smelled of men's cologne and new leather.

And in the end, they did both. They went to Aspen with the kids for the week between Christmas and New Year, and a month later, he took Sarah away for a romantic week in Jamaica at Round Hill, in their own villa, overlooking Montego Bay. They laughed about their honeymoon in Bermuda, about how they had never left their room, and barely managed to stay in the dining room long enough to have dinner. This vacation was no different. They played tennis and swam and lay on the beach every morning, but by late afternoon, they were making passionate love in the privacy of the villa. And four nights out of six they made special arrangements for room service. It was the most romantic trip they had ever taken, and they both felt reborn when they left Jamaica. Sarah was always amazed to realize how passionately she still loved him. She had known him for twelve years, been married to him for eight, and yet she felt as though their romance was still fresh, and it was obvious that Oliver felt the same about Sarah. He devoured her with the energy of an eighteen-year-old, and more than that, he loved to talk to her for hours. The sex they shared had always been great, but with the years came new vistas, new ideas, new horizons, and their ideas were no longer as diverse or as sharply polarized as they once had been. With the years, they had grown slowly together, and he teased her about becoming more conservative, while he had slowly become a little more liberal. But he felt as though they had slowly become one person, with one mind, one heart, and one direction.

They returned from Jamaica in a kind of haze, mellowed, slowed down from their usual pace, and the morning after they returned, Oliver sat at breakfast and admitted that he hated to leave her and go to the office. They exchanged a secret look over the children's heads at breakfast. She had burned the toast, left lumps the size of eggs in the Cream of Wheat, and the bacon was almost raw when she served it.

"Great breakfast, Mom!" Benjamin teased. "You must have had a terrific time on vacation, you forgot how to cook!" He guffawed at his own joke, and Melissa giggled. She was still much shyer than Benjamin, and at five she worshiped him as her first and only hero, after her father.

The children left for school in their car pools, and Oliver to catch his train, and Sarah found it impossible to get going. She was disorganized all day, and she felt as though she couldn't get anything done. By dinner-time, she still hadn't left the house, and had puttered around all day, getting nothing accomplished. She assumed it was the price of having had too good a time on vacation.

But the condition persisted for weeks. She barely managed to crawl through the days, and just doing car pools and chauffeuring the kids from here to there seemed to sap all the energy she had, and by ten o'clock at night she was in bed, gently snoring.

"It must be old age," she groaned to Oliver one Saturday morning as she attempted to sort through a stack of bills, and unable to do even that without feeling exhausted and distracted.

"Maybe you're anemic." She had been once or twice before, and it seemed a simple explanation of what was becoming an annoying problem. She hadn't accomplished anything in a month, and she had two spring benefits to put on, and all of it seemed like too much trouble.

On Monday morning, she went into the doctor's office for a blood test and a checkup, and for no reason she could think of, when she picked up the children that afternoon she already felt better.

"I think it's all in my head," she reported to Oliver when he called to say he had to work late and wouldn't be home for dinner. "I went in for a checkup today, and I already feel better."

"What did he say?"

"Nothing much." She didn't tell him that the doctor had asked if she was depressed, or unhappy, or if she and Ollie were having trouble. Apparently one of the early signs of depression was chronic exhaustion. Whatever it was, it was nothing serious, she was sure of that. Even the doctor said she seemed to be in good health, she had even gained five pounds in three weeks since their trip to Jamaica. It was no wonder, all she did was sit around and sleep. Even her diligent reading had been neglected, and she hadn't gotten back to her weekly tennis game again. She had promised to the next day, and was on her way out the door, feeling tired, but with racket in hand, when the doctor called her.

"Everything's fine, Sarah." He had called her himself, which worried her at first, but then she decided it was just a kindness after all the years she'd known him. "You're in good health, no anemia, no major problems." She could almost hear him smiling, and she was so tired, it annoyed her.

"Then why am I so goddamn tired all the time? I can hardly put one foot after another."

"Your memory is failing you, my dear."

"Terrific. You're telling me I'm getting senile? Great. That's just what I wanted to hear at nine-fifteen in the morning."

"How about some good news then?"

"Like what?"

"Like a new baby." He sounded as though he had just announced a million-dollar gift and she felt as though she was going to faint dead away in her kitchen, tennis racket in hand, as she listened.

"Are you kidding? In this house, that's no joke. My children are practically grown . . . I . . . I can't . . . shit!" She sat down heavily in a convenient chair, fighting back tears. He couldn't mean it. But she knew he did. And suddenly she knew what she had been unwilling to face. Denial had kept her from knowing the truth. She hadn't missed a period because she was anemic or overworked or overage. She was pregnant. She hadn't even told Ollie. She had told herself it was nothing. Some nothing. But this time there was no doubt what she would do. This was 1979. Her children were a reasonable age. She was thirty-one years old. And abortions were legal. This time Oliver was not going to talk her out of it. She was *not* going to have a baby. "How pregnant am I?" But she knew . . . it had to be . . . it had happened in Jamaica . . . just like it had happened in Bermuda when she conceived Benjamin on their honeymoon . . . goddamn vacation.

"When was your last period?" She calculated rapidly backward and told him. In medical parlance, she was six weeks pregnant. In "people talk," it was only about a month, which meant she had plenty of time to get an abortion. For a moment, she even wondered about getting one without saying anything to Ollie. But she wasn't going to mention it to their doctor. She would call her gynecologist and get an appointment. "Congratulations, Sarah. You're a lucky girl. I hope Oliver will be happy."

"I'm sure he will be." Her voice felt like lead in her throat as she thanked him and hung up, and with shaking fingers dialed her gynecologist and made an appointment for the following morning. And then, in a panic, she remembered her tennis partners waiting for her on the court at the Westchester Country Club. She would have liked not to go, but it wouldn't have been fair to them, and she hurried out the door and turned the key in the ignition of her station wagon. And as she did, she caught a glimpse of herself in the mirror. This couldn't be happening to her . . . it couldn't be . . . it wasn't fair . . . when she grew up she was going to be a writer . . . when . . . if . . . or maybe not. Maybe all she'd ever be was a housewife. The ultimate condemnation when she was in college. The thing she had never wanted to be, and now was. That was all she was, wasn't it? A housewife. She said it out loud in the car as though it were a dirty word . . . a baby . . . Jesus Christ . . . a baby . . . and what did it matter if it would be different this time, if they could afford help, if the house was big enough to accommodate all of them. The baby would still scream all night, still need to be bathed and dressed and fed and taken care of, and nurtured, and driven around and taken to the orthodontist one day. She would never get a chance to do what she wanted now. Never. She felt as though the unborn child, the mere knowledge of it, were threatening her very existence. And she wouldn't let it.

She forced the car into reverse and shot out of the driveway, and ten minutes later she was at the tennis courts, looking pale, and feeling sick, knowing what she did now.

She managed to keep the patter of conversation somehow, and that night she was grateful that Ollie had to stay late at the office, working on a presentation for a new client. A very big one. But what did it matter now how big his clients were? In Sarah's mind, her life was over.

She was asleep when he got home that night, and managed somehow to get through breakfast the next morning. He asked her what was bothering her, and she told him she had a splitting headache.

"Did you find out about those tests yet? I'll bet you really are anemic." He looked suddenly worried, and instead of loving him for it, she hated him as she thought of what he had planted inside her.

"Not yet. They haven't called." She turned away to put the plates in the dishwasher so he wouldn't see the lie in her eyes, and a few minutes later he was gone, and the children had been picked up by their car pools. And an hour later she was at the gynecologist's office, planning for her abortion, but the doctor threw her a curve, and asked her how Ollie felt about what she was doing. "I . . . he . . . uh . . ." She couldn't lie to the man. He knew her too well, and in addition to that, she liked him. She looked directly at him with a strange light in her eye, and silently dared him to defy her. "I haven't told him."

"About the abortion or the baby?" He looked startled. He had always thought that they had a very happy marriage, the kind in which two people confide easily and openly in each other.

"Neither one. And I'm not going to." His face set as he listened to her and he slowly shook his head in disapproval.

"I think you're making a mistake, Sarah. He has a right to know. It's his child too." And then he had an uncomfortable thought. Perhaps there were things about them he didn't know. Anything was possible. "It is . . . isn't it?"

She smiled in answer. "Of course it is. I just don't want to have it." She told him all the reasons why and he made no comment, but when she was through, he repeated again that he thought she should discuss it with her husband. He urged her to think about it, and after she had he would make the appointment for her, but not before.

"You're still a very young woman. You're certainly not too old to have this baby."

"I want my freedom. In eleven years, my son will be in college, and my daughter two years later. If I have this baby, I'll be tied down for another twenty years. I'm not ready to make that kind of commitment." It sounded incredibly selfish, even to her ears, but she couldn't help it. That was how she felt. And no one was going to change that.

"Is that what Oliver feels too?" She didn't answer for a long moment. She didn't want to tell him that Ollie had always wanted more children.

"I haven't discussed it with him."

"Well, I think you should. Call me in a few days, Sarah. You have time to make the decision and still do things safely."

"Time isn't going to change anything." She felt defiant and angry and let down as she left his office. He was the one who was supposed to solve the problem for her and now he wasn't.

She went home and cried, and when Oliver came home at eleven o'clock that night, she was in bed, feigning another headache. The children were long since asleep, and she had left the TV on in the bedroom, droning at her as she waited for him to come home, but still sure she wouldn't tell him.

"How'd it go today? You look tired." She looked up at him sadly as he walked into the bedroom.

"It went okay," he said as he sat down on the edge of

the bed and smiled at her and loosened his tie. The blond hair looked tousled by the wind, and he was tired, but he still looked unbearably handsome. How could he look like that? Life was so simple for him. All he had to do was go to an office every day and deal with real people in a real world. He got to have all the fun, while she spent every waking hour with women and children. There were things about life that weren't fair, and in her eyes, that was one of them. There were times when she wished she were a man, when she wished she had lived her life differently, when she wished she had gotten a job years before, instead of doing what she'd done. But this was so easy. She had taken the easy way out. She had had two kids, moved to the suburbs, and given up her dreams. And now she was having another baby . . . but she wasn't, she told herself rapidly . . . she was having an abortion. "What's wrong, Sarrie?" He looked worried as he bent to kiss her. He knew her too well, and he could see the anguish in her eyes, the anguish not born of guilt for what she wanted to do, but of anger at what had happened.

"Nothing. I'm tired too."

"The kids give you a hard time today?"

"No . . . they were fine."

"So what's wrong?" he persisted.

"Nothing," she lied.

"Bullshit." He took off his jacket, opened his shirt, and moved closer to her on the bed. "Don't try and kid me. You're worried sick about something." And then a sudden wave of terror hit him. It had happened to a guy he knew at the office six months before. They discovered that his wife had cancer and four months later she was dead, leaving him devastated and alone with three children. Oliver knew he couldn't have lived through it if he lost Sarah. He had loved her for too long. She was everything to him. "Did the tests come back? Is there something I should know?"

For an instant she thought of what the doctor had said . . . You should tell him, Sarah . . . he has a right to know . . . it's his baby too . . . But I don't want to! something inside her screamed. "The tests were fine." And then, forced by the honesty they had always shared, she let herself be pressed into telling him something she knew she'd regret later. "More or less."

The pain of worry sliced through him like a knife as he gently took her hand in his own. "What does that mean?" He could barely speak and he never took his eyes from hers. "What did they tell you?"

She realized instantly what he thought and knew she couldn't cause him any more worry. She didn't want any more of his children, but she loved him. "It's nothing like that. Don't look so scared." She leaned over to kiss him, and as he held her she could feel him tremble.

"Then what is it?"

She spoke in a whisper, from an abyss of despair, then slowly raised her eyes to his again, still wanting not to tell him. "I'm pregnant."

For an instant, neither of them moved as her words sank in, and his whole body seemed to go slack from the tension that had seized him when she started speaking. "Oh my God . . . why in hell didn't you tell me?" He sat back and grinned and then his smile faded as he read the look in her eyes. She looked as though she would have preferred having cancer.

"I didn't know until yesterday. Stupid, I guess. It must have happened in Jamaica."

He couldn't repress a grin and for an instant she wanted to hit him. "I'll be damned. I never even thought of that. I guess it's been a while, my memory is rusty." His voice and eyes were gentle, but she pulled her hand from his and lay back against the pillows, as though to get as far away from him as she could. It was all his fault.

"I'm having an abortion."

"Oh? When did you decide that?"

"Within about thirty seconds of hearing the news. Ollie, I can't do this."

"Is something wrong?"

She shook her head slowly, suddenly knowing what a bitter fight it was going to be between them, but she wasn't willing to lose this time. She was not going to have this baby. "I'm too old. And it isn't even fair to the children."

"That's crap, and you know it. They'd probably be thrilled if we told them."

"Well, we're not going to. It's going to be all over in a few days."

"Is that right?" He got up and started to pace the room. "Simple as that, is it? What is it with you? Every time you get pregnant, we have to go through this fucking insanity about abortion."

"It's not insanity. It is *my* sanity. I don't want another baby. You go to the office every day, you have your own life. I'm stuck out here playing car pool and PTA mom, and I'm not going to re-up for another twenty years. I've done ten, and the way I see it, I'm halfway through, and you're not going to change that."

"And then what? What's so worthwhile killing this baby for? You're going to become a brain surgeon maybe? For chrissake, you're doing important things here, you're raising our children. Is that too big a sacrifice for Miss Cliffie to make for God and Country? I know you used to think you should be in SoHo with the Great Unwashed, writing poems and the Great American Novel. Personally, I think this has a little more merit, and I thought that by now you'd figured that much out too. For chrissake, Sarah, grow up!"

"I have grown up, God damn you. I've grown up, grown out, and grown old, and I'm not going to throw my life away for everyone else forever. Give *me* a chance, for chrissake. What about *me*? There are more than just kids in this world, Oliver, or hadn't you noticed?"

"I notice that you have a damn easy life out here. While I work my balls off in New York, you play tennis with your friends, and make cookies with Melissa, and that's what you should be doing. But don't tell me what a fucking hardship that is, Sarah, I just don't buy it. And a baby isn't going to change any of that."

"Bullshit!"

The fight raged until two in the morning, and the next night, and the next night, and the night after. It raged through the weekend and into the following week, with tears on both sides, and slamming doors, and ugly accusations. It finally boiled down to Oliver begging Sarah to have the baby, and eventually throwing up his hands, and telling her to do whatever the hell she wanted.

She scheduled the abortion twice, and even made the mistake of calling her sister in Grosse Pointe, which turned into an even bigger fight when her sister told her she thought she was indecent, immoral, and more than likely crazy.

It went on for weeks, and in the end, they were both drained, damaged, disillusioned, but somehow they managed to piece it all back together and Sarah did not have the abortion. But Oliver agreed that after this one, she could have her tubes tied. He thought it was an unfortunate choice, but he also realized that neither of them could survive another attack like this one on the very foundations of their marriage, and Sarah assured him that under no circumstances was she going to be having another surprise baby when she was forty.

The baby came on Election Day, with Oliver standing in the delivery room, encouraging Sarah, who told him she hated him every time she had a contraction, and she had assured Ollie almost hourly for the past eight months that she was never going to give a damn about this baby. He told her he would love it for both of them, and the children were thrilled at the prospect. Benjamin was eight by then and intrigued and excited by the whole thing, and to Melissa, at six, it was like having a live doll to play with. Only Sarah had remained unenthusiastic about the impending arrival. And as the baby's head appeared, Oliver watched in wonder as Samuel Watson made his way into the world, with a loud cry and a look of amazement at his father. They handed the baby to Oliver first and he gently gave him to Sarah, who lay with tears streaming down her cheeks, remembering all the ugly things she had said about this baby. He had black hair and Ollie's green eyes, and creamy skin, and a look in his eyes that somehow foretold great wisdom and great humor. He was the kind of baby you fell in love with the moment you saw him, and as fervently as she had resisted him, Sarah fell as ardently in love with him from the instant she held him. He was "her" baby, no crier, no screamer, an easy, peaceful, happy baby, right from the first. He became her great passion in life, and she regaled Oliver nightly with tales of Sam's accomplishment and genius. He was just simply a very delicious baby, and everyone was crazy about him right from the first, Ollie, Sarah, his brother and sister, his grandparents. He was terrific, and he proved Ollie right, although he was gracious enough never to say it, but they both knew. Ollie had been right, and they were both grateful that Sarah had had him. Everything about him was easy and lovable and fun, and he never became the burden Sarah had feared he would be.

To make matters easier, Ollie had hired a housekeeper for her, a local woman who'd worked for a bishop for fifteen years and wanted to find a household with a little life and fun. She loved Melissa and Benjamin, and like everyone else, she fell in love with Sam the minute she saw him. He had round cherub cheeks and a smile to match, and fat little arms and legs that begged you to squeeze and hold and kiss him. And more often than not Agnes, his benevolent guardian, and Sarah, his adoring mother, found themselves each kissing one chubby cheek as the three noses met and they laughed and Sam squealed with amusement. Agnes was exactly what Sarah had needed, she only wished she had had her when Benjamin was screaming the walls down on Second Avenue with colic, but they couldn't have afforded her then anyway. Now everything was different. And as Ollie had predicted, it was all surprisingly easy.

Sarah didn't have to make breakfast anymore. She didn't have to make dinner anymore. She didn't vacuum or clean or do laundry. They had a cleaning woman twice a week, and the miraculous Agnes. She was happy living in a tiny little room they built onto what had once been a deck, outside the guest room, which was now the baby's bedroom. And day and night, he was surrounded by his sister checking up on him, his brother bringing him baseball mitts and footballs, Sarah, Oliver, and Agnes. And amazingly, he did not become a spoiled brat, but instead, he was a remarkably pleasant child, who remained the joy of the house, and brought sunshine into everyone's life around him. The nightmare of the child that would destroy Sarah's life never materialized, but by the same token he provided her no excuses. He needed no special extra time, he caused no trouble in school, he was just as happy to play with Agnes or Melissa as he was with her, or most especially Benjamin or his father, and Sarah had no excuse now.

And before she knew it, Benjamin was suddenly seventeen and in his last year of high school, Melissa fifteen and permanently grafted to a telephone she would drag inexplicably into an upstairs closet, to sit huddled on the floor amid old ski clothes to speak to boys no one had ever heard of, and Sam was nine, content to play in his own room, busy with his own routine, and singularly undemanding of his mother's attention—all of which left Sarah with no reason whatsoever why she couldn't write. She couldn't blame the blank pages or the silence of the typewriter on the children.

And as she sat watching the snow fall, she wondered what she would say to Ollie. She wished he wouldn't ask her how the writing was going. For almost two years now, he had evidenced sincere concern and it was driving her crazy. She couldn't tell him that nothing was coming, that it was going nowhere, that at forty-one her worst fears had come true. Her life really was over. She had never felt so stale and old and tired, and this time she knew she wasn't pregnant. As promised, and agreed, she had had her tubes tied years before, after Sam's arrival. This was something very different. This was the slow, demoralizing realization that your life is going nowhere, that the dreams you had at twenty had dissipated years before and were very likely never real in the first place. She was never going to be a writer now. At thirty-five, knowing that would have destroyed her, at thirty-nine, it might have killed her. At forty-one, it filled her with sadness. There was nothing left now, except the ordinariness of her life, while Ollie climbed to greatness. It was an odd feeling. Even her children were more important than she was. Everyone had something going in their lives. Benjamin was an outstanding athlete and a terrific student. Melissa was incredibly artistic and, surprisingly, a real beauty. She talked about becoming an actress sometimes, and both she and Benjamin talked about Harvard. Sam sang with the choir and had the voice of an angel, but more than that, he had the soul of someone so warm and dear that the whole world loved him. And what did she have? The children. Ollie. The house. The fact that she'd gone to Radcliffe twenty years before. So what? Who cared? Who knew? Who remembered? She had only one hope left, and even that was a slim one, another slice of unreality in her pie of nothingness. There was no way she could do it anyway. How? She lived here. They needed her. Or did they? They had Agnes . . . but she couldn't do that to Ollie . . . She smiled sadly to herself as Agnes let the dog out and he bounded through the snow, barking and leaping. They were all so happy. All of them. Even Agnes. But why did she feel so empty? What was gone? What had she lost? What had she never had? What did she want now? Something. Everything. She wanted all of it. Fame. Success. Fulfillment. Big stuff. Big guns. And she knew she would never have it. She would sit here forever, watching the snow fall, while life passed her by, and Ollie brought in new clients. She had her own Mercedes now, she had two fur coats. She had three terrific children, thanks to Ollie's persistence, and one fantastic husband, and nothing of her own that mattered. No talent. No accomplishment. It was all gone now. The girl that she had been was gone forever.

"The mail is in, Mrs. Watson," Agnes spoke softly as she set it down on the desk beside her.

"Thanks, Agnes. Anything that looks good?"

"Mostly bills. And I think a school letter for Benjamin. It's addressed to you though." Benjamin was in the process of filling out his Harvard application for the following year, but he hadn't even sent it in yet. They wouldn't be writing to him, nor to Sarah about him. This was something different and she knew it. She knew what the answer was going to be, but her hand trembled anyway as she reached out and took it from Agnes. She stood very still for a moment, staring at it, thinking back . . . to when things were different . . . but that was all gone now. All gone. She had to force herself to remember that, as she tore it open, with her back to Agnes, and then walked slowly into the living room, to stand amid the sunny chintzes and bright flowered prints that brought them summer and spring even in the midst of winter.

She opened the letter slowly, as though peeling away a shell, as though breaking open her life . . . but she didn't let herself think that. She sat down slowly in her chair, never seeing Agnes watching her, with a puzzled look in her eyes as Sarah read . . . slowly . . . painfully . . . and then felt her breath catch in amazement. It couldn't be. It was wrong. She had read it wrong. It had to be. But it wasn't. The words were there. My God . . . the words were there . . . and suddenly she felt her body fill, as though with light and music. She didn't feel empty anymore. It was as though there was something inside her now. Better than a baby. It was herself . . . She was there. She was back again. And she read the line again, and again, and again.

. . . "We are pleased to inform you that you have been accepted for the master's program at Harvard University" . . . pleased to inform you . . . pleased to inform you . . . the words blurred as the tears rolled slowly down her cheeks. It was a dream, only a dream. There was no way she could do it. She couldn't leave them. Couldn't go back to school. And yet she had applied months before, in September, when the children went back to school and she was bored and lonely. Just to try it . . . just to see if . . . and now they were telling her they wanted her. But she couldn't. But as she looked up she saw the snow still falling outside, the dog still barking and cavorting and Agnes watching her from the doorway. She knew she had to. They'd understand. They'd have to understand . . . it wouldn't be for very long . . . and then she would be a person again. A person of her own. She would be real . . . She would be Sarah.

Chapter 2

"Bad news in that letter, Mrs. Watson?" Agnes had seen Sarah's face go pale as she watched her, and then she had seen tears glistening on her cheeks as Sarah stared out the window. There was no way that Agnes could understand all that she was feeling now. The excitement . . . the disbelief . . . the hope . . . and the terror. She had left her alone in the den with her own thoughts, and it was a full hour before Sarah walked into the kitchen.

"No . . . no . . . just a surprise . . ." Sarah looked vague, almost shell-shocked, neither happy nor sad, as she wandered distractedly around the kitchen, straightening things out without seeing them, pushing a chair into the table, picking a tiny piece of paper off the floor. It was as though she didn't know what to do now. As though she were seeing her home for the first time, or the last. What in hell was she going to do? She couldn't go back to Harvard now. She couldn't possibly leave them. She silently wondered why she had even applied. It was ridiculous, a pipe dream, Ollie would laugh at her . . . and yet . . . somehow it wasn't funny now. It was frightening and sad and wonderful, and an opportunity she didn't want to give up, even for them. She had never felt so torn in her life. And she knew she couldn't tell Ollie. Not yet. Maybe after the holidays. Christmas was only two weeks away. She could tell him after that. Maybe they'd go skiing for a few days and she could tell him then. But what in God's name would she tell him? . . . I want to go back to school, Ol . . . I'm moving up to Boston for a year or two . . . I have to get out of here . . . but tears filled her eyes again, and for a desperate moment, she knew she didn't want to leave them.

Agnes was watching her, not believing what she had said. There had to have been more than a surprise in the letter she'd read. Or if it was, it couldn't have been a good one.

"What time are the kids coming home?" Sarah looked vaguely at the spare little woman bustling around the kitchen, making preparations for dinner. Usually she was grateful for her; suddenly now, Agnes was making her feel useless. Her shining white hair was pulled tightly back in a bun, her face set, lips pursed as she set the kitchen table. The children ate in the kitchen with her whenever she and Oliver went out, and sometimes when Oliver and Sarah were at home, they all ate in the kitchen together. But most of the time when she and Ollie were home, they ate in the dining room. It was something Oliver liked to do, he liked the ceremony of it, the tradition of sitting down together in a civilized way, and talking about what they'd done all day. It was his way of getting away from the pressures of work, and keeping up with what they did, especially the children. But tonight she and Ollie were going out with friends, to a new restaurant in nearby Rye. The phone broke into Sarah's thoughts before Agnes could answer her, and Sarah hurried to answer it. Maybe it was Ollie. She suddenly wanted to be near to him, to hear his voice, to keep him close to her. Suddenly, in a single moment, with the letter she'd just read, everything was changing.

The call was from their friends. They had to cancel their dinner date that night. She had a terrible sore throat, and he had to stay late at the office. Sarah turned toward Agnes with a pensive look. "I guess we'll stay home tonight and eat with the kids. The people we were having dinner with just canceled."

Agnes nodded, watching her, and then spoke up. "Why don't you go out with Mr. Watson anyway?" Sarah looked as though she needed the distraction. And Sarah smiled at her. The two women knew each other well, and yet Agnes always kept a respectful distance. She wasn't afraid to speak her mind, to give them hell when she thought she should, particularly for the children's sake, yet even when she railed at them, which she sometimes did, they were "Mr. and Mrs. Watson." "Mr. Watson isn't very fond of meat loaf."

Sarah grinned at her. She was right. He wasn't. Maybe they should go out. But suddenly she didn't want to be alone with him. And as she tried to decide, she heard the front door slam and a voice call out, and a moment later, Benjamin strode into the cozy kitchen. At seventeen, he was six feet tall, with bright red hair, and his mother's dark blue eyes. His cheeks were red from the cold, and he pulled his watch cap from his head and threw it on the table.

"Disgusting boy!" Agnes waved a wooden spoon at him, looking fierce, but the love she felt for him was evident in her eyes. "Get that hat off my kitchen table!"

He laughed, and grinned warmly at her, stuffing the hat in the pocket of his peacoat. "Sorry, Aggie . . . Hi, Mom." Instead of the hat, he tossed an armload of books onto the table. "Boy, it's cold out there." His hands were red, he never wore gloves, and he had walked the last block home, a friend had dropped him off. And he strode straight to the refrigerator to give himself sustenance until dinner. He ate constantly, portions that would have frightened anyone, yet he was thin as a rail, and had his father's spare frame and powerful shoulders.

"Stay out of there. You'll be eating dinner in less than an hour." Agnes waved the spoon again and he grinned.

"Just a snack, Aggie . . . it's okay . . . I'm starving." He stuffed a handful of salami into his mouth as Sarah looked at him. He was a man, and a handsome one. He had his own life, own friends, and in a few months he'd be in college. Did he really need her now? Would it make a difference to him? Suddenly she couldn't imagine that her presence there meant anything to him, as he turned to look at her, struck by the somber look in her eyes. "Something wrong, Mom?"

"No, no," she shook her head fervently, just as she

had when Agnes had asked her. "I was just trying to decide whether or not to go out to dinner with your father. What are you up to tonight? Still studying for exams?"

He nodded. He was a good student, a fine young man, a person she admired, her firstborn, and still the most like her in many ways, although he was less rebellious than she had been at his age. "Yeah, my last one's tomorrow. Chemistry. I'm going over to Bill's to study with him tonight. Can I have the car?" That was all he needed from her in truth, their refrigerator and her car keys.

She smiled slowly at him. She would miss him if she went. She would miss all of them . . . especially Sam . . . oh God . . . and Ollie . . . "Sure . . . just be sure you drive carefully. If it gets any colder, this stuff'll turn to ice. Can't he come here, come to think of it?" But Benjamin was quick to shake his head, always determined, just as she was.

"He came here the last three times. I told him I'd go there tonight. Mel's going to be out anyway. Did she call you?"

Their mother shook her head. "Not yet." She never did. She always forgot to call. She did exactly as she pleased, and always had, without making a fuss about it. She led her own life. At fifteen, Melissa was the soul of independence. "What do you mean, 'she's out tonight'? It's a Tuesday." She had only just been allowed to date since that September, and it was confined to one weekend night, with boys her parents had met, under circumstances they approved of. "And how's she getting home?"

"I told her I'd pick her up." He picked up an apple

from the basket on the kitchen counter and took a bite. "She has rehearsal tonight. She's in some play with the drama club. She's okay, Mom." They both heard the front door slam again, and Sarah saw Agnes glance at the clock with a private smile, as she glanced hurriedly at her meat loaf.

There was suddenly the heavy sound of boots, as though a man had arrived in their midst, a wild *woof!* and a muffled crash, the slamming of another door, more barking, and then suddenly Sam and Andy, the Irish setter, exploded into the kitchen. The dog was leaving paw prints everywhere, leaping on the boy with the shining dark hair and green eyes just like his father's. He wore a broad, happy-go-lucky smile, his hair was wet, and his boots and the dog's feet had dragged in tons of snow, which were rapidly turning into puddles on the kitchen floor, as Andy leapt to lick his face, and put two paws on Sam's shoulders.

"Hi, guys! Boy, it smells good in here. What's for dinner? Meat loaf?"

Agnes turned to smile broadly at him, and then saw the disaster he was rapidly making of her kitchen, as Sarah and Benjamin laughed. Sam was hopeless, he could turn any room into a trash heap in a matter of moments.

"Get out of here, you wicked boy! And where's your hat? You'll catch your death with wet hair like that!" She waved the wooden spoon at him as she had at Benjamin before, but this time with greater zeal, and hurried off to get him a towel, clucking and growling and scolding.

"Hi, Mom." He hurried over to kiss her, Andy wagging his tail ferociously as he watched and Sam played with him, kicking off his boots then and leaving them in a heap in the middle of the kitchen floor, where Andy found them with delight and fled with one of them to the living room couch, where he deposited it amid shrieks from Agnes.

"Get out of here! Both of you! Go upstairs and take a bath!" she called after him, as he hurried up the stairs with Andy in hot pursuit, as Sam left his coat on the floor at the foot of the stairs and Sarah called after him.

"Come back and pick up your stuff!" But he was already long gone, down the hall, with Andy barking after him, and Agnes was already busy mopping up her kitchen. Benjamin hurried up the stairs to his own room to organize his books for that night, and when Sarah walked slowly up after them, she couldn't help thinking how much she would miss them.

The phone rang as she reached the master bedroom. It was Melissa calling to say what Sarah already knew, that she was staying at school late to rehearse with the drama club, and Benjamin would pick her up on his way home. And then Ollie called, and he wanted to go out that night, even without their friends, just as Agnes had suggested.

"We'll have a quiet dinner, just the two of us. I think I'd like that better anyway." She could feel the warmth of his voice all the way from New York, and there were tears in her eyes when she hung up the phone. What was she going to say to him? Nothing. Not tonight. She'd have to wait. She had already promised herself she wouldn't tell him till after Christmas.

She puttered around their room, straightening things, listening to the sounds of the children beyond, touching familiar objects, and thinking about her husband. And then she lay down on their bed, thinking of all of them, of what they meant to her. And yet they were costing her something, too, without knowing it, without meaning to, each one in his or her own way had taken something from her, and given something back too . . . but suddenly what they gave her wasn't enough, and it was no longer what she wanted. It was a terrible thing to admit. A terrible thing to say to them, and she knew she never could. But she wanted her own life now. She was ready for it. She wanted to be more than Agnes was, standing in the kitchen waiting for them to come home every day, and eventually waiting for them to leave forever. It wouldn't be long now. Benjamin would be gone in the fall. And Melissa two years after that, and then there was Sam . . . but she'd be through with what she wanted to do long before he left home. So what difference did it make? Why couldn't she do what she wanted to for a change, yet while saying that to herself, she felt unbearably guilty.

The phone broke into her thoughts again and it was her father-in-law, sounding distressed and tired. He had had problems with his heart of late, and Phyllis hadn't been well either.

"Hi, George, what's up?"

"Is Oliver there?" He was curt with her this time, which was unlike him.

"No, he's not." She frowned worriedly, she was fond of him, although she was less so of Phyllis. "Is something wrong?"

"I . . . no . . . actually, I'm not sure. Phyllis went out shopping at noon, by herself, and she hasn't come home yet. And with this weather . . . well, I was concerned, and she hasn't called. It's just not like her." She was sixty-nine years old, and strong, but lately they had all found her a little distracted. She had had pneumonia a few months before, and afterward she hadn't seemed quite herself, and Sarah knew that George worried endlessly about her. At seventy-two, he seemed somehow more alert than his wife, yet at the same time much frailer. He was still handsome, like his son, tall and straight with gentle eyes and a lovely smile, and yet there were times when he seemed older than he was, and Oliver worried about him.

"I'm sure she's just forgotten the time. You know how women are when they go shopping." Sarah wanted to reassure him. It wasn't good for his heart to fret about every little thing, and undoubtedly Phyllis would walk in at any moment.

"I was wondering if I ought to go looking for her. I thought maybe Oliver . . ." Lately, he was relying on Ollie more, which wasn't like him either.

"I'll have him call the minute he comes home." And that would mean the end of their dinner out, unless she came back before. But on the other hand, maybe it was just as well. Suddenly, Sarah didn't want to be alone with her husband.

But George called again before Oliver got home. Phyllis was home safe and sound. She'd had trouble getting a cab, and didn't have the change to call. He didn't tell Sarah that she looked disheveled to him somehow, and the cabdriver had told him she'd had trouble remembering her address, and when George questioned her, he realized with shock that she no longer knew their phone number, and that was why she hadn't called him. "I'm sorry I troubled you, my dear."

"Don't be silly, George. You can call us anytime. You know that."

"Thank you." At the other end, he cast a worried glance at his wife, humming to herself as she wandered aimlessly around the kitchen. Lately, he had been cooking for her, but they both pretended that it was because he liked having something to do, and he liked to say that he was a better cook than she was. "Give Oliver my love when he comes home, and if he has time, please ask him to call me."

"I will," she promised, and promptly forgot when Oliver got home a few minutes later. He was hurrying to shower and dress and insisted that he wanted to take her out to dinner. "But Sam will be all alone tonight." She wanted desperately to stay home, not to face him alone across a table. There was nothing she could say to him. Not yet. And it was easier to hide here in their own home. To hide behind the children and the television set. To hide behind anything. Anything was better than having to face him.

"Is Agnes going out?" Ollie questioned her as he shaved, watching the news at the same time, barely glancing at her, but pleased at the prospect of their evening together. He had a surprise for her. He had just gotten a big promotion and a raise. The top of the ladder, at his firm, was in clear sight now. At forty-four, Oliver Watson was the stuff that business legends were made of. He had it all, he knew, and he was grateful for that, a job he loved, a wife he adored, and three kids he was crazy about. What more was there in life? Absolutely nothing he could think of.

"No, Agnes'll be here, but I thought . . ."

"Don't. Get dressed." He gently patted her behind as she walked past him, and then stopped her and put his arms around her as he turned off his razor. "I love you, do you know that?" She did. Only too well. And she loved him, too, which made everything she wanted to do now that much harder.

"I love you too." Her eyes were sad and he pulled her closer.

"You sure don't look happy about it. Tough day today?"

"Not really." There was no tough anymore. The kids were busy and almost gone, Agnes took care of the house, she had been slowing down her committee work for the past two years, to give herself time to write, which she never did anyway. What could be tough in the perfect life? Nothing, except constant emptiness and total boredom. "Just tired, I guess. Oh . . . I almost forgot. Your father called. He wants you to call him."

"Everything okay?" He worried about his parents a lot. They were getting old, and his father seemed so frail ever since his heart attack. "Is he feeling all right?"

"He sounded fine. Once your mother got back. He called because she went shopping this afternoon and she was late coming back. I think he was worried about her in this weather."

"He worries too much about everything. That's why he had that heart attack. She can take care of herself, I keep telling him that. He keeps insisting that she gets confused, but I think she's a lot less confused than he thinks. I'll call him when we get home, if it's not too late. Come on," he urged her on with a smile, "hurry up. Our reservation's at seven."

They kissed Sam good night when they left, and gave Agnes the phone number of the restaurant. Benjamin was already gone, and he hadn't said good-bye to them. He had taken the keys to Sarah's car and left right after devouring most of the meat loaf, two plates of vegetables, and a piece of Agnes's apple pie. And Sarah felt sure that as soon as he got to Bill's he would eat again, and probably finish off the pie when he got home that night. She used to worry that he'd get fat, but there seemed to be no fear of that, he was a bottomless pit, and if it hadn't been for the broad shoulders, he would have looked like the proverbial beanpole.

The restaurant was lovely when they arrived, cozy, quaint, with French Provincial decor and a fire roaring in a fireplace. The food was good, and Oliver ordered an excellent California Chardonnay. They both relaxed and Sarah listened as he told her about the promotion and the raise. It was strange listening to him now. For years, she had lived vicariously through him, and now suddenly she had her own life. It was like listening to someone else. She was pleased for him, but his success was no longer a shared accomplishment. It was his alone. She knew that now. And as they finished their meal, he sat back and looked at her, sensing that something had changed, but not sure what it was. He usually read her well, but not tonight. There was something distant and sad about the way she looked at him, and he suddenly felt a finger of fear touch his heart. What if she were having an affair? Even a passing one . . . one of those suburban wives' involvements with the insurance man, or the orthodontist, or one of their friends. He couldn't believe it of her. She had always been so loyal to him, it was the way she was, straight-arrow and sure and honest, it was part of what he loved so much about her. It couldn't be that. And he had never cheated on her. But he just couldn't figure out what was going on with her, and as he ordered champagne and dessert, he looked at her in the candlelight and thought she had never looked lovelier or younger. At forty-one, she was better-looking than most women at thirty. The dark red hair still shone, her figure was great, her waistline almost as trim as it had been before their babies.

"What's bothering you, sweetheart?" His voice was a caress as he reached out and took her hand. He was a good man, a decent one, she knew that, and she also knew how much he loved her.

"Nothing. Why? What makes you say that? I had a wonderful time tonight." She was lying, but she didn't want him to know. He always did anyway. He knew her too well. Twenty-two years was a long, long time.

"I'd say on a scale of ten, tonight was about a two in your book. Maybe a one. If you count going to the dentist as a zero."

She laughed at him, and he chuckled as he poured her champagne. "You're crazy, you know that?" she accused him.

"Yeah. About you. Imagine an old fart like me still being nuts about his wife. Pretty amusing, huh, after eighteen years of marriage."

"I take it forty-four is an 'old fart' now? When did you decide that?"

He lowered his voice conspiratorially as he answered. "When I couldn't make love to you the third time last Sunday night. I think that pushed me over the edge into that category forever."

She grinned. Their lovemaking was almost always terrific. "I thought twice in an hour and a half wasn't too shabby myself. Besides, you'd had a hell of a lot of wine to drink. Don't forget that."

He looked at the empty wine bottle and the champagne in front of them and grinned at her. "I guess that blows tonight, too, huh?"

"I don't know. Maybe we ought to go home and check it out before you're too far gone." She was laughing at him, glad they'd gone out to dinner after all. It had relieved some of her tension.

"Thanks a lot. But I want to know what's bothering you first."

"Absolutely nothing." And at that precise moment, she was being honest.

"Maybe not now, but a little while ago, something was. You looked like your best friend had died when I came home."

"No, I didn't." But she had been feeling some of that. He was her best friend, after all, and if she went back to school, in some ways she would lose him. "Don't be silly, Ol."

"Don't try to bullshit me. Something's worrying you, or preoccupying you. Is it your writing?" He knew she hadn't written anything in two years, but it didn't matter to him. He just wanted her to be happy.

"Maybe. I'm not getting anywhere with that. Maybe I can't write anymore. Maybe that was just a flash in my youth." She shrugged and for the first time in two years, it didn't seem to matter.

"I don't believe that, Sarah. You were good. I think it'll come back to you in time. Maybe you just haven't figured out what you want to write about. Maybe you ought to get out in the world more . . . do something different . . ." Without knowing it, he was opening the door to her, but she was terrified to walk through it. No matter what she did, or said, or how she said it, once she told him, everything in their lives would be changed forever.

"I've been thinking about that." She advanced cautiously.

"And?" He waited.

"What do you mean 'and'?" She was scared of him. It was rare for her. But for the first time in her life, she was terrified of her husband.

"You never think about anything without coming to some kind of conclusion, or taking action."

"You know me too well." She smiled, suddenly looking sad again, and desperately not wanting to tell him.

"What aren't you telling me, Sarrie? Not knowing what's on your mind is driving me crazy."

"Nothing is on my mind." But she wasn't convincing either of them, and she was going around in circles. "Maybe it's just midlife crisis."

"That again?" He grinned. "You went through that two years ago, and you only get one go around. Next time it's my turn. Come on, baby . . . what is it?"

"I don't know, Ollie . . ."

"Is it us?" His eyes looked sad as he asked her.

"Of course not. How could it be us? You're wonderful . . . it's just me, I guess. Growing pains. Or the lack of them. I feel like I've been stagnant ever since we got married." He waited, holding his breath, the champagne, and the wine, and the party atmosphere all but forgotten. "I haven't done anything. And you've accomplished so much."

"Don't be ridiculous. I'm a guy like a million other ad men."

"The hell you are. Look at you. Look at what you just told me over dinner. In five years, you'll be the head of Hinkley, Burrows, and Dawson, if it takes you that long, which I doubt. You're one of the biggest success stories in the business."

"That doesn't mean anything, Sarah. You know that. It's transitory. It's nice. But so what? You've raised three great kids. That's a hell of a lot more important."

"But what difference does that make now? They've grown up, or practically, in a year or two they'll be gone. Mel and Benjamin anyway, and then what? I sit and wait around for Sam to go, too, and then I spend the rest of my life watching soap operas and talking to Agnes?" Her eyes filled with tears at the prospect, and he laughed. He had never known her to watch daytime TV. She was far more likely to bury herself in Baudelaire or Kafka.

"You paint a mighty gloomy picture, my love. Nothing's stopping you from what you want to do." He meant it, but he had no concept of the scope of her ambitions. He never had. She had buried them all long before, left them behind somewhere in a duffel bag or an old trunk, with her Radcliffe diploma.

"You don't really mean that."

"Of course I do. You can do volunteer work, get a part-time job, write short stories again. You can do absolutely anything you set your mind to."

She took a breath. The time was now, whether she

was ready or not. She had to tell him. "I want to go back to school." Her voice was barely audible across the narrow table.

"I think that's a great idea." He looked relieved. She was not in love with someone else. All she wanted was to take some courses. "You could go to the state university right in Purchase. Hell, if you spread it out over time, you could even get your master's." But the way he said it suddenly annoyed her. She could go to a local school, and "spread it out over time." How much time? Ten years? Twenty? She could be one of those grandmothers taking creative-writing courses and producing nothing.

"That isn't what I had in mind." Her voice was suddenly firm and much stronger. He was the enemy now, the one who had kept her from everything she wanted.

"What were you thinking of?" He looked confused.

She closed her eyes for an instant, and then opened them and looked at him. "I've been accepted for the master's program at Harvard." There was an endless silence between them as he stared at her and tried to understand what she was saying.

"What is that supposed to mean?" Suddenly he didn't understand anything. What was she saying to him, this woman he thought he knew, who had lain next to him for two decades. Suddenly, in the blink of an eye, she had become a stranger. "When did you apply for that?"

"At the end of August." She spoke very quietly. The determination he remembered from her youth was burning in her eyes again. Right before him, she was becoming another person.

"That's nice. It would have been nice of you to mention it. And what did you intend to do about it if you were accepted?"

"I never thought I would be. I just did it for the hell of it . . . I guess when Benjamin started talking about applying to Harvard."

"How touching, a mother-and-son team. And now? Now what are you going to do?" His heart was pounding and he suddenly wished they were at home, so he could pace the room, and not sit stuck in a corner of a restaurant at a table that had instantly become claustrophobic. "What are you telling me? You're not serious about this, are you?"

Her eyes met his like blue ice, as she nodded slowly. "Yes, I am, Ollie."

"You're going back to Cambridge?" He had lived there for seven years and she for four, but that was lifetimes ago. Never in his life had he ever considered going back there.

"I'm thinking about it." She was doing more than that, but she couldn't face telling him yet. It was too brutal.

"And what am I supposed to do? Quit my job and come with you?"

"I don't know. I haven't figured that out yet. I don't expect you to do anything. This is my decision."

"Is it? *Is it?* And what about us? What do you expect us to do while you play student again? May I remind you that Melissa will be home for another two years, and Sam for nine, or had you forgotten?" He was furious now, and he signaled the waiter for the check with an impatient gesture. She was crazy. That was what she was. Crazy. He would have preferred that she tell him she was having an affair. That would have been easier to deal with, or at least he thought so at the moment.

"I haven't forgotten any of that. I just need to think this out." She spoke quietly, as he peeled off a wad of bills and left it on the table.

"You need a good shrink, that's what you need. You're acting like a bored, neurotic housewife." He stood up and she glared at him, the full frustration of the past twenty years boiling up in her until she could no longer contain it.

"You don't know anything about me." She stood, facing him, as the waiters watched politely from the distance, and the diners nearby pretended not to listen. "You don't know what it's like, giving up everything you've ever dreamed of. You've got it all, a career, a family, a wife waiting for you at home like a faithful little dog, waiting to bring you the newspaper and fetch your slippers. Well, what about me, God damn it! When do I get mine? When do I get to do what I want to do? When you're dead, when the kids are gone, when I'm ninety? Well, I'm not going to wait that long. I want it *now,* before I'm too old to do anything worthwhile, before I'm too old to give a damn anymore, or enjoy it. I'm not going to sit around and wait until you start calling our children because you can't figure out whether I got lost when I went shopping, or I was so goddamn tired of my life I just decided not to come home again. I'm not waiting for that, Oliver Watson!" A woman at a nearby table wanted to stand up and cheer, she had four children and had given up the dream of medical school to marry a man who had cheated on her for twenty years and took her totally for granted. But Oliver stalked out of the restaurant, and Sarah picked up her coat and bag and walked out behind him. They were in the parking lot before he spoke to her again and there were tears in his eyes this time, but she wasn't sure if they were from the cold or hurt and anger. It was hard to tell. But what she didn't understand was that she was destroying everything he believed in. He had been good to her, he loved her, he loved their kids, he had never wanted her to work, because he wanted to take care of her, to love, honor, cherish, and protect her. And now she hated him for it and wanted to go back to school, but worse than that, if she went back to Harvard, she would have to leave them. It wasn't school he objected to, it was where it was, and what she would have to do to them to get there.

"Are you telling me you're leaving me? Is that what this is about? Are you walking out on us? And just exactly how long have you known that?"

"I only got the letter of acceptance this afternoon, Oliver. I haven't even absorbed it yet myself. And no, I'm not leaving you." She tried to calm down. "I can come home for vacations and weekends."

"Oh for chrissake . . . and what are we supposed to do? What about Mel and Sam?"

"They have Agnes." They stood in the snow, shouting at each other, and Sarah wished with all her heart that she had waited to tell him. She hadn't even sorted it out herself yet.

"And what about me? I have Agnes too? She'll be thrilled to hear it."

Sarah smiled at him. Even in anguish, he was decent

and funny. "Come on, Ollie . . . let's just let this thing cool down. We both need to think about it."

"No, we don't." His face was suddenly more serious than she had ever seen it. "There should be absolutely nothing to think about. You're a married woman with a husband and three kids. There's no way you can go to a school almost two hundred miles away, unless you walk out on us, plain and simple."

"It's not that simple. Don't make it that simple, Ollie. What if I really need to do this?"

"You're being self-indulgent." He unlocked the car, yanked open the door, and slid behind the wheel, and when she got in, he stared at her, with fresh questions. "How exactly do you intend to pay for this, or are you expecting me to put you and Benjamin through Harvard?" It was going to be something of a strain on them having one child in college, let alone two when Mel went. And adding Sarah to their burdens seemed even more absurd, but she had long since figured that out, in case she was ever accepted.

"I still have the money my grandmother left me. With the exception of the new roof we put on the house, I've never touched it."

"I thought that money was earmarked for the kids. We agreed that money was sacred."

"Maybe it'll mean more to them to have a mother who does something worthwhile with her life, like writing something that might mean something to them one day, or getting a job that does someone some good, or doing something useful."

"It's a lovely thought, but frankly I think your children would rather have a mother than a literary example." He sounded bitter as he drove the short distance to the house, and then sat huddled in the car, outside the house in the driveway. "You've already made up your mind, haven't you? You're going to do it, aren't you, Sarrie?" He sounded so sad, and this time when he turned to look at her, she knew that the tears in his eyes weren't from the wind, they were from what she had told him.

Her eyes were damp too as she hesitated, looking out at the snow, and then she turned to face him. "I think maybe I have to, Ollie . . . I don't know if I can ever explain it . . . but I have to. It won't be for long, I promise . . . I'll work as hard as I can, as fast as I can." But she wasn't kidding anyone. They both knew it was an intense two-year program.

"How can you do this?" He wanted to say "to me," but it sounded too selfish.

"I have to." Her voice was a whisper as a car pulled up behind them, and the lights from the headlights behind them lit up their faces. She could see tears rolling down his cheeks and all she wanted to do was hold him. "I'm so sorry . . . I didn't want to tell you now . . . I wanted to tell you after Christmas."

"What difference does it make?" He glanced behind them at Benjamin and Melissa getting out of the other car, and then back at his wife, the wife he was about to lose, who was leaving them to go back to school, and might never come back, no matter what she said. He knew that nothing would ever be the same again. They both did. "What are you going to tell them?"

The kids waited for them to get out, watching them, and chatting in the cold night air, as Sarah glanced at them, with a stone in her heart. "I don't know yet. Let's get through the holiday first." Oliver nodded, and opened the door, wiping the tears from his cheeks hurriedly so his children wouldn't see them.

"Hi, Dad. How was dinner?" Benjamin appeared to be in high spirits, and Melissa, all legs and long blond hair, was smiling. She still had her stage makeup on. It had been a dress rehearsal for the play, and she'd loved it.

"It was fun," Sarah answered quickly for him, smiling brightly. "It's a cute place." Oliver glanced at her, wondering how she could do it, how she could talk to them at all, how she could pretend, how she could face them. Maybe there were things about her he didn't know, had never known, and maybe didn't want to.

He walked into the house, said good night to the kids, and walked slowly upstairs, feeling old and tired, and disillusioned, and he watched her as she quietly closed their bedroom door and faced him. "I'm sorry, Ollie . . . I really am."

"So am I." He still didn't believe it. Maybe she'd change her mind. Maybe it was change of life. Or a brain tumor. Or a sign of a major depression. Maybe she was crazy, maybe she always had been. But he didn't care what she was. She was his wife and he loved her. He wanted her to stay, to take back the things she had said, to tell him she couldn't leave him for anything . . . him . . . not just the children . . . him . . . but as she stood watching him with somber eyes, he knew she wouldn't do it. She meant what she had said. She was going back to Harvard. She was leaving them. And as the realization cut through to his heart like a knife, he wondered what he would do without her. He wanted to cry just thinking about it, he wanted to die as he lay in bed that night, next to her, feeling her warmth beside him. But it was as though she was already gone. He lay next to her, aching for her, longing for the years that had flown past, and wanting her more than he ever had, but he rolled slowly on his side, away from her so she wouldn't see him cry, and never touched her.

Chapter 3

The days before Christmas seemed to crawl past, and Oliver almost hated to come home now. He alternated between hating her and loving her more than he ever had before, and trying to think of ways to change her mind. But the decision had been made now. They talked about it constantly, late at night, when the children were in bed, and he saw a brutal stubbornness in Sarah that he had thought she had given up years before. But in her mind, she was fighting for her life now.

She promised that nothing would change, that she would come home every Friday night, that she loved him as she had before, yet they both knew she was kidding herself. She would have papers to write, exams to study for, there was no way she could commute, and coming home to bury herself in her books would only frustrate him and the children. Things *had* to change when she went back to school. It was inevitable, whether she wanted to face it or not. He tried to convince her to go to a different school, somewhere closer to home, even Columbia would be better than going all the way back to Harvard. But she was determined to go back there. He wondered at times if it was to recapture her youth, to turn the clock back to a simpler time, and yet he liked their life so much better now. And he could never understand how she would be able to leave the children.

They still knew nothing of their mother's plans. The older ones sensed a certain tension in the air, and Melissa asked her more than once if she and Dad had had a fight, but Sarah just brushed them off with a carefree air. She was determined not to spoil Christmas for them, and she knew her announcement was going to upset them. She had decided to tell them the day after Christmas and Ollie agreed because he thought he could still change her mind. They went to Melissa's play and then decorated the Christmas tree in what seemed like perfect harmony, singing carols, making jokes, while Oliver and Benjamin struggled with the lights, and Sam ate the popcorn faster than Melissa and Sarah could string it. Watching them, Oliver felt as though his heart would break. She couldn't do this to them, it wasn't fair, and how was he going to take care of them? And no matter how dear she was, Agnes was only hired help after all. And he worked in New York all day long. He had visions of Benjamin and Melissa running wild and Sam going into a decline, while their mother played graduate student at Harvard.

It was Christmas Eve before he sat down alone with her, in front of a roaring fire in the library, and faced her soberly and asked her not to go through with her plans. He had already decided that if he had to, he was going to beg her.

"You just can't do this to them." He had lost ten pounds in two weeks, and the strain in the air was killing both of them, but Sarah was adamant. She had written to accept the week before, and she was leaving in two weeks to find a place to stay in Boston. Her classes started on the fifteenth of January. All that remained was to get through Christmas, pack her things, and tell the children.

"Ollie, let's not go through this again."

He wanted to jump up and shake her. But she was withdrawn from him, as though she couldn't bear facing the pain she knew she had caused him.

The children had hung their stockings near the tree, and late that night, he and Sarah brought the presents down. She and Agnes had been wrapping them for weeks. She had gone all out this year, almost as though it were their final Christmas. Ollie had bought her an emerald ring at Van Cleef the week before, it was beautiful and something he knew she had always wanted. It was a plain band set with small diamond baguettes, and in the center a beautifully cut square emerald. He wanted to give it to her that night, but suddenly it seemed more like a bribe than a gift, and he was sorry he had bought it.

When they went to bed that night, Sarah set the alarm for six. She wanted to get up early to stuff the turkey. Agnes would be up early to do most of the work anyway, but Sarah wanted to do the turkey herself, another final gift to them, and it was a family tradition.

She lay in bed, after they turned out the lights, thinking quietly, and listening to Ollie breathe. She knew he was awake, and could imagine only too easily what he was thinking. He had been beside himself for the past two weeks. They had argued, cried, talked, discussed, and still she knew she was doing the right thing, for herself anyway. Now all she wanted was to get it over with, to start her new life, and get away from them, and the pain she knew she was causing Ollie.

"I wish you'd stop acting as though I were leaving here for good." Her voice was gentle in the darkness.

"You are though, aren't you?" His voice sounded so sad, she couldn't bear to hear it.

"I told you. I'll come home every weekend I can, and there are plenty of vacations."

"And how long do you think that will last? You can't commute and go to school. I just don't understand how you can do this." He had said that a thousand times in the last two weeks, and silently he kept searching for another reason, for something he had done, or failed to do, it had to be that. She couldn't just want an entirely different life, away from them, if she really loved him.

"Maybe after it's all over it'll make more sense to you. Maybe if I make something of myself as a result of this, then you'll respect what I've done. If that happens, then it'll be worth it."

"I respect you now. I always have." He turned to look at her in the moonlight. She looked as lovely as she always had to him, maybe more so now with the pain of losing her a constant reminder of how much he loved her. And then, already aching for them, for what they didn't know and he did, "When exactly are you going to tell the children?"

"I thought tomorrow night, after your parents go home."

"It's a hell of a way to wind up Christmas."

"I don't think I ought to wait any longer. The children know something's going on. Mel's been suspicious all week, and Benjamin's been gone. With him, that's always a sign that he knows something's wrong and doesn't know how to face it."

"And how do you think they're going to feel after they hear the news?"

"Like we do, probably. Scared, confused, maybe excited for me. I think Benjamin and Mel will be able to understand. I'm worried about Sam, though." She spoke softly and turned to look at Ollie, reaching quietly for his hand, and her voice trembled when she spoke again, thinking of their last baby. "Take good care of him, Ollie . . . he needs you more than he needs me. . . ."

"He needs you too. I only see him a couple of hours a day and all we talk about is football, baseball, and homework."

"That's a start. Maybe you'll all be closer after this."

"I thought we were." That was the part that hurt most. He had thought they had everything. The perfect family. The perfect life. The perfect marriage. "I always thought everything was so just right between us . . . I never understood how you felt about all this . . . I mean . . . well, I did when you got pregnant, but I always thought that after that, and even before

Sam, you were happy." It hurt him so much to think that he hadn't given her everything she wanted.

"I was . . . I have been . . . I just wanted something you couldn't give me. It has to come from within, and I guess I never found it." She felt so guilty for making him feel inadequate. He had always been the perfect husband.

"And if you don't find it now?"

"I give up, I guess." But she knew she would. She already had in part. Just making the decision to go had changed her.

"I think you could find it right here. Maybe all you needed was more freedom."

She moved closer to him in their comfortable bed, and he put an arm around her. "I had all the freedom I needed. I just didn't know what to do with it."

"Oh baby . . ." He buried his face in her hair, and his eyes filled with tears again, but as she laid her face against his chest, he could feel her tears and her shoulders tremble. "Why are we doing this? Can't we just turn the clock back a few weeks and forget this ever happened?"

Even through her tears she shook her head and then looked up at him. "I don't think so. I would always feel I'd missed something. I'll come back . . . I promise . . . I swear. I love you too much not to." But something in his heart told him it just wouldn't happen no matter what she said. It was safer to keep her at home, to never let her go. Once gone, anything could happen.

They lay for a long time, holding each other tight, their faces side by side, their lips meeting from time to time, and at last his hunger for her got the best of him.

For the first time in two weeks, he took her with a passion and a longing that had been long since forgotten. There was a desperation to their lovemaking that had never been there before, a thirst, a loneliness, an insatiable hunger. And she felt it, too, along with guilt, regret, and a sorrow that almost overwhelmed her as they shuddered in unison and lay side by side kissing afterward, until finally he slept in her arms . . . Oliver . . . the boy she had loved long since . . . the man he had become . . . the love that had begun and now might end at Harvard.

Chapter 4

Christmas morning was a frantic rush. The table, the turkey, the presents, the phone calls from Chicago, and three calls from the Watsons. George called to say that Phyllis wasn't quite herself, and Oliver brushed it off as his father getting too wound up again over nothing. They were expected at noon, and arrived at almost two o'clock, with armloads of gifts for everyone, including a cashmere shawl for Agnes, and a huge soup bone for Andy. And contrary to George's warnings, Phyllis seemed remarkably well and looked lovely in a new purple wool dress she'd bought the day she'd gone shopping for hours and hours and worried her husband.

They opened presents for what seemed like ages, and Sarah was stunned by the emerald ring Ollie had given her early that morning when he sat at the kitchen table, at the crack of dawn, watching her stuff the turkey. She had given him a sheepskin coat, some tapes she knew he wanted, some ties and socks, and silly things, and a beautiful new black leather briefcase. And as a joke, he'd given her a funny little red "school bag," to remind her that she was just "a kid to him," and a gold compass to find her way home, inscribed with the words *Come Home Soon. I Love You. Ollie.*

"What's that for, Dad?" Sam had inquired, noticing the gift when Sarah opened it. "You and Mom going camping? That's a pretty fancy compass."

"Your mom's a pretty fancy woman. I just thought it might be useful if she got lost sometime." He smiled, and Sam laughed, and Sarah gently reached out to touch Ollie. She kissed him tenderly, and afterward he followed her out to the kitchen to help carve the turkey.

The meal itself was an uneventful one, except that halfway through, Grandma Phyllis started to get nervous. She seemed to jump out of her seat every chance she got, helping to carry plates that didn't need to go anywhere, bringing things in from the kitchen that didn't belong, and asking everyone ten times if they were ready for another helping.

"What's the matter with Grandma?" Sam whispered to his father at one point, when Phyllis had scurried after Agnes, insisting that she was going to help her. "She never used to like to help in the kitchen that much." Oliver had noticed it too, but imagined that she was just ill at ease about something. She seemed unusually agitated.

"I think she just wants to help your mom and Agnes.

Old people get like that sometimes. They want everyone to know that they're still useful."

"Oh." Sam nodded, satisfied, but the others had noticed it too. And Mel looked worried as she glanced at her mother. Sarah only shook her head, not wanting the questions to form in words. It was suddenly obvious to her that her mother-in-law had some kind of a problem.

But the meal went smoothly other than that. And everyone ate too many helpings of everything, and then collapsed in the living room, while Sarah, Agnes, and Phyllis tidied up the kitchen. Melissa joined them for a while, but then came to sit with the men and her two brothers.

She looked worriedly at Grandpa George, and sat down next to him when she returned. "What's the matter with Grandma? She seems so nervous."

"She gets like that sometimes, agitated. It's difficult to calm her down, sometimes it's just better to let her wear herself out as long as she's not doing any harm. Is she okay out there?"

"I think so. She's running around the kitchen like a whirlwind." But the truth was she wasn't really doing anything, just talking incessantly and moving dirty plates from here to there and back again without getting anything accomplished. Sarah and Agnes had noticed it, too, but no one had said anything, and eventually they had told Mel to go on into the other room. And with that, her grandmother had looked up, at the sound of her name, looking straight at her only female grandchild.

"Mel? Is she here? Oh I'd love to see her, where is she?" Melissa had been stunned into silence and her mother had motioned her to go into the other room, but she was still shaken when she sat down next to her grandfather, and asked for an explanation.

"She's so confused. I've never seen her like that before."

"It's been happening to her more and more often." George Watson looked sadly at his son. It was exactly what he had been trying to explain to Ollie. Yet sometimes she was right as rain, and he wondered if he himself was imagining her confusion. It was hard to know what to think. One day she seemed totally out of control, and the next she seemed fine again, and sometimes she changed from hour to hour. It was both frightening and confusing. "I don't know what it is, Mel. I wish I did. Old age, I suppose, but she seems too young for that." Phyllis Watson was only sixty-nine years old, and her husband was three years older.

And a few minutes later, Phyllis and Sarah walked back into the room, and the older woman seemed much calmer. She sat down quietly in a chair, and chatted with Benjamin, who was telling her about applying to Harvard. He was applying to Princeton, too, Stanford on the West Coast, Brown, Duke, and Georgetown. With his grades and athletic skill, he had a host of great schools to choose from. But he still hoped that he would get into Harvard, and now so did Sarah. It would be exciting to be in school with him. Maybe if that happened, he would forgive her for leaving home eight months before he left for college. Ollie had even suggested that she wait until Benjamin left for school, but she didn't want to postpone anything. She had waited too many years for this to be willing to wait another hour. It was the kind of reaction Phyllis had foretold years before, but now she might not even remember or understand that.

"How soon will you hear from all those schools?" George Watson was excited for his grandson.

"Probably not until late April."

"That's a long time to wait, for a boy your age."

"Yes, it is." Benjamin smiled and looked at his father lovingly. "Dad and I are going to tour the schools this spring while I wait. I know most of them, but I've never been to Duke, or Stanford."

"That's much too far away. I still think you should go to Princeton." George's old school, and everyone smiled. George always thought that everyone should go to Princeton.

"I might, if I don't get into Harvard. Maybe you'll get Mel to go there one day." She groaned and threw a half-eaten cookie at him.

"You know I want to go to UCLA and study drama."

"Yeah, if you don't get married first." He usually said "knocked up," but he wouldn't have dared in front of his parents. She was having a hot romance with a boy in his class, and although he didn't think she had gone "all the way" yet, he suspected that things were getting closer. But she had also recently become aware of his new romance, with a good-looking blond girl with a sensational figure, Sandra Carter.

The evening wore on, and eventually the senior Watsons went home, and just after they did, Oliver looked questioningly at Sarah. She had been oddly quiet for the last half hour, and he knew she was thinking about what she would say to the children. In a way, they were all so tired that it would have been better to wait another day, but she had thought about it for so long that now she wanted to tell them.

Benjamin was about to ask her for the keys to the car, and Melissa wanted to call a friend, and Sam was already yawning when Agnes appeared in the doorway.

"It's time for Sam to go to bed. I'll take him up if you want, Mrs. Watson." Everything in the kitchen was put away and she wanted to retire to her room, to enjoy the new television set the Watsons had given her for Christmas.

"I'll take him up in a while. We want to talk first. Thank you, Agnes." Sarah smiled at her, and for an instant Agnes stopped, there was something odd in her employer's eyes, but she only nodded and wished them all a merry Christmas, before going to her room for the night. Sam looked up at his mother with wide, tired eyes.

"What are we going to talk about?"

"Mom . . . can I . . . I was supposed to go out . . ." Benjamin looked anxious to get out as he glanced at his new watch, and Sarah shook her head this time.

"I'd like you to wait. There's something I want to talk to you all about."

"Something wrong?" He looked puzzled, and Mel looked down at them, she was already halfway up the stairs, but Sarah waited as they all gathered again and sat down. This seemed like official business now, and Oliver took a chair across the room, near the fire, wondering what she would say to them, and how they would take it.

"I don't quite know where to start." Sarah felt

breathless suddenly, as she looked at all of them, her tall, handsome son, her daughter so grown up now, yet still a child, and Sam cuddled sleepily into the couch beside her. "There's something I've wanted to do for a long time, and I'm going to do it now, but it's not going to be easy for any of us. It's a big change. But the first thing I want you all to know is how much I love you, how much I care . . . but something I've always believed, and told all of you, is that you have to be true to yourself," she squeezed Sam's hand, and avoided Oliver's eyes as she went on, "you have to do what you think is right, even if it's hard to do sometimes." She took another breath and there was dead silence in the room as they waited. They were frightened of what she was going to say. She looked so serious suddenly, and Benjamin noticed that their father looked pale. Maybe they were getting divorced, or having another kid, a baby wouldn't be so bad, a divorce would be the end of the world. None of them could imagine what it was. "I'm going back to school." She sighed as she said the words.

"You are?" Mel looked stunned.

"Where?" Benjamin asked.

"Why?" Sam wanted to know. It sounded dumb to him. School was for kids, and he couldn't wait to get out. Imagine going back when you were grown up. It sure wasn't something he'd want to do at her age. "Is Dad going back to school too?"

Sarah smiled, but Oliver did not. It would have been easier for all of them if he were. Then they would all have gone to Cambridge. But she was the only one moving on, they were staying right here, with their safe, comfortable lives. Only she needed to sail out of port, out of the safe harbor of their lives, into unknown waters. But the thought exhilarated more than frightened her. One day she would explain that to them, but not now. Now they needed to know how it would affect them. And it would. There was no denying that. Especially Sam, who sat looking up expectantly at her. It tore at her heart, just looking at him. But still, she knew she had to leave them.

"No, Dad's not going back to school. Just me. I'm going back to Harvard in a couple of weeks."

"Harvard?" Benjamin looked shocked. "You? Why?" He didn't understand. How could she go to school in Boston? And then slowly he understood. He glanced at his father's eyes and saw it all, the loneliness, the pain, the sorrow she had put there, but there was something anguished and sad in her eyes now too.

"I'm going to come home as often as I can. And you'll still have Dad and Agnes to take care of you."

"You mean you're leaving us?" Sam sat bolt upright next to her, his eyes wide and instantly filled with terror. "Like for good?"

"No, not for good," she was quick to add. "Just for a while. I can come home for weekends and vacations." She decided to tell them the truth. She owed them that much. "The program is for two years."

"Two *years*?" Sam started to cry and for a moment no one else spoke as she tried to put her arms around him and he wrenched away, running into the middle of the room, toward his father. "You're going away and leaving us? Why? Don't you love us anymore?" She got up and reached out to him but he wanted none of it, and there were tears bright in her eyes now too. She had expected it to be hard, but not like this, and suddenly she ached at the pain she was causing all of them, yet she still knew it was what she had to do, for her own sake.

"Of course I love you, Sam . . . all of you . . . I just need to do this . . . for myself . . ." She tried to explain, but he couldn't hear her through his sobs, he had run to Mel and was clinging to her now as she started to cry too. She hung on to her little brother as though they both might drown, and looked up at her mother with accusing eyes.

"Why, Mom?" They were the two most painful words she had ever heard, and she looked to Oliver for help, but he said nothing now. He was as heartbroken over it as their children.

"It's hard to explain. It's just something I've wanted to do for a long time."

"Is it you and Dad?" Mel asked through her tears as she held on to Sam. "Are you getting divorced?"

"No, we're not. Nothing's going to change. I just need to go away for a while, to accomplish something for myself, to be someone on my own, without all of you." She didn't tell them they were dragging her down, that they kept her from creating anything on her own. It would have been unfair to them, but so was this. It was easy to see that now. In a way Oliver had been right, he always was, but she knew that she was right too. They'd survive, and she'd come back to them a better person. If she stayed, she would die. She knew that for sure now.

"Can't you go to school here?" Benjamin asked her quietly. He looked shocked too. But he was too old to cry. He just kept looking at her, as though wanting to understand, sure that there was another reason for all this. Maybe they were getting divorced and didn't want to tell the kids. But then why didn't she take the kids with her? It just didn't make sense. All he knew was that their family was falling apart, and he wasn't sure why. But he wanted to believe that she had good reasons for this. He loved her so much. He wanted to understand her side, too, but he couldn't.

"I don't think I could get anything done here, Benjamin. Harvard is the right place for me." She smiled sadly, feeling Sam's sobs tear through her guts like a physical pain, but not daring to approach him. Every time she tried, he flailed out wildly at her. And Oliver was keeping his distance from him too. "Maybe we'll both be there together in the fall."

"That would be nice." Benjamin smiled at her. He would always believe in her, and the things she did, but inside he was staggering from the blow. He felt as if his whole life had been blown apart in a single moment. It had never dawned on him that either of his parents would go anywhere. They were there to stay . . . or maybe not after all. But he would never have thought that she would be the one to go. He could hardly think as he sat in his chair trying to stay calm, watching Oliver in the corner of the room, and then he stood up and looked at his dad, and asked him point-blank, "Dad, what do you think about this?"

"It's your mother's decision, Son. We can't stand in her way. And she hasn't given us much choice. She believes she's doing the right thing, and we just have to make the best of it and support her." He met Sarah's eyes then, and for him something had changed. She had hurt his children now, not just him, and he would never forget that, but he also knew that he would always love her. "We're going to miss you, Sarrie." The beauty of Christmas was forgotten now, the laughter, and the traditions and the gifts. This was the hardest night of their lives, but it could have been worse. Something could have happened to one of them. This was just for a while, or so she said. Two years. It seemed like an eternity to them now, as Sarah attempted to approach Mel and Sam again. Sam just cried more and Mel held up her hand to keep her away and looked at both her parents with equal anger.

"I think you're lying to us. I think you're leaving for good, and you don't have the guts to tell us. But if you are, why aren't you taking us with you?"

"Because I'm not. And what would you do in Cambridge? Lose all your friends here? Go to a new school? Live in a tiny apartment with me while I write papers and study for exams? Benjamin's in his senior year, you have two more to go. Do you really want to shake all that up? And I couldn't take care of you while I'm going to school. You're much better off here with Daddy and Aggie, in your own home, going to a school you love, with friends you've had for years, in familiar surroundings."

"You're walking out on us." Mel's eyes were filled with shards of anger and pain, and Sam's sobs had never dimmed once. Mel turned on her father then. "You must have done something awful to her to make her walk out on us like this." She hated them both and knew she always would. Forever.

Sarah was quick to his defense. "That's not true, Mel. Your father has nothing to do with this."

"People don't just go away to school. Not grown-ups anyway. You must hate us all a lot to go." Sam's sobs grew to a wail, and Mel stood up and held him in her arms. And then he turned to look at his mother again, his face ravaged by tears, and she took no step toward him this time. He was no longer hers. He was theirs now.

Sam could hardly speak through his sobs. "Iss . . . iss . . . that true? Do . . . do . . . you . . . hate us, Mom?" Her heart broke at the thought and tears spilled down her cheeks as she shook her head.

"No, I don't. I love you with all my heart . . . all of you, and Daddy." She was crying now, and Oliver turned away from all of them, as they stood silently watching each other, not knowing what to do. Their family had been destroyed in one fell swoop. And then, quietly, he walked over to Mel and took Sam in his arms, and Sam clung to him as he had years before, when he was a baby.

"It's gonna be all right, Son . . . we're gonna be okay." He bent and tried to kiss Mel, but she pulled away from him, and ran up to her room, and an instant later they heard the door slam, and then slowly Oliver walked up the stairs with Sam, and Sarah and Benjamin were left alone. He looked at her, still in shock, unable to believe what he'd heard, yet knowing it was true.

"Mom . . . why?"

He was old enough to talk to openly and she always had. "I'm not sure I know. I just know I can't do this anymore, and that seems right. That's all I know. I want to be more than this. More than someone who drives car pools and waits for Sam to come home from school." For a moment, it sounded to Ben as though she hated being their mother.

"But couldn't you wait?" Other moms did.

"Not long enough. I have to do it now." She blew her nose, but the tears wouldn't stop. It was awful hurting them, but without meaning to, they were hurting her too. They had for years. And so had Ollie.

Benjamin nodded, wishing he understood. He loved her and wished her well, but secretly he thought it was a terrible thing to do. He couldn't imagine leaving a child. He had never thought she would do a thing like that. But she had, and she was, and now everything was changed. What was left? Nothing. A bunch of kids. A father who worked all the time. And a hired woman to cook for them. Suddenly, he couldn't wait to get out in the fall. He would have left sooner if he could. He had no family anymore. Just a bunch of people he lived with. It was almost as if she'd died, only worse, because she could have stayed if she wanted to. And it was knowing that she didn't want to that really hurt him. All that crap about how she cared about them. If she did, she'd stay, but she was going. That said it all. He looked down at his feet, and then back up at her, feeling guilty for his thoughts, and wanting to get out of the house as fast as he could. He had always believed in her, even more than in his dad, and suddenly she was screwing all of them. Just like that. Him, Mel, Sam, even his dad. He felt sorry for him, but there was nothing he could do to change it.

"I'm sorry to ask you now . . . I was wondering if . . . do you think Dad would mind if I took the car for a while?"

She shook her head, wondering what he really thought. He had always been the one she was closest to. "I'm sure it's okay." It was as though suddenly she no longer had any authority. She had turned in her keys. It was a glimpse of what coming back on weekends would be like. They wouldn't be used to having her around, she wouldn't have any authority over them anymore. It wasn't going to be easy, no matter what she did. "Are you all right?" She was worried about him. She knew that even if he wasn't saying much, he was hard hit. And he was still only seventeen, after all. She didn't want him going out and getting drunk and then trying to drive home, or some other wild idea. "Where are you going at this hour?" It was after ten o'clock on Christmas night and she wasn't crazy about the idea of having him on the roads.

"Just to see a friend. I'll be back in a while."

"Okay." She nodded and he turned to go, and then suddenly she reached out to him and grabbed his hand. "I love you . . . please always remember that . . ." She was crying again, and he wanted to say something to her, but he didn't. She had hurt him too much, hurt all of them. All he could do was nod, and walk to the front door as he picked up his coat. And a moment later he was gone. She shuddered as the front door slammed, and then she walked slowly up the stairs to their bedroom. She could still hear sobs coming from Mel's room, and the door was locked when she tried, and Mel wouldn't answer her, and there was no sound from Sam's, and she didn't dare go in and wake him. She walked into her own room, and sat down on the bed, feeling as if she'd been hit by a truck, and it was an hour later when Oliver finally came in. He found her lying on the bed, staring at the wall, her eyes still full of tears.

"How is he?" She hadn't even gone to him. He was Oliver's now, no longer hers. They all were. She might as well be gone and then she realized that she should leave as soon as possible. It would probably be easier for all of them, now that they knew she was going.

"He's asleep." Oliver sank down in a chair with an exhausted sigh. It had been a long day, and an endless night, and he didn't want to play games with her anymore. She was ruining their lives, all for what she wanted. His mother had been right. But it was too late now. They were in it up to their necks, and if his kids were going to survive, he had to start swimming fast. He had just gotten his feet wet with Sam, and there was still Mel to worry about, and Benjamin. He had seen the look in the boy's eyes. Even at seventeen he was badly shaken up by what Sarah had done. "I don't know if any of them are ever going to recover from this."

"Don't say things like that. I feel bad enough as it is."

"Maybe not. Maybe if you felt bad enough, you wouldn't do it. They're never going to trust anyone again, least of all me. If their own mother walks out on them, what do you suppose they're going to expect from the rest of the world? Just what do you think this is going to do to them, make them better people? Hell, no. They'll be lucky if they survive. We all will."

"What if I'd died?"

"That would have been easier for them. At least it wouldn't have been your choice, and even that apparently makes kids feel rejected."

"Thanks a lot. So you're telling me that I'm the ultimate bad guy, is that it?" She was angry again. He was trying to beat her with guilt, and she felt guilty enough already.

"Maybe I am telling you that, Sarah. Maybe you are. Maybe you're just a real selfish bitch, and you don't give a damn about any of us. That's possible, isn't it?"

"Maybe. Are you telling me you don't want me back?"

"Don't put words in my mouth." The trouble was, he did, he always would, no matter what she did to him and the kids, but he hated her now for what she had just done to them. Sam had held on to him like a drowning child, and he was. He was going to hurt for a long, long time, and Oliver meant what he had said. He wondered if all of them would be marked by this for life. Surely Sam would, particularly if she didn't come back to stay, which Oliver realized was entirely possible, even though she denied that now, but things were going to change for her once she was at Harvard again. There were going to be other people in her life, and Oliver and the kids would be far, far from there. There were no guarantees now, for either of them.

"I think I should leave in the next few days. It's too hard on all of us if I stay for the next two weeks."

"That's up to you." He walked into the bathroom and got undressed. He suddenly didn't feel close to her anymore. They had made love only the night before, and now she seemed like a stranger to him. A stranger who had walked into his house and emotionally abused his kids. "When do you think you'll go?" he asked when he came back and sat down on the bed.

"Day after tomorrow maybe. I have to get organized."

"Maybe I should take the kids away so they don't see you leave."

"That might be a thought." She looked at him sadly then, there was nothing left to say. They had said it all, the accusations, the regrets, the apologies, the explanations, and now the tears. "I don't know what to say to you anymore." Especially after tonight, after watching their children cry. And yet she was still going.

"Neither do I." She looked numb and broken.

They lay in silence in the dark, and at last, at 2:00 A.M., he fell asleep. But Sarah lay wide awake until the dawn, and it was only then that she heard Benjamin come in. But she said nothing to him. He was a good boy, and he'd had a hard time. This was going to be hard for him too. He was still only a boy, or so she thought.

He had become a man that night, and it had been a strange and beautiful experience for him. Sandra's parents had been away, and he had made love to her for the first time. It was as though he had been given a woman of his own in exchange for the one he had lost earlier that evening. It was an odd, bittersweet night for him, and after that they had talked long into the night, about what was happening at home, and how he felt about it. He could talk to Sandra, as he could to no one else, and then they had made love again, and at last he had come home, to his own bed, to think of the new love he had, and what it meant, and the mother he had lost, and suddenly that seemed a little less awesome to him, because of Sandra.

Sarah lay listening to the sounds of the house as they all slept, wishing she was one of them again. But she wasn't anymore. It was as though she were someone else, and the only thing left was to get on with her new life now. She was still excited about that, in spite of what it had cost in hearts and lives. And as they all slept, she got up and bĕgan to pack. She packed everything she wanted in three suitcases and when Oliver got up in the morning, she was through. She had showered and dressed, and made a reservation on a plane. She had called a hotel in Cambridge where she had once stayed. And she had made up her mind to leave by that afternoon at the latest.

"Where are you going at this hour?" Oliver looked surprised to see her dressed when he got up, and he sensed that a lot had gone on while he slept.

"Nowhere yet. I'm leaving tonight. I'll tell the kids when they get up. They can't be much more upset than they already are. Why don't you take them away somewhere for a breather?"

"I'll try. I'll see what I can do." He showered and changed and made some calls. And at breakfast they both told them that Sarah was leaving sooner than she'd planned, and he was taking them skiing in Vermont. He asked Agnes to pack for Sam, and for a moment Benjamin seemed to hold back. He said there were some things he wanted to do for school during the rest of the vacation.

"During Christmas break?" Oliver looked skeptical and wondered if it was a girl.

"How long will we be gone?"

"Three or four days." Long enough to distract everyone if that was possible, and then back to the pall that would have fallen over the house when she left. It was already there now. They had looked shocked when she said she was leaving that day, but they were already so numb from the pain of the night before that nothing surprised them now, and they just nodded over the breakfasts they barely touched. Benjamin looked tired and didn't say much, he hardly ate, and Mel wasn't speaking to anyone, and Sam looked constantly at his father, as though to be sure he was still there and hadn't left them.

In the end, Benjamin agreed to come to Vermont with them and they managed to leave the house by four, before Sarah left for the airport. The good-byes were terrible, and Sam was crying again when they left her. Agnes stood in the doorway rigid with dismay, and even Benjamin had tears in his eyes this time, Sarah couldn't even speak, and Oliver was crying openly as they drove away. He looked in the mirror only once, and almost felt his heart physically break as he saw her standing there, in front of the house, her arm lifted in a last wave. His whole life was gone, in one moment, the woman he loved, and everything he had built. Vanished, in exchange for the insanity she wanted. And he figured it didn't hurt for his kids to see him cry. He was hurting as badly as they were, and as he looked down at Sam, he smiled through his tears, and pulled the boy closer to him.

"Come on, champ, we're gonna be okay, you know. And so is Mom." There were still tears in his eyes as he tried to smile at Sam and the other children.

"Will we ever see her again?" It was just what Ollie had feared. Sam trusted nothing and no one now, but Ollie wasn't sure he did himself, who could blame him?

"Of course we will. And one of these days we won't feel quite this bad. It hurts like hell right now though, doesn't it?" His voice choked up again, and in the backseat Benjamin blew his nose. Mel was crying, too, but she was lost in her own thoughts, and said nothing to any of them, and hadn't since that morning.

It was going to be odd being mother and father to them, odd doing the things she had done for them . . . taking them to the doctor . . . the orthodontist . . . buying Sam's shoes . . . when would he find the time for all of it? How would he manage without her? But more importantly than that, how would he live without the woman he loved, without her hand and her life and her comfort and her laughter? It was a long quiet drive to Vermont, and no one spoke until they were well into Massachusetts and stopped for dinner.

Sarah was in Boston by then, and on her way to Cambridge, to start a new life. The life she had wanted, without them.

Chapter 5

In the end, the skiing was fun, and after the first few days they all started to come to life again, although some of them more slowly than others. Sam had nightmares at night, and he cried easily now, but he laughed, too, and he had a great time skiing with his father. And Benjamin even entered a downhill race before they went home, but whenever he wasn't skiing, he was calling friends, as though they alone held the solution to all his problems. Only Mel remained withdrawn, skiing halfheartedly and avoiding the rest of them. She was the only female in their midst now, and Oliver tried to boost her spirits repeatedly, but she wouldn't even let him get near her. She seemed to have nothing to say to them, the only one she ever spoke to was Sam, and even with him she was painfully quiet.

Oliver kept busy with all of them, renting skis and boots for them, loading and unloading the car, organizing meals, tucking Sam into bed, keeping an eye on Mel, making sure everyone was properly dressed, and by eight o'clock at night he was exhausted. He could barely get through their evening meal, and at night he fell into bed with Sam. He had decided to share a room with him, in case the child was too lonely. And Sam wet the bed twice, which kept Oliver busy even at night, changing sheets, turning the mattress around, and finding fresh blankets. It was obvious that Sam was deeply distressed, as they all were, but Ollie had his hands so full with them that he hardly had time to think of Sarah. It was only at night, as he lay in bed, that he could feel the ache in his heart, and when he woke in the morning, the pain of the memory of her struck him with the weight of a mountain. It was a little bit as though she had died, and it was only on the third day they were in Vermont that Ollie even brought her name up. He said something about "Mom," and their heads spun around, each of them wearing the clear evidence of their pain, and he was instantly sorry he had said it.

It was New Year's Day when they drove back, and they were all in better spirits, and looked incredibly healthy. It was when they got home that it hit them again. The house was too quiet, the dog was asleep, and even Aggie was out. And Oliver realized that they had all secretly hoped that Sarah would be waiting for them, but she wasn't. She was long gone, and even though Oliver had her number at the hotel in Cambridge, he didn't call her that night. He put Sam to bed, after Mel helped him make dinner. Benjamin went out. He appeared in the kitchen dressed for what looked like a date as the others sat at the kitchen table.

"So soon?" Ollie smiled. None of them had even unpacked. "Must be someone special."

Benjamin smiled noncommittally at his father. "Just a friend. Can I borrow the car, Dad?"

"Don't come home late, Son. And be careful. There will still be a lot of drunks on the road tonight." At least he was grateful that his son was cautious and he knew he never drove if he drank. More than once, Benjamin had called them to pick him up, even if he'd just had a beer or two with friends. Sarah had drummed that into him, that and a lot of other things. She had left her mark on all of them, and now she was gone, and Oliver wondered when she would come home for the much promised weekend. She'd only been gone for six days, and it already felt like a lifetime.

It was strange going to bed alone that night, and he lay in bed thinking about her, as he had all week, and trying to pretend to himself that he really wasn't. At midnight, he finally turned on the light, and tried reading some papers he had brought home from the office. His boss had been a good sport about giving him the week off on such short notice, and he was in better shape now, but not much. He was still awake when Benjamin came home at one o'clock, and stopped in the doorway to say good night. Oliver had left the door open so he could hear Sam, and Benjamin stood looking sadly at him, as he put the car keys down on a table.

"It must be hard on you, Dad . . . I mean . . . with Mom gone."

Oliver nodded. There wasn't much he could say to him. It was hard on all of them. "I guess we'll get used to it, and she'll come home soon." But he didn't sound convinced, and Benjamin nodded. "Did you have a good time tonight? It's kind of late to be coming home at this hour on a school night."

"Yeah . . . I kind of lost track of the time. Sorry, Dad." He smiled and said good night. An hour later Oliver heard Sam crying, and he hurried into his bedroom. The boy was still asleep, and Ollie sat down next to him and stroked his head. His dark hair was damp, and eventually he settled down again. But at four o'clock, Oliver felt him slip into bed beside him. The child cuddled up next to him, and Ollie thought about carrying him back to his room, but in truth he found he was grateful to have him near him, and he turned over and went back to sleep. And father and son slept peacefully until morning.

At breakfast the next day, there was the usual chaos. Aggie cooked waffles and bacon for everyone, which was usually a weekend treat, saved only for special occasions. It was as though she knew they needed something special now, and she had packed an extra nice lunch for Sam, with all his favorites. She was going to drive his car pool now, and Ollie left for the train feeling disorganized and rushed, which was unlike him. He had been busy leaving instructions for everyone, and reminded everyone to come home on time and get to work on their homework. That was what Sarah did, wasn't it? Or was it? Everything had always seemed so peaceful when she was there, so in control, and so happy when he left for the office. And once there, he was greeted by a week's stack of work and reports on pending projects. He couldn't leave until seven o'clock that night, and it was close to nine when he got home. Benjamin was out again, Mel was on the phone with friends, and Sam was watching TV in his father's bed, having forgotten to do his homework, and Aggie hadn't pressed him. She told Oliver she hadn't wanted to upset him.

"Can I sleep with you, Dad?"

"Don't you think you should sleep in your own bed, Son?" He was afraid it might become a nightly habit.

"Just tonight? . . . please . . . I promise, I'll be good."

Oliver smiled at him, and stooped to kiss the top of his head. "I'd be a lot happier if you'd done your homework."

"I forgot."

"Apparently." He took off his coat and tie, set down his briefcase near the desk, and sat down on the bed next to Sam, wondering if Sarah had called, but not daring to ask him. "What'd you do today?"

"Nothing much. Aggie let me watch TV when I got home." They both knew Sarah had never let him do that. Things were changing rapidly without her, a little too much so for Ollie.

"Where's Benjamin?"

"Out." Sam looked unconcerned.

"So I gathered." And he was going to have to handle that too. He was not allowed to go out on weekday nights, even if this was his senior year. He was only seventeen, and Ollie wasn't about to let him run wild without Sarah. "Tell you what, champ. I'll let you sleep here tonight, but that's it. Tomorrow you go back to your own bed. Deal?"

"Deal." They shook hands on it as the child grinned, and Oliver turned off the light.

"I'm going to go downstairs to get something to eat. Get some sleep."

"G'night, Dad." He looked happy as he snuggled into the big bed, taking over the half that had been Sarah's.

"Sleep tight . . ." Oliver stood looking at him for a long moment from the doorway. "I love you." He whispered the words, and then went to check on Mel. She had dragged the hall phone into her bedroom, and there was disorder everywhere, clothes, books, hot rollers, shoes. It was a wonder she could get into the room at all, and she looked up at her father with a curious look as he waited for her to end the call. But she only covered the receiver with her hand.

"You want something, Dad?"

"Yes. Hello and a kiss might be nice. Have you done your homework?"

"Hello. And yes, I have." She sounded annoyed even to be asked the question.

"Want to keep me company while I eat dinner?" She hesitated, and then nodded, looking none too pleased. She would have preferred staying on the phone with her friend, but her father had made it sound like a command performance. The truth was, he didn't want to eat alone, and she was the only candidate in the house, other than Aggie.

"Okay. I'll be right down." He picked his way gingerly across the room, and went downstairs to find the dinner Aggie had left him. She had wrapped the plate in tinfoil and left it in the oven to stay warm, but when he uncovered it, there wasn't much there he wanted.

The lamb chops were overcooked, the baked potato was still hard, and the broccoli had died hours before. Even the smell of it didn't appeal to him, and he threw it all out and made himself fried eggs and fresh-squeezed orange juice, waiting for Mel to join him. He gave up eventually and by the time she came down, he was finished eating.

"Where's Benjamin?" He thought she might know, but she only shrugged.

"With friends, I guess."

"On a weekday night? That's not very smart." She shrugged again, and looked pained to be baby-sitting for her father. "Are you spending any time with Sam when you get home?" He worried about Sam most of all, especially when it was hard for him to get home on time. The child needed more in his life now than just Aggie.

"I have a lot of homework to do, Dad."

"That didn't look like homework to me just now, in your bedroom."

"He's in bed, isn't he?"

"He wasn't when I got home. He needs you now, Mel. We all do." He smiled. "You're the lady of the house now that Mom's gone." But it was a responsibility she had never wanted. She wanted to be free to be with her friends, or at least talk to them. It wasn't her fault her Mom had gone. It was his. If he hadn't done whatever he did that she still couldn't figure out, Sarah would probably never have left them. "I want you to spend time with him. Talk to him, keep him company for a little while, check his homework."

"Why? He's got Aggie."

"That's not the same thing. Come on, Mel, be nice to

him. You always used to treat him like your baby." She had even cradled him the night Sarah told them she was leaving. But now, it was as though she wanted no part of any of them. Like Sarah, she had divorced herself from all of them. And Oliver suddenly wondered if Benjamin was having the same reaction. He seemed to want to be out all the time, and that was going to have to stop too. He just wished he had more time with all of them, to help them cope with their reactions and their problems. The phone rang as he was talking to her, and he almost sighed when he heard his father on the line. He was too tired to talk to him now. It was after ten o'clock, and he wanted to shower and climb into bed with Sam. It had been a brutal day at the office, and coming home at night was no longer easy either.

"Hi, Dad. How are you?"

"I'm all right." He seemed to hesitate, and Oliver watched Mel escape while he talked to his father. "But your mother's not."

"Oh? Is she sick?" For once, Oliver was too tired to be very worried.

"It's a long story, Son." The older man sighed as Oliver waited for the news. "She had a brain scan this afternoon."

"My God . . . what for?"

"She's been acting confused . . . and she got lost last week while you were gone. I mean really lost this time, and she fell off some steps and sprained her ankle." Oliver felt suddenly guilty for not calling from Vermont, but he had had his hands full too. "She's lucky, I suppose, at her age, she could have broken her hip, or worse." But it couldn't be much worse than what they had told him.

"Dad, they don't do brain scans for a sprained ankle. What is it?" His father seemed to be wandering too, and Oliver was too tired to listen to a long story.

He seemed to hesitate again. "I was wondering if . . . could I drive over to see you?"

"Now?" Oliver sounded stunned. "Dad, what's wrong?"

"I just need to talk, that's all. And our neighbor Margaret Porter will keep an eye on her. She's been a great help. Her husband had the same kind of problems."

"What problems? What are you talking about? What did they find?" Oliver sounded impatient with him, which was rare, but he was so tired and suddenly very worried.

"No tumors, nothing like that. That was a possibility, of course. Look . . . if it's too late . . ." But it was obvious that he needed to talk to someone, and Ollie didn't have the heart to tell him not to come over.

"No, it's fine, Dad, come on over."

He put a pot of coffee on and made himself a cup, wondering again where Benjamin was and when he was coming home. It was too late to be out on a school night, and he was anxious to tell him just that. But his father arrived first, looking worn and pale. He looked years older than he had just a week before on Christmas, and it reminded Oliver again of his father's weak heart. He wondered if he should be out driving alone at night, but he didn't want to upset him now by asking.

"Come on in, Dad." He hoped the doorbell hadn't

woken Sam, as he escorted his father into the big, friendly kitchen. His father declined the coffee, but took a cup of instant decaf, and let himself slowly down into one of the kitchen chairs, as Ollie watched him. "You look worn out." He probably shouldn't have let him come, but he had thought his father needed to talk, and he was right. He slowly told Oliver the results of the brain scan.

"She has Alzheimer's, Son. Her brain is visibly shrinking, according to the scan. They can't be sure of course, but that and her recent behavior seem to confirm the diagnosis."

"That's ridiculous." Oliver didn't want to believe it. "Get another diagnosis." But George Watson only shook his head. He knew better.

"There's no point. I know they're right. You don't know the things she's been doing lately. She gets lost, she gets confused, she forgets simple things she's known all her life, like how to use a phone, the names of friends." Tears filled his eyes. "Sometimes she even gets confused about who I am. She's not sure if I'm me, or you. She called me Oliver for days last week, and then she flew into a rage when I tried to correct her. She uses language I've never heard her use before. Sometimes I'm embarrassed to take her out in public. She called the bank teller we see every week a 'fucking asshole' the other day. The poor woman almost fainted." Oliver smiled in spite of himself. But it wasn't funny. It was sad. And then suddenly George looked around with a puzzled air. "Where's Sarah? In bed?"

For a moment, Oliver thought of telling him she was out, but there was no point hiding the truth from him.

He had to find out sometime. The odd thing was that he felt ashamed of it, as though he had failed to keep his wife, as though it were clearly all his fault. "She's gone, Dad."

"Gone where?" His father looked blank. "Gone out?"

"No, gone back to school. To Harvard."

"She left you?" George looked stunned. "When did that happen? She was here with you on Christmas . . ." It seemed impossible to comprehend, but he suddenly saw the sorrow in his son's eyes, and now he understood it. "Oh God, Ollie . . . I'm so sorry . . . When did all this come up?"

"She told me about three weeks ago. She enrolled in their master's program last fall, but I think there's more to it than that. She says she's coming back, but I'm not sure of that. I think she's kidding herself more than she's kidding us. I don't know what to believe yet. We'll have to wait and see what happens."

"How are the children taking it?"

"On the surface, pretty well. I took them skiing last week, and it did us all a lot of good. That's why I didn't call you. She left the day after Christmas. But in reality, I think we're all still in shock. Mel blames it all on me, Sam has nightmares every night, and Benjamin seems to be handling it by hiding out with his friends day and night. Maybe I'm not sure I blame him. Maybe if that had happened to me at his age, I'd have done the same thing." But the idea of his mother leaving them was inconceivable to both of them, and it brought their thoughts back to her, after Oliver's astounding revelation. "What are you going to do about Mom?"

"I'm not sure what I can do. They said that at the rate she's going, she could degenerate pretty rapidly. Eventually, she won't recognize anyone, she won't know me." His eyes filled with tears again, he couldn't bear to think of it. He felt as though he were losing her day by day, and the thought of it made him feel all the more sharply Oliver's pain over losing Sarah. But he was young enough, he'd find someone else one day. Phyllis was the only woman George had ever loved, and after forty-seven years he couldn't bear the thought of losing her. He took out a linen handkerchief, blew his nose, and took a deep breath as he went on again. "They said it could take six months or a year, or a lot less, before she's in a totally removed state. They just don't know. But they think it will be hard to keep her at home once that happens. I don't know what to do . . ." His voice quavered and Oliver's heart went out to him. He reached out and took his hand. It was hard for him to believe they were talking about his own mother, the woman who had always been so intelligent and strong, and now she was forgetting everything she had ever known and breaking his father's heart in the process.

"You can't let yourself get too overwrought about this, or it'll make you sick too."

"That's what Margaret says. She's the neighbor I told you about. She's always been very good to us. Her husband suffered from Alzheimer's for years, and she finally had to put him in a home. She had two heart attacks herself, and she couldn't take care of him herself anymore. He was like that for six years, and he finally passed away last August." He looked miserably at his son. "Ollie . . . I can't stand the thought of losing her . . . of her not remembering anything . . . it's like watching her fade away bit by bit, and she's so difficult now. And she was always so good-natured."

"I thought she seemed a little agitated on Christmas Day, but I didn't realize anything like this was happening. I was too wrapped up in my own problems, I guess. What can I do to help?" It was hideous, he was losing his mother and his wife, and his daughter would hardly speak to him. The women in his life were fading fast, but he had to think of his father now, and not himself. "What can I do for you, Dad?"

"Just be there, I guess." The two men's eyes met and held, and Oliver felt a closeness to him he hadn't felt in years.

"I love you, Dad." He wasn't ashamed to say it now, although years before, the words might have embarrassed his father. When Oliver was young, his father had been very stern. But he had softened over the years, and he needed his son desperately now, more than he'd ever needed anyone.

"I love you too, Son." They were both crying openly, and George blew his nose again, as Oliver heard the front door open and close quietly, and he turned to see Benjamin walking swiftly up the stairs and he called out to him.

"Not so fast, young man. Where've you been until eleven-thirty at night on a weekday?"

Benjamin turned, looking flushed from the cold and embarrassment, and then he looked surprised to see his grandfather sitting there. "Out with friends . . . sorry, Dad. I didn't think you'd mind. Hi, Grampa, what are you doing here? Something wrong?"

"Your grandmother's not well." Oliver was suddenly

stern, and feeling strong again. His father's warmth seemed to give him new strength, at least someone still cared about him. And his father needed him, and so did the kids, even if Sarah didn't need him anymore. "And you know damn well you're not allowed to go out on a school night. You pull that again and you're grounded for two weeks. Got that, mister?"

"Okay, okay . . . I told you I was sorry." Oliver nodded. The boy looked odd. Not drunk or stoned, but as though there was something different about him suddenly. He seemed more of a man, and he didn't seem inclined to argue. "What's wrong with Grandma?"

His grandfather looked up unhappily, and Oliver spoke up quickly for him. "Your grandmother's been having some problems."

"Will she be okay?" Benjamin looked suddenly young and very frightened. It was as though he couldn't bear the thought of losing anyone else. He looked worriedly at the two men, and Oliver patted his shoulder. "She'll be okay. Your grandpa needs some support, that's all. Maybe you can find some spare time for him, away from all those friends that are so appealing."

"Sure, Grampa. I'll come over and visit this weekend." The boy was fond of him, and George Watson was crazy about his grandchildren. Sometimes Oliver thought he liked them better than he had his only son. He was mellower now and better able to enjoy them.

"Your grandmother and I would like that." He stood up, feeling tired and old, and touched the boy's arm, as though it might restore some youth to him. "Thank you both. I'd better be getting home now. Mrs. Porter will be wanting to get home. I left your grandmother with her." He walked slowly to the front door, with Benjamin and Oliver following.

"Will you be all right, Dad?" Oliver wondered if he should drive him home, but his father insisted that he preferred his independence. "Call when you get home then."

"Don't be foolish!" George snapped. "I'm fine. It's your mother who's not well." But his face softened again then, and he hugged Oliver to him. "Thank you, Son . . for everything . . . and . . . I'm sorry about . . ." He glanced at Benjamin, and his look took them both in. ". . . about Sarah. Call if you need anything. When your mother's feeling a little better, maybe Sam could come over and spend a weekend." But it didn't sound as though she was going to be getting any better.

Both men watched George drive away, and Oliver sighed as he closed the front door. Nothing was simple anymore. For anyone. It was sobering to think about the problem with his mother. He turned to look at Benjamin then, wondering what was going on in his life that he wasn't sharing.

"So where are you going these days when you're out till all hours?" He eyed him carefully as they turned out the lights and headed upstairs.

"Just out with friends. Same old crowd." But something in the way he moved his mouth told Ollie he was lying.

"I wish I thought you were telling me the truth."

Benjamin gave a start and turned to look at him. "What makes you say that?"

"It's a girl, isn't it?" Oliver was smarter than he

knew, and Benjamin looked away with an odd smile that said it all.

"Maybe it is. It's no big deal." But it was. A very big deal. His first affair, and he was crazy about her. They were spending every minute they could in bed. Her parents were out all the time. Both her parents worked, and they seemed to go out a lot, and she was the last child at home, so they had plenty of free time to themselves, and they knew exactly what to do with it. Sandra was his first big love. She was a pretty girl from his school. They were in the same chemistry class, and he was helping her pass it. She was on academic probation all the time, unlike him, and she didn't really care. She was a lot more interested in him, and he loved the way her body felt when he touched her. He loved everything about her.

"Why don't you bring her around sometime? Does Mel know her too? I'd like to meet her."

"Yeah . . . maybe . . . sometime . . . G'night, Dad." He disappeared swiftly into his room, and Oliver smiled to himself as he walked into his bedroom, and saw Sam, just as the telephone started ringing. He hurried into the bathroom with it, with the long cord Sarah had had installed so she could talk on the phone while she was in the tub, and in a hushed voice he answered. He thought that maybe it would be his father. But his heart stopped. It was Sarah.

"Hello?"

"Is that you?"

"Yes." A long pause while he tried to regain his composure. "How are you, Sarah?"

"I'm fine. I found an apartment today. How are the kids?"

"Holding up." He listened, aching for her, and then suddenly hating her again for leaving. "It hasn't been easy for them." She ignored the remark.

"How was skiing?"

"Fine. The kids had a good time." But it wasn't the same without you . . . he wanted to say the words to her, but he didn't. Instead, he said the one thing that he had promised himself he wouldn't. "When are you coming home for the weekend?"

"I just left a week ago." Gone, the promise to return every weekend. He had known it would be like this, but she had so ardently denied it. And now she suddenly sounded so callous and so different. It was hard to believe she had actually cried with him before she left. Now she sounded like a casual acquaintance, calling to say hi, instead of his wife of eighteen years, having just moved to a hotel near Boston. "I thought we ought to give everyone time to adjust. After last week, I think we all need a breather." That was why she had left them in the first place, for a "breather."

"And how long will that be?" He hated himself for pressing her, but he found that he couldn't help it. "A week? A month? A year? I think the children need to see you."

"I need to see them too. But I think we ought to give it a few weeks, give them a chance to settle down." *And what about me?* He wanted to shout the words at her, but he didn't.

"They miss you a lot." And so did he.

"I miss them too." She sounded uncomfortable, as though she were anxious to get off. She couldn't stand the guilt of talking to him. "I just wanted to give you the address of my new apartment. I'll move in on Saturday, and as soon as I have a phone, I'll call you."

"And in the meantime? What if there's an emergency with the children?" The very mention of it panicked him, but he had a right to know where she was. He needed to know, if only for his own sake.

"I don't know. You can leave a message for me at the hotel. And after that, I guess you could send a telegram to that address if you had to. It shouldn't take me long to get a phone in."

The ice in his voice was only to hide the pain. "That sounds like a ridiculous arrangement."

"It's the best I can do. Look, I've got to go."

"Why? Is someone waiting for you?" He hated himself for saying that too, but as he listened to her, he was passionately jealous.

"Don't be ridiculous. It's late, that's all. Look, Ol . . . I miss you . . ." It was the cruelest thing she could have said. She didn't have to be there at all. She had gone by choice, she had torn his heart right through his guts, and now she dared to tell him she missed him.

"You've got a lot of gall, Sarah. I don't understand the game you're playing."

"There's no game. You know exactly why I came here. I need to do this."

"You also said you'd come home every weekend. You lied."

"I didn't lie. But I've thought it over, and I just think it would be hard on everyone. You, me, the children."

"This ridiculous sabbatical of yours is also hard on everyone, and what am I supposed to do while you're gone? Lock myself in the bathroom with *Playboy*?"

"Ollie . . . don't . . . please . . . it's hard for both of us." But it was her choice, not his.

"I didn't walk out on you. I never would have done this."

"I had no choice."

"You're full of shit. My mother was right years ago. You're selfish."

"Let's not start that again. For chrissake, Ollie, it's after midnight." And then, suddenly, she was curious, "Why are you whispering?" She had expected him to be in bed, but there was an echo as they talked.

"Sam's in our bed. I'm in the bathroom."

"Is he sick?" She sounded suddenly concerned, and it only made him angry. What would she have done if he was? Fly home? Maybe he should tell her Sam was sick after all. But the truth was worse.

"He has nightmares every night. And he's been wetting his bed. He wanted to sleep with me tonight."

There was a long silence as she envisioned them in what had only days ago been her bed, and then she spoke softly. "He's lucky to have you. Take care. I'll call you as soon as I get the phone."

He wanted to say more to her, but it was obvious that she didn't. "Take care of yourself." He wanted to tell her he still loved her, but he didn't say that either. She was kidding herself about everything, about coming back to them, about not being gone for good, about coming home for weekends and vacations. She had left them, that was the simple truth of it. She had walked out on all of them. And the worst of it was that he knew, no matter what, no matter why, no matter how, he would always love her.

Chapter 6

The first weeks without her were hard. And it seemed as though every morning breakfast was a disaster. The eggs were never quite right, the orange juice was too pulpy, the toast too dark or too light, and even Ollie's coffee tasted different to him. It was ridiculous, he knew. Aggie had been cooking for them for ten years, and they loved her, but they had grown used to Sarah's breakfasts. Sam seemed to whine all the time, more than once Ollie saw him kick the dog, Mel remained sullen throughout, and Benjamin no longer graced them with his presence. Instead he flew out the door, insisting that he never ate breakfast. And suddenly Oliver always seemed to be arguing with them. Mel wanted to go out *both* weekend nights, Benjamin was still coming home too late during the week, but claiming that he was studying with friends, and Sam was restless at night and always wound up in Ollie's bed, which was comforting at first, but after a while got on his nerves. The peaceful family they had been had vanished.

Sarah eventually called when she got her phone, two weeks later than promised, and she still hadn't come home to see them. She thought it was too soon, and now all their conversations were brief and bitter. And she seemed almost afraid of the kids, as though she couldn't bring herself to comfort them. She was keeping up the pretense that she would come home to them one day, smarter, better educated, and successful. But Ollie knew better. Overnight the marriage he had cherished for eighteen years had wound up in the trash. And it affected the way he saw everything, the house, the kids, their friends, even his clients at the office. He was angry at everyone, at her of course, and himself as well, secretly convinced, as Mel still was, that he had done something wrong, and it was his fault.

Their friends called and invited him out, word had gotten around slowly, once Aggie started driving Sarah's car pool. But he didn't want to see anyone. They were curious, and gossipy, and just too damn nosy. And in the midst of it all, George seemed to be calling night and day, with horrifying reports of Ollie's mother's backward progress. She was even more forgetful now, a danger to herself in some ways, and George was distraught and clinging to his son for comfort. But Ollie could barely keep his own life afloat. It was hard enough coping with the children. He thought of taking all of them to a shrink, but when he called Sam's teacher to talk about it, she insisted that everything they were feeling was normal. It was understandable that Sam was difficult and argumentative and whiny, his grades were suffering in school, and so were Mel's. And it was obvious that she still blamed her father for her mother's absence. The school psychologist said that was healthy too. She needed someone to blame it on, other than herself, and he was a convenient scapegoat. And it was equally normal that Benjamin would seek refuge with his friends, to escape the home that was now so different without her. It would all blow over in time, the experts said, they'd all adjust, but there were times when Ollie wondered if he would survive it.

He came home exhausted every night, drained by the day at work, to find the house disrupted, the children unhappy and fighting. His dinners were no longer edible, wrapped in tinfoil and kept in the oven too long. And when Sarah called, he wanted to throw the phone at the wall and scream. He didn't want to hear about her classes or why she wasn't coming home *again* this weekend. He wanted her to come back and sleep with him, love him, cook for him, and take charge of their children. Aggie was great, but what she could offer them fell far short of all the little special things provided by their mother.

He was sitting in his office one afternoon, staring out the window, at the rain and sleet that were typical of late January in New York, and wondering if she ever would come back. Right then, he'd have settled for a weekend. She'd been gone a month by then, and he was so lonely, he almost thought he couldn't stand it.

"There's a happy face . . . can I come in?" It was Daphne Hutchinson, an assistant vice-president of the firm, he'd known her for four years, and they were currently working together on a presentation for a new client. She was a good-looking woman with dark hair she wore pulled back tightly in a bun. She was well-dressed in a chic, European way, everything was very spare and neat about her. And she always wore a great scarf, an expensive pair of shoes, or a piece of discreet but handsome jewelry. He liked her, she was quick and smart, discreet, hardworking, and for whatever reason she had never been married. She was thirty-eight years old, and her interest in striking up a friendship with Oliver over the years had never been more than platonic. She had made it clear to everyone at the firm, from the first, that office romances weren't her style, and through thick and thin and some serious attempts, she had stuck by what she said at the beginning. Oliver respected her for that, and it made her easy to work with. "I've got some of the mock-ups for next week," she was carrying a large portfolio, but she looked hesitant, "but you don't look much in the mood. Should I come back?" She had heard a rumor that Sarah had left, and she had seen the strain in his face for weeks, but they had never discussed it.

"That's okay, Daph, come on in. I guess now's as good a time as any."

She was worried about him as she walked in. He seemed to have lost weight, his face was pale, and he looked desperately unhappy. She sat down and showed him the work, but he seemed unable to concentrate, and finally she suggested they forget it and offered him a cup of coffee. "Anything I can do? I may not look like much," she said, grinning amiably, "but I've got tremendous shoulders."

He smiled at her. She had great stature in many ways, and lots of style, and he almost forgot how tiny she was. She was a terrific woman, and once again he found himself wondering why she had never married. Too busy perhaps, or too wrapped up in her work. It happened to a lot of them, and then suddenly at forty they panicked. But she didn't look as though she was panicking. She seemed content and self-possessed, and her eyes were kind as he sat back in his chair with a sigh and shook his head. "I don't know, Daph . . . I guess you've heard . . ." His eyes bore into hers like two pools of green pain and she had to resist an urge to put her arms around him. "Sarah left last month to go back to school . . . in Boston . . ."

"That's not the end of the world, you know. I thought it was worse than that." She had heard they were getting a divorce, but she didn't say that to Ollie.

"I think most likely it is worse than that, but she hasn't got the guts to admit it. We haven't seen her in almost five weeks, and the kids are going nuts on me. So am I. I go crazy every night trying to get out of here, and it's six or seven o'clock most nights. Eight before I get home, and by then everyone's out of control, my dinner's turned to sock, we yell at each other, they cry, and then it all starts again the next morning."

"It doesn't sound like much fun. Why don't you take an apartment in New York for a while, at least you'd be closer to work, and the change might do the kids good." He hadn't even thought about it, but he couldn't see the point of doing that now, putting them through the trauma of changing friends and schools. And he knew they all needed the comfort of familiar surroundings.

"I'm just barely managing to keep our heads above water, let alone think of moving." He told her about Mel's fury at him, Benjamin's disappearing act, and Sam's wetting the bed on and off, and sleeping with him every night.

"You need a break, kid. Why don't you take them somewhere? Why don't you go to the Caribbean for a week, or Hawaii, someplace hot and sunny and happy?" Was there such a place? Would any of them ever be happy again? It seemed difficult to believe and he was faintly embarrassed to be dumping on her, but she didn't seem to mind it.

"I guess I keep hoping that if we stay right where we are, she'll come back, and we can turn the clock back."

"It doesn't usually work like that."

"Yeah." He ran a tired hand through his hair. "I've noticed. I'm sorry to bore you with all this. It just gets to me sometimes. It makes it hard to concentrate on work. But at least it's nice to get out of the house. It's so depressing being there at night, and weekends are worse. It's as though we've all been smashed apart and don't know how to find each other anymore. It wasn't like that before. . . ." But now he could barely remember how it had been. It seemed as though they had been living through the agony of her absence for a lifetime.

"Can I do anything?" She'd never met his kids, but she would have been willing to. She had a lot of free time on her hands on the weekends. "I'll be happy to meet them sometime. Maybe it would do them good, or do you think they'd feel I was trying to grab you from their mother?"

"I'm not sure they'd even notice." But they both

knew that wasn't the case. He smiled at her, grateful for the sympathetic ear. "Maybe you could come out sometime for the day. It might be fun for all of us, when things settle down a little bit, if they ever do. My mother's been sick lately too. It's like when one thing goes wrong, everything falls apart all at once. Did you ever notice that?" He grinned the boyish smile that melted women's hearts and she laughed.

"Are you kidding? It's the story of my life. How's the dog?"

"The dog?" He looked surprised that she would ask. "Fine. Why?"

"Watch out for him. This'll be the time he'll develop distemper and bite fourteen of your neighbors." They both laughed and he sighed again.

"I never thought anything like this would happen to us, Daph. She took me completely by surprise. I wasn't ready for this, and neither were the kids. I thought we had the perfect life."

"It happens like that sometimes. People get sick, they die, things change, they suddenly fall in love with someone else, or do some other crazy thing like this. It's not fair, but that's the way it is. You just have to make the best of it, and one day you'll look back, and maybe you'll understand why it happened."

"It was me, I guess." He still believed that, it had to be. "Maybe she felt neglected, or ignored, or taken for granted."

"Or stifled, or bored, or maybe she just wasn't such a great person after all." She was closer to the truth than she knew, but Oliver wasn't ready to admit that. "Maybe she just wanted her own life for a change. It's hard to know the reasons why people do things. It must be even harder for your kids to understand." She was a wise woman for her years, and Oliver remembered again how much he had always liked her, not in a flirtatious way, but she offered the sound, valuable stuff that solid friendships were made of. It had been years since he'd had a woman as a friend, not since he had married Sarah.

"If I don't understand it myself, it's not surprising that they don't. And she isn't helping matters by staying away. When she left, she promised to come home every weekend."

"That's rough, too, but maybe this is better for all of you. By the time she comes back to visit, you'll all be more settled." He laughed bitterly at the thought. It seemed an unlikely prospect.

"There is no such thing at our house. Everyone starts complaining at breakfast, and when I come home they're still at it, or they're not there at all, which is worse. I never realized the kids could be such a handful. They've always been so easy and so good, so well adjusted and happy. And now . . . I hardly recognize them when I go home at night, the complaints, the moodiness, the arguments, the whining. I can hardly wait to get back here." And once in the office, he couldn't stand being there either. Maybe she was right. Maybe they should take another vacation.

"Don't let this become your life." She said it with a knowing look in her eyes. "You pay a price for that too. Give her a chance, if she comes back, great. If she doesn't, get your life squared away. Your *real* life. Not this bullshit. It's no substitute for a real live person. I speak from experience. Believe me."

"Is that why you never got married, Daphne?" Under the circumstances, it no longer seemed quite so rude to ask her.

"More or less. That and a few other complications. I swore to myself I'd build a career until I was thirty, and after that some other things happened to keep me occupied, and I took refuge in my work again. And then . . . well, it's a long story, but suffice it to say this is it for me. I love it, it works for me. But it's not much of a life for most folks. And you've got kids. You need more than just this in your life. Your kids will be gone one day, and that desk isn't much company after midnight." Everyone knew that she stayed as late as ten o'clock some nights. But it was also why she made the best presentations. She worked like a dog on what she did, and she was brilliant at it.

"You're a wise woman." He smiled at her and looked at his watch. "Think we should take another stab at that stuff you brought in?" It was almost five o'clock, and he was thinking about going home, but it was still a little bit too early.

"Why don't you go home early for a change? It might do your kids good, and you too. Take them out to dinner somewhere."

He looked surprised by the idea, he had never even thought of it, he was so desperately clinging to their old routines. "That's a great idea. Thank you. You don't mind if we do that stuff again tomorrow?"

"Don't be silly. I'll have more to show you." She got up and walked to the door, and looked over her shoulder at him. "Hang in there, kid. The storms may hit all at once, but the good news is they don't last forever."

"You swear?"

She held up two fingers with a grin. "Scout's honor."

She left and he dialed the house, and Agnes answered. "Hi, Aggie." He felt happier than he had in days. "Don't bother to cook dinner tonight. I thought I'd come home and take the kids out." He loved Daphne's idea, she really was one hell of a smart woman.

"Oh." Agnes sounded as though he had taken her by surprise.

"Is something wrong?" Reality was beginning to hit him again. Nothing was easy now. Not even taking the kids out to dinner.

"Melissa is at rehearsal again, and Benjamin has basketball practice tonight. And Sam is in bed with a fever."

"Christ . . . sorry . . . all right, never mind. We'll do it another time." And then, frowning, "Is Sam all right?"

"It's nothing. Just a cold and a touch of the flu. I suspected he was coming down with something yesterday. The school called and had me pick him up right after I dropped him off this morning." And she hadn't called him. His kid was sick, and he didn't even know. Poor Sam.

"Where is he?"

"In your bed, Mr. Watson. He refused to get into his own, and I didn't think you'd mind."

"That's fine." A sick child in bed with him. It was a far cry from the life that bed had once known, but all of that seemed to be over. He hung up, looking glum, and Daphne appeared again in his doorway.

"Oh-oh, looks like bad news again. The dog?"

Ollie laughed. She had a cheering effect on him, almost like a favorite sister. "Not yet. Sam. He has a fever. The others are out. Scratch dinner tonight." And then he had an idea. "Listen, would you like to come out on Sunday? We could take the kids out then."

"Are you sure they wouldn't mind?"

"Positive. They'd love it. We'll go to a little Italian restaurant they love. They have great seafood and terrific pasta. How about it?"

"It sounds like fun. And let's make a deal, if their mother comes home for the weekend unexpectedly, it's off, no qualms, no hard feelings, no problems. Okay?"

"Miss Hutchinson, you're much too easy to get along with."

"It's my stock in trade. How do you think I got this far? It ain't my looks." She was modest as well as smart, and she had a great sense of humor.

"Baloney."

She waved and hurried off again, and as he got ready to leave, he wondered why he wasn't physically attracted to her. She was a good-looking girl, and she had a great figure although she was small, and she carefully disguised her shape with businesslike suits and simple dresses. He wondered if he just wasn't ready yet, after all, as far as he knew, he was still married to Sarah. But it was more than that. Daphne put out a vibe that said "I'll be your friend anytime, but don't come too close, pal. Don't touch me." He wondered what was behind it, if anything, if it was just her policy at work, or if it was more than that. Maybe one day he'd ask her.

He got home at seven-fifteen, and Sam was sound asleep in his bed, his little head hot and dry with fever.

The other two were out, and he went downstairs to make himself fried eggs again. There was no dinner left for him. Aggie had made Sam chicken soup and French toast and she figured Ollie could fend for himself. He did, and waited for the others to come home, but it was a long wait. Melissa came in at ten, looking happy and excited. She loved the play, and had a major role, but as soon as she saw Oliver, her face closed up, and she hurried to her room without speaking. It was a lonely feeling, as she closed her door, and it was after midnight when her older brother got home, and Oliver was sitting in the den, quietly waiting.

He heard the front door close and walked swiftly out to him, with a look on his face that said it all. Benjamin was in big trouble.

"Where've you been?"

"I have basketball practice on Tuesday nights." His eyes told his father nothing, but he looked healthy and strong, and everything about him shrieked of independence.

"Until midnight?" Ollie wasn't about to buy the story.

"I stopped for a hamburger afterward. Big deal."

"No, not 'big deal.' I don't know what's going on with you, but you seem to have the impression that now that your mother's gone, you can do anything you please. Well, that's not the case. The same rules stand. Nothing has changed here, except that she's gone. I still expect you to come home, and stay home on weekday nights, do your work, interact with the rest of the family, and be here when I get home. Is that clear?"

"Yeah, sure. But what difference does it make?" He looked furious.

"Because we're still a family. With or without her. And Sam and Mel need you too . . . and so do I . . ."

"That's crap, Dad. All Sam wants is Mom. And Mel spends half her life on the phone, and the other half locked in her room. You don't come home till nine o'clock and when you do, you're too tired to even talk to us. So why the hell should I sit around here wasting my time?"

Oliver was hurt by his words and it showed. "Because you live here. And I don't come home at nine o'clock. I make it home by eight at least. I break my back to catch that train every night, and I expect you to be here. I'm not going to tell you that again, Benjamin. This has been going on for a month now. You're out every night. I'm going to ground you for a month if you don't knock it off."

"The hell you will." Benjamin looked suddenly furious, and Oliver was shocked. His son had never answered him that way before, he would never have dared. And suddenly he openly defied him.

"That's it, mister. You win the prize. As of this minute, you're grounded."

"Bullshit, Dad!" For an instant, Benjamin looked as though he was going to punch him.

"Don't argue with me." Their voices were raised, and neither of them had seen Mel come quietly downstairs, and she stood watching them now from the kitchen doorway. "Your mom may not be here, but I still make the rules here."

"Says who?" An angry voice came from beyond them, and they both turned in surprise to see Melissa watching. "What gives you the right to push us around? You're never here anyway. You don't give a damn about us. If you did, you'd never have chased Mom away in the first place. It's all your fault she left, and now you expect us to pick up the pieces."

He wanted to cry, listening to both of them. They didn't understand any of it. How could they? "Listen, I want you both to know something." Tears stood out in his eyes as he faced them. "I would have done anything to keep your mother here, and as much as I blame myself for what she did, I suspect that some part of her always wanted to do that, to go back to school, to get away from all of us and lead her own life. But whether it's my fault or not, I love you all very much." His voice trembled painfully and he wondered if he could go on, but he did, "and I love her too. We can't let this family fall apart now, it means too much to all of us . . . I need you kids . . ." He began to cry, and Mel looked suddenly horrified, "I need you very much . . . and I love you. . . ." He turned away, and felt Benjamin's hand on his shoulder, and a moment later he felt Melissa close to him, and then her arms around him.

"We love you, Dad." She whispered hoarsely, and Benjamin said nothing but stood close to them. "I'm sorry we've been so awful." She glanced at her older brother and there were tears in his eyes, too, but no matter how sorry he felt for his father, he had his own life now, and his own problems.

"I'm sorry." It was several minutes before he could speak again. "It's hard for all of us. And it's probably hard for her too." He wanted to be fair to her, not to turn the children against her.

"Why hasn't she come home like she said she would? Why doesn't she ever call us?" Melissa asked plaintively as the three of them walked slowly into the kitchen. Sarah had hardly called them since moving to Boston.

"I don't know, sweetheart. I guess there's more work than she thought there would be. I kind of thought that might happen." But he hadn't expected her to stay away from them for five weeks. That was cruel to Sam, to all of them, and he had told her that repeatedly on the phone, but she just kept saying that she wasn't ready to come home yet. Having made the break, painful as it was, she was flying free now, no matter how much it hurt them. "She'll come home one of these days."

Melissa nodded pensively and sat down at the kitchen table. "But it won't be the same anymore, will it?"

"Maybe not. But maybe different won't be so bad. Maybe one day, when we get through this, it'll be better."

"Everything was so good before though." She looked up at him and he nodded. At least they had made contact again, at least something was going right. He turned to look at his son then. "What about you? What's happening with you, Benjamin?" Oliver could sense that there was a lot going on, but nothing his son was going to tell him. And that was new for him too. He had always been so easy and so open.

"Nothing much." And then, looking awkward, "I'd better get to bed now." He turned to leave the room, and Oliver wanted to reach out and stop him.

"Benjamin . . ." The boy stopped. Oliver had

sensed something. "Is something wrong? Do you want to talk to me alone before you go to bed?" He hesitated, and then shook his head.

"No, thanks, Dad. I'm fine." And then, anxiously, "Am I still grounded?"

Oliver didn't hesitate for a beat. It was important that they all understand he was in control now, or they'd all go wild. And for their own good, he couldn't let that happen. "Yes, you are, Son. I'm sorry. In by dinner every night, weekends included. For a month. I warned you before." He was unbending, but his eyes told Benjamin that he was doing it because he loved him.

Benjamin nodded and left the room, and neither of them knew the sense of desperation Oliver had just created. He had to be with her at night . . . had to . . . she needed him. And he needed her too. He didn't know how they were going to survive it.

Oliver looked at Melissa after Benjamin left, and walked slowly over to where she sat and bent to kiss her. "I love you, sweetheart. I really do. I think we all need to be patient right now. Things are bound to get better."

She nodded slowly, looking up at her father. She knew more about Benjamin than she was willing to tell. She had seen him a thousand times with Sandra, and she also knew he was cutting classes. Word got around quickly in their school, even between sophomores and seniors. And she suspected how serious he was about the girl, serious enough to defy their father.

Sam didn't stir that night, as Oliver slept beside him, and in the morning the fever was gone, and everyone seemed calmer as he left for work with a lighter heart.

He was sorry for having had to ground Benjamin, but it was for his own good, and he thought that Benjamin could understand that. The breakthrough with Mel had been worth the agonies of the night before, and suddenly as he got to work, and found a message on his desk, he remembered his invitation to Daphne the night before, to come out on Sunday, and for the first time in a month, he was excited at the prospect of the weekend.

Chapter 7

Daphne came out on the train on Sunday, and he picked her up and brought her back to the house, as they chatted on the way about the children. Mel had been friendlier to him all week, Sam still had a little cold, and Benjamin had barely spoken to him since Oliver had told him he was grounded. But he was respecting the rules finally. He was in every night by dinnertime, and in his room the moment after.

"I warn you, they're not an easy group these days, but they're good kids." He smiled at her, glad she had come out. Sarah hadn't called in days, and they were all feeling the strain of her silence, particularly Ollie.

"I'll try to let them know I'm no threat." Daphne smiled at him again, she was wearing beautifully cut black leather pants and a fur jacket.

"What makes you say that?" He wasn't sure why,

but she seemed to want him to know that she had no romantic interest whatsoever.

"I say that because I like to keep things straight, and honest."

"Is there some reason why you're not interested in men?" He tried to sound casual, and he certainly had no immediate interest in her, but it might be nice to go out with her one day. She had a lot to offer any man, brains, looks, charm, wit. He really liked her. "I know you make a point of never dating anyone at the office."

"That's because I learned my lesson a long time ago. The hard way." She decided to tell him. She wanted to, maybe because she also found him attractive. "Three years into my first job, after I graduated from Smith, I fell in love with the chairman of the board of the ad agency I worked for." She smiled quietly and he whistled as he looked at her.

"You don't mess around, do you?"

"He was one of the most exciting men in advertising. He still is. He was forty-six years old then. Married, with two kids. He lived in Greenwich. And he was Catholic."

"No divorce."

"Very good. You win the prize: two hundred dollars." She didn't sound bitter about it, just matter-of-fact. She wanted Oliver to know about it, although she never told anyone. There were those who knew, and most people didn't. "Actually, his family owned the firm. He's a terrific man. And I fell head over heels in love, and told myself it didn't matter that he was married." She stopped and watched the countryside as though remembering, and Oliver urged her on. He wanted to know the rest, what the guy had done to her to make her so gun-shy about men. It seemed a shame to waste her life alone, although she clearly didn't seem unhappy.

"And? How long did it last? What happened?"

"We had a great time. We traveled. We met on Tuesday and Thursday nights, in an apartment he kept in town. It doesn't sound very nice, but I guess you could say I became his mistress. And eventually, he canned me."

"Charming."

"He figured that someone would find out, and a few did, but most didn't. We were very discreet. And he was always honest with me. He loved his wife, and his kids, they were still little then. His wife was only a few years older than I was. But he loved me too. And I loved him. And I was willing to accept what little he could give me." She didn't look angry as she spoke about him and Ollie was surprised at how calm she was about it.

"How long has it been since you've seen him?"

She laughed as she looked at him. "Three days. He got me another job. We have an apartment. We spend three nights a week together now, and that's all it will ever be. It's been thirteen years in March, and it may sound crazy to you, but I'm happy, and I love him." She looked perfectly content and Oliver was stunned. She was involved with a married man, and seemed perfectly happy about it.

"Are you serious? You don't mind, Daph?"

"Of course I do. The kids are in college now. And his wife is busy with the garden club and about sixteen charities. I guess there's something about their life he likes, because he's never wavered for a minute. I know he'll never leave her."

"But that's a stinking deal for you. You deserve more than that."

"Who says? If I married someone else, we could wind up divorced, or unhappy. There are no guarantees with anyone. I used to think I wanted kids, but I had a problem five years ago, and now I can't anyway. I guess this is enough for me. Maybe I'm strange, or abnormal, but it works for us. And that, my friend, is the story of me. I thought you ought to know." She smiled gently at him. "Because I like you."

"I like you too." He grinned sheepishly. "I think you've just broken my heart." But in a way, he was relieved. It took the pressure off him, too, and now they could really be friends. "Do you think he'll ever leave his wife?"

"I doubt it. I'm not even sure I'd marry him if he did. We're comfortable like this. I have my own life, my career, my friends, and him. It just gets a little rough sometimes on holidays and weekends. But maybe what we have is more precious to us because we know its limitations." She was even wiser than he'd thought, and he admired her, for her honesty as much as the rest.

"I wish I could be as philosophical as you are."

"Maybe you will be one day." He wondered if he could ever be satisfied with two days a week with Sarah. He didn't think so. He wanted so much more than that. He wanted what he had had with her before, and it didn't look as though he was going to get it.

He pulled up in front of the house, and turned to

face her. "Thank you for telling me." And he really meant it.

"I trust you." It was her way of asking him not to share her secret, but she already knew he wouldn't. "I thought you ought to know. I didn't want your kids to worry about us."

"Great." He grinned. "What should I tell them when I introduce you? Hey, kids, it's okay, she's involved with a married man and she loves him." His face sobered then, and his eyes were gentle. "You're a terrific woman, Daph. If there's anything I can ever do for you, if you need a friend . . . just yell. . . ."

"Don't worry. I will. Sometimes it gets pretty lonely. But you learn to fend for yourself, not to reach for the phone at night, not to call him when you think you have appendicitis. You call friends, you learn to take care of yourself. I think it's been good for me."

He shook his head. "I don't think I'll ever be that grown up." At forty-four, he still expected Sarah to take care of him if he had a headache.

"Don't worry about it. I'm probably just crazy. My parents think I am anyway."

"Do they know?" He was amazed. They were obviously very liberal.

"I told them years ago. My mother cried for months, but now they're used to it. Thank God my brother has six children. That took the heat off me." They both laughed then and got out of the car, and Andy instantly leapt all over the leather pants, but she didn't seem to mind it.

When they walked into the house, Sam was watching TV, and Mel was doing something in the kitchen with Agnes, and Oliver ushered Daphne in, and introduced her to Sam. She looked casual and at ease, and Sam looked her over with interest.

"You work with my dad?"

"I sure do. And I've got a nephew your age. He watches wrestling too." She seemed to be up-to-date on the rages popular with nine-year-olds, and Sam nodded his approval. She was okay.

"My dad took me to a match last year. It was great."

"I took Sean once too. He loved it. I thought it was pretty awful." Sam laughed at her, and Melissa emerged slowly from the kitchen, and Oliver introduced her.

"Daphne Hutchinson, my daughter, Melissa." They shook hands properly, and Agnes quietly disappeared, wondering if he was already going out with other women. Things had certainly changed around here, but after what Mrs. Watson had done, she could hardly blame him. He needed a wife, and if she was too foolish to hang on to a good thing, then someone else deserved her good fortune.

The two ladies chatted easily, and Ollie could see that Melissa was carefully looking her over. She approved of the leather pants, the shining hair, the fur jacket, and the black Hermès bag, hanging casually from her shoulder. Daphne was very chic on her own time, too, and now Oliver understood why. There was a certain aura that came from an older man buying gifts for her, and introducing her to the finer things. Even her jewelry was too expensive for most single women. The story Daphne had told him still amazed him. But it was interesting too. But it was as though Melissa sensed that this woman was no threat, that there was nothing except friendship between her and her father. She had eyed her carefully at first, and the messages Daphne had sent out were only of friendship and nonsexual interest.

"Where's Benjamin?" Ollie asked finally.

"Out, I guess." Mel answered. "What do you expect?" She shrugged and grinned at Daphne.

"I have an older brother too. I hated him for about eighteen years. He's improved a lot, though, with old age." He was exactly the same age as Oliver now, which may have been part of why she liked him.

The four of them sat and talked for hours in the cozy living room, and eventually went for a walk with Andy, and just before dinnertime, Benjamin came home, looking rumpled and distracted. He had gone to play touch football with friends allegedly, but as always, he had wound up at Sandra's. Her parents were separated now too and it made things easier for them. Her mother was never home, and her father had moved to Philadelphia.

Benjamin was cool with Daphne when they met, and barely spoke to any of them on the way to dinner. They went to the Italian restaurant Oliver had told her about, and they had a good time, laughing and talking and telling jokes, and finally even Benjamin warmed up, although he cast frequent inquiring looks at his father and Daphne.

They went back to the house for the dessert Agnes had promised to prepare for them, and Andy was lying in front of the fireplace as they ate apple pie à la mode and homemade cookies. It had been a perfect day, the first they'd had in a long time, and they all looked happy.

The phone rang as they were listening to Sam tell

ghost stories, and Oliver went to answer. It was his father, and the others could only hear Ollie's half of the conversation.

"Yes . . . all right, Dad . . . slow down . . . where is she? Are you all right? . . . I'll be right over. . . . Stay there. I'll pick you up. I don't want you driving home alone. You can leave the car there and pick it up tomorrow." He hung up, with a frantic air, and the children looked frightened, and he was quick to reassure them, although as he set down the phone, his own hands were shaking. "It's all right. It's Grandma. She had a little accident. She took the car out alone, and hit a neighbor. No one's badly hurt. She's just shaken up, and they're going to keep her in the hospital tonight, just to watch her. Grandpa's just upset. Fortunately the guy she hit was quick, and jumped onto the hood of the car, all he got was a broken ankle. It could have been a lot worse for both of them."

"I thought she wasn't supposed to drive anymore," Melissa said, still looking worried.

"She isn't. Grandpa was in the garage, putting away some tools, and she decided to do an errand." He didn't tell them that she had told the doctor she'd been going to pick her son up at school, and his father had been crying when he called him. The doctors had just told him that they felt it was time to put her in a home where she could have constant supervision. "I hate to do this," he said, looking at Daphne, "but I've got to go over there to see him. I think he's probably more shaken up than she is. Do you want me to drop you off at the station on the way?" The train wasn't due for another hour, but he didn't want to leave her stranded.

"I can take a cab. You just go." She looked at the three young faces around her. "I can stay here with the children, if they'll have me." Mel and Sam looked thrilled, and Benjamin said nothing.

"That would be great." He smiled at her, and instructed Mel to call a cab at nine-fifteen. It would get her to the station in plenty of time to catch the nine-thirty. "Benjamin can even drive you."

"A cab will be fine. I'm sure Benjamin has better things to do with his time than drive old ladies to the station." She had sensed his reticence and didn't want to impose on him. And a moment later, Oliver left, and Benjamin disappeared to his own quarters, leaving her and the two younger children alone.

Sam went to get more pie, and Mel ran upstairs to get the script for the play to show her. Agnes had gone to bed, as she was wont to do, right after cleaning up the kitchen, and Daphne was alone in the living room when the phone rang, and rang and rang, and nervously she looked around, and finally decided to answer, fearing that it might be Ollie, and he would worry if he got no answer. Maybe he had forgotten something. In any case, she picked it up, and there was a sudden silence on the other end, and then a female voice that asked for Ollie.

"I'm sorry, he's out. May I take a message?" She sounded businesslike, and all her instincts told her it was Sarah. And she was right.

"Are the children there?" She sounded annoyed.

"Certainly. Would you like me to get them?"

"I . . . yes . . ." And then, "Excuse me, but who are you?"

Daphne didn't miss a beat as Mel walked into the

room and Daphne spoke into the phone. "The baby-sitter. I'll let you speak to Melissa now." She handed the phone to Mel with a gentle smile, and then walked into the kitchen to see how Sam was doing. He was butchering the pie and dropping big gobs of apple into his mouth, while attempting to cut another piece for Daphne. "Your mom's on the phone, I think. She's talking to Mel."

"She is?" He looked startled and dropped what he was doing to run into the other room as Daphne watched him. And it was a full ten minutes before they returned, looking subdued, and Daphne ached for them. She could see in their eyes how desperately they missed her and Sam was wiping his eyes on his sleeve. He had obviously been crying. And Melissa looked sobered by the conversation too.

"More pie for anyone?" Daphne wanted to distract them, but wasn't sure how, as Mel looked at her with questioning eyes.

"Why did you tell her you were the sitter?"

Daphne looked her square in the eye, honest with her, as she had been with Ollie. "Because I didn't want to upset her. Your dad and I are just friends, Mel. There's someone in my life I love very much, and your dad and I will never be more than friends. There was no point upsetting your mother, or causing a misunderstanding between them. Things are hard enough for all of you right now as they are, without my adding to the trouble."

Mel nodded at her, silently grateful. "She said she's not coming home next weekend 'cause she has a paper to write." And as she said the words, Sam started to cry softly. And without thinking, Daphne pulled him close to her and held him. She had defused any fears they might have had by telling them about the man she loved, and she was glad she had, and gladder still she had told Ollie before. These were not people to hurt, but to love and nurture. And it made her angry knowing that their own mother had left them.

"Maybe it's too painful for her to come back just yet." She was trying to be fair, but Mel looked angry.

"Then why can't we go and see her?" Sam asked reasonably.

"I don't know, Sam." Daphne wiped his tears, and the three of them sat down at the kitchen table, their appetite gone, the apple pie forgotten.

"She says her apartment is not ready yet and there's no place for us to sleep, but that's stupid." He stopped crying, and the three of them talked, and nine-fifteen passed without their notice.

"Oh dear." When she glanced at her watch again, it was nine-thirty. "Is there another train?" She could always take a cab into New York if she had to.

But Melissa nodded. "At eleven."

"I guess I'll catch that then."

"Good." Sam clung to her hand, but the two children looked suddenly exhausted. She put Sam to bed shortly after that, and chatted with Mel until shortly after ten, and then suggested she go to bed, she could take care of herself for another half hour before she called a cab. And Mel finally went upstairs, with her own thoughts. And Ollie came home at ten-thirty, and was surprised to see Daphne still there, quietly reading.

"How's your father?"

"All right, I guess." Ollie looked tired. He had put

his own father to bed, like a child, and promised to come back the next day to help him decide what to do about his mother. "It's an awful situation. My mother has Alzheimer's, and it's killing my father."

"Oh God, how terrible." She was grateful that her own parents were still youthful and healthy. They were seventy and seventy-five, but they both still looked like fifty. And then she remembered the call from Sarah. "Your wife called, by the way."

"Oh Christ . . ." He ran a hand through his hair, wondering if the kids had told her Daphne was there, but she read the look in his eyes and was quick to reassure him. "What did they tell her?"

"I don't know. I wasn't in the room when they talked to her. But no one was around when the phone rang, I answered it, and told her I was the sitter." She smiled and he grinned at her.

"Thanks for that." And then, with worried eyes again, "How were the kids afterward?"

"Upset. I gather she told them she couldn't come home next weekend, and she can't have them up there. Sam was crying. But he was all right when I put him to bed."

"You are truly an amazing woman." He glanced at his watch then with regret. "I hate to do this, but I'd better get you to the station for the train. We'll just make it."

"I had a terrific day, Oliver." She thanked him on the way to the station.

"So did I. I'm sorry I had to run out at the end."

"Don't worry about it. You have your hands full. But things will look up one of these days."

"If I live that long." He smiled tiredly.

He waited for the train with her, and gave her a brotherly hug before she left, and told her he'd see her the following day at the office. She waved as the train pulled away, and he drove slowly home, sorry that things weren't different. Maybe if she'd been free, he told himself, but he knew it was a lie. No matter how free Daphne might have been, how attractive, how intelligent, all he wanted was Sarah. He dialed her number when he got home, but when the phone rang at her end, there was no answer.

Chapter 8

George Watson put his wife in a convalescent home the week after that. It was one that specialized in patients with Alzheimer's and various forms of dementia. Outwardly, it was cheerful and pleasant, but a glimpse of the patients living there depressed Oliver beyond words, when he went to see his mother. She didn't recognize him this time, and thought George was her son, and not her husband.

The old man dried his eyes as they left, and Oliver took his arm in the bitter wind, and drove him home, and he felt as though he was deserting him as he left him that night and went back to his children.

It seemed odd, when he thought about it, that he and his father were both losing their wives at the same time, although in different ways. It was heartbreaking for both of them. But at least Oliver had the children to keep him occupied, and his work to distract him. His father had nothing, except loneliness and memories, and the painful visits he made to the home every afternoon to see Phyllis.

And then the big day came. Sarah called on Valentine's Day, and announced that she wanted to see the children the following weekend. In Boston.

"Why don't you come here?" She had been gone for seven weeks, and, like the children, Oliver was aching to see her and have her at home with them.

"I want them to see where I live." He wanted to object, but he didn't. Instead, he agreed and called her back when he had figured out their approximate time of arrival in Boston.

"We should get to your place around eleven o'clock Saturday morning, if we take a nine A.M. shuttle." He would have liked to make it on Friday night, but it was too complicated with schools and work, and she had suggested Saturday morning. "Do you have room for all of us?" He smiled for the first time in weeks, and at her end, there was an odd silence.

"I wasn't . . . I thought Mel and Benjamin could sleep on two old couches in my living room. And . . . I was going to have Sam sleep with me . . ." Her voice trailed off as Oliver listened, his hand frozen to the phone as the words reverberated in his head, Sam . . . sleep with *me* she had said, not with *us.*

"Where does that leave us, or should I say me?" He decided to be blunt with her. He wanted to know where he stood, once and for all. He couldn't stand the torture of not knowing any longer.

"I thought maybe . . ." her voice was barely more than a whisper, ". . . you'd want to stay at a hotel. It

. . . it might be easier that way, Ollie." There were tears in her eyes when she said it, but there was a weight on his heart as he heard her.

"Easier for who? It seems to me you were the one promising that nothing would change, not so long ago, you were saying you weren't leaving for good. Or had you forgotten?"

"I didn't forget. Things just change when you get away and get some perspective." Then why didn't things change for him? Why did he still want her so badly? He wanted to shake her until her teeth rattled in her head, and then he wanted to kiss her until she begged him to take her. But she wasn't going to do that again. Not ever.

"So you're telling me it's over. Is that it, Sarah?" His voice was too loud, and his heart was pounding.

"I'm just asking you to stay in a hotel, Ollie . . . this time . . ."

"*Stop that!* Stop playing with me, dammit!" It was a cruel side to her he had never even known was there.

"I'm sorry . . . I'm as confused as you are." And at that precise moment, she meant it.

"The hell you are, Sarah. You know *exactly* what you're doing. You knew it the day you left here."

"I just want to be alone with the children this weekend."

"Fine." His voice turned to ice. "I'll drop them off at your place at eleven." And with that, he hung up the phone before she could torture him any further. It was going to be a lonely weekend for him, while she and the children had their happy reunion.

He could have let them go alone, but he didn't want to. He wanted to be with them, particularly afterward, for the trip home. He also knew in his heart of hearts that he wanted to be near her. He was also particularly worried about Sam, and moderately so about the others. Benjamin was unenthusiastic about going, he was going to miss a game, but Oliver told him he thought he should go. Mel was excited to go, and Sam was ecstatic. But he wondered how they would all feel after they saw her.

The flight to Boston had a festive air, as Oliver sat quietly across the aisle from them, and when they drove to her address on Brattle Street, he was incredibly nervous. He had told her he would drop them off, and when she opened the door, he thought his heart would stop when he saw her. She looked as lovely as she had before, only more so. Her hair was loose and longer, and her jeans clung to her in a way that made Ollie ache, but he tried to maintain his composure in front of the children. She kissed him lightly on the cheek, hugged the children, and took them inside to the lunch she had waiting for them as Oliver drove off in the cab, aching for her with every ounce of his body.

She lived in a small apartment, with a comfortable living room and a tiny bedroom, and behind it a shaggy garden, and as the children slurped soup, gobbled their food, and stared happily at her, everyone talked at once with the relief of releasing long-pent-up fears and emotions. Sam stayed glued to her, and even Benjamin looked more relaxed than he had in a long time. Everyone looked happy, except Oliver, alone in his hotel room.

It had finally happened, she had turned him away. She didn't love him anymore. And the reality of it almost killed him. He cried as he remembered the past and walked for hours on the Harvard campus. He went to all the places they had gone to years before, and realized as he walked back to his hotel that he was still crying. He didn't understand. She had told him nothing would change between them, yet now she had shut him out. It was all over and they had become strangers. He felt like an abandoned child. And that night, as he sat alone in his hotel room, he called her.

He could hear the ruckus of music and voices and laughter in the background, and it only made him lonelier for her than before. "I'm sorry, Sarah. I didn't mean to interrupt your time with the children."

"That's okay. They're making popcorn in the kitchen. Why don't I call you later?" And when she did, it was after midnight.

"What's happening to us?" He had to ask her, had to know, after two months all he could do was think about her and he still wanted her back more than ever. If she really wasn't coming back to him, he had to know it. "I don't understand this. When you left, you said you'd come home every weekend. Now, after almost two months, you keep me at arm's length and act as though we're divorced."

"I don't know either, Ollie." Her voice was soft, a familiar caress he wanted to forget, but couldn't. "Things changed for me once I got here. I realized how badly I wanted this, and that I couldn't go back to what we had before. Maybe I'll be able to one day . . . but it'll have to be very different."

"How? Tell me . . . I need to know. . . ." He hated himself for it, but he was crying again. Something terrible had happened that weekend and he knew it. She was in control of everything he cared about and wanted, and he was helpless to change it, or make her come home to him.

"I don't know the answers either. I just know I need to be here."

"And us? Why this? Why couldn't I stay there?" He had no shame, no pride. He loved her too much and wanted her too badly.

"I think I'm afraid to see you."

"But that's crazy. *Why?*"

"I don't know. Maybe you want too much from me, Oliver. It's almost as though I'm someone else now. Someone I used to be, and was going to be. Someone who's been asleep for all these years, put away, and forgotten, but now I'm alive again. And I don't want to give that up. For anyone. Not even you."

"And the people we were together? Have you forgotten them so soon?" It had only been seven weeks, and she made it sound like forever.

"I'm not that person anymore. I'm not sure I ever could be. I think that's why I'm afraid to see you. I don't want to let you down. But I'm not the same person anymore, Ollie. Maybe I haven't been in a long time, and just didn't know it."

His breath caught, but he had to ask her. "Is there someone else?" Already? So soon? But there could be. And she looked so beautiful when he dropped the kids off. Years had dropped from her when she left Purchase, and she had been pretty to him then, but now she was even more so.

"No, there isn't." But she seemed to hesitate as she said it. "Not yet. But I want to be free to see other people." Jesus. He couldn't believe she was saying these words. But she was. It was over.

"I guess that says it all, doesn't it? Do you want to file for a divorce?" His hand shook on the phone as he asked her.

"Not yet. I don't know what I want. Not yet." He had wanted her to scream in terror at the prospect, but it was obvious that she was considering it. And it was equally obvious that their life together was over in any case.

"Let me know when you figure it out. I think you're a damn fool though, Sarah. We had something wonderful for eighteen years, and you're throwing it out the window." He sounded bitter and sad as he wiped the tears from his cheeks, torn between sorrow and fury.

"Ollie . . ." She sounded as though she was crying too. "I still love you."

"I don't want to hear it." It was too painful now, too much for him. "I'll pick the kids up tomorrow at four. Just send them downstairs, I'll have a cab waiting." Suddenly, he didn't want to see her again. And as he set the phone down gently next to the bed, he felt as though he had set his heart down with it. The woman he had known and loved as Sarah Watson was no more. She was gone. If she had ever existed.

Chapter 9

When he picked the children up the following afternoon, his heart was pounding as the cab waited. He got out and rang the bell and then slid back into the taxi. He was anxious to see them again, to have them back with him, to not be alone for a moment longer. Sunday alone in Boston had been dismal without them. And this had been a weekend he would always remember.

Melissa was the first to emerge, looking confident and grown up and very pretty. She waved at her father in the cab, and he was relieved to see that she was in good spirits. It had done her good to see her mother at last. Benjamin came next, looking serious and subdued, but he was always that way now. He had changed drastically in the two months since she had left them. Or maybe he was just growing up. Oliver wasn't sure, and he worried about him. And then came

Sam, dragging his feet and carrying a large, awkwardly wrapped bundle. She had given him a teddy bear, unsure if he would like the gift, but he had slept with it the night before, and clutched it now like a sacred treasure.

Benjamin slid into the front seat, and Mel had already gotten into the cab, as Sam reached his father with wide, sad eyes, and it was easy to see he'd been crying.

"Hi, big guy, whatcha got?"

"Mom gave me a teddy bear. Just for good luck . . . you know . . ." He was embarrassed to admit how much he loved it. And she had instinctively picked the right thing for him. She knew them all well, and Oliver could still smell her perfume on the boy as he hugged him. It made his heart ache just to smell it and think of her. And then, as Sam climbed over him, bumping his overnight bag across their legs, Oliver glanced up, and saw her standing in the doorway. She was waving to them, and for an instant, he wanted to jump out of the cab and run back and hold her and take her back with them. Maybe he could still bring her to her senses, and if not, at least he could touch her and feel her and smell her. But he forced himself to look away, and in a hoarse voice told the driver to head for the airport. He glanced back in spite of himself as they drove away, and she looked pretty and young as she continued to wave from the doorway, and suddenly, as he watched her, he felt Melissa slip something into his hand. It was a little white silk pouch, and when he opened it, he saw the emerald ring he had given Sarah for Christmas. There was a little note that asked him to save it for Melissa. And that too was a powerful statement. It had been a brutal weekend for him, and he slipped the pouch in his pocket without saying a word, his jaw hard, his eyes cold, as he looked out the window.

Oliver said nothing for a long time, and just listened as the children rattled on, about the dinner she'd cooked, and the popcorn, and how much they'd liked the apartment. Even Sam seemed more at ease now. And it was obvious it had done him a world of good to see their mother. They all looked well groomed, and Sam's hair was combed just the way Oliver liked it. And it was painful for him just seeing them that way, so obviously fresh from her hands, as though newly born, and only just then sprung from her. He didn't want to hear about how wonderful it had been, how great she looked, how cute the garden was, or how hard her courses. He only wanted to hear how desperately she missed all of them, and most of all him, how soon she was coming back, how much she hated Boston, and that she'd been wrong to go there. But he knew now that he would never hear that.

The flight back to New York was rough, but the children didn't even seem to notice, and they got home at eight o'clock that night. Aggie was waiting for them, and offered to cook them dinner. They told Aggie all about Boston then, and what their mom had done, what she had said, what she thought, and about everything that she was doing. And finally, halfway through the meal, Ollie couldn't stand it anymore. He stood up and threw his napkin down as the children stared at him in amazement.

"I'm sick and tired of hearing about all that! I'm glad you had a great time, but dammit, can't you talk about anything else?" They looked crushed and he was suddenly overwhelmed with embarrassment. "I'm sorry . . . I'm . . . never mind . . ." He left them and went upstairs, closing the door to his room, and then sitting there, in the darkness, staring out into the moonlight. But it was so painful listening to them, hearing about her all the time. They had found her again. And he had lost her. There was no turning the clock back now, no getting away from it. She didn't love him anymore, no matter what she said on the phone. It was over. Forever.

He sat there, in the dark, on his bed, for what seemed like a long time, and then he lay down in the darkness and stared up at the ceiling. It was a longer time still before he heard a knock at the door. It was Mel, and she opened the door a crack, but at first she didn't see him. "Dad?" She stepped into the room, and then she saw him there, lying on his bed in the moonlight. "I'm sorry . . . we didn't mean to upset you . . . it's just . . ."

"I know, baby, I know. You have a right to be excited. She's your mom. I just got a little crazy for a minute. Even dads go berserk sometimes." He sat up and smiled at her and then turned on the light, feeling awkward that she had found him sulking in the darkness. "I just miss her a lot . . . just like you did. . . ."

"She says she still loves you, Dad." Mel was suddenly so sad for him and the look in his eyes was just awful.

"That's nice, sweetheart. I love her too. It's just hard to understand sometimes when things change." . . . when you lose someone you love so much . . . when you feel as though your whole life is over . . . "I'll get used to it."

Melissa nodded. She had promised her mother she would do everything she could to help, and she was going to. She put Sam to bed that night, with his teddy bear, and told him to leave Daddy alone for a change, and sleep in his own bed.

"Is Dad sick?" She shook her head. "He acted weird tonight." Sam looked very worried.

"He's just upset, that's all. I think it was hard for him to see Mommy."

"I thought it was great." He grinned happily, holding the bear, and Mel smiled at him, feeling a thousand years older.

"So did I. But I think it's harder for them."

Sam nodded, as though he understood, too, but in truth, he really didn't. And then he asked his sister what he didn't dare to ask either of his parents. "Mel . . . do you think she'll come back? . . . I mean, like before . . . here, to Dad, and everything. . . ."

His sister hesitated for a long time before answering him, searching her own heart and mind, but like her father, she already knew the answer. "I don't know . . . but I don't think so."

Sam nodded again, better able to cope with it now, now that he had been to visit her, and she had promised he could come back in a few weeks. She hadn't said anything about coming back to see them in Purchase. "Do you think Dad's mad at her?"

Mel shook her head. "No. I think he's just sad. That's why he weirded out tonight."

Sam nodded and lay back on his pillow. "G'night, Mel . . . I love you." She bent to kiss him and gently stroked his hair, just as Sarah had in Boston.

"I love you, too, even though you're a brat sometimes." They both laughed and she turned off the light and closed the door, and when she went back to her room, she saw Benjamin climbing out the window, and dropping swiftly to the ground. She watched him, but she made no sound or sign. She just pulled down her shade, and went to lie on her own bed. She had a lot to think about. That night, they all did. They all lay awake for a long time that night, thinking about Sarah. And wherever Benjamin had gone, Mel figured it was his own business. But it was also easy to guess his whereabouts. Despite the restriction still in force, he had gone to Sandra's.

Chapter 10

Daphne walked into Oliver's office the next morning, shortly after ten o'clock, and at first she thought he looked all right. She knew he had taken the children to Boston to see Sarah for the weekend.

"How was it?" But as soon as the words were out of her mouth, she could see the answer in his eyes. He looked as though he'd been hit by lightning.

"Don't ask."

"I'm sorry." And she was, for him and the children.

"So am I. Do you have the slides put together yet?" She nodded, and they avoided any further mention of the subject. They worked straight through until four o'clock, and for once he found relief in his work. It was wonderful not to be thinking of Sarah, or even the children.

He got home at nine o'clock that night, and later

every night after that. They had a rush presentation to put out for a major client. But for once, the children seemed all right. And three weeks after the first visit, Sarah invited the children back to Boston again, but this time Oliver didn't go with them. Mel went with Sam instead. Benjamin had already made plans to go skiing with friends, and didn't want to change that.

On Friday night when Ollie got home late, the house was quiet and dark, even Aggie had taken a few days off, and had gone to stay with her sister in New Jersey. It was odd being alone without all of them, but in some ways it was a relief too. It had been three months since Sarah left, three months of caring and crying and worrying about them, of being responsible every hour of the day and rushing back and forth between Purchase and his office. Sometimes he had to admit that Daphne was right. It would have been easier to move to New York, but he didn't think any of them were ready for that. Maybe in a year or two . . . it was odd thinking that far ahead now, without her. His life looked like an empty wasteland.

He had dinner with his father on Saturday night, and on Sunday afternoon, he went to visit his mother. She was a depressing sight, and all she talked about was wanting to go home, to work in her garden. She wasn't fully aware of where she was, but there were moments when she seemed more lucid than others.

"You doing all right, Dad?" he asked him the night they went out.

"More or less." The older man smiled. "It gets awfully lonely without her."

Ollie sighed and smiled ruefully at him. "I know what you mean, Dad." It still seemed ironic that they were both losing their wives at the same time. Ironic and tragic and endlessly painful.

"At least you have the children to keep you company."

"You should come down and see them more. Sam is dying to see you."

"Maybe tomorrow afternoon." But Ollie had explained that they were in Boston with their mother.

They returned in good spirits again this time, but Mel had warned Sam not to talk about it too much with Daddy. And she had particularly told him not to mention Jean-Pierre. He was a friend of their mom's, who had dropped by to meet them on Saturday night, and Mel secretly thought he had a crush on their mother. He was twenty-five years old, and a graduate student from France, and he had made everyone laugh, and told lots of jokes, and made pizza from scratch. Sam thought he was a great guy, but Mel assured him that Daddy wouldn't want to hear it.

"Do you think he's going out with Mom?" Sam was always curious, and he thought he'd seen them kissing once in the kitchen when he went in for a Coke.

But Mel was quick to demolish his theories. "Don't be stupid."

And they were both excited, because Sarah had promised to take them away for spring vacation. "Where do you think we'll go?" Sam asked.

"I don't know, we'll see."

In the end, she decided on a week of spring skiing in Massachusetts, and she was taking all of them. Even Benjamin had agreed to go with her. And it was only five days before they left that Oliver got the call at the office. It was Benjamin's school. He had been cutting classes for months, and was close to flunking out, and they wanted Oliver to know he was being put on academic probation.

"Benjamin?" He looked stunned. He had come out of a meeting to take the call, fearing that he'd gotten hurt. "I can't believe that. He's always been on the honor roll."

"Not anymore, Mr. Watson." The assistant headmaster had called him himself. "Since January, we've scarcely seen him in class, and this term he has incompletes in almost every subject."

"Why didn't you tell me before now? Why did you wait this long?" Oliver was shocked and angry, at the boy, at himself, at the school, at Sarah for starting it all. It seemed as though the misery was never-ending.

"We've been sending you notices for three months, and you've never responded."

"Son of a bitch . . ." Oliver knew instantly what must have happened. Benjamin must have taken them so Oliver wouldn't know what was going on. "What about his college applications?"

"I just don't know. We'll have to notify the schools he's applied to, of course, but he's always been a strong student before this. We realize that there are mitigating factors. Perhaps if he agrees to do summer school . . . and, of course, it will all depend on his grades from this point on. His last term is going to be very important."

"I understand." Oliver closed his eyes, trying to absorb it all. "Is there some other problem in school I should know about?" He sensed that there was more and he was suddenly almost frightened to hear it.

"Well, some things aren't really in our province . . ."

"What does that mean?"

"I was referring to the Carter girl. We feel that she's part of Benjamin's problem. She's had her own problems this year, a broken home, and she's not . . . well, she's certainly not the student Benjamin is, or was, but I think their involvement provides a great deal too much distraction. There's even talk of her dropping out. But we had already told her mother she wouldn't be graduating with her class. . . ." Damn . . . Oliver had put him on restriction and told him to be home by dinnertime, and he had cut classes to hang out with some dumb girl, she was even a dropout, or almost.

"I'll take care of it. I'd appreciate it very much if we could do something about this so that it doesn't affect Benjamin's college applications." He was due to hear from them any day . . . Harvard . . . Princeton . . . Yale . . . and now he was on academic probation.

"Perhaps if you could spend more time at home with him. We realize how difficult that is now, with Mrs. Watson gone . . ." The words cut him to the quick, he was doing everything he could now, to be with the kids, but again Benjamin's words rang in his ears . . . *you don't come home till nine o'clock every night.* . . .

"I'll do what I can. And I'll speak to him tonight."

"Very well, and we'll keep you apprised of the situation at our end."

"Next time, just call me at the office."

"Of course."

Oliver hung up, and sat for a moment with head bowed, feeling breathless. And then, not knowing what else to do, he dialed Sarah in Boston. But fortunately she was out. And it wasn't her problem anyway. She had deserted all of them. The problem was his now.

He left the office that afternoon at four o'clock, and was home before six. He was there when Benjamin walked through the door, looking pleased with himself, carrying his books, and with a single glance of steel, his father stopped him.

"Come into the den, please, Benjamin."

"Something wrong?" It was obvious from his father's face that there was, but he never suspected what was coming. As he walked through the den door, Oliver gave him a ferocious slap. It was the first time in his life he had struck any of his children except for a single spanking when Benjamin was four, and had put a fork into an electrical outlet. He had wanted to make an impression on him then, and he did this time too. But more than that, the gesture was born of guilt and frustration. Benjamin almost reeled from the shock of it, and his face grew red as he sat down without a sound and Oliver closed the door. He knew now that his father had found out, or some of it at least. And he suspected what was coming.

"I'm sorry . . . I didn't mean to do that . . . but I feel as though I've been cheated. I got a call from your school today, from Mr. Young . . . what the hell have you been up to?"

"I . . . I'm sorry, Dad. . . ." He stared at the floor and then finally back up at him. "I just couldn't . . . I don't know."

"Do you know you're being put on academic probation?" Benjamin nodded. "Do you realize you may never get into a decent college after this? Or you may have to forfeit a year, or at the very least do summer school? And what the hell happened to all the notices they supposedly sent me?"

"I threw them out." He was honest with him, and he looked about ten years old again, as he looked unhappily at his father. "I figured I'd get everything in control again, and you'd never have to know."

Oliver paced the room, and then stopped to stare at him. "And what does that girl have to do with this? I think her name is Sandra Carter." In truth it was emblazoned in his mind, and he had suspected for a long time that Benjamin's current romance was out of hand, but he had never for a moment suspected it would go this far. "I presume you're sleeping with her. How long has that been going on?"

For a long time, Benjamin stared at the floor and didn't answer.

"Answer me, dammit. What's going on with her? Young said she was thinking of dropping out. What kind of a girl is she and why haven't I met her?"

"She's a nice girl, Dad." Benjamin suddenly looked up at him with defiance. "I love her, and she needs me." He chose not to answer his father's second question.

"That's nice. As a fellow dropout?"

"She's not going to drop out . . . yet . . . she's just had a hard time . . . her father walked out on her mom, and . . . never mind. It's a long story."

"I'm touched. And your mother walked out on you, so the two of you walk into the sunset hand in hand,

and flunk out of school. And then what, you pump gas for the rest of your life, while she goes to work as a cocktail waitress? That isn't what I expect of you, or what you want for yourself. You deserve more than that, and she probably does too. For chrissake, Benjamin, get hold of yourself." His face hardened into rigid lines his son had never seen before, but the last three and a half months had extracted a price from him and it showed. "I want you to stop seeing the girl. Now! Do you hear me? And if you don't, I'll send you away to goddamn military school if I have to. I'm not going to let you throw your life away like this, just because you're upset and we've all had a hard time. Life is going to throw a lot of curves at you, Son. It's what you do with them that will make or break you."

Benjamin looked at him quietly, as stubborn as his father, worse, as stubborn as Sarah. "I'll pull my grades up, Dad, and I'll stop cutting school. But I'm not going to stop seeing Sandra."

"The hell you won't, if I tell you to. Do you understand me?"

Benjamin stood up, his red hair and blue eyes blazing at his father. "I won't stop seeing her. I'm telling you that honestly. And you can't make me. I'll move out."

"Is that your final word on this subject?"

Benjamin only nodded.

"Fine. You're on full restriction till the end of school, until I see those grades look the way they did before, until the school tells me you haven't missed five minutes of class to take a pee, until you graduate, and get into the kind of college you deserve. And then we'll see about Sandra." The two men stood glaring at each other, and neither of them wavered. "Now go to your room. And I warn you, Benjamin Watson, I'm going to be checking on you night and day, so don't screw around. I'll call the girl's mother if I have to."

"Don't bother. She's never there."

Oliver nodded, still desperately unhappy with his oldest son, and startled by his defiant devotion to the girl. "She sounds charming."

"May I go now?"

"Please do . . ." And then, as Benjamin reached the door, in a softer voice, "And I'm sorry I hit you. I'm afraid I've reached my limits, too, and this nonsense from you isn't helping." Benjamin nodded and left the room, closing the door behind him, as Oliver let himself slowly down into a chair, feeling his entire body tremble.

But the following week, after a great deal of thought, he realized what he had to do, or what he could do, to at least improve the situation. He went to the headmaster of the school and spoke to him, and at first they weren't sure, but finally they said that if Oliver could get him into a comparable school, they would agree to what he was suggesting. It was the only thing he could do, and it would be hard on the kids at first, but it might be just what the doctor ordered for all of them. Oliver sent them all to Sarah for their school holiday, and although Benjamin refused to go at first, Oliver forced him. He threatened him in every possible way, until the boy finally left with the others. And miraculously, during the week the kids were gone, Oliver spoke to four different schools, and found one very good one that was willing to take him. He was going to move them all to New York as soon as he could, rent an apartment, and put them in new schools. It would get Benjamin away from the girl, and whatever friends were distracting him, and it would mean Oliver could be home every night by six o'clock in the evening. It was what Daphne had suggested two months before, and he had said he would never do, or at least not for several years, but now it was an idea born of desperation.

Both schools involved agreed to the plan, and the one in Purchase even agreed to let him graduate with his class if he did well in New York for the remaining two months of school, passed all his exams, and agreed to go to summer school back in Purchase. It was perfect. Without further ado, Mel was accepted by an exclusive Upper East Side girls' school, and Collegiate agreed to take Sam. They were all excellent moves, albeit a little hasty. And in the last two days before they came home, Oliver pounded the pavements with Daphne, and came up with a very attractive apartment, a year's sublet from a banker who was moving to Paris with his wife and kids. It had four good-sized bedrooms and a pleasant view, an elevator man, a doorman, a big elaborate kitchen, and behind it a very respectable room for Agnes to live. It was going to cost him a fortune, but as far as Oliver was concerned it was worth it. In ten days, he had made all his moves. All that remained now was to break the news to the children when they got home from their vacation with their mother.

He and Daphne sat in the living room after he'd signed the lease, and she eyed him with concern. For a man who hadn't been willing to make any changes at all two months before, he was moving very quickly now. He had been ever since he'd realized that Sarah wasn't coming home.

"I think it'll do us all good." He was defending himself to her, although he didn't have to.

"So do I. But what do you think the kids'll say?"

"What can they say? I can't keep track of Benjamin while I'm commuting. And if it's a disaster between now and June, we can always move back to Purchase and I'll put the kids back in their old schools in the fall. But maybe this is what I should have done right from the beginning."

She nodded again. He was right. It wasn't written in stone, and at least it was a good try at turning the tides that were drowning Benjamin in Purchase. "You don't think it's too radical?"

"Are you telling me I'm crazy?" He smiled nervously at her, wondering the same thing himself, and amazed at what he'd accomplished since the kids left on vacation with their mother. He was dreading telling them, and yet he was excited too. It was an exciting new life for all of them, whatever the reasons that had led him to do it. And it seemed like the best solution to Benjamin's problems.

"I think you've done the right thing, if that helps at all. But I also think it'll be another big adjustment for them."

"Maybe a good one this time." He walked around the living room. The apartment was handsome, and he thought the children would like their rooms, particularly Melissa. Their new home was on East 84th Street, on a tree-lined street, two blocks from Central Park. It was everything Oliver had wanted, once he made up his mind to look for an apartment in town. "What do you think, Daph? Do you really think I'm nuts?" He was suddenly afraid to tell the children. What if they went crazy again, but he'd been so sure it was the right decision when he made it.

"I don't think you're crazy, and I think it'll be fine. Just don't expect them to jump up and down and tell you what a great idea it is. It'll scare them at first, no matter how easy you try to make it for them. Give them time to adjust."

"I know. That's what I was just thinking."

But he was in no way prepared for the violence of their reactions. He told them the next day, when they came home from their vacation with Sarah. He picked them up at the airport and drove them into town, telling them he had a surprise for them, but refusing to tell them what it was. They were in high spirits as they drove in, telling him everything they'd done, and seen, and how good the skiing had been with their mother. But for once, it didn't upset him. He was suddenly excited about what he was going to show them in New York.

"Are we going to see Daphne, Dad?" It was Melissa asking him and he only shook his head and continued driving. He had told Agnes that morning, and she'd been startled, but she'd agreed to come. She didn't mind moving to New York with them, as long as she was with the children.

They drove up in front of the building and he found a parking place, and escorted them in, as they looked around in curiosity.

"Who lives here, Dad?" Sam wanted to know, and Ollie shook his head, walked into the elevator, and asked for seven.

"Yes, sir." The elevator man smiled. The doorman had recognized him at once when he let them in. They were the new tenants in 7H, which was why he hadn't asked them where they were going.

Oliver stood in front of the apartment and pressed the bell, and when no one answered, he shrugged his shoulders, and took the key out of his pocket, opened the door, and swung it wide for his children, as they stood watching him with startled eyes, wondering if he'd gone crazy.

"Come on in, you guys."

"Whose apartment is this?" Mel was whispering and afraid to go in, but Sam wandered right in and looked around. There was no one home, and he signaled to the others to join him.

And then suddenly, Benjamin understood, and he looked worried as he walked in. But Mel began exclaiming over how pretty the antiques were.

"I'm glad you like it, sweetheart." Ollie smiled. "These are our new New York digs. How do you like them?"

"Wow!" She looked thrilled. "When are we going to use this, Daddy?" They had never had an apartment in New York before, and suddenly Sam looked worried.

"Aren't you going to come home during the week anymore, Dad?"

"Of course I am. A lot earlier than before too. We're all going to live here until the end of the school year, and then we'll come back again in September." He was trying to make it sound like an adventure to them, but it was suddenly sinking in, and they all looked frightened.

"You mean we're moving here?" Mel looked horrified. "What about our friends?"

"You can see them on weekends, and in the summer. And if we hate it, we won't come back next year. But I think we ought to at least try it."

"You mean I have to change schools *now*?" She couldn't believe what he was saying. And there was no hiding the truth from her. He nodded his head, and looked at all their faces. Sam looked stunned, and Mel sat down in a chair and started to cry. Benjamin said nothing at all, but his face hardened into a block of ice as he looked at his father. He knew it was partially due to him, but that did nothing to mitigate his anger. He had no right to do this to them, no right at all. It was bad enough that their mother had gone, but now they had to change schools, and move to New York. Suddenly, everything was going to be different. But that was just exactly what Oliver wanted. Especially for him, and Benjamin knew it.

"Come on, guys, it'll be fun. Think of it as a whole exciting new life."

"What about Aggie?" Sam looked suddenly doubly worried. He didn't want to lose anyone else he loved, but his father was quick to reassure him.

"She's coming too."

"And Andy?"

"He can come, too, as long as he behaves. If he chews up all the furniture, we'll have to leave him with Grandpa and pick him up on weekends."

"He'll be good. I swear." Sam's eyes were wide, but at least he wasn't crying. "Can I see my room?"

"Sure." Ollie was pleased. At least Sam was trying, even if the older ones weren't. Melissa was still playing

Camille, and Benjamin was staring sullenly out the window. "It doesn't look like much now, but when we bring some of your stuff in it'll look great." Fortunately the man who owned the apartment had two sons and a daughter, and there were two masculine-looking rooms, and a pink one. But Melissa refused to even come and see it. It was twice the size of her room at home, and much more sophisticated than what she was used to. And Sam reported on it to her when he returned to the living room.

"It's okay, Mel . . . it's pink . . . you'll like it . . ."

"I don't care. I'm not moving here. I'll stay with Carole or Debbie."

"No, you won't." Oliver's voice was quiet and firm. "You'll move here with the rest of us. And I've gotten you into an excellent school. I know it's a tough change, but it's for the best right now, really, Mel, believe me."

Benjamin suddenly wheeled on them then as his father finished speaking. "What he's saying is that he wants to keep an eye on me at close range, and he wants to keep me away from Sandra. What about weekends, Dad? Is she off-limits then too?" His voice was bitter and angry.

"She's off-limits until your grades improve. I told you, I'm not fooling around with you. All your chances for a decent college are about to go right out the window."

"I don't care about that. It doesn't mean anything."

"It meant a lot to you when you sent in your applications, or had you forgotten?"

"Things have changed a lot since then," he muttered darkly, and walked back to the window.

"Well, has everyone seen as much as they want to?" Oliver managed in spite of all of it to sound cheerful, but only Sam was willing to go along with it.

"Is there a backyard?"

Oliver smiled at him. "Not exactly. There's Central Park two blocks away. That ought to do in a pinch." Sam nodded in agreement. "Shall we go?" Melissa hurried to the door, and Benjamin followed more slowly, looking pensive. And it was a quiet drive back to Purchase, all of them lost in their own thoughts, and only Sam occasionally asking questions.

Agnes had dinner waiting for them at home, and Sam told her all about the apartment. "I can play ball in Central Park . . . and I've got a pretty big room . . . and we're coming back here as soon as school gets out, for the summer. What's my school called, Dad?"

"Collegiate."

"Collegiate," he repeated, as Aggie listened intently, and kept an eye on the two others. Neither Benjamin nor Mel had said a word since they'd sat down at the table. "When are we moving again?"

"Next weekend." As he said the words, Melissa collapsed into a flood of tears again, and a few minutes later, Benjamin left the table. He quietly took the car keys from the hall table, and without saying a word, a moment later, he drove away, as Oliver watched him.

Mel never emerged from her room again that night, and the door was locked when he tried it. Only Sam was pleased about the move. To him it was something new and exciting. And after putting him to bed, Oliver went back downstairs to wait for Benjamin to come home. They were going to have a serious talk about his acts of defiance.

He didn't come home until 2:00 A.M., and Ollie was still waiting for him, getting more and more worried. And at last, he heard the crunch of the gravel in the driveway and the car stop outside. The door opened quietly, and Oliver walked out into the hall to meet him.

"Do you want to come out to the kitchen and talk?" It was a purely rhetorical question.

"There's nothing to talk about."

"There seems to be a lot, enough to keep you out till two A.M., or is that another kind of conversation?" He led the way to the kitchen without waiting for an answer, and pulled out two chairs, but it was a moment before Benjamin sat down, and it was obvious he didn't want to. "What's going on, Benjamin?"

"Nothing I want to talk about with you." Suddenly they were enemies. It had happened overnight, but it was no less disappointing or painful.

"Why are you so angry with me? Because of Mom? Do you still blame that on me?"

"That's your business. What I do is mine. I don't like you telling me what to do. I'm too old for that."

"You're seventeen years old, you're not a grown-up yet, even if you'd like to be. And you can't go on breaking all the rules, sooner or later you're going to pay a hell of a price for it. There are always rules in life, whether you like them or not. Right now, you may not even get into college."

"Fuck college." His words startled Ollie.

"What's that all about?"

"I have more important things to think about." For a

moment, Oliver wondered if he was drunk, but he didn't appear to be, and Ollie suspected he wasn't.

"Like what? That girl? . . . Sandra Carter? At your age, that's a passing thing, Benjamin. And if it isn't, you're going to have to wait a long time before you can do anything about it. You've got to finish school, go to college, get a job, make a living to support a wife and kids. You've got a long road ahead of you, and you'd better stay on track now or you're going to be in deep shit before you know it." Benjamin seemed to sag a little as he listened, and then he looked up at his father.

"I'm not moving to New York with you. I won't."

"You have no choice. You have to. I'm closing the house here, except for weekends. And I won't let you live here alone, it's as simple as that. And if you want to know the truth, we're moving there partly because of you, so you can get your act together before it's too late, and I can spend more time with all of you in the evenings."

"It's too late for that now. And I'm not going."

"Why not?" There was an endless silence in the room while Oliver waited. And then, finally, the boy answered.

"I can't leave Sandra."

"Why not? What if I let you see her on weekends?"

"Her mom's moving to California, and she won't have anywhere to stay." Oliver almost groaned at the picture he was painting.

"Isn't Sandra going with her?"

"They don't get along. And she hates her dad. She won't go to Philadelphia to live with him either."

"So what's she going to do?"

"Drop out of school and get a job and stay here, but I don't want to leave her alone."

"That's noble of you. But she sounds very independent."

"She isn't. She needs me." It was the first time he had opened up and talked about her, and Oliver was touched, but also frightened by what he was hearing. She didn't sound like the kind of girl anyone should be involved with. She sounded like trouble. "I can't leave her, Dad."

"You're going to have to leave her in the fall when you go to college anyway. You might as well deal with it now, before it becomes an even bigger problem." But Benjamin only smiled at the irony of his words.

"I can't go." He was adamant and Oliver was suddenly confused.

"To college or New York?" This really was a new one.

"Either one." Benjamin looked stubborn and almost desperate.

"But *why*?" There was another long silence, and finally Benjamin looked up at him, and decided to tell him all of it. He had carried it alone for long enough, and if his father wanted to know so badly, then he would tell him.

"Because she's pregnant."

"Oh my God . . . oh my *God*! . . . why the hell didn't you tell me?"

"I don't know . . . I didn't think you'd want to know . . . and anyway, it's my problem." He hung his head, feeling the full burden of it, as he had for months.

"Is that why her mother is leaving her and going to California?"

"In part. But they also don't get along, and her mother has a new boyfriend."

"And what does she think about her daughter being pregnant?"

"She figures it's Sandra's problem, not hers. She told her to get an abortion."

"And? . . . will she?"

Benjamin shook his head, and looked at his father with everything he believed in, in his eyes, his heart on his sleeve, and the values of his father. "I wouldn't let her."

"For God's sake, Benjamin . . ." Oliver got up and began to pace the kitchen. "You wouldn't let her? Why not? What on earth is a seventeen-year-old girl going to do with a baby? Or is she willing to give it up for adoption?"

Benjamin shook his head again. "She says she wants to keep it."

"Benjamin, please make sense. You're ruining three lives, not just one. Get the girl to have an abortion."

"She can't."

"Why not?"

"She's four months pregnant."

He sat down again with a thud. "What a mess you've gotten yourself into, no wonder you're cutting classes and flunking out, but I've got news for you, we'll wade through this mess together, but you're moving to New York with me next week, come hell or high water."

"Dad, I already told you." Benjamin stood up, looking impatient. "I'm not going to leave her. She's alone and pregnant, and that's my kid she's carrying around.

I care about her, and the baby." And then suddenly, his eyes filled with tears, he was tired, and drained, and he didn't want to argue anymore, things were tough enough for him without taking on his father too. "Daddy, I love her . . . please don't interfere in this." Benjamin didn't tell him he'd offered to marry the girl, but Sandra thought marriage was dumb. She didn't want to end up divorced like her parents.

Oliver went to him and put an arm around him. "You have to be sensible . . . you have to do the right things . . . for both of you. And throwing your life away isn't going to help anybody. Where is she living now?" A thousand possibilities were running through Ollie's mind as they spoke, and one of them was paying for her upkeep in a home for unwed mothers.

"At home, but she's moving into an apartment in Port Chester. I've been helping her pay the rent."

"That's noble of you, but she's going to need a lot more than that very shortly. Do you have any idea how expensive babies are? How much it costs to have one?"

"What do you suggest, Dad?" He sounded suddenly bitter again, "that we get an abortion because it's cheaper? That's my baby inside her. I love it and I love her, and I'm not giving either of them up, do you understand that? And I'm not moving to New York. I'll get my grades up here, without going anywhere. I can always stay with her if I have to."

"I don't know what to say to you anymore. Are you sure she's four months pregnant?" Benjamin nodded and it depressed Oliver to realize that their little "accident" had coincided with Sarah's departure. They had all gone nuts for a while, but Benjamin's craziness would last a lifetime. "Will she give it up?"

Benjamin shook his head again. "No, we won't, Dad. It's funny, I always thought you were against abortion." The blow hit hard. He was the man who had fought Sarah each time to save his three children, and yet now he wanted Benjamin's baby to be aborted. But this was so different.

"In most circumstances, I am. But what you're doing is going to destroy your life, and I care more about you than that baby."

"That baby is a part of me, and a part of you, and Mom . . . and Sandra . . . and I'm not going to let anyone kill it."

"How are you going to support it?"

"I can take a job after school if I have to. And Sandra can work too. She's not doing this to get something out of me, Dad. It just happened and now we're dealing with it the best we can." And that wasn't great, and even he knew it.

"How long have you known?" It certainly explained his seriousness in recent months, and constant disappearances, and his defiance.

"A while. A couple of months, I guess. She wasn't sure at first, because she's never very regular, and then I made her go to a clinic."

"That's something, I guess. And now? Is she getting adequate medical care?"

"I take her to the doctor once a month." It was incredible . . . his baby . . . his firstborn . . . was becoming a father. "That's enough, isn't it?" He looked suddenly worried again.

"For now. Do you think she'd go into a home for

unwed mothers? They could take care of her, and eventually help her make arrangements for the baby."

"What kind of arrangements?" Benjamin sounded instantly suspicious.

"That's up to her . . . and you . . . but it would be a decent place to live, with girls in the same situation."

Benjamin nodded. It was a thought anyway. "I'll ask her."

"When's the baby due anyway?"

"Late September."

"You'll be away in school by then."

"Maybe." But that was a whole other fight, and both of them were too tired for that. It was after four o'clock in the morning and they were both exhausted.

"Go to bed. We'll talk tomorrow." He touched Benjamin's shoulder with a look of tenderness and sorrow. "I'm sorry, Son. I'm so sorry this happened to both of you. We'll work it out somehow."

"Thanks, Dad." But neither of them looked convinced as they went upstairs to bed, with their own thoughts, and their own troubles. And the doors to their bedrooms closed softly behind them.

Chapter 11

They talked long into the night almost every night that week, and got nowhere. One night, Oliver even went to see Sandra, and he was saddened when he saw the girl. She was pretty and not too bright, frightened and alone, and from another world. She clung to Benjamin as if he were the only person who could save her. And one thing she was adamant about, just as Benjamin was, she was going to have their baby.

It filled Oliver with despair, and in the end, he called Sarah.

"Are you aware of what's going on in the life of your oldest son?" It sounded like a soap opera even to him, but something had to be done about it, he couldn't spend the rest of his life with that girl, and their baby.

"He called me last night. I don't think you should interfere."

"Are you crazy?" He wanted to strangle her with the telephone cord. "Don't you understand what this will do to his life?"

"What do you want him to do? Kill the girl?"

"Don't be an ass, for chrissake," he couldn't believe what he was hearing from her, "she should get rid of it, or at least put the baby up for adoption. And Benjamin should come to his senses."

"This doesn't sound like the Oliver I know . . . since when did you become such a champion for abortion?"

"Since my seventeen-year-old son knocked up his seventeen-year-old girlfriend, and proposed to ruin both their lives by being noble."

"You have no right to interfere with what he thinks is right."

"I can't believe I'm hearing this from you. What's happening to you? Don't you care about his education? Don't you realize that he wants to give up school now, drop out of high school, and completely forget college?"

"He'll come around. Wait until the kid starts screaming day and night, like he did. He'll be begging you to help him escape, but in the meantime he has to do what he thinks is right."

"I think you're as crazy as he is. It must be genetic. And is that the kind of advice you're giving him?"

"I told him to do whatever he believed in."

"That's nonsense."

"What are you telling him to do?"

"To pull up his socks, drag up his grades, get his ass back in school, and let the girl go to a home for unwed mothers, and have the baby put up for adoption."

"It's certainly nice and tidy anyway. Too bad he doesn't agree with you."

"He doesn't have to agree with me, Sarah. He's a minor. He has to do what we tell him to do."

"Not if he tells you to go to hell, which he will if you push him too hard."

"Just like you did?" He was furious with her, she was playing with Benjamin's life with her goddamn liberal ideas.

"We're not talking about us, we're talking about him."

"We're talking about one of our kids ruining his life, and you're talking garbage."

"Face reality, Oliver, it's his kid, his life, and he's going to do exactly what he wants to do, whether you like it or not, so don't give yourself ulcers over it." It was hopeless talking to her, and eventually he hung up, even more frustrated than before.

And on Saturday morning, Benjamin came to his father as the moving van appeared in the driveway. They were sending small things to New York, some linens, and the clothes they needed.

"Ready to go, Son?" Oliver tried to sound cheerful, and as though nothing were wrong, as though that might make a difference and convince him. But Benjamin looked quiet and determined.

"I came to say good-bye to you, Dad." There was an endless silence between them.

"You have to come with us, Son. For your own sake. And maybe even for Sandra's."

"I'm not going. I'm staying here. I've made my decision. I'm dropping out of school right now. I've got a job in a restaurant, and I can stay at Sandra's apartment with her." In a way, Oliver had forced his hand with the move to New York, and he was almost sorry.

"And if I let you stay in the house? Will you go back to school?"

"I'm sick of school. I want to take care of Sandra."

"Benjamin, please . . . you can take better care of her if you get an education."

"I can always go back to school later."

"Does the school know about this yet?" Benjamin dashed the last of his father's hopes as he nodded.

"I told them yesterday afternoon."

"What did they say?"

"They wished us luck. Sandra had already told her homeroom teacher about the baby."

"I can't believe you're doing this."

"I want to be with her . . . and my kid . . . Dad, you would have done the same thing."

"Possibly, but not in the same way. You're doing the right thing, but in the wrong way and for the wrong reasons."

"I'm doing the best I can."

"I know you are. What if you take a high school equivalency test, take some time off now and go to college in the fall. That's still a possibility, you know."

"Yes, but it's not what I want anymore, Dad. I want to be out in the real world. I've got real responsibilities of my own, and a woman I love . . . and a baby in September." It was ridiculous thinking about it, and yet it was real. Oliver wanted to cry standing on his front lawn, watching the moving men carrying boxes in and out of the house, under Aggie's directions. It was all crazy. In four months, Sarah had destroyed their lives, and now none of it would ever be the same.

He suddenly wondered why the hell he was moving to New York, if Benjamin wasn't even coming. And yet, there were things he liked about the idea, like being able to get home earlier at night, and spending more time with Mel and Sam. Mel had calmed down in the last week, knowing that the move was only for two months for now, and on a trial basis, and they would come back to Purchase for weekends, and for the whole summer. And what made it even more interesting was that all of her friends were impressed and were dying to come and see her in the city. "Dad, I've got to go. I start work at two o'clock, and Sandra's waiting for me at the apartment."

"Will you call me?"

"Sure. Come and see us when you're in town."

"I love you, Benjamin. I really, really love you." He threw his arms around the boy, and held him close as they both cried.

"Thanks, Dad. Everything'll be all right . . ." Oliver nodded, but he didn't believe it. Nothing would ever be all right again, or at least not for a long, long time.

Oliver watched the boy drive away with tears rolling down his cheeks, and he waved at him slowly, and then Benjamin was out of sight, and his father walked slowly back into the house. He had brought the whole damn mess to a head without meaning to, and now Benjamin was a dropout, working in a restaurant and living with a floozy, but maybe something good would come of it, one day . . . one far-off, distant day. . . .

Inside the house, like it or not, everything was chaos. Moving men were everywhere, the dog was barking frantically, and Sam was so excited, he could hardly stand it, as he ran around the house clutching his bear. Mel stayed on the phone almost until the instant they left, and Aggie insisted on leaving everything in order. But finally they got out, and with a last look at the house they loved, followed the moving van to new adventure in New York. There was a plant from Daphne waiting for them there, and fruit and cookies for the kids, and a box of dog biscuits for Andy. It was the perfect welcome, and Mel squealed excitedly as she saw her room, and made a dash for the phone there.

But as they settled in, all Oliver could think about was Benjamin in his new life, a life he'd bitterly regret one day, if it took that long for him to regret it. And Oliver felt as though, one by one, he was losing the people he loved most dearly.

Chapter 12

The move to New York was the best thing he had done for them in years, Oliver realized within a matter of days. Sam loved his new school, and he had an easy time making friends. And Mel was crazy about her new school, spending time with Daphne whenever she could, going to Bloomingdale's, and calling everyone she knew at home to report each new development in her glamorous new life in the city. And best of all, Oliver managed to get home before dinner every night, and spend the kind of time with the kids that he wanted to. Mel was still on the phone most of the time, but she knew he was there. And he and Sam had hours to talk and read and play games, and with the warmer weather in early May, they sometimes went to the park to play ball after they ate dinner. It was the perfect life. Except for Benjamin, whom Ollie missed constantly, and worried about most of the time. He had lost two people now, although he made a point of seeing the boy every week when they went home to Purchase for the weekends. He wanted him to come over and have dinner with them, but Ben was working at night, and it almost broke his father's heart when he stopped in to see him at the restaurant, working as a busboy for a tiny salary. He renewed his offer to let him stay at the house, much as he disliked the idea of his living alone, and he begged him to go back to school. But Benjamin wouldn't leave Sandra now. And when Ollie glimpsed her one Saturday afternoon, he was shocked. She looked more than five months pregnant, and Oliver wondered if the baby was really his son's. He asked Benjamin as much when he had the chance, but the boy only looked hurt and insisted that it was his baby. He said he was sure of it. And Oliver didn't want to press him.

The hardest blow of all came when the college letters began rolling in. Oliver would find them at the house on the weekend. Benjamin still wanted to get his mail there. The school had never notified them that Benjamin had dropped out, and he had been accepted by all except Duke. He could have gone to Harvard, or Princeton, or Yale, and instead he was scraping other people's food off plates in a restaurant, and at eighteen he was going to be a father. It almost broke Ollie's heart to think about it. Oliver answered all of the letters himself, explaining to all that because of difficult family circumstances at the time, he was unable to accept, but he would like to reapply the following year. Ollie still hoped to get him to New York to finish school. A year would be lost in his life, but no more. And he didn't bring it up with Benjamin again. It was a sensitive subject, and he seemed totally wrapped up in his life with Sandra.

"How about coming to New York for a few days sometime?" Oliver would have done anything to lure him there, but the boy was serious about his responsibilities, and he always declined, explaining that he couldn't leave Sandra alone, and Oliver never extended the invitation to her. Benjamin hadn't been to Boston, either, to see his mother since he'd left home, but he seemed to talk to her from time to time. But Mel and Sam visited her, once they were settled in their new home. They seemed quieter about things this time when they came back, and Oliver had the feeling that Sam was unhappy about something. He tried to ask Mel about it once, but she was vague, saying only that Mom was pretty busy with school. But Oliver sensed that there was something else, and one evening it came out, as he and Sam were playing cards. It was a quiet night, and they were alone. For once, Mel was studying in her room.

"What do you think about French people, Dad?" It was an odd question and his father looked up with a puzzled frown.

"French people? They're okay. Why?"

"Nothing. I just wondered, that's all." But Ollie sensed that there was more, and the boy wanted to talk, but was afraid to.

"Is there a French boy at your school?"

Sam shook his head and discarded again, stroking Andy's head as he waited for his father to play. He loved the evenings they shared now. He was really beginning to enjoy their new life. But he still missed his mother and Benjamin, as all three of them did. "Mom's got this friend. . . ." The words came out as he played, and stared at the cards, and suddenly all of his father's antennae went up. So that was it. She had a boyfriend.

"What kind of friend?"

The child shrugged, and picked another card. "I don't know. He's okay, I guess." Mel just happened to be walking by, and she stopped, trying to catch Sam's eye, but he wasn't looking at her, and Oliver looked up and saw the look on her face as she slowly wandered toward them.

"Who's winning?" She tried to distract them both from what Sam had just said. She knew they weren't supposed to talk about it, although Sarah hadn't said that to them, but it was understood between them.

"Sam is. We were just having a little chat."

"Yeah." Mel looked at Sam disapprovingly. "So I heard."

"Your mom has a new French friend?"

"Oh, he's not new," Sam was quick to add. "He was there before. We met him another time too. But he's staying with Mom now. You know, kind of like a friend. He's from France, and his name's Jean-Pierre. He's twenty-five, and he's here on an exchange program for two years."

"How nice for him." Oliver's face set in a thin line as he picked another card without even seeing what it was. "Nice for Mom, too, I guess. What's he like?" He hated to pump the child, but he wanted to know now. She was living with a twenty-five-year-old man, and exposing her children to him. It made him furious just thinking of it.

"It was no big deal, Dad. He slept on the couch when we were there." And when you're not, he wanted to ask. Then where does he sleep? But they all knew that. Even Sam had commented on it to Mel on the way back, wanting to know if she thought their mother was in love with him. And she had made him once again promise not to tell their father.

"That's nice," he repeated again. "Is he a nice guy?"

"He's okay." Sam seemed unimpressed. "He makes a big fuss over Mom. I guess that's what French guys do. He brought her flowers and stuff, and he made us eat 'croissants.' I like English muffins better, but they were okay. It was no big deal." Except to Oliver, who felt as though there were smoke coming from his ears. He could hardly wait to put Sam to bed, and it seemed like hours when he was finally free of him, and Mel intercepted him then, suspecting how he felt about what Sam had said.

"He shouldn't have told you all that. I'm sorry, Dad. I think he's just a friend of Mom's. It was just a little weird with him staying there."

"I'll bet it was."

"He said his lease had run out, and Mom was letting him sleep on the couch until he found another place to live. He was nice to us. I don't think it means anything." Her eyes were big and sad, and they both knew it meant a lot more than she was admitting to her father. It meant Sarah had moved on, and there was a man in her life, unlike Oliver, who still longed for her every night, and hadn't had a date since she left, and still didn't want to.

"Don't worry about it, Mel." He tried to look more relaxed about it than he felt, for her sake if nothing else. "Your mother has a right to do whatever she wants now. She's a free agent. We both are, I guess."

"But you never go out, do you, Dad?" As she looked at him, she seemed proud of him and he smiled at her. It was an odd thing to be proud of him for.

"I just never get around to it, I guess. I'm too busy worrying about all of you."

"Maybe you should one of these days. Daphne says it would be good for you."

"Oh she does, does she? Well, tell her to mind her own business, I have enough confusion in my life without adding that."

And then, his daughter looked at him, knowing the truth. And she was sorry for him. "You're still in love with Mom, aren't you, Dad?"

He hesitated for a long moment, feeling foolish for saying it, but then he nodded as he spoke, "Yes, I am, Mel. Sometimes I think I always will be. But there's no point in that now. It's all over for us." It was time she knew, and he suspected they all did anyway. It was five months since she'd left and nothing had turned out as she'd promised. No weekends, no vacations, she hardly ever called now. And now he knew why, if she was living with a twenty-five-year-old boy from France named Jean-Pierre.

"I kind of thought it was." Mel looked sad for him. "Are you going to get divorced?"

"One of these days, I guess. I'm in no rush. I'll see what your mom wants to do." And after Mel went to bed, he called her that night, remembering what Sam had said, and he didn't beat around the bush with his wife. There was no point to that. It was long past the time to play games with her.

"Don't you think it's a little tasteless to have a man staying with you when the kids are there?" There was no rage in his voice this time, just disgust. She was no longer the woman he knew and loved. She was someone else. And she belonged to a boy named Jean-Pierre. But she was the mother of his children, too, and that concerned him more.

"Oh . . . that . . . he's just a friend, Ollie. And he slept on the couch. The kids slept in my room with me."

"I don't think you fooled anyone. They both know what's going on. At least Mel does, I can promise you that, and I think Sam has a pretty fair idea too. Doesn't that bother you? Doesn't it embarrass you to have your lover staying there?" It was an accusation now, and what really burned him was the guy's age. "I feel like I don't know you anymore. And I'm not even sure I want to."

"That's your business now, Oliver. And how I live my life, and with whom, is mine. It might do them good if your own life were a little more normal."

"I see. What does that mean? I should drag in nineteen-year-old girls just to prove my manhood to them?"

"I'm not proving anything. We're good friends. Age is of no importance."

"I don't give a damn. A certain decorum is, at least when my children are around. Just see that you maintain it."

"Don't threaten me, Oliver. I'm not one of your children. I'm not your maid. I don't work for you anymore. And if that's what you mean when you say you don't know me, you're right. You never did. All I was

was a hired hand to keep your kids in line, and do your laundry."

"That's a rotten thing to say. We had a hell of a lot more than that, and you know it. We wouldn't have stayed together for damn near twenty years if all you were to me was a maid."

"Maybe neither of us ever noticed."

"And what's different now, other than the fact that you've deserted your children? What's so much better? Who cooks? Who cleans? Who takes the garbage out? Someone has to do it. I did my work. You did yours. And together we built something terrific, until you knocked it down, and walked all over it, and us, on the way out. It was a stinking thing to do, to all of us, and especially me. But at least I know what we had. We had something beautiful and worthwhile and decent. Don't denigrate it now just because you walked out."

There was a long silence at her end, and for a moment, he wasn't sure if she was crying. "I'm sorry . . . maybe you're right . . . I just . . . I'm sorry, Ollie . . . I couldn't hack it. . . ."

His voice was gentler again. "I'm sorry you couldn't." His voice was sweet and gruff, "I loved you so damn much, Sarah, when you left I thought it would kill me."

She smiled through her tears. "You're too good and too strong to ever let anything get you down for long. Ollie, you don't even know it, but you're a winner."

"So what happened?" He grinned ruefully. "It doesn't look to me like I won. Last time I looked, you weren't hanging around my bedroom."

"Maybe you did win. Maybe this time you'll get

something better. Someone better suited to you, and what you want. You should have married some terrible, light-hearted bright girl who wanted to make you a beautiful home and give you lots of children."

"That's what I had with you."

"But it wasn't real. I only did it because I had to. That's what was wrong with it. I wanted to be doing this, leading a bohemian life with no responsibilities other than to myself. I don't want to own anyone or anything. I never did. I just wanted to be free. And I am now."

"The bitch of it is I never knew . . . I never realized . . ."

"Neither did I for a long time. I guess that's why you didn't either."

"Are you happy now?" He needed to know that, for his own peace of mind. She had turned their life upside down, but if she had found what she'd been looking for, maybe it was worth it. Just maybe.

"I think I am. Happier anyway. I'll be a lot more so when I accomplish something that I think is worthwhile."

"You already did . . . you just don't know it. You gave me twenty great years, three beautiful kids. Maybe that's enough. Maybe you can't count on anything forever."

"Some things you can. I'm sure of it. Next time you'll know what you're looking for, and what you don't want, and so will I."

"And your French friend? Is he it?" He didn't see how he could be at twenty-five, but she was a strange woman. Maybe that was what she wanted now.

"He's all right for now. It's a very existential arrangement."

Oliver smiled again. He had heard the words before, a long time since. "You sound just the way you did when you lived in SoHo. Just make sure you're going ahead and not back. You can't go back, Sarrie. It doesn't work."

"I know. That's why I never came home." He understood now. It still made him sad, but at least he understood it.

"Do you want me to file?" It was the first time he had ever asked her directly, and for the first time it didn't break his heart to say the words. Maybe he was finally ready.

"When you have time. I'm in no hurry."

"I'm sorry, sweetheart . . ." He felt tears sting his eyes.

"Don't be." And then she said good night, and he was left alone with his memories and his regrets, and his fantasies about Jean-Pierre . . . the lucky bastard . . .

Sam crept back into his father's bed that night, for the first time since he'd come to New York, and Oliver didn't mind. It was comforting to have him near him.

And that weekend they went to Purchase, but they didn't see Benjamin. The children were busy with their friends, and Sarah's garden was in full bloom, so Aggie had her hands full clipping things she wanted to take back to the city, and on Saturday morning, as Oliver lay in bed, quietly dreaming, the phone rang.

It was George, and as Oliver listened, he sat bolt upright in bed. His father wasn't making much sense, all he could understand was that his mother had been hit by a bus and was in a coma. She was back in the hospital again, and his father was crying, his voice jagged and broken.

"I'll be right there, Dad. When did it happen?" It had happened at eight o'clock that morning.

He was at the hospital in under an hour, his hair barely combed, in khaki pants and the shirt he'd worn the night before, and he found his father crying softly in the hall, and when he saw Oliver, he held out his arms like a lost child.

"God, Dad, what happened?"

"It's all my fault. She was better for a few days, and I insisted on bringing her home for the weekend." But he missed her so much, he longed for her next to him in the bed they'd shared for almost half a century, and when she had seemed better to him, he had deluded himself that it would do her good to go home for a few days. The doctors had tried to discourage him, but he had insisted he could care for her as well as they could. "She must have gotten up before I woke up. When I did, I saw her there fully dressed. She looked a little confused, she said she was going to make breakfast. I thought it was good for her to do something familiar like that, so I let her. I got up and showered and shaved, and when I went into the kitchen she wasn't there. The front door was open, and I couldn't find her. I looked for her everywhere, in the garden, in the shed. I drove all over the neighborhood, and then . . ." He started to sob again, "I saw the ambulance . . . the bus driver said she had walked right into him. He hit the brakes as hard as he could and he couldn't stop in time. She was barely alive when they brought her in, and they just don't know . . . Oh,

Ollie, it's as though I killed her. I wanted so badly to turn back the clock, to pretend to myself that she was all right again, and of course she wasn't, and now . . ." She was in intensive care, and when Ollie saw her, he was badly shaken. She had sustained tremendous head injuries, and broken most of her bones. But mercifully, they said she had been unconscious from the moment she'd been hit, if that was any comfort.

The two men waited in the hall, and at noon, Oliver insisted on taking his father to the cafeteria for lunch. They saw her every hour for a moment or two, but there was no change, and by midnight it was clear to both of them that their vigil was fruitless. The doctors held out no hope, and just before dawn she had a massive stroke. His father had gone home by then, while Oliver still waited. He had called home several times and reported to Aggie on the situation. He didn't want her to tell the children yet. She had told them he'd gone back to the city for an emergency at work. He didn't want to upset them for the moment.

The doctor came to speak to him at six o'clock as he dozed in the hall. He had seen his mother for the last time two hours before. In the intensive care unit there was neither night nor day, there were only bright lights and the humming of machines, the pumping of respirators and the occasional whine of a computer, and a few sad, lonely groans. But his mother hadn't even stirred when he saw her.

The doctor touched his arm and he woke instantly. "Yes?"

"Mr. Watson . . . your mother has had a massive cerebral hemorrhage."

"Is she? . . . has she? . . ." It was terrifying to say

the words even now. At forty-four, he still wanted his mother. Alive. Forever.

"Her heart is still pumping, and we have her on the respirator. But there are no brain waves. I'm afraid the fight is over." She was legally dead, but technically, with their help, she was still breathing. "We can keep her on the machines as long as you like, but there's really no point. It's up to you now." He wondered if his father would want him to make the decision for him, and then suddenly he knew he wouldn't. "What would you like us to do? We can wait, if you'd like to consult your father." Oliver nodded, feeling a sharp pain of loneliness knife through him. His wife had left him five months before, and now he was about to lose his mother. But he couldn't think of it selfishly now. He had to think of George and what it would mean to him to lose his wife of forty-seven years. It was going to be brutal. But in truth she had left him months before, when she began fading. Often, she even forgot who he was. And she would have grown rapidly worse over the next year. Maybe, in a terrible way, this was better.

"I'll call him." But as he walked to the phone, he thought better of it, and he walked outside to find his car in the balmy spring morning. It was beautiful outside, the air was sweet, the sun was warm, and the birds were already singing. It was hard to believe that for all intents and purposes she had already died, and now he had to go and tell his father.

He let himself into the house with a key he kept for emergencies, and walked quietly into his parents' bedroom. It was as it always had been, except that his father lay alone in the old four-poster they had had since their wedding day.

"Dad?" he whispered, and his father stirred, and then he reached out gently and touched him. "Dad . . ." He was afraid to scare him. At seventy-two, he had a weak heart, his lungs were frail, but he still had dignity and strength and his son's respect. He woke up with a start, and looked at Ollie.

"Is it? . . . Is she . . ." He looked suddenly terrified as he sat up.

"She's still there, but we need to talk."

"Why? What is it?"

"Why don't you wake up for a minute." He still had the startled look of someone roused from a sound sleep.

"I'm awake. Has something happened?"

"Mom had a stroke." Ollie sighed as he sat down carefully on the bed and held his father's hand. "They're keeping her going on the machines. But, Dad . . . that's all that's left . . ." He hated to say the words, but they were the simple truth. "She's brain dead."

"What do they want us to do?"

"They can take her off the machines, that's up to you."

"And then she'll die?" Ollie nodded, and the tears coursed slowly down the old man's cheeks as he sank slowly back against his pillows. "She was so beautiful, Oliver . . . so sweet when she was young . . . so lovely when I married her. How can they ask me to kill her? It's not fair. How can I do that to her?" There was a sad sob and Oliver had to fight back his own tears as he watched him.

"Do you want me to take care of it? I just thought you'd want to know . . . I'm sorry, Dad." They were both crying, but the truth was that the woman they loved had died a while ago. There was really nothing left now.

George sat slowly up again and wiped his eyes. "I want to be there when they do it."

"No," his son objected instantly. "I don't want you to do that."

"That's not your decision to make, it's mine. I owe it to her. I've been there for her for almost fifty years, and I'm not going to let her down now." The tears began again. "Oliver, I love her."

"I know you do, Dad. And she knew that too. She loved you too. You don't have to put yourself through this."

"It's all my fault this happened."

Oliver took the old man's hands hard in his own. "I want you to listen to me. There was nothing left of Mom, nothing that we knew and loved. She was gone, she had been for a long time, and what happened yesterday wasn't your fault. Maybe in a way it's better like this. If she had lived, she would have shriveled up and died, she wouldn't have known who anyone was, she wouldn't have remembered any of the things she cared about or loved . . . you . . . her grandchildren . . . me . . . her friends . . . her house . . . her garden. She would have been a vegetable in a nursing home, and she would have hated that if she'd known. Now she's been spared that. Accept that as the hand of fate, as God's will, if you want to call it that, and stop blaming yourself. None of it is in your control. Whatever you do now, whatever happened, it was meant to be this way. And when we let her go, she'll be free."

The old man nodded, grateful for his son's words. Maybe he was right. And in any case, none of it could be changed now.

George Watson dressed carefully in a dark pin-striped suit, with a starched white shirt, and a navy blue tie Phyllis had bought for him ten years before. He looked distinguished and in control as they left the house and he looked around for a last time, as though expecting to see her, and then he looked at his son and shook his head.

"It's so odd to think that she was here just yesterday morning."

But Ollie only shook his head in answer. "No, she wasn't, Dad. She hasn't been here in a long, long time. You know that."

George nodded, and they drove to the hospital in silence. It was a beautiful morning . . . a beautiful morning to die, Oliver kept thinking. And then they walked up the steps and took the elevator to the fourth floor, and asked to see the doctor on duty. It was the same man who had spoken to Oliver only two hours before, and there had been no change in Mrs. Watson's condition, except that she had had several seizures, which was expected after the hemorrhage. Nothing of any import had changed. She was brain dead, and she would remain that way forever, and only their machine was keeping her alive for the moment.

"My father wanted to be here himself," Oliver explained.

"I understand." The young doctor was kind and sympathetic.

"I want to be there when you . . . when . . ." His voice quavered and he couldn't say the words, as the doctor nodded his understanding. He had been through it dozens of times before, but somehow he wasn't hardened to it yet.

There was a nurse with her when they walked in, and the machines were pulsing and beeping. The line on the monitor traveled in a single straight line, and they all knew that that was her final condemnation. But she looked peaceful as she lay sleeping there. Her eyes were closed, her hair was clean, her hands lay at her sides, as George reached out and took one. He brought it to his lips and kissed her fingers.

"I love you, Phyllis . . . I always, always will . . . and one day we'll be together again." The doctor and Ollie turned away, the son with tears flowing down his cheeks, wishing that everything could be different, that she could live a long, long time, that nothing had changed, that she would have lived to see Sam grow up and have children of his own. "Sleep peacefully, my darling," George whispered for the last time, and then he looked up expectantly at the doctor. He continued to hold her hand, and the machines were turned off. And quietly, peacefully, with her husband holding her hand in death as he had in life, Phyllis Watson stopped breathing.

For a long moment, George closed his eyes, and then he bent to kiss her, laid her hand down, touched her cheek for a lingering moment, and looked at her for a long, long time, imprinting that last look on his heart forever. And then he walked outside blinded by tears. Forty-seven years of the life they shared, the love that had bonded them as one for most of their lives, had ended. But there was something beautiful about the way it had been done, because of the people they had been. Even the doctor was touched, as he left them to sign the papers. Oliver made him sit down on a chair in the hall, and then he drove him home again. He stayed with his father till noon, and then went home briefly to begin making the arrangements.

The children were waiting for him there, and Mel knew instantly that something had happened. Her father looked disheveled and exhausted, and Aggie's story had never rung true to her. "What happened, Dad?"

Tears filled his eyes. "Grandma just died, sweetheart. And it was very sad, and kind of beautiful at the same time. It's going to be very hard on Grandpa." Mel started to cry, and a moment later, sensing something, Sam joined them. Ollie told him and he cried too. He was going to miss her so much.

"Can we go see Grandpa?"

"In a while. I have some things to do first." There was the funeral to arrange, the final details at the hospital to wind up. And that afternoon, he decided to send them home on the train with Agnes. He called Daphne before he did, and asked her to drop in on them at the apartment. She told him how sorry she was. It didn't seem fair that all of this should be happening to him, she said, and he was touched and grateful.

He called Benjamin, too, and told him the news, and suggested he look in on his grandfather when he could. He told him he'd let him know when the funeral was. He thought it might be Wednesday.

And then he went back to his father's home and Ollie was relieved to see that Mrs. Porter, their faithful neighbor, was there, taking care of his father. She was quiet and polite and kind to him, and she was very sweet. Finally when he returned home, alone and exhausted, Sarah called him. She told him how sorry she was, and apologized in advance for not coming to the funeral, she had exams.

"I'll explain it to Dad."

"Tell him how sorry I am." She herself was crying.

"Thanks, Sarah." And for once he felt nothing for her. All he could think of was his father's face as he had held his mother's hand, the look of love and gentleness he cast on her. It was what he wanted in his life, too, and he hoped that one day he would find it. But he knew now that it wouldn't be with Sarah.

He went back to his father's house in the morning, and by then, all the arrangements were made. The kids came back out on Tuesday night, and the funeral was Wednesday. It was a sweet, simple affair, with the music his mother had loved, and armfuls of lovely flowers from her own garden. And then, as they lowered the casket slowly into the ground, and left her there, he took his father home, to live alone, to face his grief, to end his days without the woman he had cherished.

Chapter 13

It was June before they all caught their breath again. School let out, and they moved back to the country for the summer. George came to visit them from time to time, and he seemed tired and much older. And it was obvious that he was desperately lonely, more so than he had been when Phyllis was at the rest home. At least then he could visit her, but all he could do now was talk about her to his family and friends.

Ollie was commuting again, a decision he had made for the summer. And it made him doubly glad now that he had taken the New York apartment. It was just as difficult going home late to the kids at night, but it didn't seem quite as bad in the summer. They swam in the pool when he got home, and the kids went to bed later than they did in the winter.

They celebrated the Fourth of July with a few

friends and a barbecue, and in two weeks, Mel and Sam were joining Sarah for the rest of the summer. She was taking them to France, to travel there for a month with Jean-Pierre. She had called to tell him that, and he decided to let her. The kids were old enough to understand. Mel was sixteen and Sam almost ten, and they were excited about going.

George even came to the barbecue, and brought Margaret Porter, the pleasant neighbor they had all met before. She was an attractive woman with gray hair and a lively mind. She had been a nurse in her youth, and her late husband had been a doctor, and she seemed to take good care of Ollie's father. She made a point of seeing that he sat down when he should, without making an issue of it, brought him his food, and joked amiably with him and their friends and George seemed to like it. He talked about Phyllis a lot, and Ollie knew he still felt guilty about the accident that had ultimately killed her. But he seemed to be recovering. They all were, in their own way, from the blows of the past year. Even Ollie felt more himself now. He had filed for divorce in June, and at Daphne's constant urging, he had gone on a date, which had proven to be a disaster. He had gone out with a creative type from another agency, and afterward insisted the girl was a kook. She had wanted him to try cocaine, and her favorite sport was women's wrestling. Daphne had teased him about it a lot, but at least it was a beginning.

Benjamin and Sandra also came to the barbecue, and by then she was seven months pregnant. Ollie felt sorry for her, she wasn't bright, and her childish face looked ridiculous on the huge body. She talked about the baby a lot, and for a moment Ollie was terrified, wondering if they were going to get married too. But when he asked, Benjamin said they had no plans for that yet. He thought they were both too young.

Mel tried to talk to her several times, but she seemed to have nothing to say, and Mel finally gave up, and went back to chatting with her friends. Daphne had come out, too, and she and Margaret Porter spent a lot of time at the poolside talking.

"I had a lovely time," Daphne told Ollie before she left. "A real old-fashioned Fourth of July, with good friends. You can't ask for more than that in life." She smiled happily and he laughed, remembering bygone days.

"I could. But I guess I won't. Another date like the one I had, and it might kill me." They both laughed, remembering the lady wrestling fan.

"Your father seems to be doing all right, and I like his friend. She's a very interesting woman. She and her husband traveled a lot in the Far East, and they set up a clinic for two years in Kenya."

"She seems to be good for Dad. That's something at least. I just wish Benjamin would sort himself out. That girl is sweet, but she'll destroy his life, if he lets her."

"Give him a chance. He's trying to do the right thing. He just doesn't know what that is yet."

"It's hard to imagine him with a kid of his own. He's still a child himself, and she looks like she's fourteen years old. And God, Daph, she's so pathetically stupid."

"She's just out of her element here, and you have to admit, she's at a hell of a disadvantage. She knows what you all think of her, what Benjamin has given up to be with her. That's a hell of a burden for her."

Ollie smiled at his friend ruefully. "Speaking of which, she looks like she's having triplets."

"Don't be unkind," she scolded.

"Why not? She's ruining my son's life."

"Maybe not. Maybe the baby will be terrific."

"I'd still like her to give it up."

Daphne shook her head, she had talked to both of them, and she knew better. "I don't think Benjamin would let her. He's too much like you, too moral, too decent, too anxious to stand up for what he believes in and do the right thing for everyone. He's a great kid. Everything'll be all right."

"What makes you so sure?"

"He's your kid, isn't he?" And then she had gone back to New York, and the others had left shortly after. And Ollie had helped Agnes clean up, and in spite of himself, as he lay alone by the pool late that night, he found himself thinking of Sarah, wondering what she was doing then. The Fourth of July had always been special to them. And they would have been married nineteen years that summer. It made him think of other things as well . . . his parents . . . and his father . . . and Margaret Porter. He wondered if his father was interested in her, or just grateful for her help, and happy to have someone to talk to. Maybe a little of both. It was odd to think of his father interested in anyone, except his late wife.

It was funny how they all had someone now . . . Sarah had Jean-Pierre, his father had Margaret for whatever it was worth, and even his son had the girl who was carrying his baby. And Oliver was alone, waiting for someone to walk into his life and make it whole again. He wondered if it would ever happen.

"Dad?" It was Mel, whispering in the dark, looking for him. "Are you out there?"

"I'm at the pool. What's up?"

"I just wondered if you were okay." She wandered over and sat down next to him.

"I'm fine, sweetheart." He touched the long blond hair and smiled. She was a sweet girl, and things were good between them again. She seemed to have settled down a lot since their move to New York, and she was closer to him again. Closer than she was to Sarah. "It was nice today, wasn't it?"

"Yes, it was." And then, echoing his own thoughts, "What do you think of Grandpa's friend?"

"Margaret? I like her."

"Do you think he'll marry her?" Mel seemed intrigued and Ollie smiled at her.

"I doubt it. He loved Grandma too much for that. You don't find that more than once in a lifetime."

"I just wondered." And then, with fresh concern, "Do you think Mom will marry Jean-Pierre? . . . he's so young for her . . ." Although she would never have said that to her mother.

"I don't think so, sweetheart. I think she's just having fun."

Melissa nodded, relieved. "God, isn't poor Sandra awful?"

He nodded his agreement, suddenly amused that they were dissecting everyone after the guests left, the way married couples did. It made him feel less lonely. "It drives me crazy to see Benjamin wasting his life with her, working as a busboy to support her."

"What'll they do with the baby?"

"God knows. I think they should give it up, but Benjamin insists they want it. And then what? I'll be damned if I'll let them get married."

"I don't really think he wants to. He's just trying to be nice to her. But he looks pretty bored with her too. And she kept looking at the other guys who came by. I don't think she knows what she wants. God, Daddy . . . imagine being seventeen and having a baby!"

"Keep that in mind, my dear, if the call of the wild ever strikes!" He wagged a finger at her and she laughed, blushing in the darkness.

"Don't worry. I'm not that stupid." He wasn't quite sure what that meant. If it meant she would never do it, or if she did, she would be more careful. He made a mental note to himself to have Daphne talk to her on the subject, before she went to France for the summer.

"Is Sam asleep?"

"Out like a light."

"Maybe we should go to bed too." He stood up and stretched and they walked slowly inside holding hands. It had been a beautiful day, sunny and hot, and now the night was cool. It was exactly the way he liked it.

He kissed her good night outside her room, and lay in his own bed that night, thinking of what the last year had been like. How much had changed, how different they all were. Only a year before, on the Fourth of July, everything had been so different. Sarah had been there, his mother . . . Benjamin still seemed like a child. They had all grown up that year, or some of them anyway. He didn't know about Sarah. He suspected that she was still groping. But he felt as though he had found his feet at last, and as he drifted off to sleep, he found himself wondering again about his father and Margaret Porter.

Chapter 14

In July, Mel and Sam left for Europe with Sarah and her French friend, and Oliver moved back to the apartment in New York. There was no point commuting every night now with the kids gone. It was easier for him to stay late at work, and then go back to 84th Street. He and Daphne spent a lot of time working together, and they had a standing spaghetti date now on Monday and Friday nights. She was with her friend the other three weekday nights, and now and then she would talk to Ollie about him. "Why do you do that to yourself?" he scolded more than once. "At your age, you should get married and be with someone who can give you more than three nights a week. Daph, you deserve it."

She always shrugged and laughed. She was happy as things were. He was a wonderful man, she said, and she didn't want more than that. He was intelligent and kind and generous to her, and she loved him. And without children, marriage didn't seem quite as important to her.

"You'll be sorry one day."

But she didn't agree with him. What she had was right for her, even though she missed him when she wasn't with him. "I don't think so, Ollie." He admitted to her how lonely it was being alone, without the kids. He missed having someone to talk to at night, and the companionship he had known for nearly twenty years with Sarah.

He only went out to Purchase now to visit Benjamin and his father. Sandra was getting bigger by the hour. And for the first time in his life, Benjamin looked pale to him. He never got out in the sun anymore. He was always working. He had two jobs now. One pumping gas, and the other at night as a busboy. He was trying to save enough money to get her decent maternity care, pay for the apartment they shared, and have enough on hand to support their baby. And when he had offered to help them, Benjamin had refused it.

"It's my responsibility now, Dad. Not yours."

"This is ridiculous. You're a child. You should be in school, being supported and getting an education." But he was learning other things, about how tough life was when you were eighteen, and had a family to support and hadn't even finished high school. Sandra had had to stop work finally, her ankles were swollen to the size of melons, and the doctor was afraid she was becoming toxemic. Benjamin went home at lunchtime to prepare her meals, and she would lie on the couch and watch TV, while he cooked, complaining all the while that she never saw him anymore. He came home at night as early as he could, but he usually worked till two o'clock in the morning. And just thinking about it drove Oliver wild. He kept trying to give him money to ease his burdens, and finally he found a simpler solution. He gave it to Sandra, and she was always happy to take whatever he gave. He urged them to go to the house and at least use the pool, but Sandra didn't want to go anywhere, and Benjamin didn't have time. He was too busy working.

He was not unlike his mother, Oliver thought to himself one day, after writing a $500 check to Sandra and telling her to buy whatever she needed for the baby. Sarah hadn't taken a penny from him either since she left. She was supporting herself on the money her grandmother had left, and she insisted it wasn't right for Ollie to support her. Things were tight for her, and the children reported constantly about things they couldn't do when they visited her, because "Mom couldn't afford it," but that was the lifestyle Sarah had always wanted. The life that he had provided for her didn't matter to her anymore. She had given mountains of clothes to Mel, and left the rest at the house in Purchase. She lived in blue jeans and T-shirts and sandals. And she and Jean-Pierre were proud of the fact that they were traveling through Europe on a shoestring. He had had several postcards from the kids since they left, but they never called, and he was never quite sure where they were. It made him nervous from time to time, but Sarah had only said that they would stay with relatives of Jean-Pierre's in France, and youth hostels in the other countries where they traveled. It was certainly going to be a different experience for them, but it might be good for them too. And he trusted her to take good care of them. She was their mother, after all, and he had always trusted her. But now, with all of them gone, he was stunned at how much he missed them. It was almost a physical pain when he went home at night to the empty apartment. He had given Aggie the summer off, and hired a weekly cleaning service to take care of the apartment. The house in Purchase was closed, and the dog was staying with his father. It was company for him at least. And when Oliver took the train up to see him one Sunday afternoon, he was touched to find his father lovingly tending his late wife's garden. He had always hated gardening, but now it was vital to him to maintain the roses that had meant so much to her.

"Are you doing all right, Dad?"

"I'm fine. It's awfully quiet here, especially with you and the children gone. Margaret and I go out to dinner from time to time, but I have a lot of work to do, to get your mother's estate in order." The tax work he had to do for probate seemed to keep him busy, and she had had some stocks that he wanted to transfer now to Ollie's children.

Ollie felt sad after he'd spent the afternoon with him, and he went back on the train that night feeling pensive. His car was in the shop, and it was odd riding home on the train instead of driving. He took a seat in the parlor car, and picked up the book he had brought with him, and it was several stops before the seat next to him was occupied. He glanced up and saw a young woman with long dark hair and a deep tan slide into place beside him.

"Sorry," she apologized, as she bumped him with her bag. She seemed to have assorted weekend equipment with her, and a tennis racket strapped to an overnight bag poked him in the leg repeatedly until she moved it. "Sorry about all this stuff." He nodded and assured her it was all right, and went back to his book, as she pulled out what looked like a manuscript and began to make notations. And more than once he sensed her watching him, until finally he looked up and smiled, and realized that she was very attractive. She had blue eyes, and a smattering of freckles on a face that couldn't have been more than twenty-five or -six years old. Her hair was pulled back, and she wore no makeup.

"How do you like the book?" she asked once as they pulled into another station.

"Not bad." It was the hit of the summer, and he liked it, although he usually preferred not to read fiction. But Daphne had given it to him and insisted that he would enjoy it. "Is that your manuscript you're working on?" He was curious about her, and she laughed, shaking her head, and for an instant she seemed a little older. She was actually thirty years old, but her natural good looks reminded him of some of Mel's friends. She had a deep, friendly voice, and intelligent eyes, as she explained what she was reading and why.

"I'm an editor, and we published the book you're reading. That's why I asked if you like it. Do you live out here?" She was curious about him, but she seemed interested in everyone. She was open and easy, and he noticed in her summer dress that she had very pretty arms and shoulders.

"I used to live out here. I live in the city now. Most of the time anyway."

Ah, she decided for herself. A weekend father. "Visiting your kids?"

He shook his head, amused by her straightforward questions. "No. My father."

"Me too." She smiled. "He and his wife just had a baby." She explained that he was sixty-three years old, and married for the third time. Her mother had remarried too, and was living in London.

"Sounds like an interesting family."

"It is." She grinned. "His wife is four years younger than I am. Daddy's never been one to waste time." She didn't tell him that her mother was married to Lord Bronson, and the talk of Europe with their castles and country homes, and glamorous parties. She had wanted to get away from all that, and had gone to work in New York, like the rest of the world. She had no great fondness for the jet-set life of her parents. "And what do you do?"

He suddenly laughed at her. She was a funny girl. Funny and open and nice and extremely attractive. "I'm in advertising." She wondered then if he was married, but she didn't ask him.

"So's my dad." She seemed amused. "Robert Townsend, maybe you know him."

So that was who she was. Townsend was one of the most important men in the business. "I've met him. I can't say I really know him." And then, he decided to introduce himself to her. "I'm Oliver Watson."

She shook his hand with a firm grip of her own. "Megan Townsend." She put her manuscript away then, and they chatted the rest of the way in. He liked talking to her, and he forgot about his book, and offered her a ride home when they arrived at Grand Central Station in New York.

She lived on Park and 69th, only fifteen blocks from his apartment, and after he dropped her off, he stopped the cab and decided to walk home. It was a warm night, and he liked being in New York during the summer. The city was almost deserted, except for a few real devotees, the hardworking stiffs like himself, and a handful of tourists.

The phone was ringing when he got home, and he assumed it was Daphne. No one else ever called, now that the children were gone, except occasionally his father. But he was startled when he heard the voice of the woman he had just dropped off. It was Megan Townsend.

"Hi there, I just had a thought. Want to come back for a drink and a salad? I'm not much of a cook, but I can manage that. I just thought . . ." She sounded suddenly unsure, and it crossed her mind that he might be married. At his age, most men were, but she figured that if she was barking up the wrong tree, he would tell her. He had looked like a pretty straightforward guy.

"That would be very nice." It was a new experience for him, being picked up by a woman, and invited over for dinner on a Sunday night. It hadn't even occurred to him to ask for her number, and he realized then that Daphne was right. He was desperately out of practice. "Can I bring anything?"

"I'm all set. Say eight o'clock?"

"That's great," and then, "I'm glad you called."

"It's not exactly the thing to do, I guess," she

laughed into the phone, seeming perfectly at ease with what she had done, and he wondered if she did it often, "but life's too short. I liked talking to you on the train."

"So did I."

And then she decided to ask him before wasting too much time. Married men weren't her thing, although for an occasional dinner she didn't mind. "By the way, are you married?"

"I . . ." He didn't quite know how to answer her. He was, but not in any way that counted anymore, and he decided to tell her the truth. "I am . . . but I've been separated for seven months."

His answer seemed satisfactory to her. "I figured you were out visiting your kids today when I first saw you."

"They're in Europe for the summer, two of them anyway. The other one is in Port Chester, working." But he didn't tell her that Benjamin was eighteen and living with a fellow dropout while they waited for the birth of their baby.

"See you at eight." She hung up with a smile, pleased with what she'd done, and Oliver looked pleased too, as he strolled back down Park Avenue half an hour later.

Her apartment was on the top floor, with a very pretty penthouse garden. It was in a small, exclusive building and Oliver suspected correctly that it was a co-op. This was no ordinary working girl, and he knew that Robert Townsend was not only a major advertising success, but he was also from a very prominent family in Boston. And Megan's breeding was stamped all over her, from her hair to her shoes, to her well-bred voice, to the expensive white silk shirt she'd put on with a pair of jeans to greet him. Her hair was hanging loose, and he loved the way it flowed down her back and over her shoulders. She wasn't just pretty, he realized now, she was beautiful, and very striking. She had put some makeup on, and she escorted him into the airy living room, which was all done in white and chrome, with a black-and-white marble floor, and two zebra rugs tossed casually under an enormous glass table. There was one mirrored wall to reflect the view, and the glass table in the tiny dining room was set for two. And somehow, even though she wore only jeans and a silk shirt, she had an aura of great sophistication.

"This is quite a place!" He marveled at the view, and she led him out onto the terrace as she handed him a gin and tonic.

"It's my only case of excessive indulgence." Her father had wanted to buy her a town house for her thirtieth birthday, earlier that year, but she had steadfastly refused it. She loved the place she had, and it was big enough, and Oliver certainly understood why she liked it. "I spend an awful lot of time here. I spend most of my weekends here, buried in manuscripts." She laughed easily and he smiled.

"I can think of worse fates." And then he decided to play her game. There was a great deal he suddenly wanted to know about Megan Townsend. "What about you? Married? Divorced? The mother of twelve?" although that at least seemed more than unlikely. Everything about her screamed that she was unencumbered and single.

"Never married. No kids. No cats, dogs, or birds.

And no currently married lovers." They both laughed, and he grinned ruefully.

"I guess that leaves me out."

"Are you going back to your wife?" she inquired, as they sat on two white Brown Jordan deck chairs outside.

"No, I'm not." He met her eyes squarely, but he didn't tell her that until recently, he would have liked to. "Our lives have gone in very separate directions. She's a graduate student at Harvard now, and an aspiring writer."

"That sounds admirable."

"Not really." There was still a trace of bitterness in his voice, whenever he talked about Sarah to strangers. "She walked out on me and three children to get there."

"Sounds like heavy stuff."

"It was."

"And still is?" She was quick, and she seemed anxious to get to know him.

"Sometimes. But better lately. You can't hang on to anger forever," he smiled sadly, "although I tried to for a long time. She kept insisting she was coming back, but I think that charade is finally behind us. And the kids are adjusting . . . so am I. . . ." He smiled at her, and then suddenly laughed at himself. "Although, I have to admit to you, this is the first 'date' I've had in twenty years. You may find my dating manners a little rusty."

"You haven't been out with anyone since she left?" Megan was impressed. The woman who'd left him must have been quite something. She'd never been without a man in her life for more than a month, and she was sure she didn't want to be. Her last lover had departed only three weeks before, after a comfortable six months, commuting between her penthouse and his Fifth Avenue town house. She moved with a racy crowd, but something about Oliver had intrigued her, his looks, his charm, and something that had suggested to her that he was very lonely. "Are you serious?"

And then suddenly he remembered the lady wrestling fan, and laughed again. "No, I lied . . . I had a date a couple of months ago, and it was a disaster. It almost cured me."

"Good Lord, Oliver," she laughed and set down the remains of her gin and tonic, "You're practically a virgin."

"You might say that." He laughed and for a moment, wondered if he had gotten in over his head this time. He hadn't made love to a woman in seven months, and suddenly he wondered what would happen if he tried. Maybe it wouldn't even work. For seven months, he hadn't wanted anyone but Sarah. And he hadn't slept with anyone else in twenty years before that. He had never cheated on his wife, and this girl seemed somehow as though she was used to getting any man she wanted. Suddenly a little boy in him wanted to run home as fast as he could, and he felt like Sam as he stood up and went to admire the view again, while she went back inside to finish putting together the promised salad.

"I warn you, I can't cook. Caesar salad and carpaccio are the full limit of my skills. After that, it's strictly pizza and Chinese takeout."

"I can hardly wait. I like them all." And he liked her, too, although she frightened him a little bit.

They sat down to dinner in the dining room, and talked about her work, and his, and he began to feel more at ease again, and then eventually she asked about his children, and he tried to describe them to her.

"They were all pretty hard hit when their mother left, and I was too. But I think they're coming out of it now." All except Benjamin and the disaster he had created for himself with Sandra.

"And what about you? How do you feel now?" She seemed a little mellower after some good French white wine, and he had relaxed too. It was easier to talk to her now, as they mused about life over their simple dinner.

"I don't know. I don't think about it much anymore. I just keep busy with my work and the kids. I haven't thought about how I feel in a while. Maybe that's a good sign."

"Do you still miss her?"

"Sure. But after twenty-two years, I'd be crazy not to. We were married for eighteen years, and dated for four years before that. That's a long time in anyone's life. In my case, it's half a lifetime."

"You're forty-four?" She smiled, and he nodded. "I figured you for about thirty-nine."

"I figured you for twenty-five."

"I'm thirty." They both laughed.

"And how does that feel? As terrifying as they say? Sarah hated turning thirty, she felt as though her whole life was behind her. But that was nothing compared to thirty-nine . . . and forty . . . and forty-one. . . . I think that's what got to her finally. She was panicked that she would never accomplish anything before she got really old, so she ran. The dumb thing was that she had accomplished a lot, or at least I thought so anyway, but she didn't."

"I'm not hung up about those things, but I guess that's because I'm not married and bogged down by kids. I've done exactly what I've wanted to do all my life. I guess you could say I was spoiled rotten." She said it with a look of glee, and he laughed, suspecting she was right, as he glanced around the expensively appointed apartment.

"What's important to you? I mean, what do you really care about?"

Myself, she almost said out loud, and then decided to be a little less honest. "My work, I guess. My freedom. Having my own life to do exactly as I please with. I don't share well, and I don't do well with having to live up to other people's expectations. We all play by our own rules, and I like mine. I don't see why one *has* to do anything, get married, have kids, conform to certain rules. I do it my way, and I like that."

"You are spoiled," he said matter-of-factly, but for the moment, he wasn't sure that he minded.

"My mother always told me not to play by anyone else's rules, and I never have. I always seem to be able to look beyond that. Sometimes it's a strength, and sometimes it's a terrible weakness. And sometimes it's a handicap because I don't understand why people complicate life so much. You have to do what you want to do in life, that's the only thing that matters."

"And if you hurt people in the process?" She was treading on sensitive ground, but she was also smart enough to know it.

"Sometimes that's the price you pay. You have to

live with that, but you have to live with yourself, too, and sometimes that's more important."

"I think that's how Sarah felt. But I don't agree with that. Sometimes you owe other people more than you owe yourself, and you just have to tough it out and do what's right for them, even if it costs you." It was the basic difference between him and his wife, and possibly the difference between him and Megan.

"The only person I owe anything to is me, and that's how I like it for now. That's why I don't have kids, and I'm not compelled to be married, although I'm thirty. I think that's what we're really talking about. In a sense, I do agree with you. If you have kids, you owe a lot to them, and not just to yourself. And if you don't want to live up to them, you shouldn't have them. I don't want all that responsibility, which is why I don't have them. But your wife did. I suppose the basic mistake she made was marrying you and having children in the first place." She was more astute than she knew, and she had hit Sarah's philosophies bluntly on the head, much to Oliver's amazement.

"That was my fault, I guess. I talked her into all of it. And then . . . twenty years later, she reverted to what she had been when we met . . . and bolted. . . ."

"You can't blame yourself for that. It was her responsibility too. You didn't force her to marry you at gunpoint. You were doing what you believed in, for you. You can't be responsible in life for other people's behavior." She was a totally independent woman, attached to no one and nothing, but at least she was honest about it.

"What does your family think about the way you

live?" He was curious about that, too, and for a moment, she looked pensive.

"Oh, I suppose it annoys them. But they've given up on me. My father keeps getting married and having kids. He had two with my mother, four with his second wife, and he's just had his seventh child. My mother just gets married, but forgets to have kids, which is fortunate, because she really doesn't like them. She's sort of an Auntie Mame. My sister and I spent most of our lives in expensive boarding schools, from the time we were seven. They would have sent us sooner if they could, but the schools wouldn't take us."

"How awful." Oliver looked horrified. He couldn't even imagine sending his children away. At seven, Sam had still been a baby. "Did it affect you?" But he realized, as soon as he had said it, that it was a stupid question. There were obviously reasons why she was attached to nothing and no one now.

"I suppose it did. I'm not very good at forming what the English call 'lasting attachments.' People come and go. They always have in my life, and I'm used to it . . . with a few exceptions." She looked suddenly sad, and began to clear the table.

"Are you and your sister close?"

She stopped and looked at him oddly. "We were. Very close. She was the only person I could ever count on. We were identical twins, if you can imagine that. Double trouble, as it were. Except that she was everything I wasn't. Good, kind, well-behaved, decent, polite, she played everything by the rules, and believed anything anyone told her. She fell in love with a married man at twenty-one. And committed suicide when he wouldn't leave his wife." Everything had changed for Megan after that, and Oliver could see it in her eyes as she told the story.

"I'm sorry."

"So am I. I've never had another friend like her. It was like losing half of myself. The better half. She was all the good things, all the sweet things I never was and never would be."

"You're too hard on yourself." He spoke to her very softly, and his kindness only made it more painful.

"Not really. I'm honest. If it had been me, I'd have killed the son of a bitch, or shot his wife. I wouldn't have killed myself." And then, with a look of anguish, "When they did the autopsy, they found out she was four months pregnant. She never told me. I was here in school. She was staying in London with my mother." She looked at him with hardened eyes. "Would you like coffee?"

"Yes, please." It was an amazing tale. It was incredible to realize the things that happened in people's lives, the tragedies, the pain, the miracles, the moments that changed a lifetime. He suspected that Megan had been very different before her sister died, but he would never know that.

He followed her out to the kitchen, and she looked up at him with a warm smile. "You're a nice man, Oliver Watson. I don't usually tell people the story of my life, certainly not the first time I meet them."

"I'm honored that you did." It explained a lot about her.

They went back out to the terrace to drink the pungent brew she extracted from the espresso machine, and she sat very close to him as they looked at the view. And he sensed that she wanted something from him, but something that he wasn't ready to give her. It was too soon for him, and he was still afraid of what it would be like to reach out to a woman who wasn't Sarah.

"Would you like to have lunch sometime this week?"

"I'd like that very much." She smiled. He was so sweet and innocent, and yet so strong and so decent and so kind. He was everything she had always feared and never wanted. "Would you like to spend the night with me here?" It was a blunt question and the question took him by surprise as he set his cup down. He looked over at her with a smile that made him look handsome and boyish at the same time.

"If I say no, will you understand that it's not a rejection? I don't like rushing into things. You deserve more than that. We both do."

"I don't want anything more than that." She was honest with him. It was one of her few virtues.

"I do. And so should you. We spend the night, we have some fun, we wander off, so what? What has it given us? Even if we only spend one night together, it would be nicer for both of us if it meant something."

"Don't put too much weight on all that."

"Would it be simpler to say I'm not ready? Or does that make me sound like a loser?"

"Remember what I said, Oliver? You have to play by your own rules. Those are yours. I have mine. I'll settle for lunch, if you're not too shocked at being propositioned."

He laughed, feeling more comfortable again. Anything seemed acceptable to her, she was flexible and undemanding, and so sexy, he wanted to kick himself for not taking her up on her offer then and there before she could change her mind.

"I'll call you tomorrow." He stood up. It was time to go. Before he did something he would regret later, even if she didn't. "Thank you for a wonderful dinner."

"Anytime." She watched him closely as they walked to the door, and then looked into his eyes with something few men saw. Although she had bedded down with many, there were few who knew her. "Oliver . . . thank you . . . for everything. . . ."

"I didn't do anything, except eat and talk, and enjoy being with you. You don't need to thank me."

"Thank you for being who you are . . . even if you never call me." She was used to that, usually after a night of unbound passion. As she had said to him, people came and went in her life. She was used to it. But if he didn't call her, she would somehow miss him.

"I'll call you." And with that, he bent, and took her in his arms and kissed her. She was the first woman he had kissed since his wife had left, and her mouth was inviting and warm, and her body strong and appealing. He wanted to make love to her more than anything, but he also knew he had to go. He wanted to think about this. She was too powerful a woman to be taken lightly.

"Good night," she whispered as the elevator came, and he smiled as he looked her straight in the eye as the doors closed. She stood there for a long time, and then she walked slowly back into her apartment and closed the door. She went back to the terrace, and sat down, thinking about him . . . and the sister she hadn't talked about in years. And without knowing why, or for which of them, she began to cry softly.

Chapter 15

He called her, as promised, first thing the next morning, and invited her to lunch at the Four Seasons that day. He had lain in bed thinking about her for hours the night before, and hating himself for not staying and making love to her. He had had everything in the world handed to him on a silver platter, and he had run away. He felt like a total fool, and he was sure that Megan shared his opinion.

They met at the Four Seasons at noon, and she was wearing a bright red silk dress and high-heeled black patent leather sandals, and he thought she was the sexiest woman he had ever seen. It made him feel like an even bigger fool about the night before, and he told her as much as they settled down at their table. The fountain in the middle of the room was issuing a delicate spray, and there were people everywhere from his business and her own. It was hardly a discreet place for them to meet, but neither of them had any reason to keep secrets.

She told him about the new book she was interested in publishing, and he explained to her at length about one of their new clients. And it was three o'clock before they looked around and realized that they were the only people left in the room. Megan laughed and Oliver looked faintly embarrassed.

"How about dinner tomorrow night?" he asked as they left.

"Can you cook?"

"No." He laughed. "But I can fake it. What would you like? Pizza? Chinese? Pastrami sandwich? Cheeseburger from Hamburger Heaven?"

She laughed at him. "Why don't I pick up some things at my favorite deli and we can make a mess of it together?"

"Sounds great." He loved the idea, the coziness of it, and most of all the prospect of seeing her again.

"Do you like moussaka?"

"I love it." But he was a lot more interested in her than the meal, and he kissed her lightly on the cheek as he put her in a cab and walked back to his office.

"New client?" Daphne asked him at four o'clock when she dropped by his office with some storyboards to show him.

"Who?"

"That knockout I saw you with at lunch." She grinned happily at him across his desk and he blushed and pretended to concentrate on the storyboards for the commercial.

"What are you doing? Spying on me?"

"Do I smell spring in the air? Or is that her perfume?"

"Mind your own business. It's probably Raid. I found a cockroach under my desk this morning."

"A likely story. Even the plastic plants can't breathe in this place, let alone a nice healthy cockroach. She's gorgeous. Who is she?"

"Just a girl I met the other day."

"Very nice. Serious?" She was like a sister to him, and he loved her for it.

"Not yet. And probably never. She's one of those great independent women like my ex-wife, she believes in careers and freedom and not getting too attached to anyone." But it was the first time he had called Sarah that, and that in itself was a step in the right direction.

"She sounds like big trouble. Just have a good time before she breaks your heart."

"I'm getting there."

"Congratulations."

"Thank you. Now, do you mind if we get back to work, or would you rather play advice to the lovelorn?"

"Don't be so touchy." But they forewent their dinner date that night, and they both worked late. And when he went home, he called Megan. She was out, but her answering machine was on. He left his name and just said he'd called to say hello, and reconfirmed their date for the following evening.

She arrived promptly at eight, arms laden with goodies, and they unpacked them together in his kitchen.

"This is a nice place," she said politely, but it was

nothing like hers, and it still had the impersonal feeling of someone else's apartment. Only the children had impressed their personalities on their rooms, but Ollie had done nothing much about the rest, and with Aggie away, there weren't even flowers. He had thought about it too late, after he got home, and was opening a bottle of wine for their dinner.

"How was your day?"

"Not bad. How was yours?" She looked relaxed and happy in a white silk skirt slit almost to her thigh, and a turquoise blouse that made her honey-tanned skin look even darker.

He told her what he had done all day, and it was nice having someone to share it with, as they ate the moussaka at the kitchen table.

"It must be lonely for you here, with the children gone."

He smiled at her, wondering if it was an invitation to go back to her place. "It gets a little quiet without them. But I've been working pretty late most nights." And he suddenly had the feeling that he wouldn't be doing that for much longer.

They talked about crazy things, polo, and baseball, her parents again, and her dislike of the English. He suspected that it was due to the man who had caused the suicide of her sister. She had strong opinions about everything, and when she helped him clear the dishes, he noticed the slit in her skirt again, and felt an irresistible wave of arousal.

They sat in the living room afterward, drinking wine, and talking, and then suddenly, without knowing how it had happened, he found himself kissing her and they were lying on the couch, and he wanted desperately to make love to her. Her skirt was around her waist, her thighs bare, and as his hand passed over the satin of her flesh, he realized that she had worn nothing but her body beneath the skirt, and he groaned with desire as he felt her. His fingers found what he was looking for, and she moaned softly, as the years fell away from him and he was young again, young and in love and overwhelmed with passion. He pulled off her blouse, and she magically undid the skirt, and she lay naked and splendid beneath his hands, and the sight of her took his breath away she was so lovely.

"My God, Megan . . . my God . . ." And then expertly, teasingly, tauntingly, she peeled his clothes from him, and they lay on the couch making love as he had never made love before. She did things to him that he had never dared dream of, and she filled him with a desire so powerful that he took her with force, and came like an earthquake inside her. And then he lay over her, feeling her body tremble, and then begin to writhe slowly. He couldn't believe she wanted more, but she guided his hands back to her, and then pushed his head between her legs, and his tongue caressed the places where she wanted him. She moaned and she cried and she shuddered, and in a moment he entered her again, and they lay making love for hours, again and again. She pulled him to the floor, and then he led her to his bedroom. And at last they lay spent, side by side, and she laughed her deep, throaty laughter, and pulled him to her again as he groaned.

"Good God, woman, you're going to kill me."

"But what a way to die!" They both laughed, and a

little while later, she ran a bath for him, and then they made love in the bathtub. It was an unforgettable night for both of them, and as the sun came up, they were soaking happily in the bathtub. She was nothing like anyone he had ever known, she was overwhelmed with desire, and brought the same out in him. He had never thought himself capable of the feats she had had him perform, but he had loved it.

"Do you realize, we've been making love for ten straight hours? It's seven o'clock in the morning." He was astonished at what they'd done. Astonished, and pleased with himself and with her. It was nothing like his lovemaking with Sarah, and he had thought their love life had been perfect.

"After seven months, don't you think you deserve it?" She smiled at him and he laughed.

"I hadn't looked at it that way. Maybe we should try again." But he was only joking. And she wasn't. She sat astride him in the bathtub as he laughed and rode him again, and much to his amazement, within moments he was aching for her again, and they rolled and splashed and cavorted like two dolphins in the bath-tub, and then he pressed her against the side of the tub and ground himself into her as she moaned, out of control, begging him not to stop, and finally screaming as they both exploded from the depths of the warm, soapy water. "Oh Megan . . . what you do to me! . . ." His voice was deep and hoarse as he kissed her neck and she opened her eyes to look at him and stroke the blond hair that was disheveled from their passion. "I've never known anyone like you."

"It's never been like this for me before." She had

never said that to anyone, and she really meant it. "You're remarkable, Oliver."

"You're pretty terrific yourself." He could hardly make himself get dressed to go to work, and once he was fully dressed again and they were ready to leave, she grabbed him, and began stroking him where he should have been exhausted, but wasn't. "I can't believe this . . . Megan . . . we're never going to get out of here. . . ." And he was beginning to think they shouldn't.

"Maybe we should both call in sick," she whispered as she pulled him to the hall floor, and began to bite his neck and nibble his face, and taunt him as she stroked him. He took her with force again, more force than he knew he had and more strength than he could believe was left after almost twelve hours of making love to Megan Townsend.

And in the end, they did exactly as she suggested. They both called in sick, and spent the day in bed, and on the floor, and on the couch, and in the bathtub. They even made love leaning against the wall in the kitchen, when they finally went in to reheat some moussaka. It was a kind of madness that had overtaken both of them, and that night they lay in bed and he held her close as she fed him chocolate chip cookies.

"Do you think we should call a doctor?" he asked happily. "Maybe it's a disease . . . or we've been drugged . . ."

"Maybe it's the chocolate chip cookies."

"Mmm . . . good . . . give me more . . ." It was difficult to even imagine being apart again, or ever being able to keep their clothes on. And then, he suddenly wondered something he should have thought of the day before, and asked her if she was worried about getting pregnant.

"Nope." She looked perfectly relaxed. "I had my tubes tied nine years ago."

"At twenty-one?" He looked shocked, and then he remembered. That had been when her sister had died, four months pregnant.

"I knew I never wanted kids anyway, and I wasn't going to let some asshole do to me what had happened to Priscilla."

"And you've never regretted it? What if you want children one day?"

"I won't. And if I do, I can adopt them. But I doubt if I'd ever do that. I just don't want that kind of headache. Why? Do you want more kids?"

"I used to. But Sarah never wanted more children. She had her tubes tied, too, when we had Sam. I always regretted it, but she never did."

"Would you want more kids now?" She didn't look worried, just intrigued. She couldn't imagine wanting any more children, or any at all, for her own sake.

"I'm not sure. It's a little late now. But I suppose I wouldn't mind if it happened."

"Well, don't count on me." She grinned and lay back against her pillows.

And then, feeling easy and open with her, he confided in her about Benjamin. "My eighteen-year-old son is expecting a baby in September. It's a hell of a mess. He's working as a busboy and supporting the girl. They both dropped out of high school, when he could have gone to Harvard."

"Maybe he will one day." But she looked suddenly

sorry for Ollie. It was obvious how upset he was about the boy. "Will they keep the baby?"

"They want to. I've done everything I could to discourage them. At least, thank God, they're not getting married." He was grateful for Sandra's persistence on that score.

"Maybe they'll come to their senses when they're faced with the reality of it. Babies are only cute in diaper ads. The rest of the time they're little monsters."

"And how many babies have you known, Miss Townsend?"

"As few as possible, thank you very much." She rolled over and got a firm grip on his favorite member, and then pulled back the blanket and moved down to play her tongue gently around it. "Personally, I prefer daddies to babies . . ."

"How lucky for me." He smiled and closed his eyes, and then pulled her to him to reciprocate in kind. But that night, they finally fell asleep, exhausted, just after midnight. It had been a marathon day, and one he would never forget. The miracle of Megan Townsend.

Chapter 16

The romance blazed on through the hottest month of the year. The weather was torrid in August, and so was their passion. They alternated between his apartment and hers, and one night, even spent the night making love on the terrace. But fortunately, they were higher than the other buildings around them.

He hardly ever had time to see Daphne anymore, but she knew what was going on, and she was happy for him. He had a perennially glazed look in his eyes, and he was constantly vague and absentminded, and she hoped, for his sake, that he was screwing his brains out.

They had driven out to Purchase one day, so he could see Benjamin and his father, and he had dropped Megan off at her father's, and then picked her up to take her back to the city. But they didn't stop at the house. Somehow he didn't want to go there with her. It was still too full of memories of Sarah.

But he seldom thought of her now. He was obsessed with Megan, and their lovemaking, and her body. And on a blazing Sunday afternoon, they were walking around naked in his apartment, when the phone rang. He couldn't imagine who it was. Probably Daphne, checking up on him, although she seldom called him now. She didn't want to disturb him.

The crackle of long-distance wires met his ears when he picked it up, and then the phone went dead, and it rang again, and an overseas operator told him there was a collect call from San Remo. He could hardly hear anything, and he smiled, as Megan paraded before him. And for a moment, he felt sad, thinking of the adjustments they'd have to make. The children were due home the following weekend.

"Hello?" He could hear a sound in the distance. It sounded like crying, but he knew it was only static.

"Hello?" he shouted and then suddenly he heard Mel crying and saying over and over, "Daddy . . ."

"Melissa? Melissa! Talk to me!" The line faded on them, and then she came back, with an echo, but a little clearer. "What is it? What happened?"

". . . an accident . . ." Oh God . . . no . . . Sam . . . not Sam . . . please . . . and not even Sarah . . .

"Baby, I can't hear you! Talk louder!" His eyes filled with tears as he waited, and Megan watched. He had totally forgotten her, in his desperation to understand his daughter.

". . . an accident . . . killed . . . Mommy . . ." Oh Jesus. It was Sarah. . . .

He stood up as though that would improve the connection and shouted into the phone as loud as he could. In Italy, it was midnight. "What happened to your mother?"

". . . a car . . . driving . . . we're in San Remo . . . Jean-Pierre . . ."

"Melissa, is your mother hurt?" And Megan saw in his face then that he still loved her, but after twenty years, she didn't blame him. And she stood paralyzed with fear too. It reminded her of the call she'd gotten almost ten years before . . . from her mother . . . Darling . . . oh darling . . . it's Priscilla . . .

"Mom's all right. . . ." The tears spilled down his cheeks as he heard the words.

"Sam? What about Sam?"

". . . Sam broke his arm . . . Daddy, it was so awful . . ." And then she began crying again, and he could understand nothing. But if Sam was alive . . . he was alive, wasn't he? . . . and Sarah . . . and Melissa was on the phone . . . "A car hit us . . . full on . . . the driver was killed . . . and two kids . . . and Jean-Pierre . . . Jean-Pierre was killed instantly . . . oh Daddy . . . it was so awful . . ." Oh Jesus . . . poor man . . . but at least the children were alive. His children anyway, if not the others. It was a terrible, selfish way to look at it, but he was deeply grateful.

"Baby, are you all right? . . . are you hurt?"

". . . I'm fine . . ."

"Where's Mom?"

"At the hospital . . . told me to call you . . . we have to go back to France for the funeral . . . We'll be home on Friday."

"But you're all right? You're sure? Was Mommy hurt?"

". . . black eye . . . all cut up . . . but she's okay. . . ." It was like playing telegraph, but they were alive, even if bruised and broken. And they had seen their mother's lover die, and another man, and two children. He shuddered at the thought of it.

"Do you want me to come over?"

". . . don't think so . . . we're going to be staying . . . with Jean-Pierre's parents . . . going back tonight . . . Mom says you have the number."

"I have it. I'll call you. And, baby . . ." he began to cry as he held the phone in a trembling hand, ". . . I love you . . . tell Sam I love him too . . . and tell Mommy I'm sorry."

Mel was crying again, and eventually the connection got so bad, they had to hang up. Ollie looked badly shaken as he hung up the phone and stared up at Megan. He had totally forgotten her as he talked to his daughter.

"Are they all right?" She was standing naked, and lovely, before him, as she handed him a glass of brandy.

"I think so. We had a terrible connection. There's been an accident . . . several people were killed, from what I could understand. My wife's friend was killed instantly. He was driving. In San Remo."

"Jesus. How awful." She sat down next to him, and took a sip of the brandy he hadn't touched. "Were the kids hurt?"

"Sam broke his arm. I think Melissa's all right. Sarah got cut up, but I think they're all right. It must have been grim." And then, still shaken, he looked at

Megan. "When she started talking, I thought . . . I thought Sam . . . or maybe even Sarah . . . It's a terrible thing to say with other people getting killed, but I'm glad it wasn't."

"I know." She put an arm around him and held him close, and for a long time, they just sat there. They stayed at his place that night, in case the children called again, and for the first time in a month, they didn't make love at all. All he could think about were his children. And slowly, the shock of it brought them both back to their senses. Their wild idyll was going to change when the children came home. He couldn't stay out all night, and she couldn't stay at the apartment with him, and they would have to be far more circumspect around his children. In a way, it made them want to do as much as they could, while they were still alone, and in another way, the realization of what was coming so soon had already changed things.

And by Thursday night, they were both nervous and depressed. They lay awake all night, making love and talking, and wishing that things could be different.

"We could get married one day," he said, only half jokingly, and she looked at him with mock horror.

"Don't be silly. That's a little extreme, isn't it?"

"Would it be?" He had never known anyone like her, and he was totally under her spell for the moment.

"For me, it would. Oliver, I can't marry anyone. I'm not the type, and you know it."

"You heat up a great moussaka."

"Then marry the guy at the deli where they made it."

"He can't be as cute as you, although I've never met him."

"Be serious. What would I do with a husband and three children?"

He pretended to think it over and she laughed. "I could think of a few things . . ."

"You don't need to be married for that, fortunately." They had had a glorious month, but she was already acting as though it was over. "I just don't want more than this."

"Maybe one day you will."

"If I do, you'll be the first to know. I promise."

"Seriously?"

"As serious as I can be about subjects like this. I told you before, marriage is not for me. And you don't need another wife to run shrieking out the door. You need some wonderful, smart, beautiful girl who's going to love you to pieces and take care of your kids, and give you fourteen more babies."

"What a thought. I think you're confusing me with your father."

"Not quite. But I am definitely not what the doctor ordered, Oliver. I know what I am, and some of it's all right, and some of it isn't. In my own way, I'm probably a lot like your wife, and that's exactly what you don't need. Be honest."

He wondered if she was right, and if he had found himself a newer, somewhat racier edition of Sarah. He had never thought of that, but it was possible, although the idea depressed him. "What happens now?"

"We enjoy it for what it is, for as long as we can, and when it gets too complicated for either of us, we say good-bye, with a kiss and a hug and a thank-you."

"Simple as that?"

"Simple as that."

"I don't buy that. You grow attached to people in life. Don't you think after a month of being together all the time we've grown attached to each other now?"

"Sure. But don't confuse great sex with good loving. The two do not always go hand in hand. I like you, I care about you, maybe I even love you. But it's going to be different when the children come home. Maybe too different for both of us, and if it is, we just have to accept it and move on. You can't kill yourself over things like that in life. It's not worth it." She was so damn casual, so nonchalant, just as she had been when she picked him up on the train, and called to invite him to dinner. As long as it was fun, it was fine, but when it wasn't fun anymore, just toss it. She was right. He had told himself he was falling in love with her. But maybe she was right there, too, maybe what he was really in love with was her body.

"Maybe you're right. I just don't know." And they made love again that night, but this time it was different. And the next morning she went back to her own place, taking with her all traces of herself that for the past month she had left at his apartment. Her makeup, her deodorant, the pills she used in case she got a migraine, the perfume he had bought her, her hot rollers, her Tampax, and the few dresses she had left in his closet. It made him lonely just seeing the empty space, and he was reminded again of the pain of losing Sarah. Why did everything have to end? Why did it all change and move on? He wanted to hang on to all of it forever.

But the point was driven home with even greater force when he saw his children get off the plane, and Sarah behind them. She had a look of shock on her face he'd never seen there before, and grief and loneliness. It was worse than any pain she'd ever felt for him, and her eyes looked woefully out at him, surrounded by two vicious shiners, and a bandage on her chin that covered fourteen stitches. Sam looked frightened as well, and he was clinging to his mother's hand with his good arm, the other was in a cast from fingertip to shoulder. And Melissa started crying the moment she saw him. She flew into his arms, sobbing incoherently, and a moment later, Sam was there, too, the awkward arm in a sling, as he clung to his daddy.

And then Oliver looked up at the woman who had been his wife, and was no more, and he knew with full force how much she had loved the boy who had died in San Remo.

"I'm sorry, Sarrie . . . I'm so sorry . . ." It was like losing a part of himself, seeing her so broken. "Is there anything I can do?" They walked slowly to the baggage claim as she shook her head, and Melissa talked about the funeral. Jean-Pierre had been an only child and it had been awful.

Oliver nodded, and tried to comfort them, and then looked over Sam's head at Sarah. "Do you want to stay at the house in Purchase? We could stay in town, except for the Labor Day weekend."

But she only shook her head and smiled. She seemed quieter, and not older, but wiser. "I start school on Monday. I want to go back. I have a lot to do." And she didn't tell him that that summer she had finally started her novel. "But thank you anyway. The kids are going to come up in a few weeks, and I'll be all right." But she dreaded going through his things when she got back to the apartment in Cambridge. It suddenly made her more aware of what Oliver had gone through when she had left. In a way, that had been a little bit like dying. She had loved Jean-Pierre like a son and a friend, a lover, and a father, and she had been able to give him everything she had denied Oliver in recent years, because he wanted nothing from her. He had taught her a lot about giving and loving . . . and dying . . .

Sarah flew straight on to Boston, once the children were in Oliver's hands, and they took a cab into the city. They were quiet and subdued and upset and Oliver asked Sam if his arm hurt, and told him he wanted to take him to an American doctor. He already had an appointment for later that afternoon, but when they went, the orthopedist assured him that the arm had been properly set in San Remo. And Mel had grown taller and blonder and lovelier over the summer, despite the trauma.

And it was so good being back with them again, it suddenly reminded him of how much he had missed them, without knowing it. And suddenly he wondered about the madness of his affair with Megan. They were going to the house in Purchase the next day, for the weekend, and he had invited Megan out for the day on Sunday, to meet his children. And Aggie was coming back on Monday. In the meantime, they were going to fend for themselves. And he cooked them scrambled eggs and toast when they got back to the apartment. And little by little, they told him everything they'd done that summer. They'd had a great time until the accident. And listening to them made him realize again how distant from his life Sarah was now. He wasn't even sure anymore if he still loved her.

The children went to bed right after they ate, and Sam even fell asleep at the kitchen table. The time difference had caught up with him, and they were both exhausted.

Oliver tucked Sam into bed, careful to prop the arm on a pillow as they'd been told to do by the doctor, and then he went to check on Melissa, who was wearing a puzzled frown as she held up a mysterious object in her bedroom. "What's that?" It was a woman's blouse, with a bra tangled in with it, and as she held it up, his face froze and he could smell Megan's perfume. He had forgotten the time he had chased her into Mel's room and almost torn her clothes off as they laughed, and then rushed back to his bedroom eventually to make love in the bathtub.

"I don't know . . ." He didn't know what to say to her. He couldn't begin to explain what had gone on in the past month, not to his sixteen-year-old daughter. "Is it yours?" He tried to look innocent, and she was almost young enough to believe him.

"No, it's not." She sounded like an accusing wife. And then he slapped his head, feeling like a fool in a sitcom.

"I know what that is. I let Daphne stay here one weekend, when I was in Purchase. They were painting her apartment." Melissa looked instantly relieved, and he kissed her good night, and retreated to his own room, feeling as though he had just escaped a life sentence.

He called Megan late that night and told her how

much he missed her. He could hardly wait until Sunday. And the next morning, the three of them left for the country. They opened the house, which smelled hot and musty, and put the air-conditioning on, and went to buy groceries, and after lunch they went to his father's to pick up Andy. And they found their grandfather looking extremely well, and once again puttering around his wife's garden, but this time his neighbor, Margaret Porter, was helping. She had a new haircut, and he was wearing a new pale blue linen blazer, and as Ollie and the children drove up, they'd been laughing. It was nice seeing him so happy again. And Oliver was relieved. Every time he saw him now, he couldn't get the picture out of his mind of his father holding his mother's hand when she died, and kissing her good-bye. It broke his heart, but finally, after three months, George was looking a lot better.

"Welcome home!" he shouted to the kids, and Margaret went inside to get lemonade and homemade cookies. It was almost like old times, except that Sam said the cookies were better. And Margaret smiled, and stuck up for her late friend.

"Your grandmother was the best cook I ever knew. She made the best lemon meringue pie I ever tasted." George smiled thinking about it, and it brought back memories to Ollie of his childhood.

"What have you been up to, Dad?" Ollie asked as they sat outside under the old elm tree. They had never put in a pool, and George insisted they didn't miss it. And if he wanted to swim, they could always go to visit the children in Purchase.

"We've been busy. The garden's a lot of work. And

we went into New York last week. Margaret had some business to take care of, and we went to an off-Broadway play. It was very good actually." He sounded surprised, and smiled as he glanced at Margaret, and Oliver looked surprised too. His father had always hated going to the theater. And then George looked at Sam. "How did you do that, son?" Sam told them about the accident, and Melissa added her details, and the two elders were horrified, and as grateful as Oliver had been that they'd survived it. "It makes you realize how precious life is," he said to the two young people. "And how short. Your friend was only twenty-five years old. That's a terrible shame . . . terrible . . ." Ollie saw him take Margaret's hand, and wondered what that meant, and a moment later she took the children inside for more lemonade and a fresh batch of cookies.

"You're looking well, Dad," Oliver said pointedly after the children were gone, wondering if there was a reason for it, and he was suddenly reminded of his own fling with Megan. Maybe his father was having a little flirtation with his neighbor. But there was no harm in that. They were both lonely people in their seventies and they had a right to a little friendly company now and then, and he knew how lonely his father was without his mother.

"I've been well, Son. Margaret takes very good care of me. She used to be a nurse, you know. And her husband was a doctor."

"I remember."

"We'd like to take you to dinner sometime. Maybe in the city. Margaret likes to go into New York from time to time. She says it keeps her young. And I'm not sure if that's what does it, but she has more energy than a woman half her age. She's a terrific girl." Oliver smiled at the idea of calling a woman of seventy-odd years a girl, but what the hell, and then he almost fell out of his chair, as his father looked at him and smiled, with mischief in his eyes. "We're getting married next month, Oliver. I know that will be difficult for you to understand. But we're not young. We don't have much time, for all we know. And we don't want to waste what's left. I think your mother would have understood it."

"You're *what*?" Oliver turned in his chair to stare at him. "Mom has been gone for three months, and you're marrying your next-door neighbor?" Had he gone crazy? Was he senile? What was wrong with him? How could he even consider such a thing? It was disgusting.

"You can't be serious." Oliver was livid, and he looked it.

"I am serious. I have a right to more than just sit alone in a chair, don't you think? Or does it offend you to think of people our age getting 'involved,' as you young people call it. We could have an affair, but I think I owe her the decency of marriage."

"You owe Mom the decency of respecting her memory. She's not even cold in her grave yet!" He stood up and started to pace up and down as George Watson calmly watched him, and from the kitchen window Margaret saw what was going on with a worried eye. She had told George it would be like that, and he had told her they had a right to their own lives. They weren't dead yet, though they might be soon, but he didn't want to waste the time they had left. And although it was different from his life with Phyllis, he loved her.

"I have every respect for your mother, Oliver. But I have a right to my own life too. So do you. And one day you'll probably remarry. You can't spend the rest of your life mourning Sarah."

"Thank you for the advice." It was inconceivable. Until a few weeks before, he had been sitting around in chaste celibacy and his father had been having an *affair* with his neighbor. "I think you ought to give this a great deal of thought."

"I have. We're getting married on the fourteenth, and we'd like you and the children to come, if you will."

"I'll do nothing of the sort. And I want you to come to your senses." But as he said it, Margaret returned to them with George's straw hat, and a cool drink, and the heart pill he took every afternoon, and even Oliver couldn't miss the gentle loving of the look that passed between them.

But he was stiff and unyielding until they left, he hurried the children into the car, thanked Margaret politely, and halfway back to Purchase, remembered that they had forgotten Andy. He called his father when he got home, and told him he'd pick the dog up the following weekend.

"That's fine. We enjoy having him here." And then, "I'm sorry I upset you, Oliver. I understand what you must feel. But try to see it from my point of view too. And she's a wonderful woman."

"I'm happy for you, Dad," he said through clenched teeth. "But I still think you're being hasty."

"Perhaps. But we have to do what we think is right. And at our age, there isn't much time left. Not good time anyway. You never know what grief is just around the corner."

"All the more reason not to rush into anything."

"That depends on how you look at it. Tell me that when you're my age." And Oliver realized as he hung up, that it disgusted him to think of his father making love to Margaret Porter. And he said as much to Megan that night, when he called her.

"Don't be ridiculous. Do you think your sex drive will die before you do? I certainly hope not. He's right, and he's smart. Why should he sit alone? You have your own life, your kids do too. He has a right to do more than spend the rest of his life alone, reminiscing about your mother. Is that what you really want him to do?" It wasn't, and yet it was, and her view on the subject annoyed him.

"You're as bad as he is. I think you're both oversexed." And then he told her about Mel finding her blouse and bra, and she only laughed.

"I remember that night well," she said mischievously.

"So do I. Christ, how I miss you. I'm practically having withdrawals."

"We'll catch a quickie tomorrow in the pool." The thought of it, with his children afoot, almost made him shudder. Things were definitely going to be very different.

"We may have to wait until Monday."

"Don't count on it. We'll think of something." He

smiled as he put down the phone, and wondered if she was right about his father. But he didn't even want to think about that. Imagine his father getting married at his age! The very idea of it was revolting.

Chapter 17

Oliver picked Megan up at the train and she was wearing short shorts and a little halter top in white with black polka dots, and all he wanted to do was tear off her clothes and make love to her in the car, but he restrained himself while she laughed, and stroked his crotch as they drove home to the children.

"Stop that . . . Megan Townsend, you are driving me crazy!"

"That, my dear, is the whole point." And then, as though switching gears, she told him all about Friday's successful auction. . . .

The kids were in the pool when they drove up, with Sam's arm in a huge garbage bag so he could swim, and Mel lying on a raft in a new bikini she had bought in the south of France. And both children looked up with interest as their father approached them with

Megan. He introduced everyone, and then took Megan inside to change, but as he showed her the small dressing room, she pulled him swiftly into it with her, and reached her hand into his shorts and began caressing him until he groaned in a whisper.

"Megan . . . don't! . . . the kids . . ."

"Shh . . . they'll never know the difference." She had missed him as much as he had missed her. After a month of orgasmic feasting, they had gone three whole days without each other. And she had the door locked and his pants down around his knees in a moment, as she licked and sucked and kissed, and he pulled off her halter, and then slid down her shorts. And as usual, she had nothing beneath them. And then she was on her knees, kissing him, and he gently pushed her down, and made frantic love to her on the dressing room floor, as she shuddered and moaned, and just as he came with a sound of animal pleasure, he could hear Sam start to shout, and bang on several doors looking for him, and then start to pound on the dressing room door, as Oliver jumped a foot and stared at Megan wild-eyed. He put a finger to his lips, begging her not to give him away as she giggled.

"Dad! Are you in there?" It was a tiny room, and Oliver was sure the child could hear his breathing. He shook his head, wanting Megan to say he wasn't.

"No, he's not. I'll be right out." She spoke from the floor, with his father on top of her, awash with terror.

"Okay. Do you know where he is?"

"I don't know. He said he was going to get something."

"Okay." And then more door slamming and he was gone, and Ollie leapt to his feet, threw cold water on his face, pulled up his pants, and tried to straighten his hair as she laughed at him.

"I told you we'd manage it somehow."

"Megan, you're crazy!" He was whispering, convinced the child knew, but she wasn't frightened.

"Relax. He's ten years old, he has no idea what his father is up to."

"Don't be so sure." He kissed her quickly and unlocked the door, as she casually fished in her bag for her bikini. "I'll see you at the pool." He just hoped she would behave herself there or Mel would be horrified. But on the other hand, she had just spent the summer with her mother and her twenty-five-year-old lover. He had a right to his own life, didn't he, and just as the thought crossed his mind, he heard the echo of his father's words . . . but this was different, wasn't it? Or was it?

And he found Sam waiting for him in the kitchen. He had wanted a Coke and couldn't find one. "Where were you, Dad?"

"I was in the garage, looking for a wrench."

"What for?" Oh God, leave me alone, I don't know . . . it had been so simple while they were away, and now this was so crazy.

He poured Sam a Coke, and went back to the pool, where Megan was slowly easing herself into the water in a minuscule red bikini. Her cascade of dark hair was piled high on her head, and Mel was watching her with a look of female appraisal.

The two women never spoke, and Oliver felt like a large puppy dog, circling the pool, watching them both, keeping an eye on Sam, and feeling incredibly nervous.

"I like your bathing suit," Megan said to Mel. It was pink and ruffled and comparatively pure compared to her own, which was barely more than two tiny patches on her breasts, and a loincloth with a thong. But she wore it well. She had an incredible body.

"I got it in France."

"Did you have a good time?"

"All right." She didn't want to talk about the accident anymore, and she didn't think Megan knew. Her father had said she was a casual friend he hadn't seen in a while. "We've only been home for two days." Megan swam past her with long, smooth strokes, and a few minutes later, Mel left her raft, to make a spectacular dive. It was as though there was a competition between the two, and the tension around the pool was dense all afternoon, particularly between the two women.

They had hot dogs for lunch, and Megan began talking about spending time in England as a child. But it was obvious Mel wasn't impressed. And Megan made no particular effort with her or Sam. It made Oliver uncomfortable watching all of them, and he was almost relieved when they dropped her off at her place, that evening, in town. Her eyes blew him a kiss, and she disappeared with a wave, as Mel visibly relaxed in the car, and Sam snorted.

"She's nice, isn't she?" Ollie said, regretting the words almost as soon as they were out of his mouth. Mel turned on him like a snake, with a look of fury.

"She looks like a whore."

"Melissa!"

"Did you see that bathing suit?"

"Yeah." Sam grinned, and then looked chastened as his sister shot him a quelling look in the backseat.

"She's a very nice girl," Oliver defended as they drove home.

"I don't think she likes kids very much," Sam offered.

"What makes you say that?"

"I don't know." He shrugged. "She didn't say very much. But she sure looks good, doesn't she, Dad?"

"She's smart too. She's an editor with a publishing house."

"So what? All she cares about is flaunting her body around." Mel had sensed her sexuality, and had hated it, unlike her male relatives, whose eyes had been glued to her all afternoon.

Oliver let the subject rest, and that night after Sam was in bed, Mel came out of her room with a frown. "I guess you can give her these." She handed him the blouse and bra she'd found in her room two days before. "They're hers, aren't they, Dad?"

"What makes you say that?" He felt as though he'd been caught in the act, as though he'd defiled their home, which he had. But he had a right to do what he wanted to, didn't he? After all, he was a grown man. "I told you, they're Daph's."

"No, they're not. Daphne's got much bigger boobs. These are Megan's." She spoke accusingly and he could feel himself blush as he looked at his daughter.

"Look, Mel, there are some things that grown-ups do, that just don't involve kids, and are better left alone."

"She's a tramp." Mel's eyes blazed at him, but now he was angry.

"Don't say that! You don't even know the girl."

"No, and I don't want to. And she doesn't give a damn about us. She just has her tongue hanging out over you, like a dog or something. I can't stand her." The rivalry of two women fighting over him seemed strange as he listened to her. And he couldn't help wondering why she hated Megan. Except that he had to admit, Megan had made no special effort to win them over. She had talked mostly to him, and only occasionally to his children. It hadn't really turned out the way he had wanted.

"She's just a friend, that's all. It's no big deal, Mel. Relax."

"You mean that?" She looked relieved.

"What?"

"You're not in love with her?"

"I don't know. I like her."

"Well, she doesn't like you as much. She likes herself more." He wondered if Mel was right, and if she was being jealous or perceptive.

"Don't worry about it." But then as she left the room, he found himself thinking again about his father. Was he being a jealous child, like Mel, or was he right to object to his marrying Margaret Porter? And what right did he have to interfere? Was he going to keep him company at night and on weekends? Was he going to be there for him, bringing him his heart pills? Oliver wanted his own life, and his father had a right to the same, however much it made Oliver lonely for his mother.

Ollie decided to call him that night, and when he did, Margaret answered. It made him jump for a minute, and then he relaxed and asked to speak to his father.

"Hi, Dad . . . I just wanted to tell you that . . ." He didn't know how to say it. "I love you very much, that's all. You do what's right for you, and forget about the rest. You're old enough to know what you want by now, and what you need. And if she makes you happy," tears stung his eyes as he said the words, "go for it! You have my blessing!"

There was a little sob at the other end, and then George Watson cleared his throat and thanked him. "She's a fine woman, Son . . . not your mother, by any means," as he said it, he hoped Margaret couldn't hear him, but he owed Oliver that much. Phyllis had been his mother, after all, "but she's a good soul, and I love her."

"Good luck to you both."

"Will you come to our wedding?"

"Damn right I will."

"September fourteenth. Now don't forget it." Oliver laughed. His father sounded young again, and he was happy for him. What the hell, he had a right to it. More power to him if he could find a woman he loved and be happy with her.

He called Megan after he hung up, feeling better again, but she was out, and he felt his heart give a little tug as he left his name on the machine, and then lay on the empty bed she had left him. He wondered if it had all been a crazy dream, and if Mel was right. But Megan had never pretended to be anything other than she was. She was out to have a good time, and not hurt anyone. She didn't want anything more than that . . . she didn't want ties . . . or husbands . . . or homes . . . or children . . . and as he lay there thinking about her, he wondered if his summer romance was over. It had been fun, but it wasn't going to be easy now. And Megan wasn't going to hang around, waiting for him. And the kids sure as hell hadn't taken to her. Sometimes, life just wasn't easy.

Chapter 18

The Labor Day weekend was a nice homecoming for all of them. They had a barbecue near the pool, as they always did, and the children invited friends, and his father came over with Margaret. They brought cookies and treats, and homemade bread, and they brought the dog, and this time Oliver congratulated them both, and let his father announce it to the children. They were a little startled at first, but they took their cue from their dad, and if he thought it was all right, then they guessed it was too. Even Daphne came. And she had agreed to spend the weekend. Only Megan had declined. She had gone to East Hampton instead, which bothered Ollie, but he couldn't convince her to come. She just said it wasn't her scene, kids and dogs and barbecues, and she didn't want to intrude on them. But the truth was that it bored her. He hadn't seen her all week, and he was going crazy without her, but she was working late and so was he. The kids were home, and he was waiting for them to settle down again, which she seemed to think wasn't important.

Benjamin and Sandra came to the barbecue, though, and this time the girl looked truly pathetic. Her face was bloated to twice its size, she could barely walk, she was so large, and it was hard to believe she had ever been pretty. Benjamin looked thin and pale, in comparison, and he was feeling the load of his two jobs, and Sandra did nothing but complain, and sometimes he thought he would go crazy. His father handed him a beer, after Mel took Sandra into the house to lie down for a while, and Oliver looked at Benjamin carefully, wondering when he was going to admit he couldn't hack it anymore, or if he was going to let it kill him.

"How's it going, Son?"

"Okay, I guess. I'm going to have to get another job pretty soon. They're closing the gas station down, and letting me go in a few weeks. And the restaurant doesn't pay enough. But I've got some pretty good leads, and after the baby's born, Sandra says she'll go back to work pretty quickly." He tried to sound hopeful, but it was obvious to his father that he was getting seriously discouraged, and who wouldn't have? At the age of eighteen, to be expecting a child, supporting a seventeen-year-old pseudo wife, and working two jobs, was hardly anyone's idea of a happy life, least of all his father's.

"Are you going to let me help you out before it kills us both, or are you going to be stubborn?" The boy smiled, looking older and wiser than he had before. He had learned a lot in the last few months, but none of it easy or fun, and seeing him like this was a weight on his father's heart.

"We'll see, Dad. The baby'll be here in three weeks, and after that, things'll be okay."

"Having a baby around isn't easy."

"Yeah, I know. We've been taking a class at the Y about how to take care of it, and Lamaze and all that stuff. I want to be there at the delivery, to help Sandra." He was going all the way with what he'd taken on, and Oliver had to admire him, if nothing else, but he was desperately worried about him.

"Will you call me if you need help with anything?"

"Sure."

"Promise?"

Benjamin grinned again, and for a fraction of an instant, looked almost like his old self. "Sure I will, Dad. Thanks."

They joined the others after that and talked about Grandpa's wedding. Benjamin promised to come, and Oliver offered to give the bride away. Daphne was happy for them, and later on, in a quiet moment, she asked Oliver what was happening with Megan, but he only shrugged unhappily and told her he didn't know for the moment.

"She came out to meet the kids last week and it was not exactly a glowing success. She's not into that kind of thing, and right now I've got my hands full. It was different while they were gone. But now, I don't know, Daph."

"She doesn't sound like the warm maternal type, but perhaps that wasn't the main thrust of your interest."

Oliver smiled at his friend, and then laughed. "You might say that."

"Well, at least it got you out of your shell." It certainly had done that. He smiled again. "That's nice about your father."

"It seems kind of crazy, doesn't it, Daph? Benjamin is about to have a kid, my dad's getting married, and I'm sitting around by myself."

"That'll change one of these days." But he was in no rush. If the affair with Megan ended, it wouldn't be the end of the world. He wasn't even divorced, and he still couldn't imagine getting remarried. He was busy with his life, with his children, and his work. The rest could wait for the moment.

They swam late into the night, and the children sang, and his father left eventually, and Benjamin had to get to work. Daphne helped Oliver clean up, and Aggie was back after a relaxing summer. And it felt somehow as though they'd all come a long way since the summer began. And it hurt only briefly when he remembered the year before when Sarah was there and life had been so simple and sane. Nothing was quite as simple anymore. And nothing was sure now. But life was sweet, and he was grateful for what he had. If he never had more than this again, even that might be all right.

He finally saw Megan at her place the night they got home, and after making love for hours, they finally talked things out, and she admitted to him that she'd gone to East Hampton with an old lover. It hurt to have her tell him that, and yet, he had suspected it anyway.

"It's over, isn't it?"

"Not really." She lay languidly in her bed and looked at him. "I'd be happy to see you anytime. But I'm not going to play mommy to your kids, if that's what you want. And you don't have the kind of time for me you did when they were away. That's just the way things go sometimes, Oliver. But between us, nothing's changed." She was so casual about it all, everything was easy and unattached and purely sexual. He had loved that about her at first, and yet now, it didn't seem enough. He didn't want to share her with anyone else, didn't want to have to have a life separate from his children. But it was too difficult being with someone who didn't really care about them, and whom they resented. And he knew now that she would make no effort for them. She really didn't want to. It was part of her all-out effort to stay unattached. In the end, she had won. But it was a losing game.

"I'm sad things worked out this way," he told her honestly as he dressed, and this time she didn't fight to take his clothes off. It had changed for her, too, whether she admitted it or not.

"There was really no other way it could have gone. I told you that from the first. You don't need a woman like me, Oliver. You deserve better than that. You deserved better than Sarah. Don't settle for less this time, my friend. If you do, you'll always get hurt, and you don't deserve that."

"Why don't you want more than that?" Why didn't she? Why were they so different?

"I'm not made that way, I guess. Priscilla was . . . but I never was. It's too painful, I suppose. I'm not willing to take those risks, to throw my heart out there, to take chances with my life and my heart. I just want to have a good time, Ollie. That's all I want. Simple as that." And it had been that. A good time. A great time. A wild, wonderful time, and he could have gone on forever, except that eventually the moussaka would have gone stale. One needed more than that. At least he did, even if she didn't.

"What do I say as I leave?" he asked her sadly, as he stood in the hall, fully dressed, knowing he wouldn't be back again. "Thank you?"

"You say, 'so long,' 'see you around,' 'thanks for a good time.' "

"Thank you for more than that . . . thank you for something very special. You're very special. Don't forget that. And maybe one of these days, you'll get brave."

"Don't count on it." She kissed him lightly on the lips and pressed the button for the elevator. And as the doors closed, he saw her for the last time, wrapped in a white satin kimono, smiling at him, the mane of dark hair ebony against her ivory face.

He knew he was going to miss her. And he felt sad for her as he walked home that night. Sad for what she would never have, for what she didn't want, for what she was afraid to reach out for. And far above, she stood on the terrace, watching him, and she gave a silent wave. She walked back into her living room, and turned on the music. She finished the brandy he had left, and sat down alone on the couch, remembering how his flesh had felt when she touched him.

"You would have liked him a lot," she whispered to the memory of the twin who was long gone. He would have been perfect for her, and Megan would have teased her, about how decent he was, and how square and how tame. Megan smiled to herself, thinking of them both, and then she walked slowly back to her bedroom. She had work to do and another book auction to run the next day. There was no point thinking about the past. She forced them both from her heart, like furniture she no longer had room for, took a shower, brushed her teeth, turned the light out, and went to bed, knowing that it had been nice for a while, but it was over with Oliver Watson. She didn't cry, she didn't mourn. She was used to handling these things, and as she drifted off to sleep, she forced herself to think of something else. Her moment with Oliver was over.

Chapter 19

George Watson's wedding to Margaret Porter was exactly what it should have been. It was tender and sweet and simple, and there were tears in Daphne's eyes as the couple took their vows. Weddings always did that to her, probably because she'd never had one. But this one particularly so, because they were both such dear people.

The bride wore a simple beige lace dress and carried a bouquet of tiny beige orchids. She wore a small, elegant hat, and Oliver gave her away, as promised, and then stood next to his children with damp eyes, as the organ played.

The ceremony was brief and to the point, and afterward they all went to the house in Purchase for a small reception. Oliver had decided to do that for them, and he had invited a few of their close friends. Many of them had been shocked at first, and then, like Oliver, they had mellowed. It was difficult to deny them the joy they obviously shared, and plainly deserved.

It was a sunny September afternoon, and the bride and groom left at five o'clock to drive into the city. They were spending the night at the Plaza Hotel and then flying to San Francisco for two weeks. Margaret had relatives there, and they wanted to go to the opera. They were going to spend a few days in Carmel, and then go back to San Francisco and fly home. It sounded like the perfect trip for them, and Margaret hadn't said so, but she didn't want to be far from "civilization." With George's heart, she liked keeping near places where she knew he could get competent medical care. But he looked in need of nothing but her kind hand, as they left for the city, with the guests throwing rose petals after them, as the two old people beamed and waved.

"It was perfect, absolutely perfect!" Daphne raved as they sat in the living room afterward. "Maybe I'll get married when I'm their age." Oliver shook his head and grinned.

"You would do something like that. Maybe I'll join you." He had told her about the end of the romance with Megan. And she wasn't surprised, although she was sorry for him. It had been a good distraction over the past two months, and now that it was over he had that lonely look again, although he claimed that he was happy.

"You just have to go back to the drawing board again."

"What a pain in the ass." The prospect of dating again filled him with despair. But he also recognized that the fling with Megan had been more than a little exhausting, and unusual to say the least. Someone who lived by more ordinary norms might be easier in the long run.

He drove Daphne to the station that night, because she insisted she had to get back. There was a luncheon she had to go to the next day, and her friend's wife was out of town, so she wanted to spend the night with him. He never accompanied her anywhere. He was careful not to be seen with her. But she accepted that, as she did everything else about him.

"He's a lucky bastard," Oliver had said to her more than once, and she only laughed. She wanted nothing more than she shared with him. She loved him totally and was content to live with his restrictions. And Oliver had long since stopped trying to convince her to look for someone else.

Later that night, he was chatting with Mel, as they sat in the living room talking about the wedding, when the phone rang, and she grabbed it, convinced it was one of her friends. She looked surprised when it wasn't, and handed it to her father instead. It was Benjamin, and he had asked only for their father. So she handed him the phone, kissed him, and went up to bed.

" 'Night, Dad."

"See you in the morning, sweetheart. Sleep tight." And then he turned his attention to her older brother. "What's up, Benjamin?" They had seen him only that afternoon at the wedding. He had taken the day off, and he had come alone. Sandra wasn't feeling well. She had the flu, Benjamin had said, which was unfortunate, given her condition. The baby was due in another ten days, and Benjamin was showing the strain. He looked absolutely awful.

"Hi, Dad." Benjamin sounded terse. "She's in labor. We're at the hospital. We've been here since eight o'clock."

"Everything okay?" It brought back memories of when they had been born, and how excited he had been, but Benjamin sounded scared more than excited.

"It's not going so great. She's not making any progress . . . and, Dad . . . she's having such a hard time. They gave her some stuff, but it isn't doing anything to help the pain."

"What about your Lamaze?"

"She doesn't want to do it. And . . . Dad . . . they think the baby is having problems." Oh Jesus. A damaged baby.

"Do you want me to come down?"

"Yeah . . . I . . . I'm sorry, I know it's late. Would you?"

"Sure." Benjamin gave him the name of the hospital. "I'll be right there." He hurried out of the house, grabbing his car keys on the way, and glad that Benjamin had called him. At least he was reaching out to him now, and maybe he could do something to help. He couldn't do anything to help Sandra, of course, and he was sorry for her. She had no family to take care of her, no mother to hold her hand. But at least he could be there for Benjamin, and the doctors could do the rest for Sandra.

When he got there, Benjamin was pacing nervously in the corridor, wearing green pajamas and a white gown over them, and a funny green shower cap on his head. His father smiled at the sight of him, remembering the Halloween he'd dressed up as a doctor. He'd been four years old then, and he hardly looked older than that to Ollie now. "You look like Dr. Kildare. How is she?"

"Awful. She was screaming and screaming. They asked me to leave so they could check her again and she kept begging me not to . . . I don't know what to do for her, Dad."

"Relax, Son. It'll be all right. Do you want a cup of coffee?"

Benjamin shook his head, and Ollie went to get a cup for himself. He had had a lot of wine at the wedding, and he didn't want to get sleepy when Benjamin needed him. And as he came back with the steaming cup, there were two doctors in similar garb conferring with his son. Oliver stood at a little distance from them, and he saw Benjamin close his eyes and nod his head.

"They want to do a cesarean. The baby's in trouble now. I know she didn't want that, but they say there's no choice." He pulled the shower cap slowly off his head. "They won't let me be in there with her. They're going to give her a general anesthetic."

"She'll be all right, just hang in there." He squeezed his shoulder in one powerful hand, and led him gently to a chair.

"What if the baby's not all right?" he asked miserably as he sat down next to him.

"We'll face that when the time comes, but I'll bet that baby will be just fine." He wanted to ask him again about putting it up for adoption, but he knew this wasn't the time.

It seemed to take hours as they sat there. They watched the clock drag its hands. It was already after one. And then a nurse came out and asked if Mr. Watson was there, both men stood up, and then, feeling foolish, Oliver sat back down. It was obviously Benjamin they were looking for. And the boy hurried toward the door.

"Mr. Watson?"

"Yes?"

"There's someone here who wants to meet you." And without another word, as he stood in the hallway in the middle of the night in his green pajamas, they handed him his son. He was swaddled in a tiny bundle, and he let out a wail as the nurse put him in Benjamin's hands, and then he pulled him gently toward his chest. He stood looking down at him in total amazement, as tears slid down his cheeks and he started to grin, and turned toward Oliver, holding tightly to the baby.

"It's a boy, Dad! It's a *boy*!" Oliver hurried over to see him, and as he looked down at the tiny child, he felt his heart quiver within him. It was like looking into Benjamin's face only moments after he was born. It was the same child, the same face, the same red hair and surprised eyes, and so much of Sarah, and as Oliver looked at him he realized something that had previously escaped him. This wasn't just Benjamin's child, or Sandra's, it was his grandchild as well. It was a part of him, and all of those who had come before him . . . his father . . . his mother . . . and their parents before them. It was a part of all of them, and he could no longer deny that. There were tears in his eyes, as he gently touched the child that belonged to all of them now.

"How's Sandra?" Benjamin suddenly remembered her, feeling guilty. "Is she okay?" he asked the nurse.

"She's fine. She'll be in the recovery room for a while. And now, would you like to come to the nursery with us for a little while? You can hold the baby, while we check him."

"Is he all right?"

"Everything's just fine. He weighs eight pounds, nine ounces, and his Apgars were perfect. That means he's an alert, healthy little boy." She took the baby from Benjamin, and led the way to the nursery as the new father beamed, and Oliver stayed behind. It was an amazing moment in his life. At forty-five years of age, he was suddenly a grandfather, but he was still struck by how much his grandchild looked like his own son. And then, needing to share it with someone, he walked to a pay phone, dialed the number, and charged it to his home phone.

When she answered the phone, he suddenly smiled to himself, and his voice was hoarse and gentle. "Hello, Grandma."

"Who is this?" She thought it was a crank call and was about to hang up.

"You have a grandson, Sarah." There were tears in his eyes again, as he remembered the children they had borne together.

"Oh my God. Is he all right?"

"He's perfect. Eight pounds, nine ounces, and he looks just like Benjamin when he was born."

"How's Sandra?"

"Not too great, I suspect. They had to do a cesarean.

But she'll be all right. The baby is so sweet, Sarrie . . . wait till you see him."

"They're keeping him, then?" She was wide awake now.

"Yes," he said quietly, suddenly feeling something for the baby he had never expected to feel again, almost as though it were his own baby. "I think they'll keep him." And it was impossible to disagree with Benjamin, now that he had seen his grandson.

"How's Benjamin holding up?"

"He was very nervous, but he looks like a proud papa now. Oh Sarah, you should see him." He was proud of him, and happy for him, and sad all at the same time.

"You're such an old softie, Oliver Watson. You should be having more kids of your own one of these days." It was an odd thing for her to say, but their lives were in separate worlds now.

"So I've been told. How are you, by the way?"

"I'm all right."

"Your eyes okay?"

"Still a little colorful, but they'll do. Give Benjamin my love. I'll call him tomorrow."

"Take care of yourself." He sounded sad again. Sometimes it still hurt to call her, but he was glad he had anyway. It was her grandson too. And he had wanted to tell her.

"Congratulations." She smiled into the phone, "Grampa."

"Same to you. It makes us sound ancient, doesn't it?"

"I don't know. I think I kind of like it."

He hung up then, and waited for Benjamin to

emerge. He drove him back to the house in Purchase, and it was the first time in six months that he had slept in his old room. He had left in defiance, and come home a father. It was a strange world, Oliver thought to himself, as he walked to his room, thinking of the baby that had been born that night. He wished him an easy life, an easy berth, and an easier path into manhood than his father had just had. And in his own bed Benjamin had just drifted off to sleep at last, smiling about his baby.

Chapter 20

Oliver drove them home from the hospital to the dismal apartment in Port Chester, and no amount of pleading had induced them to come home to Purchase. He suspected that Sandra would have gladly given in to the idea, but Benjamin insisted they could manage on their own. He was going to take care of her, and the baby. He had taken two weeks off from work, and by then everything was going to be in control. But whenever Oliver called them after that, the baby was screaming, and when he went to visit them the following week, Sandra looked dreadful. She was pale, with dark circles under her eyes, and was in obvious pain. Benjamin looked as though he was beside himself, and the apartment was a disaster.

It was four days later when Oliver got a call in the middle of the night at the New York apartment. It was

Benjamin. Sandra had been taken into the hospital, with an infection from the cesarean, and he was managing the baby by himself. He was in tears when he called, and Oliver went and picked him up, packed all the baby's things, and brought both of them home with him.

"Agnes can take care of Alex, and you can get some sleep for a change." This time he wasn't going to argue with him. Benjamin had never looked worse. He seemed relieved to turn things over to someone else for once, and the next day, when he came back from the office, he sat Benjamin down for a long talk. The baby was screaming all the time, and Sandra was complaining. He couldn't find a second job, and they could hardly make ends meet. Suddenly it was all crashing in on him, and he was panicking. And no matter how cute the baby was, Oliver was sorry again that they had had him.

"Son, you have to think about this carefully. Is this really what you want to do with your life? Do you really feel you can keep the baby? And more importantly, what are you going to do about yourself? Do you want to work as a busboy for the rest of your life? And what about Sandra?"

These were all the questions that had been plaguing the boy for months, and now he was overwhelmed. He admitted to his father that he didn't love Sandra anymore, he wondered if he ever had, and if he had, it hadn't been for a long time. He couldn't bear the thought of spending the rest of his life with her. But what complicated matters now was that he loved the baby.

"He's my baby, Dad. I can't leave him. I couldn't do

that to him, or to myself. But I just don't think I can stay with her for much longer . . . but if I leave her, then I have to leave Alex with her." And he had serious questions about her ability to mother the child. She seemed to have none of the instincts that he had assumed she would have. And all she thought of, as before, was herself, and not the baby.

"Why don't you give her a chance to get on her feet again? Maybe what you need to think about is supporting her, but not staying with her yourself." And just exactly how was he going to do that? Washing dishes? Pumping gas? "I'll do everything I can to help you. Why don't you just relax for a few days, and try to sort your thoughts out." But when he did, he felt responsible again. Sandra came out of the hospital, and feeling sorry for her, he took the baby and went back. Aggie was heartbroken to see him take the baby, and Oliver was equally so to see Benjamin go back again to do what he thought was right. He just wouldn't let go of what he felt were his obligations, and it broke Oliver's heart to think of him there, with the baby and the girl. He insisted on giving him five thousand dollars, and Benjamin had fought him like a tiger to give it back.

"Think of it as a loan then. I'm not going to have you starving with three of you to support. Be sensible, for chrissake." And finally, Benjamin relented, promising to pay it back to him as soon as he could manage.

And matters grew more complicated still only two weeks later. The head of Ollie's firm called him in and made a request that took him totally by surprise. The head of the Los Angeles office was dying of cancer. He was leaving within the week on permanent medical leave and someone had to take his place. More than that, they wanted to enlarge the office, and make it as important as the one in New York. They wanted "bicoastal equilibrium," as they put it, to be close to the television industry that was so important to them, and acquire bigger, better clients on the West Coast. And the chairman of the board had decided that Oliver was their main man to run it.

"For God's sake . . . but I can't do that . . . I have two kids in school here, a house, a life . . . I can't just uproot them and move three thousand miles away." And now there was Benjamin with his problems with his baby. He couldn't walk out on him, the way Sarah had done to all of them the year before. "I'll have to think this over." But the salary they mentioned, the terms, and the participation made it a deal he would have been crazy to refuse, and he knew it.

"For chrissake, Oliver, come to your senses. Take it! No one will ever make you another offer like that, and one day you'll wind up chairman of the board." Daphne tried to talk sense to him that night, as they sat in his office long after everyone else had gone home.

"But what about my kids? My house? My father?"

"Don't be ridiculous. Your father has a life of his own, and a wife who loves him. And Benjamin has his own life now too. He'll sort himself out sooner or later, whether you're here or not. He's that kind of kid. He's just like you. And Mel and Sam would love it out there. Look how good they were about moving to New York."

"But Christ, Daph, that's different. That's thirty miles from Purchase. This is three thousand miles from home."

"Not if you make a home for yourself out there. And Melissa is a junior. In two years she'll be away in college somewhere. Don't use them as an excuse. Go for it! It's a terrific offer." But Los Angeles? California? This was his home.

"I don't know. I have to think this over. I have to talk it over with the kids and see what they say."

They were both shocked when he told them, but not as horrified as he would have expected them to be. They even seemed to like the idea after they thought it over. They didn't like the idea of leaving their friends, and Sam was worried about how often he would see Sarah, but Ollie said he could send them back to visit her fairly frequently, and they could spend their vacations with her. But to Ollie, it was still a hell of a thought, and a frightening prospect. And what's more, they wanted him out there within a month, sooner if he could make it.

"Well, guys," he asked them as they talked about it for days on end. He had until the end of the week to make his mind up. "What do you say? Do we go out to California, or stay here?"

Mel and Sam exchanged a long, careful look between them, and Ollie found himself hoping that they'd say no.

"I say we do it." Mel astounded him, and Sam sat back and grinned.

"Yeah, Dad. Let's go. We can go to Disneyland every Sunday."

He sat staring at them, still stunned by their decision. "Do you mean it?" They nodded, and feeling as if he were living in a dream, the next day he went to work and told them he would go. He flew to Los Angeles that Sunday, looked for a house to rent, spent three days looking at schools, another week getting to know the people at the office, and came back to wind things up in New York.

Faithful Aggie had agreed to go with them, and he had decided not to sell the house in Purchase, but to keep it until he knew everything was right for them on the West Coast. The hardest part of all was telling Benjamin they were going, but he made a deal with him that at least relieved his mind about his son. Benjamin and Sandra agreed to move into the house in Purchase with the baby. He told them they could take care of it for him, and it would be a load off his mind if they'd "help him."

"You're sure, Dad? You're not just doing us a favor?"

"No, I'm not, Son. There's another alternative too." He held his breath. "You could leave Sandra and Alex in an apartment here, and come to the West Coast with us." But Benjamin only shook his head sadly. He wasn't leaving them. He couldn't. Sandra had no idea how to cope, and Alex was his baby.

"We'll be okay here." He had found another job, and with free rent in his father's house, that would be one less expense for them.

It all happened like a whirlwind. They packed, they went. They cried, they waved. And the week before Thanksgiving they left for Los Angeles, to begin a whole new life in California.

As the plane set down at Los Angeles airport, Oliver looked at Mel and Sam and wondered what he'd done.

"Ready?" He grinned nervously at them, praying that they'd like the house he'd rented in Bel Air. It was an incredible place with a deck, a sauna, a Jacuzzi in every bath, and a swimming pool twice the size of the one in Purchase. It had belonged to an actor who'd gone broke, and was renting it until he decided to sell it.

They picked Andy up at the baggage claim in the big cage he'd traveled in, and Aggie straightened her hat, and smiled.

There was a limousine waiting for them at the airport, and the children got into it with wide eyes, as Andy barked and wagged his tail. Oliver wondered for the hundredth time if he'd done something totally crazy. But if he had, no one seemed to mind. Not yet, at least. He sat back against the seat and took both his children's hands tightly in his own.

"I hope you like the house, guys."

"We will." Sam smiled, as he looked out the window, and Mel looked suddenly very grown up, as they drove through the Los Angeles traffic to the new home their father had found them in Bel Air. It was a whole new world, a new life for them, but they didn't seem to mind it. And as he looked out the window, only Oliver was frightened by the prospect of what they were doing.

Chapter 21

The house was exactly what the children had dreamed it would be. It was perfect for them, and Oliver was thrilled. In a matter of weeks, they had settled in, and all three of them were thriving. Even Agnes was in ecstasy over their new home, and after foraging around the local shops, she found everything she wanted.

Mel loved her school, and Sam invited two new friends to their pool to swim over Thanksgiving weekend. Only the holiday seemed a little strange for them, without Benjamin, or their grandfather, and they were a long way from Sarah too. They were going to spend the Christmas holidays with her. And it seemed amazing to them they had only been there a month, when they packed their things to leave to join her in Boston for their Christmas vacation.

Oliver drove them to the airport, and much as he knew he would miss them over the holidays, he was grateful to have a few weeks to work late at the office. He needed the time to dig into all the projects that had been waiting for him when he arrived. And the one person he really missed was Daphne. He missed her good eye, her bright mind, her clear judgment, and creative solutions to his office problems. More than once, he called her for advice, and express-mailed papers to her to see what she thought of his ideas for new campaigns, and presentations to new clients. He wished they had sent her to Los Angeles too, but he also knew she would never have gone. Her relationship with the man in New York was too important to her. She would rather have given up her job than the married man she had given up her life for thirteen years before.

The next few weeks flew by, and it was Christmas almost before they knew it. The children decorated the Christmas tree before they left, and they exchanged gifts with their father, before flying off to spend Christmas with Sarah. And suddenly as he returned to the empty house the day they left, he realized that it was going to be his first Christmas alone, the first one without them, and without Sarah. It would be easier just forgetting about it, and plunging into work. He had more than enough to occupy him in the two weeks they'd be gone. And by the next afternoon, he was startled when one of his staff knocked hesitantly on the door of his office.

"Mr. Watson, Harry Branston thought you might like to see this." The young woman put an invitation on his desk, and he glanced at it. But he was too busy to read it until several hours later. It was an invitation to a Christmas party one of the networks gave every year, for their stars, their staff, their friends, and major advertisers, and one of the biggest clients the agency had was that particular network. It seemed the politic thing to do to attend, but he didn't see how he could spare the time, and he wasn't really in the mood. He put it aside, and decided to see how his day went. It was four days hence, and the last thing on his mind that Friday afternoon, when he found the invitation in a stack of work on his desk, was to go to a party. He knew he wouldn't know anyone there, and he couldn't imagine that anyone would notice his absence. He put it aside again, and suddenly it was as though he could hear Daphne's voice urging him to go. It was exactly the kind of thing she would have told him to do, for the sake of the agency, and to establish himself as the new head of the L.A. office. "All right . . . all right . . ." he muttered, "I'll go." And then he smiled to himself, thinking of her again and how much he missed their spaghetti dinners. That had been one of the hardest things about coming to L.A. He had no friends here. And surely no one like Daphne.

He called for the office limousine, which he seldom used, but on occasions like this it was helpful. The driver would know where it was, and he wouldn't have to worry about parking.

The party was being held on one of the huge studio sets, and as the limousine glided onto the lot, a guard checked a list for his name, and then waved them on. It was all still a little bit like a dream to him, or playing a part in an unfamiliar movie.

Two young women showed him the way, and the

next thing he knew, he was in the midst of hundreds of people, festively dressed and drinking champagne, on a set that looked like a huge hotel lobby. There was a gigantic Christmas tree towering over them, and network executives were greeting everyone. He felt silly being there at first, like a new kid in school, but no one seemed to notice. He introduced himself several times, and was secretly impressed when he saw faces he knew, they were stars of successful shows, decked out in sequins and sparkles. The women were beautiful, and the men were handsome, too, and he was suddenly sorry that Mel wasn't there. She would have been awestruck by it all, and she would have loved it. He even saw the star of Sam's favorite show, a freckled-faced boy whose wisecracks Sam always repeated ad infinitum.

He turned away then to make room for someone coming through and inadvertently stepped on someone else's toes. He jumped aside with an apology on his lips, and turned to find the most beautiful woman he'd ever seen standing just behind him. Her face was flawless, her eyes were green, and her hair was the color of burnished copper. "I . . . I'm sorry . . . I didn't see . . ." He realized that he'd seen her before but he wasn't sure where. And when she looked at him, she smiled, exposing perfect teeth, but for all her incredible looks, she was perfectly at ease in a pair of red leather slacks and a simple black sweater. And she had the smile of a little girl, and not a movie star. She was surprisingly small, and everything about her seemed tiny and perfect. "I'm awfully sorry," he said again, having landed full on her foot, but she just laughed as she watched the crowd milling around them.

"Crazy, isn't it? I come every year and I always wonder why. It just looks like they call central casting and say, 'Okay, Joe, send up a bunch of bodies for a party.' Then they stick a glass of champagne in their hands and tell everyone to have a good time." She laughed again as she watched them, and then her eyes met Oliver's full on. This was a new breed to him, the perfect face, the beautifully groomed red hair, everyone in Los Angeles looked so "done up" to him, so studied in the way they dressed and made up. They made a lifetime of how they looked, and yet somehow he sensed that this girl was different.

"I know I shouldn't ask you this, I should probably know, but do you work here?"

"You could say that. You don't, though, do you?" If he had, he would have known who she was, but it didn't bother her that he didn't. In some ways, it was a lot nicer for her this way.

"I work for an ad agency." He didn't want to tell her he ran it. "I just moved out from New York a few weeks ago. It's a lot different here, but I like it a lot."

"Wait a while. It gets pretty crazy out here. I've been here for ten years, and I still feel like Alice in Wonderland." It was a sensation he was beginning to know well, and he suddenly wondered what she would look like without the carefully groomed hair and expertly applied makeup.

"Where were you from before that?"

"Nebraska." She laughed. "Would you believe? I came out here to go to UCLA and become a 'star.' And my folks still think I'm crazy for staying out here. Sometimes, so do I, but you get hooked on the action after a while. I love being in this business." She looked excited as she spoke, and he liked the look in her eyes. She was alive and full of fun, and she didn't seem to be taking any of it seriously. And then, as they were speaking, someone came up to her and asked for an autograph. She signed it without making a big fuss, smiled, thanked them, and turned back to Ollie. He was looking frankly embarrassed by then, and realized that he should have known who she was.

"All right. Tomorrow I'm going to be mortified. I'm going to find out who you are and feel like a complete jerk. Why don't you tell me now so I can feel like an ignorant fool and get it over with?" He was smiling too. "Who are you?"

"Little Red Riding Hood," she teased. "To tell you the truth, I was enjoying the fact that you didn't know me. I hate to spoil that."

"I promise I'll forget as soon as you tell me."

"Good." She held out a hand to him in formal greeting. "In that case, I'm Charlotte Sampson." She was the star of one of the network's major shows, a dramatic prime-time show that ran weekly. She had a male co-star and an audience of some eighty million viewers.

"Oh my God . . ." He did feel like a real fool, and Mel was going to die when she heard he had met her. "I can't believe it."

"Now that we've gotten that over with, who are *you*?" He had shaken her hand and forgotten to tell her his name. He couldn't believe that he hadn't recognized her, but he had never realized that she was that small, and that young and vivacious and pretty. She was very serious on the show, and she usually wore her hair in a different style, but he was staring at her again, and he felt like a real hick as he introduced himself to her at last.

"I'm sorry. You really took me by surprise. I'm Oliver Watson. This is all very Hollywood for us folks from back East. I'm afraid I'm not used to running into stars every day, let alone trampling their feet."

"Not to worry. Last time he was here my dad walked right up to Joan Collins on the set and told her she looked just like a Sunday school teacher he knew back in Nebraska. It was the first time I've ever seen her speechless. He just patted her on the back, and kept on going."

"Maybe I should try that. But you don't look like a Sunday school teacher to me." More like the girl next door. But an exceptionally beautiful one. She was really lovely, and her flame-red hair intrigued him. He could tell from the color of her creamy skin that she was a natural redhead.

"You don't look like an ad man to me. You look like one of the guys on our show." She laughed, and he could see that she did that often. She was an easygoing girl, with none of the mannerisms or affectations of someone as important and successful as she was.

"I'm afraid I don't think so."

"What brought you out here, by the way?" There were people she knew milling everywhere, waving at her, blowing kisses, making signs, but she seemed perfectly content to continue talking to Ollie.

"The agency did. Someone got sick, and they brought me in to fill in for him. It was kind of short notice, but it's worked out really well." And then suddenly, he felt very guilty. "Miss Sampson, should I be keeping you? I imagine there are a lot more important people you should be talking to than the network's ad man."

"I've already paid my dues. I came early, drank a glass of champagne, and kissed the head of the network. What more do they want? A little tap dance? I gave at the office. I'm on my time now. And I like talking to you. It's a lot easier than talking to a lot of nervous stars whose shows are slipping in the ratings." But hers wasn't, that was for sure. She had been nominated for the Emmy that year, even though she hadn't won it. Which made him feel even more a fool for not knowing who she was when he first saw her. "What have you been doing in Los Angeles, Oliver, since you got here?"

"Work . . . work some more . . . more work . . . settle in . . . to tell you the truth, I haven't seen anything except my house and my office."

"That doesn't sound like much fun. Have you been to dinner anywhere?"

"Not yet, except once with my kids. We went to the Hard Rock Café, which they loved. I felt four hundred years old, and as though I was losing my hearing."

She laughed, she liked it, but it made her feel that way too, only because it was difficult to talk there. But the decor was fabulous, and she was particularly fond of looking at Elvis Presley's old car seeming to plunge through the roof. It brought out the kid in her every time she saw it. "Have you been to Spago yet?"

"I'm afraid not."

"We'll have to go sometime." It sounded like the L.A. version of "let's have lunch sometime," and he didn't take her seriously when she said it. And then, looking interested, "How old are your kids?"

"I have a daughter who's sixteen, a son who's ten, and another son who stayed back East who's eighteen."

"That sounds nice," she smiled at him, with a faint look of regret. She really liked him. "How old's your wife?" She looked straight into his eyes, and he laughed at the directness of what she'd asked him.

"Forty-two, actually, and we're divorced." Or as good as. The papers would be final in eight weeks, and in his heart, where it mattered, the bond had been severed at last. And Charlotte Sampson grinned broadly at him when he answered.

"My, that is good news! I was beginning to worry!" He was flattered by her words, and the attention she was lavishing on him. He really felt he didn't deserve it. Maybe she was just shy, and didn't like big parties. "Are your kids here now?"

"No, they just went East a few days ago, to spend Christmas with their mother in Boston."

"I thought you said you lived in New York." She looked suddenly puzzled, "And why aren't they with you for Christmas?"

"Because they live with me all year round. And we did live in New York. But she lives in Boston. She left a year ago to go back to school, and . . ." He looked at her, Hollywood or not, he was going to tell her the truth, even though he wasn't even sure she cared, but she acted as though she did, and she seemed like a nice person. "She left us . . . me and the kids . . . so they live with me now."

She looked at him, soberly suddenly, brushing the long red hair off her shoulders. "That sounds like a long, painful story."

"It was. For a while. It's a short story now. She's happy. We're fine. You adjust to things if you have to."

"The kids too?"

He nodded. "They're doing fine. By now, I think they can weather anything. They're a good group."

"And you sound like a good father."

"Thank you, ma'am." He took a brief bow and they both laughed and one of the network heads came up to greet them both. He kissed Charlotte on both cheeks, and shook Oliver's hand, and told him he'd been keeping an eye out for him for the past hour.

"I want to introduce you to some of our friends, but I see you've already met my favorite lady."

"I attempted to trample her as I came through the door, and she was kind enough not to have me thrown out, or sue. She's probably too lame now to move, so we've been standing here chatting, while I bore her with tales of my children."

"I've enjoyed talking to you, Oliver." She looked almost hurt as the other man laughed, and then she turned to her network boss and almost pouted. "I suppose you're going to take him away now."

"I should. I'll bring him back if you like," and then he turned to Oliver with a supposed word of warning. "Watch out for her, she hates movie stars, she loves kids, and dogs, and she never forgets her lines. I don't trust women like that, do you? And what's more she's too goddamn good-looking. You should see her at four A.M., it'd make you sick, no makeup and a face like an angel."

"Come on, Howie, knock it off! You know what I look like in the morning!" She was laughing and Oliver looked amused. She looked like a good sport, and he would have loved to see her at 4:00 A.M., with or without her makeup. "He's telling lies, all lies, I hate kids and dogs." But she hadn't sounded like it when they talked about his children.

"Okay, Charlie, go play, while I take Oliver around. I'll bring him back in a little while." But when they left her, much to Oliver's regret, "Howie" introduced him to absolutely every human being of any importance on the set, and it was an hour before he got back to the spot where he had left her. And of course she was gone. He hadn't expected her to wait . . . not really . . . except that he would have loved it if she had. He quietly walked away, and went to look for his limousine, and then much to his amazement, in the distance, getting into a red Mercedes, he saw her. She was wearing her hair in two pigtails, and she had taken off her makeup , and she had an old black leather coat on. He waved to her, and she saw him and waved back, and then hesitated for a minute, as though waiting for him to approach her. He walked over to her then, wanting to tell her how much he'd enjoyed meeting her, and she smiled as he came closer.

"On your way home?" She nodded, and smiled up at him, suddenly looking like a kid. But a very pretty one as he watched her.

"I have two weeks off until after the holidays. We went on hiatus tonight. What about you? Finished with your duties in there?" She smiled easily at him and he nodded. He wanted to ask her out, but he didn't quite dare, and then he decided what the hell, all she could do was say no, even if she was Charlotte Sampson.

"Have you eaten yet?"

She shook her head, and then her face lit up. "Want to go for a pizza at Spago? I'm not sure we'll get in, but we can try. It's usually pretty crowded." That was the understatement of the year. It was usually wall-to-wall bodies, willing to wait a lifetime for Wolfgang Puck's terrific meals, and a glimpse of the stars who hung out there.

"I'd love it." He looked thrilled, and glanced over his shoulder at the limousine. "Can I give you a ride? Or should I follow you?"

"Why don't you just ride with me?"

"You wouldn't mind?" It would certainly be simpler.

She smiled warmly again. She liked the way he looked, and the way he sounded. She liked his easy air, and there was something quiet and confident about him. He looked like someone you could count on. "Of course not."

He dismissed the driver quickly then, as though he was afraid she'd change her mind, and slid into the front seat beside her. And then suddenly she turned to him. "I have a better idea. Sometimes Spago can be pretty noisy. I know another Italian place on Melrose. It's called Chianti. It's dark and no one will see us there. We can call from here, and see if they'll take us." She pointed to a small red phone hanging from the dashboard, and operated it with one hand as she started the car, while he watched with amusement. "Something wrong?"

"No. I'm just impressed."

"Yeah," she grinned. "It's a long way from Lincoln, Nebraska."

The restaurant answered on the first ring, and they would be happy to give Miss Sampson a table. And it was a perfect choice. It was small, and dark and intimate, and there was nothing "nouvelle anything" about it. It looked the way Italian restaurants used to look, and the food on the menu sounded delicious. The headwaiter took their order quickly, and they settled back side by side against the banquette, while Oliver tried to absorb it all. He was having dinner with *the* Charlotte Sampson. But this was Hollywood, wasn't it? And for the flash of an instant, he thought of Megan in New York. How different this was. That had been so sophisticated and a little decadent, and somehow this seemed so simple. But Charlotte was that kind of person. She seemed very real.

"This was a great idea." He looked pleased, and they both dove into the breadsticks. They were starving.

"It's so wonderful not to have to worry about going to work at four o'clock in the morning tomorrow. It really makes a mess of your social life sometimes. Most of the time I'm too tired to go anywhere at night, except home to bed. I take a bath, and then I crawl into bed with the next day's script, and by nine o'clock I'm out cold with the lights out."

"What about all the famous Hollywood parties?"

"They're for morons. Except the duty calls like tonight. The rest of them you can have. The ones like the one tonight are dangerous not to go to. You don't want to get anyone mad at the network."

"So I've heard. Is it really as tense as all that?"

"Sometimes, if your ratings aren't great. This is a lousy business." And then she laughed. "But I love it. I love the excitement of it, the hard work, the challenges of doing difficult scripts. There are other things

I'd like to do more, but this has been a terrific experience." She had been doing the show for two years.

"What would you rather do?"

"Professionally?" It was an interesting question. "Shakespeare probably. I did a lot of repertory in college, and summer stock after that, when I couldn't get any other work. I like live theater. The pressure of it. The demand that you remember all your lines and do it right night after night. I think the ultimate, for me, would be a Broadway play." He nodded, he could see that. It was kind of the pinnacle of the art form, but what she did had merit too. He admired her a lot for what she did. And it was harder work than it appeared. He knew that much.

"Have you done any films?"

"One." She laughed. "It was a disaster. The only person who saw it and liked it was my grandmother, in Nebraska."

They both laughed and their dinner arrived then, as they chatted on endlessly about their work, his kids, the pressures of their jobs, and how he felt about suddenly running the L.A. office. "Advertising must be rough. You screw up once, and you lose the client." She had heard horror stories for years, but he looked surprisingly calm considering the kind of pressure he worked under.

"It's no different from what you do. They don't give you much leeway either."

"That's why you need something else, so you never really care too much. There has to be something else that matters in your life."

"Like what?"

She answered without hesitation. "A husband, marriage, kids. People you love, something else you know how to do, because one day, the shows, the autographs, the hoopla, it's all gone, and you have to watch out you don't go with it." It was an intelligent way to look at what she did, and he respected her for it, but what she had just said suddenly made him wonder.

"Is there something you're not telling me, Miss Sampson? Is your husband about to walk through the door and punch me in the nose?" She laughed at the thought and shook her head as she dug into her pasta.

"No chance of that, I'm afraid. I was married once, a long time ago, when I was twenty-one. It lasted about ten minutes after I got out of college."

"What happened?"

"Simple. He was an actor. Instant death. And I've never met anyone else I wanted to marry. In this business, you don't meet too many men you'd want to spend the rest of your life with." She had also gone out with a producer for several years, but that had never come to anything. And after that, she had gone long periods without anyone, or dated people who weren't in the business. "I'm too choosy, I guess. My mom says I'm over the hill now." She looked at him soberly, but there was a twinkle of mischief. "I'll be thirty-four next month. Getting a little ripe for marriage, I guess."

He laughed openly at the remark. She looked about twenty. "I wouldn't quite say that, or is that how they look at it out here?"

"If you're over twenty-five, you're dead. By thirty you've had your first face-lift. At thirty-five, you've had two, and your eyes done at least once. Maybe twice. At forty, it's all over. See what I mean, you've got to have something else in your life." She sounded as though she meant it as he listened.

"And if not a husband and kids, then what?"

"Something to occupy your mind. I used to do a lot of volunteer work with handicapped kids. Lately, I haven't had much time though."

"I'll lend you mine."

"What are they like?" She sounded interested and he was touched. It was hard to believe she was successful and famous. She was so real and so down-to-earth, and he liked that a lot. He liked everything he had seen so far. It almost made him forget the way she looked. Her looks seemed unimportant suddenly compared to the rest. She was beautiful inside, and he liked that even better. And as he thought about it, he tried to answer her question about his children.

"Mel is intelligent and responsible, and she desperately wants to be an actress. Or at least that's what she thinks now. God knows what she'll want to be later. But she wants to major in drama at college. She's a junior in high school. She's tall and blond, and a nice kid. I think you'll like her." He suddenly assumed that the two would meet, and then wondered if he was assuming too much, but Charlotte didn't flinch when he said it. "And Sam's a cute kid, he's ten, and a little fireball. Everybody seems to love him." And then he told her about Benjamin and Sandra and the baby.

"That sounds like a heavy trip. And it must be very rough on him."

"It is. He's determined to do the right thing, if it kills him. He doesn't seem to love the girl, but he's crazy about the baby."

"So you're a grandfather then." She suddenly

looked at him with mischief in her eyes. They were the same green as his, though neither of them had noticed. "You didn't tell me that when we met." Ollie laughed at the way she said it.

"Does that make a big difference?"

"Tremendous. Wait till I tell my folks that I went out with a grandfather. They'll really wonder what I've been up to." It sounded as though she was close to them, and he liked that about her. He even told her about his father and Margaret.

"They're coming out in January to see the kids. She's the best thing that ever happened to him, although I didn't think so at first. It was a hell of a shock when he married her so soon after my mother's death."

"It's funny, no matter how old we are, where our parents are concerned, we're still children. Don't you think?"

"I do. I resented the hell out of her at first. But he has a right to some happiness in his last years."

"He could live to a ripe old age." She smiled.

"I hope he does."

"I hope I meet them," she said softly.

They finished dinner then, and chatted on for a while over coffee, and then they went back to her car, and on the way out two people stopped her for autographs. But she didn't seem to mind. She was friendly and kind, and almost grateful. He commented on it as they got back in her car, and she looked at him with her wide green eyes and a serious expression.

"You can never forget, in this business, that those people make you what you are. Without them, you're nothing. I don't ever forget it." And the beauty of it was that it hadn't gone to her head. She was amazingly modest, and almost humble.

"Thank you for having dinner with me tonight."

"I had a wonderful time, Oliver." And she looked as though she meant it.

She drove him back to the house in Bel Air and when they got there, he seemed to hesitate, not sure whether to ask her in or not, and then finally he did, but she said she was really tired. And then, suddenly, she remembered something.

"What are you doing over the holidays, with your kids gone?"

"Not much. I was going to catch up on my work at the office. This'll be my first Christmas without them."

"I usually go home too. But I just couldn't this year. I'm shooting a commercial next week, and I wanted to study the next scripts. We have a new writer. Would you like to do something on Sunday?" It was Christmas Eve, and he was trying not to think about it, but her offer sounded much too appealing to decline.

"I'd love it. We could have dinner here." Agnes was around, even with the children gone, but Charlotte had a better idea.

"How about if I make you a turkey? The real thing. Would you like that?"

"I'd love it."

"We can go to church afterward. And there are some friends I always go to visit on Christmas Day. Would you like to join me for that too?"

"Charlotte, I'd love that. But are you sure there isn't something else you'd rather do? I don't want to intrude. I'll be fine, you know." Fine, but very lonely.

"Well, I won't," she said with a soft smile. "I'll be

really disappointed if you don't come. Christmas is very important to me, and I like spending it with people I care about. I'm not into fake Christmas trees sprayed silver and all the garbage that goes with it. Your typical Hollywood Yule."

"Then I'll be there. What time?"

"Come at five o'clock. We can eat at seven, and go to church at midnight." She scribbled the address down for him, and he got out of the car, feeling dazed, as she thanked him again, and drove off with a wave. He stood for a long moment watching the little red car disappear down the hill, wondering if it had really happened. It was all like a dream. But Christmas with her was even more dreamlike.

She was waiting for him in a white hostess gown. The house was decorated beautifully. It was in the Hollywood hills, on Spring Oak Drive. And it had the cozy look of an old farm. And she laughed and said it reminded her of Nebraska. There were rough-hewn floors, beam ceilings, and huge fireplaces, one at each end of the room, and in front of them huge, overstuffed couches. The kitchen was almost as big as the living room, with another fireplace and a cozy table set for two. And there was a Christmas tree blinking brightly in the corner. And upstairs there were two handsome bedrooms, one which was obviously hers, done in pink and flowered chintzes. The other a cheerful yellow guest room, where her parents stayed when they came, which she said wasn't often enough. It didn't have one-tenth the sophistication of Megan's penthouse in New York, but it had ten times the warmth, and he loved it.

She had chilled a bottle of white wine for him, and

the turkey was roasting happily in the oven. She had made chestnut puree, mashed potatoes and yams, there were tiny peas, cranberry jelly, and lots of stuffing. And when they sat down to eat, it was a royal feast, which reminded him in a comfortable way of the Christmases he had shared at home with Sarah and, long before, his parents. He had expected to eat a pastrami sandwich in his office, or stop at Hamburger Hamlet on the way home. He had never expected this, or to be with Charlotte Sampson. It was as though she had fallen into his arms, like a gift from heaven. And as he sat down at the table, he put a small gift on the table for her. He had been so touched by her invitations that he had wanted to get her something nice for Christmas. And he had stopped at Cartier the day before to buy her a simple gold bangle. And she was deeply moved by it, and embarrassed that she hadn't gotten him a present.

"This is my gift, silly girl. A Christmas dinner right out of a fairy tale." She looked pleased that it meant so much to him, and they chatted and laughed, and after dinner he used his credit card and called the kids at Sarah's. It was odd speaking to them, and not being there, but they sounded as though they were having fun. There was a lot of laughing and squealing and passing the phone around, and it wasn't even awkward when he talked to Sarah. He wished her well, and then got off the phone. He called his father, too, and his father sounded happier than he had in a long time. It was amazing, too, to realize that Sarah had left them exactly a year before. And he said as much to Charlotte. It was easy talking to her. And she had made mince and apple pie for dessert, which she smothered with whipped cream and hard sauce.

"Do you still miss her, Oliver?" she asked as they sat looking out at the view and finishing their Christmas dinner.

But he shook his head, honest with her. "Not anymore. It's weird even remembering being married to her. She seems like a stranger now, and I guess she is. But it was brutal at first. I really thought I wouldn't survive it. But I had to for the kids. I think they were what kept me going." She nodded, it made sense to her. And she thought he was lucky to have them. "I guess we never wanted the same things, and I tried to ignore that for all those years. But she never forgot what she wanted."

"Funny how sometimes that kind of persistence is a real virtue, and other times it's a real sin, isn't it?"

"In her case, I guess getting married was just a big mistake, but I'm glad we did, or we wouldn't have had the children."

"They mean everything to you, Oliver, don't they?"

"They do," he admitted to her, "maybe too much so. I haven't done much else with myself for the last year." With the exception of Megan, and that had been a momentary aberration, a month of utter, total, and delicious madness.

"Maybe you needed the time to think, to figure out what you want now."

"I suppose so. I'm not sure I have the answer to that yet, but maybe I don't need to figure that one out for the time being." He smiled at her, and she poured him a delicious cup of steaming coffee. He felt as though he were going to explode, which was exactly what Christmas dinners were meant for. He was happy and sated, and totally enjoying being with this woman. He felt as though she had been made for him, except for the fact that she was Charlotte Sampson. "What about you?" He turned to her then. "Do you know what you're after, Charlotte?"

She grinned at him, "You know, I wish you'd call me Charlie. All my close friends do." It was amazing to be considered one of them, but he had to admit that he liked the idea. "I always think of that at year end . . . where I'm going . . . where I want to be next year, and what I want to be doing. The same thing, I guess, as long as it works," they both knew she meant the show, "and for the rest, whatever comes, whatever's right. I have my dreams, like everyone else, but a lot of them have come true already." She seemed perfectly content with her life. She wasn't seeking, or striving, or wishing she had more than she did. "I'd love to be married and have kids one day, but if that's not in the cards, then I guess it was never meant to be. You can't make yourself crazy over things like that anyway, and they only happen if they're meant to." She was strangely philosophical, and wonderfully peaceful.

He helped her clean up, and at ten o'clock they had another cup of coffee, and shortly before midnight, he drove her to Beverly Hills, to the Church of the Good Shepherd, and they sat very close to each other during the midnight service. It was exactly what it should have been, and at the end, with the lights, the trees and the incense, they all sang Christmas carols. It was one-thirty when they got out, and he drove her slowly home, feeling happy and warm and complete. So much so, he almost didn't miss the children.

He was going to drop her off when they got back, but when they got to her place, she suddenly looked at him strangely.

"I know this may sound weird to you, Oliver, but it's so lonely going home alone on Christmas Eve. Would you like to spend the night in my guest room?" They had met only two days before, and he had just shared Christmas with her, and now she was inviting him into her home, as a guest, not with the lust that Megan had shown, but with kindness and warmth and respect, and he suddenly wanted to stay more than anything in the world. He wanted to be with her, for tonight, for a week, for a year, maybe even for a lifetime.

"I'd love that, Charlie." He leaned over and kissed her then, but it was a chaste, gentle kiss, and they walked into her house hand in hand, as she led him upstairs and turned the bed down. The room had a bathroom of its own, and she kept nightclothes and a robe for friends who stayed, and fussed over him like a mother hen, and then finally left him alone with a warm smile and a "Merry Christmas." And he lay in her guest room bed for a long, long time, thinking of her and wanting to go to her, but he knew it wouldn't be fair to take advantage of her kindness now, and he lay there like a child wishing he could climb into bed with his mother, but not quite daring.

And when he awoke the next day, he could smell pancakes and sausages and hot coffee. He brushed his teeth with the new toothbrush she had left, shaved, and went downstairs in the robe, curious to see what she was up to.

"Merry Christmas, Oliver!" she called as he came through the kitchen door, and he smiled, watching her work, and two minutes later, she had a sumptuous breakfast ready. There were all the things he had smelled, and more, bacon, eggs, freshly squeezed orange juice, and coffee.

"Merry Christmas, Charlie. You may never get me out of here if you keep feeding me like this. This is some hotel you run."

She laughed happily at him. "I'm glad you like it, sir."

And then, without warning, he leaned over and kissed her. But this time the kiss was more fervent than he had dared to let it be the night before. And when she pulled away at last, they were both more than a little breathless. "My, my, Oliver, that's quite a good morning."

"It's in keeping with the quality of the breakfast." He took two bites of the eggs, and then reached for her again, suddenly unable to stay away from her any longer. She was too good to be true, and he was afraid she'd disappear before his very eyes if he didn't grab her.

"Be a good boy, Oliver," she scolded with a smile, "eat your breakfast."

"I'm not sure what I want more," he suddenly grinned like a kid in a toy shop at Christmas, "this breakfast, or you." He looked up at her again with a broad smile. "For the moment, you're winning."

"Behave yourself, or Santa won't bring you anything. Eat up."

"Yes, ma'am." Actually, he still thought Santa had put her in his stocking, and the studio head had been right, without makeup, with her hair pulled back, fresh-faced and clean, she looked absolutely gorgeous in the morning.

And after they were through, she disappeared, and came back with a little blue velvet box and set it down next to him. She had remembered it after church late the night before, and now she watched him open it with pleasure. It was a beautiful antique pocket watch, with a smooth, elegant face and roman numerals, and he stared at it in amazement.

"It was my grandfather's, Ollie . . . do you like it?"

"I love it! But you can't give me something like this!" He hardly knew her. What if he were a rotter or a cad, or she never saw him again. It didn't seem right, but as he tried to give it back to her, she refused to take it.

"I want you to have it. You're a very special man, and for me, this has been a very special Christmas. I told you, I always go home every year and this year I couldn't. And with all the people I know, there was no one I wanted to spend Christmas with here, except you . . . that says a lot . . . so that's for you . . . hang on to it . . . and remember this Christmas."

He felt tears in his eyes as he looked up to thank her, and instead he pulled her closer to him, and he kissed her even more gently this time. She tasted of orange juice and pancakes and sausages, and smelled of lavender and violets, and he wanted to hold her for a lifetime.

"I'm crazy about you, Charlie," he whispered. "Does that make any sense to you after three days? . . . excuse me, four now." They had met on Thursday, and it was now Monday.

"No," she whispered back, "and it scares me to death . . . but that's how I feel too, and I love it."

"What are we going to do, acting like two crazy kids? I just met you, and I'm falling in love with you. And you're a famous television star, what the hell are you doing with me? What is this all about?"

"I don't know," she looked pensive and almost sad, "but being on TV doesn't have anything to do with it. I know that much. I think we're just two people who met at the right time. We were just very lucky."

"Is that what it is?" Or was it more than that? Was it fate? Was it destiny? Was it lust, or loneliness? Whatever it was, it was wonderful, and at least they could talk about it like their own private secret.

"Do you want to come home with me so I can change?" he asked, smiling.

She nodded happily. It was Christmas Day, and afterward she would take him to her friends', and after that she would cook dinner for him again. She wanted it never to end, never to change, never to stop, and so did Ollie. He just wanted to be with her, and he waited while she dressed and then drove her back to his house in Bel Air. Agnes was off for the weekend, and he showed her around, showed her the kids' rooms, showed her ten thousand photographs they had brought from New York, and sat like two children themselves, for hours, poring over all of them, while he explained what was what and who was where.

"They're beautiful, Oliver."

"So are you," he whispered hoarsely, and kissed her again. He wasn't sure how long he could restrain himself. He wanted her so much, and she was so wonderful, just sitting there next to him, on the couch. "Want to sit by the pool for a while?" It was a beautiful day, sunny and warm, and maybe he wouldn't leap on her if he took her outside. He wanted to hold back, to wait, until they were both sure it was right. And they lay side by side in the sun, talking again, for a long time. There seemed to be so much to say, so much to learn, so much to explain and understand about each other.

And that afternoon, he called Benjamin, and Charlotte listened to him with a tender smile, talking to his son. The baby was fine. Sandra was out. The house was great. And they hoped to see him soon, too, and no, nothing was wrong. She smiled again as he hung up. "You're crazy about that kid, aren't you?"

"Yes." He smiled ruefully. "I just wish he'd get the hell out of that mess and get his ass out here so I could keep an eye on him. And get him to go back to school. He's wasting his life on that girl, and at his age it's a crime."

"Give him a chance. He'll sort it all out for himself in time. We all do eventually." And then, as an afterthought, "You don't suppose they'll get married, do you?"

"No, I don't." He sighed and put an arm around her and then they went to visit her friends. They were directors, both of them, and they had done some interesting things, and they had some very nice friends. Some well-known people were there, but there were a lot of anonymous ones, too, and everyone was simple and direct, and no one seemed startled to see Charlotte with Oliver, and they made him feel at home, and he had a very good time. They stayed longer than they'd planned, and at nine o'clock they went back to Bel Air, and decided to go for a swim in his pool. They hadn't had anything to eat, but they were both still full from breakfast and lunch, and all the nibbles they'd had at her friends' house.

He lent her one of Mel's suits and went to change, and when he came back, she was already in the pool, swimming smooth laps, until at last she stopped at his end.

"You're very good. Is there anything you can't do?"

"Yeah. A lot." She was smiling up at him. "I swim a lot for exercise, it keeps me in shape." And it certainly did a good job. The body he saw when she emerged to dive off the diving board startled him. Her proportions were ideal, her limbs perfectly carved. She was an incredibly beautiful girl, wet or dry, morning or night, any time of day, anytime, anywhere, and he wanted her now, here, at his pool, and he knew he couldn't do that to her. They had just met, and in some ways she was an old-fashioned girl. She dived close to him then, and came up for air near where he was swimming. "Want to race?" She was playing with him and he smiled at her. He had been captain of the swimming team a hundred years before, and she was no match for him. He beat her hands down, and then pinned her to the side of the pool and kissed her. "You're not bad yourself."

"Which skill were you referring to, my dear?" he teased.

"Both, as a matter of fact." And then she dived after him, and swam underwater to the other side, like a little fish. But suddenly he couldn't stand it anymore, and he swam after her, circling her waist with his hands, and slowly they came up for air together, and he held her close, and she put her arms around him and kissed him again.

"I'm not sure I can behave myself, if you want to know the truth." He wanted to be honest with her right from the first.

"I'm not sure I want you to, Ollie." And then she kissed him hard, and he was overcome with desire, as he peeled her bathing suit slowly from her, and ran his hands across her exquisite flesh. They were breathing as one suddenly and moving as one, as she pushed his bathing suit down, too, and cradled him with her hands.

"Oh baby . . ." he moaned as he felt her touch, "Charlotte . . . I love you . . ." he was embarrassed to have said the words, but he did. He loved the way she thought and the way she felt, and the touch of her in his hands. His fingers gently touched her inside, and then they swam slowly to the steps, hungry with desire, and he laid her gently back, and as she kissed him, he entered her and she arched her back, and then moved with him, as the warm water surrounded them, and it went on endlessly, gentle and beautiful, as if they were two people brought together by time and space and kept suspended there for as long as they could stand, and finally he lost control and shuddered as she clung to him and at the same instant she exploded too. She opened her eyes and looked up at him, and kissed him again, and said everything he had wanted to hear from the moment they met, and as crazy as it seemed, he knew it was true for both of them.

"Ollie," she whispered in the soft night air, "I love you." He led her gently from the swimming pool then, wrapped her in towels, and took her back to his room. And they lay in his bed, whispering long into the night, giggling like two kids, sharing secrets and dreams. And when he made love to her again, it was clear to both of them that it was right. For the first time in their lives, they were both where they wanted to be, with the right person at the right time in exactly the right way.

"It's all like a dream, isn't it?" she whispered to him as they drifted off to sleep like happy children.

"Merry Christmas, Charlie," he whispered back with his arm tight around her waist, and he nuzzled her neck. It was the only Christmas they had ever known, the only one they would ever want. And if it was a dream, he hoped he would never wake from it.

Chapter 22

The kids came home after two weeks in Boston, and Oliver went to pick them up, feeling happy and relaxed, and warmed by his love for Charlotte. He had missed them as much as he always did when they were away, but this time he had had a life of his own while they were gone, and the days had flown by as though by magic. He was also nervous about their return, fearing that they would sense a change in him, and hoping, too, that they would like her. He had had the experience once before of the demise of a romance, because his lady love and his children didn't get along. He still winced thinking back to the time when he had introduced them to Megan. But what he shared with Charlotte now was infinitely different. She was gentle, she was warm, she was kind and fun to be with. She cared about how he felt about things and, unlike

Megan had been, she was wildly anxious to meet his children and make friends with them.

Sam leapt into his arms the moment he was off the plane, and Mel was close behind with a big grin and a skier's tan. Sarah had taken them to New Hampshire to ski for a few days over the New Year's weekend.

"Wow, you two look great!" They had had a good time, and Mel mentioned quietly in the car on the way home that their mother was recovering slowly from Jean-Pierre. Sarah was working full tilt on her novel, and she had decided to dedicate it to Jean-Pierre. He didn't ask if there was someone else in her life. He didn't really want to know, and he felt it was Sarah's business now, not his.

"Well, Dad," Sam snuggled close to him in the car, "did you miss us?"

"Are you kidding, champ? The house was like a tomb without you two." But not always, he smiled to himself, there had been Charlotte. . . .

"It was awfully lonely without you." He smiled at Mel over Sam's head, and he noticed how womanly she had become. In the past few months, she had developed a new poise, and after two weeks away from her, he could see fresh changes in her again.

"How's Andy?" Sam inquired about the dog.

"As big a mess as ever," his father grinned, "he marched across the white couch the other day, after wading in the swimming pool. Aggie went after him with a broom, and I'm not sure who won. After that, he chewed up her curtains." They all laughed, thinking of it, and Oliver tried to sound casual as he carefully phrased his next words. "I have a friend coming for dinner tonight, just an acquaintance," he tried to sound cool but wondered if he was fooling anyone but himself, his kids were sharp, "I thought you might like to meet her."

"Someone special, Dad?" Mel wore a curious smile, and raised one eyebrow. And that was also a change. Six months before she would have been prepared to hate any woman who evidenced an interest in her father. But things were different suddenly. She was growing up, and she was almost seventeen years old. There was a boy she herself was very interested in, in school, and she had come to understand finally after the summer with her mother and Jean-Pierre, that her parents were never getting back together. It was a little harder for Sam to accept that, but he was also more innocent, and he didn't seem to notice the catch in his father's voice, but Mel had.

"Just a friend."

Mel persisted, as they drove home. "Who is she?"

"Her name is Charlie . . . Charlotte, actually . . . and she's from Nebraska." He couldn't think of what else to say, and he didn't want to appear to brag by telling her that she was an actress on a successful TV show. They'd find that out for themselves eventually anyway. Just as Aggie had. Her jaw had dropped in amazement when she first saw her. But they had made friends rapidly, and at Aggie's request, Charlie brought her autographed pictures to send to friends and little mementoes from the show. By the time the children came home, Charlotte had Aggie's full approval.

They pulled into the driveway. Aggie was waiting to hug them both, and had cookies waiting for them. Andy went wild when he saw them. Dinner wasn't for another two hours, and Sam insisted that he wanted to swim. He couldn't wait to get home to California and the pool, after two weeks in the frozen East. He said he had never been so cold in his life as he had been in Boston.

Before Mel even unpacked her bags, she headed straight for the phone to call her friends, to find out who had done what with whom and what she'd missed over the holidays while she was gone. It was obvious they were both glad to be back, and Oliver was pleased to see it. He was only sorry that neither of them had had the opportunity to see Benjamin this time. He was back working at two full-time jobs, and he and Sandra had been tied down with the baby. It sounded as though nothing had changed, when he'd asked Mel in the car, and she said she thought he sounded depressed, but maybe he was just tired. Sandra had been out after midnight, and Benjamin had been baby-sitting both times when she called him.

And promptly at seven o'clock, as Oliver waited nervously in the den, listening to the familiar noises of the children upstairs, he saw the little red Mercedes pull into the driveway. His heart leapt in his chest, and he wanted to run out to Charlie, and kiss her. But he restrained himself, and watched her get out of the car, and then went sedately to the front door to let her in, wondering if the children were watching.

"Hi, babe," he whispered as he quickly kissed her neck, and then her cheek. "I missed you." It seemed days since they'd last met, but in truth they had been together only that morning.

"I missed you too," she whispered like a conspirator, "how are they?"

"Terrific. They had a great time, but they seem happy to be back. I told them about you in the car, and so far so good." It was worse than introducing a girl to her prospective mother-in-law, but he knew how tough kids could be, particularly his own. And Charlotte was as nervous about meeting them, as he was about introducing her to them. They were like two awkward kids as he escorted her into the den, and sat at opposite ends of the room in overstuffed chairs, but they wouldn't have fooled anyone. The look that passed between them was one of pure adoration. It was a rare thing they had found in the last two weeks, and they both knew it. And Charlotte knew it was something that had to be shared.

He jumped up from the chair then, and dashed upstairs to call them, while she wandered around the room, touching things, staring into space, and staring blankly at pictures. What if they hated her, if his daughter was a brat, and his beloved Sam a little monster. But before she could turn tail and run, the dog suddenly bounded into the room, followed by Sam, then Mel, and Oliver just behind them. It was an instant attack, and the room seemed suddenly full of noise and chatter and laughter, and then they all fell silent as they saw her.

Oliver was quick to step forward and introduce them. Mel shook her hand, clearly taking stock, and seemed to approve of what she saw. In fact, she was impressed. And Sam was staring at her with narrowed eyes, as though trying to remember something, but not sure what. And there was no denying she was pretty. She had worn a sedate navy blue skirt for them, dark blue textured stockings, and pretty navy pumps, a white turtleneck sweater, and a blazer. She wore less makeup than Mel, which wasn't much, and her hair was pulled back in a long, shining ponytail. Her hair was exactly the same color as Benjamin's, which was the first thing Mel noticed.

"It's nice to meet you both," she smiled, "I've heard a lot about you from your father."

"Yeah? Like what?" Sam grinned delightedly at her. She was kind of cute, and he decided he might like her. "Did he tell you about my science experiment?" He had been particularly proud of that, and Mel groaned at the thought.

"No, don't, please . . ." She guessed correctly what was coming.

"Would you like to see it?" He smiled broadly, and Charlotte started to nod, and Mel held out a hand to stop her.

"Take my advice, don't. He grew a worm farm. It's really disgusting." She and Aggie had forced him to keep it in the garage, and he was dying to show his father's friend, as much to show off as to test her.

"I did that once," she smiled at the boy, "my mother threw it out though. I had snakes, and white mice . . . and . . . a guinea pig. Have you ever had a guinea pig, Sam?" He shook his head, duly impressed with her. She was obviously a good one. "They're terrific. Mine was a longhair. It looked kind of like a cross between a dog and a rabbit."

"Gee, that sounds great," and then to Oliver with wide eyes, "Dad, can I have one?"

"You'd better ask Aggie first. She'll probably have to clean it."

Agnes called them into dinner then, and they sat

down in the dining room at the formal table. Charlotte primly put her starched white napkin in her lap, and felt Mel's eyes taking everything in, from her shining hair, to her perfectly manicured nails.

They had hamburgers and French fries, Sam's favorite, and a big green salad and homemade muffins, and Oliver was instantly reminded of the simple meals they'd been cooking for the past two weeks in Charlotte's kitchen. He suddenly knew how much he'd miss his time alone with her, but he had already promised himself that he would spend as much time with her as he could, even after the children got back. He had a right to, after all, and they'd have to get used to it. And then suddenly, halfway through dinner, Sam let out a yell and stared at her. His mouth fell open and his eyes grew wide, and then he shook his head . . . it couldn't be . . . it wasn't her . . . or was it . . .

"Are you . . . have you ever . . ." He didn't even know how to begin to ask the question, and Charlotte gently laughed at him. She had wondered if they would figure it out, but she had figured Mel would recognize her first, but she hadn't.

"I think I am," she said modestly with a mischievous grin, "if you're asking what I think you are, Sam."

"You're on TV! Wow! . . . That's you, isn't it? I mean . . ."

"Yeah, yeah . . . that's right." She looked apologetically at both kids, feeling faintly embarrassed.

"Why didn't you tell us?" Sam seemed almost insulted, and Mel looked confused. She knew Charlotte looked familiar, but she still didn't know why and she was ashamed to ask now. Obviously she should have known and didn't. And she really felt stupid.

"It didn't seem all that important, Sam." And the beauty of it was, she meant it.

"You said you had a guinea pig! Why didn't you say you had a TV show?"

They all laughed at his reasoning, and Charlotte shook her head, and grinned. "They're not exactly the same thing, you know."

And then suddenly Mel knew, too, and her eyes grew to be enormous. "Oh my *God*! You're *Charlotte Sampson*!"

"I am." She said quietly as Aggie passed another heaping basket of the delicious muffins, and glanced at her with pride. It was as though she and Charlie were old friends, and Charlotte shot her a grateful look, and whispered, "Thanks, Aggie," as she took another muffin from the basket.

"Why didn't you tell us?" She echoed her brother's words, and Charlotte looked at her seriously.

"Would it have made you like me any better? It shouldn't, you know. That kind of thing is nice, but it isn't really very important."

"I know, but . . ." Wait till she told her friends at school that she had actually had *dinner* with *Charlotte Sampson*! Lots of kids knew famous actors here, some of them were even related to them, but she had never known any before, and as she looked Charlotte over again more carefully this time, she thought she was terrific. And so did her father. He loved the way she was handling his kids, the things she said, the way she looked, the values that made her who she was, instead of just a famous actress. "Wow, it's really exciting to meet you," Mel said honestly, and Charlotte laughed.

It was a compliment that meant something to her, especially coming from Ollie's daughter.

"Thank you, Mel. It's exciting to meet you too. I was so nervous before I came over tonight, I must have changed my clothes ten times!" Ollie was touched, and Mel looked astounded.

"You? Nervous about meeting *us*! That's amazing! What's it like being on TV?" After that, they fired a hundred questions at her, about who she knew, who she'd seen, who she worked with, what it was like being on-screen, learning lines, was she ever scared, did she really like it?

"Hey, guys, relax," Oliver intervened at last, "give Charlie a chance to eat her dinner at least." They hadn't let her come up for air since they'd figured out who she was, and suddenly into the silence Mel asked her a single question.

"How'd you meet our dad?" She was curious, no longer critical, and Charlie smiled tenderly at the question.

"Just good luck, I guess. A few weeks ago, at a network Christmas party."

And then Oliver decided to tell them the truth, or part of it anyway. He figured they were ready for it. "Charlie was nice enough to invite me for Christmas dinner on Christmas Eve." He didn't tell them he'd spent the night with her, however, or made love to her in their pool on Christmas Day, or fallen head over heels in love with her the moment they met, but Mel could see it, and even Sam suspected this was serious. They looked at each other kind of weird, more even than Mom and Jean-Pierre. But it was okay with him, he thought, Charlotte Sampson was terrific.

And as soon as they finished dessert, he invited her once again to go to the garage with him to view his worm farm. And much to Mel's horror, she went, and returned to announce it was much better than hers had been. And Sam said proudly he'd won the science prize for it, as his sister told him again that he was revolting.

At nine o'clock, Sam went to bed, and Mel stayed downstairs to talk to her about scripts and agents and acting. Charlotte confessed she had always wanted to do a Broadway play, and finally, with regret, she looked at her watch, and admitted she had a 4:00 A.M. studio call the next day to shoot a tough scene she still had to review when she went home. "There's a lot of hard work to it, Mel, if you're serious about acting as a career. But I have to admit, I love it."

"Could I come and see you on the set sometime?" Mel dared to ask, astonished at her own courage, but Charlie made them all so comfortable that it was almost like asking an old friend, and she quickly nodded.

"Sure. If your dad doesn't mind. He watched me do a commercial a couple of weeks ago, and it was fun." She smiled shyly up at him, and he touched the hand Mel couldn't see from where she stood. And she was too busy being impressed to notice the electricity between them.

"Wow, Dad, how was it?"

"Interesting. Exhausting." He looked into Charlie's eyes sympathetically. "How many takes did they do in all?"

"Thirty-two, I think. Maybe more. I forget."

"The other actor kept blowing his lines, and they had to shoot again and again," he explained to Mel.

"But it was fun watching anyway. It's incredible how many people are involved."

"You should see what goes on when they do the show, speaking of which . . ." She walked slowly toward the door, and waved good night to Mel, who flew upstairs to call her friends and tell them who she'd met. And Oliver walked her out to her car, with a look of ever-growing admiration.

"You are really incredible, do you know that? Worm farms, patience with teenage girls, is there anything else about you I should know?"

"Yes." She looked happily up at him. It had been a wonderful evening, and all her fears had been dispelled. She hoped they liked her. "I love you very much, Oliver Watson."

"I love you too, Charlie," he whispered as he kissed her. And from his bedroom window, Sam stared in amazement as he watched them, and then turned to Aggie, who was turning down his bed.

"Wow, Aggie! Dad just kissed Charlotte Sampson!" That was really something else, but Agnes only clucked at him.

"Mind your own business, young man, and go brush your teeth!"

"Do you think she really likes him?"

"I suspect she does. Your father is a fine man, who wouldn't?"

"But she's a movie star, Aggie . . . or TV, or . . . you know . . ."

"What difference does that make?" And as he went to brush his teeth, still shaking his head over it, Aggie thought they were both very lucky people. And after what she'd seen tonight, so were the children.

Chapter 23

That weekend, Charlotte drove up their driveway in her car, got out, and solemnly rang the doorbell. And when Sam answered, thrilled to see her again, she handed him an odd-shaped cage, covered by a pale blue blanket. There were odd squeaking noises from within, and a pungent smell he didn't mind, and as he pulled off the blanket, he gave a squeal of delight himself. It was a long-haired guinea pig. And she had been right, it did look like a cross between a small dog and a rabbit.

"Wow! *Wow!* . . . Look at that, Dad!" He called to his father just coming down the stairs, freshly shaved and showered, "Can I keep it?" He looked from him to Charlotte. And Charlotte looked pleadingly at the senior Watson.

"I guess you can." He smiled lovingly at her. All she did was make them happy.

"Can I keep him in my room?"

"If you can stand the smell, you can." The two adults laughed and Sam took the cage from her hand, and hurried up the stairs with it before any of them could change their mind on him.

They went to Malibu that afternoon to play on the beach, and a movie Mel wanted to see that night, some ghastly teenage horror, that Charlie said reminded her of some of her early work, and then they went to the Hard Rock Café and she didn't even seem to mind the noise. And the following week they went to Disneyland. Life was a constant holiday with her. She thought of terrific things to do, exciting events to see, and she even invited them to her house and made dinner for them, although Sam admitted reluctantly that Agnes was a better cook, but in every other way, he liked Charlie even better. The guinea pig had even been named after her, and was called Charles, and Charlie for short. And Mel had already told everyone she'd ever met that her father was going out with Charlotte Sampson.

Neither of the children objected to her, and they didn't even look upset when Oliver said he was going out at night, which wasn't often during the week, since she worked so hard and had to be on the set so early. And twice she had even stayed over on the weekend and slept in their guest room. She was a great one for decorum and behavior that wouldn't embarrass the children. And neither of them knew that late at night, their father tiptoed down the hall, and climbed into bed with her with a happy smile as she told him to *ssshhh!* and giggled.

It was, for all of them, the perfect arrangement. And

when George and Margaret came out a month after the children got home, they liked her too. At first they were enormously impressed to meet her. But they forgot quickly that she was famous. She was so unaware of herself, so discreet about her success, so warm to those she cared about, and kind to everyone, it seemed, that everyone fell in love with the woman and not the TV star. As she had said when she first met Mel, her success was nice but it wasn't the most important thing in her life. It was the people she loved who really mattered to her.

But they were all aware of her fame nonetheless, because wherever one went, people wanted her to sign autographs, or intruded at unexpected times asking her if she was . . . and telling her how much they liked the show . . . and wanting to know who Mel and Sam were . . . It annoyed them sometimes, and Oliver tried not to think about it more than he had to. But Charlie was always gracious to her fans, patient, understanding, and acted as though she had been waiting for them to come over and talk to her all day and was glad they had. Sometimes, Mel asked her how she could stand it without losing her temper.

"It's part of the job, sweetheart. You accept that when you take on this kind of work, or you'll never amount to much. You're doing this for them as much as yourself. And the day you stop caring about them, is the day you stop giving a good performance."

And most of all Oliver's father, George, thought she was absolutely charming, the prettiest girl he had ever seen, and he only prayed she would marry his son. And before he left, he asked Oliver if he'd ask her.

"Come on, Dad. We haven't even known each other

two months yet, don't rush me. Besides, she has quite a career on her hands. I don't know that she wants to settle down with an ordinary mortal and a bunch of kids." She said she did, but the truth was, he was afraid to ask her.

"I think she does. She's got real honest-to-goodness decent values."

"I know, but she could have anyone she wants in Hollywood. Give it time." He still couldn't believe his good fortune. But neither could Charlie.

And they were sitting talking quietly one night, after his father and Margaret had gone back to New York again, when the phone rang and it was Benjamin, and he was crying so hard, Ollie could hardly understand him.

"Take it easy, Son, slow down . . . that's it . . . take a deep breath . . ." He looked worriedly at Charlie, fearing an accident. He hadn't heard from him in weeks, there was never an answer when he called, and he had asked his father to look in on him when he got back, at the house in Purchase. "Benjamin, talk to me, what is it?" All he could hear was still the sound of jagged crying.

"I can't take it anymore, Dad . . . I just can't take it . . . I hate her . . ."

"What happened?"

"Nothing. I'm just so tired . . . all I do is work and pay for stuff for the baby and for her . . . she gave up her job, and she thought she was pregnant again, but she wasn't." And this time, the baby wouldn't have been his, at least, he hadn't touched her in two months. "She's been going out with Billy Webb and Johnny Pierson . . . I don't know, Dad . . . all she does is go out. Sometimes I have to take the baby to work with me. I love Alex, I don't want to leave him . . . but I can't . . ." He started to cry again. ". . . I can't do this anymore . . . I just can't. Last week I thought of killing myself. I sat in the garage for an hour, trying to get the guts to turn the car on, but I couldn't. I just kept thinking of Alex and what would happen to him if he was left with her. She doesn't give a damn, Dad. Sometimes she doesn't even remember to feed him all day and he's screaming his lungs out when I get home. Last week he almost fell in the pool when I left him alone with her for ten minutes. Dad . . . help me please . . . get me out of this. . . ." The jagged sobbing seemed to go on for hours, but when Oliver suggested he come out to California as soon as he could, Benjamin said he couldn't leave the baby. He loved him too much and Sandra would neglect him too badly.

"Why don't you bring him?"

"She says she won't let me. I told her last week, I'd take him away, and she said she'd call the police if I tried it. She says I have no right to take him, she's his mother. And if I took him, all her friends would think she'd done something really awful, and it would make her look bad. But she doesn't want to take care of him either."

"What about Sandra's mother? Do you think she'd help?"

"I don't know. Her boyfriend walked out on her, and she moved to Bakersfield from L.A."

"Do you have her number?"

"Yeah. Sandra left it on the kitchen wall." His crying had finally subsided. He was eighteen years old and staggering under an awesome burden. "You know, she hasn't even been home since yesterday morning. She's been screwing around almost since right after Alex was born," he was five and a half months old by then, "and, Dad, I tried to make it work, I really did, but I just can't," and then in a voice of shame, "Sometimes I hate her." Oliver didn't blame him a bit, and suspected that in his shoes, he might have killed her, or certainly walked out on her a long time since. But Benjamin was so determined to do the right thing, by her, and by his son. He was only grateful once again that the boy hadn't married her. At least that much was simple.

"Just relax. Why don't you go to Grampa's for the weekend?"

"What'll I do with Alex?" He sounded suddenly blank, like a helpless child. After almost a year of working two jobs, and supporting a girl who wasn't his wife, and almost six months of caring for his child, the boy was so worn out, he could hardly think straight.

"Take him with you. Margaret'll give you a hand, she was a nurse. Just pack up your stuff, and get the hell out of there. I'll call him and tell him you're coming. Now give me Sandra's mother's number." Benjamin gave it to him, and hung up after promising to pack a bag for both of them and go to his grandfather's that evening.

Oliver called his father then, and explained the situation as he repeated it to Margaret in the background, and assured his son that he would do everything he could to help the boy.

"You've got to get him out of that situation, Oliver."

"I'm going to do everything I can, Dad." He didn't

tell him that his oldest grandson had actually contemplated suicide over it, he was still too shaken over it himself. But he told Charlotte when he hung up, and she was horrified.

"Oh my God, Ollie, get him out of there. Why don't you fly back there to pick him up?"

"I want to talk to the girl's mother first, and see if she'll take in Sandra and the baby." He dialed the number in Bakersfield, and the woman answered it on the first ring. She sounded drunk, and more than a little stupid, but she knew who Oliver was, and about Sandra and Benjamin and the baby. And Oliver patiently explained that he and Benjamin felt the time had come to make some other arrangements. He asked if she would be willing to take her daughter back into her home, with her baby. And after hedging for a while, she finally asked Oliver the only question that really concerned her.

"Would ya pay for the kid, if I did? And her too?"

"I might." It would be worth anything to him to get her out of Benjamin's life, but he didn't want to tell her that. It would make her even more greedy. "It depends how much we're talking about. And I would certainly expect Sandra to work to support herself as well, unless she goes back to school, of course." But the woman seemed less than interested in her daughter's education.

"How much are we talkin' about?"

"Say five hundred a month for her and the child." It wasn't a fortune, but it was enough, particularly if she was living with her mother.

"I guess that's all right." She wanted to grab it before he changed his mind. Hell, they didn't hardly need no money for the kid, she told herself. All it ate was baby food, and she and Sandra could have some fun with the rest of the money.

"Would you be willing to sign papers agreeing to that amount?"

"Yeah. Sure."

"How soon would you be willing to take her in?"

"Hell, I don't know. I'm not working right now. I guess I could help her with the kid . . ." Her voice seemed to drift off at the other end, she wasn't crazy about the idea of living with a screaming brat, and having Sandra on her hands, again, but on the other hand the money sounded pretty good to her, unless she could do even better. "How about seven hundred, come to think of it?"

"Six." Oliver's face froze with disgust. He hated even dealing with her, and listening to her made him cringe, thinking that Benjamin had been living with her daughter.

"Okay. I'll take it."

"I'll have them on a plane to you tomorrow."

He called Margaret after that, and asked her if she could go to the house in Purchase and help the girl get on a plane to Los Angeles with the baby. And then keep Benjamin with her for the weekend. He wanted him to cool out a little bit, and he didn't want him to go through the stress of being on the same plane to L.A. with Sandra and little Alex.

Margaret sounded like an angel of mercy to him, and rapidly agreed to help. She didn't sound flustered or confused, but perfectly calm, and anxious to do everything she could to help, without upsetting Oliver's father. He thanked her from the bottom of his heart, and she assured him she'd close the house in Purchase after Benjamin left, turn on the alarm, and keep an eye on it for him after that. He hadn't wanted to sell it in any case, until he was sure they were staying in California. It was his fallback, which was why he had only rented in California.

And then he called Benjamin, who sounded as though he was waiting by the phone. "It's all taken care of, Son. I talked to her mother, and she'll be happy to take them in." He made it sound like a warmer welcome than it was, and explained that they would be providing adequate funds for the child's support, so he didn't have to worry about that. "I'll have a prepaid ticket for them at the airport tomorrow, and Margaret will come over and help her pack and take you to Grandpa's. And then I thought maybe you could spend a day or two with them, and come out here." And then he'd be home. After all these months, he'd be back in the fold again, to start a new life, or pick up the threads of his old one. It would never be quite the same for him again, Oliver knew, he couldn't erase what had happened, or forget the child, but he had a right to move on and not get buried alive with a girl he didn't love and a baby he had never really wanted. He had done the noble thing for long enough, but now that he had opened the door, Oliver was going to get him the hell out of that mess as fast as he could, before he could change his mind again. Benjamin balked at first, at the prospect of letting Sandra take the baby. But he was too tired and depressed to fight anymore, and his father kept telling him that Sandra's mother was going to take care of the baby. Benjamin sounded numb as he agreed to all of it, and then after a long moment of silence, his voice sounded sad as he thanked his father.

"I'm just going to miss Alex so much. He's so cute now, Dad. He's crawling. I don't know . . ." He seemed to hesitate again. "Maybe this isn't the right thing." But a part of him wanted relief from the responsibilities. The last few months had been a nightmare.

"You're doing the right thing," Oliver soothed, "you can visit him in Bakersfield. It's only two hours from here. This is the best thing that could happen to all of you. You, Sandra, and the baby. You can't go on struggling back there. You've done a hell of a fine job this far, and I'm proud of you. But you have to think of yourself too. At your age, without even a high school diploma under your belt, you can't offer anything to that baby."

"I know." And then, in a worried tone, "Did Sandra's mom really say she'd help her with Alex? I don't trust her to do it on her own."

"She said she would and she's not even working. Now get some sleep." And as he said the words, he could hear the baby crying in the distance. Benjamin decided to wait at the house for Sandra to come home, and Margaret was coming in the morning. "I'll talk to you tomorrow night, at Grampa's." But when he called him the next day, Margaret said he was asleep. He had been absolutely heartbroken when Sandra and the baby left. He had insisted on cleaning up the house in Purchase himself, after they left, and when he got to his grandfather's house, he had just kind of fallen apart from the shock and strain of it. Apparently his parting from Sandra had been bitter and loud. And Margaret had put him to bed like a child, and he hadn't even eaten dinner. She wondered if he should stay for a few more days, but Oliver insisted that he wanted him in California as soon as he felt up to the trip. He needed to get out of there and put as many miles as he could between himself and the past year's nightmare.

"He's a fine boy, Oliver. You should be very proud of him. He was a man till the end. And it killed him to see that child go."

"I know." He had never expected him to love the baby so much, and it certainly complicated things, but in time, perhaps things would change, perhaps the attachment wouldn't be so great, or maybe one day Sandra would be willing to give up her rights and let Benjamin adopt him. Oliver had spoken to an attorney about it and he had assured him that unless she was willing to give the baby up, and she wasn't, there was no way to wrest the child from her. They had done the right thing in letting her take him, and the appropriate thing would be to let Benjamin visit the baby. "Thank you again for taking care of all of it, Margaret," Oliver said. "I'm sorry to burden you with all that. I just didn't know who else to turn to." He had thought of calling Daphne in New York. But she was too far away, and too busy with her work. Margaret had been a godsend in handling the problem, and he was deeply grateful to her. His father was right. She was a hell of a woman.

"Your father says he's a lot like you were. Strong and kind and stubborn." It was odd to hear her say the words, Oliver had always thought Benjamin was more like his mother. "He'll get on the right track again now, don't worry about him, and I'll put him on the plane to you tomorrow or the next day."

He thanked her again, and finally hung up, to call Sandra's mother in Bakersfield and make sure that Sandra and the baby had arrived safely. She said they had and wanted to know how quickly the first check was coming.

"I put it in the mail to you yesterday, Mrs. Carter," Oliver said with disdain. "Is the baby all right?"

"He's a cute kid," she said, more to please him than out of any real emotion she had for her grandchild. And then, finally, Oliver relaxed, as he stretched out on the couch next to Charlotte, who had been through most of it with him. The ordeal was finally almost over.

He turned to her with a tired smile, as she gently stroked his hair. "It's been a year of hell for that boy, Charlie. Thank God he's free now." Though even Oliver felt a pang of sadness for little Alex. He would be more removed from their lives now.

"It must have been hard for him to call you like that. You have to give him credit for throwing in the towel while he still could."

"I do. I have a lot of respect for him. I'm just sorry he had to go through it." They had a quiet dinner alone that night, after Mel and Sam went upstairs. By then, Benjamin had called, and they all knew that their brother was arriving the next day, and Oliver had warned them he'd had a tough time, and Mel had promised to do whatever she could to make things easier for him. They all wondered what he was going to do about school, but no one knew yet.

Ollie drove Charlotte home late that night, and he only stayed for one quick drink. All they did was talk about Benjamin, and kiss for a few minutes in the kitchen. It was certainly a far cry from his wild, unbridled fling with Megan. And he smiled at her ruefully before he left, and apologized for all the confusion.

"I'm afraid you'll find, my love, that things never go quite the way you plan, with kids around. I guess I've gotten used to it over the years, but it can't be much fun for you. I haven't been very good company for the past few days."

"You've been fine, and I wouldn't have expected you to be any different." And then she had a thought, she loved being with him, and with his kids, and her heart had gone out to this boy she didn't even know yet. "Do you want me to come to the airport with you tomorrow night, or would you rather be alone with him?" She was always thoughtful about the time he needed with his kids, and he appreciated that too. There seemed to be nothing she didn't understand or wasn't willing to help with.

"There'll be plenty of time to talk after we get home. I'd like you to come with me, Charlie." He smiled, and kissed her again, and left a few minutes later, exhausted himself. He could barely imagine how Benjamin must feel after all he'd been through. But he was in no way prepared for the gaunt, pale, anguished-looking boy he picked up at the airport the next night, and all he did was put his arms around him as the boy cried, while Charlotte stood at a discreet distance. He finally wiped his eyes, and looked at his father like a long-lost friend. And Charlotte turned away so they wouldn't see her tears, as they both walked slowly over so Benjamin could meet her.

"Charlotte, I'd like you to meet my son, Benjamin."

Oliver spoke quietly, it was a somber night for them, and she understood it. But the boy made an effort to look less distraught than he was, and smiled as he shook her hand.

"My sister has told me a lot about you, and I've seen your show a lot of times. And Sam's told me about the guinea pig. You've made a big hit with my family, Miss Sampson." She was flattered by the kind speech, and gently kissed his cheek, and Oliver noticed how much the two resembled each other. Almost anyone would have thought they were related, with their bright red hair, and creamy skin, and the thin dusting of freckles.

"I'm flattered, Benjamin. But I'd be even happier if you'd call me Charlie. How was the flight out?"

"Pretty good, I think. I slept most of the way." He was still emotionally drained and totally exhausted. He had slept until noon that day, and Margaret had driven him to the airport, as she had promised his father. And then he talked quickly to his father in an undertone. "Did you talk to Sandra last night? Is the baby okay?"

"They're fine." He led him toward the baggage claim, sad to see Benjamin so worried about them. Alex was still his first concern and it was painful to see how much he missed his baby. He said as much to Charlotte, when they were alone for a minute, putting Benjamin's bags in his bedroom.

"He's not just going to forget him, Ollie."

"No, I know that. But it's time he thought of himself now."

"He will. Give him time. He's still in shock. Don't forget all he's been through."

They walked back downstairs to join the others then. All the children, including Benjamin, had stampeded into the kitchen. And when Oliver and Charlotte walked in, Benjamin was eating a club sandwich and a plate of brownies that Aggie had made him. Mel was talking excitedly to him and Sam kept shoving the guinea pig in his face, to show him how beautiful he was. And Benjamin smiled as he listened to them. It was good to be home, better than any one of them knew. He felt as though he had just spent a year on another planet.

"So how's school?" he asked Mel.

"It's great. You're gonna love it." And then she wished she could have swallowed her tongue. Her father had warned her not to press him about school, but her brother read the look in her eyes and smiled.

"Don't worry, kiddo. I'm not that uptight. But I haven't figured out what I'm going to do yet. I want to go down to Bakersfield to check on Alex first, and then I'm going to look into taking a high school equivalency test. I think I might try to get into UCLA if I can swing it." Gone the dream of Princeton and Yale and Harvard, but UCLA was a fine school, and he wanted to stay close to home for a while. Now that was all he wanted.

He told Oliver the same thing when the others had gone to bed, and Charlie told him she had gone there, too, and offered to write him a letter of recommendation, if it would help him.

"That would be great." He thanked her, and tried not to look as though he was staring at her. But he had been impressed with her all night, with how nice she was, and how pretty, and how obviously crazy about his father. She insisted on driving home herself that night, she wanted the two men to have some time alone, and Benjamin had nothing but good things to say about her after she left, which pleased his father.

"Looks like you lucked out, Dad. She's terrific."

"I think so too," he smiled, and then looked worried again as he looked over his son, as though searching for scars. But none of them showed, except in his eyes, which looked a hundred years older. "Are you okay? I mean really?"

"I'll do. Do you have a car I can borrow, Dad? I want to drive down to Bakersfield to see Alex tomorrow."

"Do you think you should? So soon, I mean. It might be hard on Sandra. Maybe you two ought to give each other a breather."

Benjamin sighed, and leaned back against the comfortable couch, relief written all over his face as he stretched his legs. "I'd be happy if I never saw her again. But I want to check on the baby."

"You're crazy about him, aren't you?" It was just like what he had felt for his own children after they were born, but he had expected this to be different, and the funny thing was that it wasn't.

"He's my son, Dad. You wouldn't expect me to feel any differently, would you?" He seemed surprised. To him, legitimacy or not was not the issue. He loved his baby.

"I guess not. I felt that way about you." It would have killed him to walk out on him, or leave him in the hands of someone he didn't trust. And suddenly, he got a glimpse of what his own son was feeling. "You can take the station wagon if you want. Just tell Aggie you're taking it, in case she needs it to buy groceries or pick Sam up."

"Thanks. And I promise, as soon as I've done that,

I'll get myself squared away with school. And if I have a long wait to get into UCLA, I'll get a job. I'm not going to sit on my ass. I want to thank you for everything you've done for me, Dad." The words brought tears to Oliver's eyes, and he gently patted him on the knee as he stood up, tired himself, and relieved to have his son back in the fold at last.

"Just make a good life for yourself, Benjamin. You'll have it all again one day. A good woman, all the children you want, at the right time, in the right way, with the right wife, if you're lucky."

Benjamin smiled at the advice, and looked up at him curiously. "You gonna marry her, Dad? I mean Charlie."

"I figured that much out." The older man smiled, and was honest with him, man to man. Benjamin wasn't a child any longer.

"I'd like to, but we haven't had much time to discuss it." He'd been skirting the subject for the last month. He knew how important her career was to her, and he was desperately afraid of rejection. He didn't want to blow it by asking her too soon, but he had known from the first night that it was right. And it was just a matter of time before he asked her. It was different from anything he'd had before, and he had feelings for her that he'd never even had for Sarah. It had always been difficult with her, he realized now, a square peg in a round hole. But this was such a perfect fit. Charlie was everything he had always dreamed of.

"She's a great girl. I really like her."

"So do I." Ollie smiled, and then showed him upstairs to his bedroom. And then he walked slowly to his own, glad to have them all under one roof again. His three little chicks that were all growing up so fast, even Sam. He never slept in his father's bed anymore. He was perfectly content in his own room, with Charlie.

Chapter 24

Benjamin drove to Bakersfield the day after he arrived, and he wasn't thrilled with what he found, but the baby was all right, and Sandra was there and her mother seemed to be keeping an eye on things, which was the best he could hope for. But the house was decrepit and unkempt, the air conditioner didn't work, and Alex was sleeping in a crib in the living room, with the TV blaring beside him. He squealed when he awoke and saw Benjamin in the room, and it was an agony leaving him again, but he was happy to get away from Sandra.

He drove back to Bel Air feeling somewhat reassured. And in the ensuing weeks, he passed his high school equivalency test, and applied to UCLA and four weeks later he was accepted. He had gotten a part-time job by then, in the bookstore on campus, and he intended to keep the job, so he could help make the monthly payments for Alex.

He had driven down to Bakersfield again, and things appeared to be the same, although Sandra was out that time, but her mother was there, drinking beer, and the baby looked happy, and Benjamin played with him for an hour, and then drove back. And this time, he didn't mention the visit to his father. He had a feeling that Oliver thought he was still too involved with the child, but he knew just as clearly that it was something he had to do, that no matter how many other children he had one day, Alex would always be his first, and an important part of his life. And he intended to stay very much in the picture. And Sandra's mother didn't seem to mind, she was very pleased with the payments that arrived punctually every month. Alex was the best thing that ever happened to her. Sandra sure knew what she was doing when she got knocked up by Benjamin Watson. The Watsons may not have been rich, but they were comfortable enough, and she knew from a little research she'd done back East that the kid's father made a hell of a good living. And then a few weeks later, she read a little item in a gossip column that really intrigued her. The old man was going out with Charlotte Sampson. It didn't mean much now, but one day, if they stopped paying their dues, a little blackmail might even be in order.

But that was the farthest thing from Ollie's mind, as the romance flourished, and they spent more and more time with each other, much to his children's delight. And finally in late April, he got up the courage to ask her.

They were having another one of their quiet, intimate dinners at Chianti, and he didn't surprise her with a ring, or ask her on bended knee. He waited until they had finished eating, and then looked at her nervously, and she giggled at him. She wasn't sure, but she thought she knew what was coming.

"How was the office today?" she teased, and he almost groaned.

"Don't do this to me . . . I wanted to talk to you about something serious. I have for a long time, but I wasn't sure how you'd feel about it . . . with your career and all. . . ."

"You want to offer me a job?" She smiled innocently.

"Oh shut up. Actually, now that you mention it . . . yes. You could call it that. A permanent position, with rotten pay, compared to what you make. A lifetime commitment, live-in, with three major handicaps, a few perks, and eventually a pension."

"Don't you dare call your children handicaps, Oliver Watson! I happen to love them." She sounded offended on their behalf, and he held her hand tightly in his own, and brought it to his lips to kiss her fingers.

"So do I. But I also happen to love you. How would you feel about getting married one of these days?" His heart pounded as he asked, and he wouldn't have been surprised if she declined, but she didn't say a word, she just kissed him.

"That's the nicest thing anyone's ever said to me," she said finally. But she still hadn't answered him, and waiting for her to was torture.

"And?"

"I think we should both think about it seriously. You more than I. I know what I'm getting, Ollie, and I love all four of you, but you've never been married to a wife with a career before, it can be pretty rough, especially a career like mine. We wouldn't have a very private life, no matter how hard we tried, and everyone would always be making a fuss about me, as long as I'm on the show anyway. And that can be a pain in the ass sometimes too." He'd already experienced it when they went out, the constant demands for autographs, the press, the well-meaning intrusions. But it didn't bother him, and he was proud of her. He didn't mind standing back and letting her be the star.

"I don't mind any of that."

"Are you sure? One day I'd like to give it all up, but to be honest with you, Ollie, not yet. I'm just not ready to. I've worked too hard for too long to give it up now before I squeeze every drop of satisfaction out of it."

"I understand that. I wouldn't expect you to give it up. I think that would be a terrible mistake."

"So do I. No matter how much I love you, I think I'd resent it. How do you think the kids would feel?" She was concerned about that too. They meant a lot to her, and to him, and she wanted it to be something they wanted, too, but Ollie only grinned.

"They said they'd divorce me if I didn't ask. And I figure they'll probably leave me and find another father if you don't accept me."

"They'd be fools if they did. They couldn't find a better one if they tried."

"That's not true. I screw up a lot."

"Yes, it is true. And I haven't seen you screw up yet. You do a hell of a job with them." Benjamin was back on the right track, Mel was doing brilliantly in school, and Sam had never been happier in his life. Things were going well for all of them. And then she smiled, shyly, as she looked up at him. "I'd like to have kids of my own one day too. One or two anyway, maybe even three if I'm not too far gone by the time I start. How would you feel about that? It would give you a pretty full house, what with the guinea pigs and white mice and worm farms and all." They both laughed, but the subject was serious, and she was right to bring it up. He frowned as he thought about it, it had crossed his mind before, but he had never really imagined having babies again. At forty-five, it was an interesting thought, and at least, she thought to herself, he hadn't gone screaming out the door yet.

"I don't know. I think I'm a little old and tired to start all over again. Kids aren't as easy as you think." He had certainly seen that in the last year, but he also knew how great were the rewards, and he didn't want to cheat her out of that. He loved her too much. And she had a lot to offer children of her own, as well as his. It was worth thinking about, if it meant convincing her about their future. "I guess I could probably be talked into it, once, anyway," he saw the look in her eyes and his heart melted as she smiled, "maybe twice. But don't push me too far. I'm a grandfather, you know."

"That doesn't count," she meant because he was still so young, but Oliver looked sad.

"To Benjamin it does."

"I just meant you're not old enough to call yourself that."

"I feel it sometimes. Except when I'm with you. I think we could do wonderful things, Charlie. There's so much I'd like to do with you. Travel, have fun, help you with your career. It's the first time in my life I've really felt it was right, right down to my toes and deep in my soul, I don't have a single doubt about us." And he felt so peaceful.

"The funny thing is, neither do I. I know how much I love you, Oliver. I just want you to be sure."

She hesitated only long enough to kiss him again, and whisper softly in his ear. "In that case you're on. But I want to wait a year from the time we met, and do it right. How about Christmas?"

"Do you mean that?" He looked stunned. His divorce had been final for a month, and Sarah had been gone for over a year, and he loved this woman with his whole heart, and now she was willing to marry him. But she was nodding and smiling and laughing suddenly, and she looked as happy as he felt.

"Of course I mean it. Do you mind waiting until Christmas?"

"A little. But I kind of like the idea of an old-fashioned engagement."

"We go on hiatus in June. We could go away for a month or two this summer. I had an offer to do a film, but it's really second-rate. I'd much rather go away somewhere with you and the children, unless Sarah's taking them somewhere."

"She is. But only in August."

They made plans through the rest of the evening, and that night when he took her home, he stayed and they made love to celebrate their engagement.

Chapter 25

The next day they told the children, and they were ecstatic. Sam wanted to know if he could come on their honeymoon, as Oliver groaned, and Charlotte asked Mel if she would be the maid of honor at their wedding. It was still eight months away, but as they talked about it, they were all like excited children.

The following day, Oliver picked her up at the studio, and when Charlotte got in the car there was a small square box on the seat, wrapped in turquoise paper and tied with a white satin ribbon. Her hands shook as she opened it and she gasped as she saw the ring sparkling inside the black suede box. It was an exquisite emerald-cut diamond, and there were tears in her eyes as she let Oliver slip it on her finger.

"Oh, Ollie . . . it's so beautiful."

"So are you." He kissed her, and held her tight, and

she snuggled close to him as they drove home to the children.

The press got hold of the news within a few days, and the producers of the show made the most of it. The PR people for the studio were all over them, wanting photographs of Charlotte with Oliver and the children. *People* magazine called, and *US*, and news of their engagement appeared in both *Newsweek* and *Time*, and suddenly even the children were being hounded. It infuriated Charlotte, and Oliver was less than pleased to discover the paparazzi outside the house on several occasions.

"How do you stand it?" he asked Charlotte more than once, and as a result, they agreed to spend their summer holiday in seclusion with the children at a borrowed villa in Trancas.

It was fairly hairy for the next few weeks, and eventually things started to calm down a little, and Sarah called, and congratulated him. She had heard the news from Sam, but she'd also read about it in the papers.

"The kids seem to be crazy about her, Ollie. I'm happy for you."

"So am I. But the press is a bit of a bore."

"You'll get used to it. That's Hollywood!" she teased, but she sounded pleased for him, and his father and Margaret were thrilled too. It was a happy time, and Oliver and Charlie had a lot to do before they left for their summer vacation in Trancas with the children.

Eventually, Charlotte finished the last of her tapings for the season, the kids finished school, and Oliver left the office for a four-week holiday and the five of them set off for Trancas. They spent a heavenly month there at the beach, and then Mel and Sam left for the East to visit their mother.

Charlie was planning to shoot a few commercials again, Oliver had to go back to work, and Ben had to get ready to start classes at UCLA at the end of August.

It was just before that that he got the call, late one afternoon, when he had come home to change and go out for dinner with Charlie and his dad. When the telephone rang, he thought his father was calling from the office. But he was surprised instead to hear Sandra's mother's voice, and she was calling for him. It almost made his heart stop to hear her.

"Is something wrong, Mrs. Carter? . . . is Alex . . ."

"He's fine, I guess." She sounded strange. She had thought a long time about the call, trying to think of some way it would bring her gain, but in the end, she had decided just to tell him. He had a right to know, and he wasn't a bad kid. And he seemed to be crazy about the boy. Maybe it was better trying to do them a favor. At least that was what she told herself as she dialed. "Sandra left the baby in the shelter yesterday morning. She's putting him up for adoption. I thought maybe you'd want to know."

"She *what*?" His heart was pounding wildly. "She can't do that. He's my son too. Where is he? I'm not going to let her do that, Mrs. Carter. I'll take care of him myself. I told her that when we were still in Purchase."

"I figured that's how you'd feel, that's why I called. I told her she should call you. But she just dumped him and ran. She left for Hawaii this morning."

"Thank you . . . thank you . . . tell them I'm going to pick him up right away . . . I'll . . . never mind . . . I'll call them myself." But when he called the shelter she'd told him about, they told him that Alexander Carter, as he was called, was now a ward of the court. Benjamin would have to prove his paternity, and file for custody, and termination of Sandra's rights. And that was up to the court now. He called his father frantically then, and had him dragged out of a meeting with a new client. He was practically hysterical by then, and Oliver told him to calm down and explain it all slowly.

"All right, all right . . . I understand now. I'll call a lawyer. Now get a hold of yourself, Benjamin. But before we do anything, I want you to think about what you really want. Do you truly want full custody of the boy? Son, it's up to you now." He finally had the chance to get out from under, if that was what he wanted. And however much it might hurt, Oliver was willing to back him up, whatever he wanted. But Benjamin knew he had only one choice. He wanted his son back, and even if it meant never going back to school, and working at any job he had to, he was going to keep his son and bring him up, no matter what it took to do it. It was the kind of sentiment one couldn't argue with, and Oliver didn't want to. He told Benjamin to sit tight and he'd call him back. He called him back half an hour later, and told him to meet him at the offices of Loeb and Loeb in Century City at four o'clock.

Benjamin was there ten minutes early and the lawyer they saw was a kindly man who had handled cases of far greater importance. But they were the attorneys for Ollie's firm, and they were willing to help them.

"If this is really what you want, young man, I don't think it's quite as complicated as it looks. I've spoken to all the parties involved today, and the authorities, and things are pretty clear. Your paternity of the child does not appear to be in question. The girl has already signed papers stating that she wants to give up the baby. If she will confirm that to us, in writing, and we've not yet been able to speak to her, then you will have sole custody of the child, and eventually her maternal rights will be terminated. That's an awesome responsibility, Benjamin, and you ought to think it over seriously before you decide to do it."

"I already have, sir. And I know that's what I want. I love him." His eyes filled with tears and with his bright red hair and freckles, he looked like a child himself. And Oliver had to fight back tears as he watched him. He had already made up his mind to do everything he could to help him.

"Mrs. Carter has told us that she will sign a statement attesting to your fine care of the boy, and your responsibility for the child. And that would pretty much wrap it up. She more or less suggested that she wouldn't mind a little 'gift' from you, or your father, but we have to be very careful about that. Child buying, or anything even remotely like it, is a criminal offense in this state, and I explained that to her. She was disappointed, but she still said she'd sign any statement we prepared. We have a court date in Bakersfield next week, and if everything goes smoothly, you should have your son back in your hands that afternoon."

"What about in the meantime?" Benjamin once again looked frantic.

"There's nothing we can do till then. He's in good hands, and he's safe." Benjamin looked unhappy about it, but there didn't seem to be anything he could do to change it, so he agreed to the court date the following week, and prayed that they'd be able to find Sandra in Maui, so she could sign whatever papers they needed to release Alex to him.

Chapter 26

The drive to Bakersfield was an anxious one for Benjamin, and Oliver took the day off to join him. Both men were silent and nervous, as they drove down, lost in their own thoughts about little Alex, and what he represented to them. . . . To Oliver, he symbolized new life and a new beginning, and it reminded him again of Charlie saying that she wanted to have children with him. Having little Alex around was going to be a reminder of what having a baby around was like, and a part of him was excited about it, while another part dreaded the chaos and confusion. But Benjamin had already promised to handle it all himself, with a little help from Agnes.

He tried to make small talk with Benjamin on the way down Highway 5, but the boy was too nervous. He and Aggie had set up a crib in his room, and he had bought six boxes of Pampers. He wanted to stop at Mrs. Carter's to get Alex's clothes, but Oliver had thought it would be better to do it on the way back. He was still afraid something might go wrong, and they wouldn't give Alex to them. They hadn't been able to reach Sandra on Maui, but the lawyer said there was a good chance they'd give him to Benjamin anyway, since she had signed the papers giving him up for adoption before she left for Hawaii.

The courthouse in Bakersfield was on Truxton Avenue, and Ollie left the car in the parking lot, and followed his son inside. It was the last week of August and the weather was blazing.

The lawyer was waiting for them inside, and Benjamin looked frightened as they took their places in the courtroom. He was wearing a navy jacket and khaki pants, a blue button-down shirt, and navy school tie. He looked like the student he might have been at Harvard. His hair was neatly combed, and Oliver smiled at him as the bailiff ordered them to rise.

"It's going to be all right, Son." Ollie pressed his hand and Benjamin smiled weakly at him.

"Thanks, Dad." But they both knew that nothing was ever certain, and the lawyer had warned them that something could go wrong. Nothing was ever guaranteed to anyone in a courtroom, and the judge looked serious as he addressed them from the bench.

The matter was set out before the court, Mrs. Carter's statement was read, and both Watsons were relieved not to see her. The papers Sandra had signed were introduced as evidence, and a probation report explained the circumstances the child would live in. He was to live in the Watson family's rented Bel Air home with Benjamin's father, sister, and younger brother, with a housekeeper to assist with the care of the child, while the father attended school at UCLA. He was to start summer school the following week, and he still had his part-time job at the bookstore. The judge looked nonplussed, and asked their attorney to approach the bench. They held a whispered conference for several minutes while the judge nodded, and then he addressed Benjamin and asked him to approach the bench as well. He told him to take the witness stand, and be sworn in, that there were some things he wanted to ask him, and Benjamin walked up the few steps with trembling knees and sat down staring at his father.

"I want you to understand, Mr. Watson, this is not a formal hearing, but this is a serious matter before the court, and a child's life hangs in the balance. Do you understand that?"

Benjamin looked pale but calm as he nodded. "Yes, sir, I do."

"The child in question, Alexander William Carter, is your son? Do you acknowledge that fact?"

"Yes, sir, I do."

"Do you currently reside with the child's mother?"

"No, sir, I don't."

"Did you ever reside with her, at any time?"

"Yes, for a year."

"And were you ever married?"

"No, we weren't."

"Have you ever supported the child, or his mother?"

"Yes, sir. For six months before Alex was born, and after that, until we broke up in March. And since then

I've . . . my dad and I have been sending her money every month. Six hundred dollars." The judge nodded and then went on with his questions.

"And are you aware of the kind of care necessary to a child his age?"

"Yes, sir, I took care of him myself until March. Sandra was . . . well, she was out a lot, and she didn't really know how to take care of a baby."

"And you did?" The judge looked skeptical, but Benjamin seemed in control of the situation.

"No, I didn't. But I had to learn. I took care of him at night after work, and sometimes I took him with me. I had two jobs then, to pay for . . . well, everything . . . Sandra quit work before the baby."

"But you took the baby to work with you?"

"Sometimes, when she was out. I didn't have anyone else to leave him with and we couldn't afford a sitter." Nothing showed on the judge's face, and no matter what happened, Oliver had never been as proud of his son as he was at that moment. He was a fine man, a boy no longer, and a hell of a good father. He deserved to have the child in his custody. He hoped now that the judge would see it that way too.

"And now, you and the baby would live with your father?"

"Yes, sir."

"Is that amenable to him? Has he agreed to this?" From where he sat Oliver nodded, and Benjamin said yes he had. "And what if you choose to leave your father's home, if, for instance, you drop out of school again, or find another girlfriend?"

"I'll take Alex with me. He's more important to me

than anything. And if I drop out of school, I'll get a job to support him, just like I did before."

"You may step down, Mr. Watson. The court calls a brief recess. We will reconvene in fifteen minutes." He rapped the gavel and was gone, as Benjamin left the stand, outwardly calm, but soaked to the skin with perspiration.

"You did great," the attorney whispered. "Just hang in there."

"Why did he call a recess?" Oliver wanted to know.

"He probably wants to read the documents again, to make sure that everything's in order. But Benjamin did just fine. I'd give him my kids if he wanted them." He smiled, trying to reassure them. And fifteen minutes later, after they had prowled the halls nervously, they took their seats again, and the judge returned.

He looked around the court, at Oliver, the attorney, and then straight at Benjamin, as he rapped his gavel. "Court is in session again. Don't rise, please stay seated," and then his eyes bore into the boy's with sober words. "What you are attempting to undertake, young man, is an awesome burden. A responsibility you can never shirk, never forget, never avoid. You can't take a day off from being a father. You can't drop out, or change your mind, or decide not to be there. For the next eighteen years, if not longer, that baby would be your responsibility solely, if the court gives you full custody. However, you appear to have fulfilled that responsibility admirably thus far. I hereby admonish you to think seriously of what you are taking on here, to remember it every day of your life, and the boy's life, and never forget for one moment what you owe your son.

"The court hereby appoints Benjamin Oliver Watson sole guardian of Alexander William Carter. You have full custody of the boy, as of this day, the twenty-ninth of August. The termination of his mother's rights has been approved by the court, and will be final within the period prescribed by law. You may change the child's name to your own as of this date, or at that time, as you choose." He looked down gently at him then and smiled, "The boy is yours, Mr. Watson." He signaled to the bailiff then, who rose and opened a door. A social worker walked in, carrying the baby, who looked content and a little startled by the unfamiliar surroundings, as his father's eyes, and his grandfather's, and even the attorney's, filled with tears. "You may take Alexander home," the judge said gently as the social worker walked straight up to Benjamin and handed Alex to his father, as the baby squealed his delight to see him there. They handed the attorney a small cardboard box with his few belongings, a pair of pajamas, a pair of overalls, and a bear Benjamin had given him when he was born. They were all crying then, and laughing as Benjamin looked up at the judge in amazement.

"Thank you, sir . . . oh thank you, sir!" And then the judge stood up, and quietly left the bench. The attorney escorted them from the courtroom, as Benjamin held the boy, and Oliver patted his son on the shoulder, and then shook the attorney's hand and thanked him. Benjamin got into the back of the car and held tightly to his baby before strapping him into the safety seat they'd brought with him.

They decided not to go back to Alice Carter's to get the rest of Alex's belongings. Suddenly, Benjamin never wanted to see her again. All he wanted was to take his son home and keep him near him forever. He even hated to start school the next day. He didn't want to leave him for a moment.

They drove home slowly for a change of pace on Highway 99, and Benjamin talked excitedly as the baby cooed. He talked about the judge, the court, and finally Sandra. The social worker had told the attorney from Loeb and Loeb that Sandra had been definite and clear. She knew she couldn't handle the responsibility of the baby, and she didn't want to try. Without Benjamin to take care of him for her, all she wanted was to escape him. The waiting period now was only a formality. No one anticipated any problems, and all Benjamin had to do now was file the paper to change the child's last name to his own, but Loeb and Loeb was going to do that for them in L.A. County.

"Well, sir, what do you think about all this?" he chatted happily with his baby. "Do you think you're going to like living with Grampa and Mel and Sam?" Alex gurgled and pointed at a passing truck as Ollie smiled proudly at him.

"If he doesn't, he can sleep in the garage with that damn noisy guinea pig of Sam's," the boy's grandfather pretended to growl. But it was obvious how much he loved him.

Mel and Sam and Aggie were waiting for them in the kitchen. They had waited there with bated breath for most of the afternoon. At first, all Mel saw was her father alone in the front seat and she thought something had gone wrong. And then suddenly, her brother got out of the backseat, holding his baby, and she let out a yell and ran to him, as Alex stared at her with wide eyes.

"Watch out . . . don't scare him . . . this is all new to him." Benjamin was fiercely protective of him, as the baby let out a wail. But Aggie had a cookie for him, and Sam held up the guinea pig to show him, as the baby started to laugh, and tried to touch its nose as it wiggled.

Aggie had found a high chair somewhere and set it up in the kitchen, as Oliver opened a bottle of champagne for his son, and even poured a few drops for Sam.

"To Alexander Watson!" he toasted with a broad smile, feeling the weight of the afternoon slip slowly from his shoulders. "May he live a long and happy life, with the best daddy of all."

"Oh no," Benjamin turned to smile at him, "That's you, Dad."

"It's both of you," Mel toasted with a smile, and everyone's eyes were damp as they grinned and looked happily at the baby.

Chapter 27

Benjamin started classes the next day, but he drove home twice to check on Alex, despite Aggie's insistence that she didn't need any help from him. But it was as though Benjamin couldn't stand being away from him again, and he needed to see him. And when he came home at the end of the day, Alexander was sitting in his high chair, happily demolishing the dinner Aggie had lovingly cooked him.

And when Charlotte came over that night, she insisted on singing to him as she rocked him and helped Benjamin put him to bed, and Mel, Aggie, and Oliver stood protectively by, and Sam dropped his favorite teddy into the baby's crib. It was the one he'd been given by Sarah the first time he'd visited her in Boston.

Alex let out a tentative wail when they all left the room, but a moment later, he was silent.

"He's going to be spoiled rotten by next week," Oliver pretended to disapprove, but it was obvious to Charlotte that Ollie was planning to become one of the chief spoilers.

"How does it feel having a baby in the house again?"

"Like good practice. He woke us all up at six o'clock this morning. But I have to admit, Benjamin is terrific with him. Better even than Aggie," he whispered.

"You look pretty adept yourself. I always feel so awkward around babies."

Oliver pulled her close to him, and that weekend they took Alex to the zoo alone, without his father. It felt terrific to both of them, and for once, no one disturbed them, or ran up to her for autographs. Several people looked, but eventually they all decided she couldn't be Charlotte Sampson. They were just a happy couple, taking their baby to the zoo, on a September Sunday. And only the large diamond on her left hand suggested that she might be someone moneyed or important, but no one even noticed.

It was particularly a relief for her because the press had been hounding her since the Emmy nominations in August. She and the show had been nominated again this year. The awards were the following week, and everyone wanted to be prepared with stories about the nominees, but Charlotte wanted to be left alone. She was afraid that too much press beforehand might jinx her. She was back at work, getting up at four every morning, and at the studio by five for hair and makeup. At night, Oliver picked her up and either took her out for a quiet dinner somewhere, or brought her back to his place for dinner with the children. They were all excited about the December wedding, and they still hadn't decided where to go for a honeymoon, Hawaii, Bora Bora, or maybe skiing. Sam felt that wherever they went, he ought to go with them, but so far Ollie wasn't buying. No guinea pigs, no kids, no babies on this honeymoon. They dealt with enough in their daily lives without dragging it all with them on their honeymoon, no matter how much he loved his children.

The following week, Charlotte's big moment was approaching and there was no way she could avoid it any longer. The press were waiting outside at the studio almost daily. They even followed her to Giorgio when she bought her dress, a slinky black sequined and beaded affair by Bob Mackie. And she had gone back to buy a dress for Mel, a beautiful pink satin Oscar de la Renta. Oliver had growled about spoiling Mel, and Charlotte had told him to mind his own business. They had had a ball, trying on gowns and giggling, as Charlotte selected several other beautiful gowns for herself, and Mel played with the hats and costume jewelry.

The big day finally came, and Charlotte and Oliver left the house with Benjamin and Mel in a block-long limousine, while Aggie and Sam settled down to watch the awards on TV. Alex was still awake when they left, happily smearing chocolate cookies all over himself, the couch, and his pajamas. He had just turned a year old the day before and had taken his first steps on his birthday.

They arrived at the Pasadena Civic Auditorium, and Charlotte looked deceptively calm as she stepped out of the car and took Ollie's arm, with Mel and Benjamin just behind them. It was the most exciting night of the children's lives, and Ollie could feel the tension too. Charlotte's palms were damp, and as the paparazzi flocked, he could feel her gently tremble. And once they took their seats in the auditorium the cameras focused in on them constantly. Dozens of stars came over to talk to them once they'd sat down, and finally the ceremony got under way with the usual assortment of lesser awards to begin with. It seemed to take hours to get to the more important ones, and by then, Sam was yawning and half asleep at home, and Alex was sound asleep in Aggie's arms, but in Pasadena, all was electricity and tension. They called out the nominees for the best show, and Mel and Benjamin let out a yell when it was hers. Both producers ran down the aisle while their wives cried, and Charlotte grinned from ear to ear as she clung tightly to Ollie. She was pleased for the producers and insisted to herself that she didn't need more than to be on a winning show, and turned her attention to the awards for best actor.

A good friend of hers won on a rival show, and she was thrilled for him. And then the big moment came. At last it was her turn. And she could hardly bear it. All her life she had told herself that fame wasn't important, and yet it was. She had worked so hard for this, and whether she won or not, in her heart of hearts, she knew she had earned it.

The cameras zoomed in on her again and again, as she held Ollie's hand, and he silently prayed for her. For her sake, he wanted her to win. The other actresses' names were called too, and then a long, long pause, while someone asked for "The envelope please," and then like a bolt of lightning through his heart he heard her name, and she stared at him, and she put a hand over her mouth, unable to believe she'd actually won this time. And he gently prodded her to her feet, and she was suddenly hurrying down the aisle toward the stage, with her flaming hair softly pulled up in curls, and the beautiful black beaded dress molding her incredible figure. "I don't believe it!" she had said before she left her seat, and she looked shaken and smiling as she addressed her colleagues and her friends at the microphone, clutching the Emmy.

"I . . . I don't know what to say," she laughed, "I don't have anything prepared because I never thought I'd win . . . I want to thank the producers and the directors and the writers and the actors and the cameramen, and all of the magical people who made this possible . . . my acting coach, John Drum, for being crazy enough to get me the job . . . my agent for talking me into it . . . Annie, you were right! . . . and most important of all," she looked straight at him, "my family . . . my soon-to-be husband, Oliver, who puts up with me so lovingly . . . and our children, Benjamin and Melissa and Sam." There were tears in her eyes then, and in Ollie's, too. Sam was too stunned to move as he watched at home. "I love you all, and I hope I can do an even better job next year." She took the Emmy then, waved to colleagues and fans, and left the stage to hurry back to her seat. The fanfare started then, the show was over, but the press almost crushed her in her seat, as Oliver shielded her, and kissed her, and she kissed him and Benjamin and Mel, and pressed their hands. It was a wild, exciting night, and they took the children home, and opened a bottle of champagne with them, and

Aggie and Sam, before she and Ollie went back to the parties where they would celebrate all night. It was an evening she would never forget. She had really made it.

The phone rang before they left, it was Margaret and his father calling to congratulate Charlotte. And Aggie was still crying tears of joy when Charlie called her own folks in Nebraska, and they were crying too. It was a magical night, and she still couldn't believe she'd won as Benjamin toasted her, and they all talked and laughed and grinned and watched a rerun of it on the news before leaving for their round of parties.

"I never thought I'd win," she said to Ollie again and again as they drove from Bel Air back to Beverly Hills.

"I knew you would!" He was so proud of her, and it was extraordinary to be a part of it with her. It was 4:00 A.M. when they finally got home, and she collapsed in her own bed, with Ollie lying next to her. The Emmy was staring at them from her dressing table across the room, and she couldn't help grinning as they watched it.

"He's pretty cute," Oliver smiled, too tired even to loosen his tie.

"Not as cute as you," she rolled over and smiled in the exquisite dress. "You look a lot better to me." She was a little drunk, and a lot overwhelmed by all that had happened.

"You're crazy, do you know that? You're the biggest star in Hollywood, and what are you doing with me?"

"Loving you. Let's get pregnant tonight."

"Behave yourself. You're about to become the mother of three kids." Three kids who were incredibly proud of her, just as their father was. "And a grandson!" They both laughed at the thought of her becoming a grandmother.

And she just beamed. It had been an unforgettable night. For all of them.

He kissed her then, and five minutes later, she was asleep in his arms, still dressed, with the Emmy staring at them in all its glory. She looked like a child as he gazed down at her, unable to believe that this remarkable woman was almost his. He left her at six o'clock in the morning to get ready to go to work. The kids were still asleep when he got home, and there was an aura of unreality about the night before. But it had happened. It was true. She had won the award, and in three months she would be his wife. It was incredible to think about. And he could hardly wait. Three months seemed much too long now . . . he smiled to himself in the shower . . . three months . . . and then he and Charlie would be married.

Chapter 28

The next week was wild, with press following her everywhere. She got a huge bonus from the show, and they upped her contract for the following year. But she got dozens of other offers too, for specials and mini-series, and movies made for TV, three feature films, and then the offer she had waited a lifetime for. Her agent called her at the studio, and she didn't know what to say to her. She wanted to do it more than anything, but she said she had to talk it over with Oliver. He had a right to a voice in the decision too. It was an important decision for her, and it meant a lot of things. Like begging her way out of her contract on the show that had brought her the Emmy. Or even breaking the contract, if she had to.

She looked nervous when he picked her up that night after work, and they were going to have a quiet evening at her place to discuss their wedding trip. He was pushing hard for Bora Bora. But before he even brought the brochures out, he knew that something had happened.

"Charlie, what's wrong?" He had good instincts for her now, and it was unusual for her to be so tense with him. But she didn't waste any time telling him. She'd been offered a Broadway play, a serious one, the kind she had always wanted to do, and it was an opportunity that might never come again. And they were going into rehearsal in December. It would mean going to New York for at least a year, more if it had a long run, maybe even at least two.

He sat looking at her, stunned, not believing his ears, or the look on her face. She was clearly torn. And he felt as though his heart would break. "What about the show?" What about me, he wanted to scream.

"I'd have to get out of my contract. My agent thinks that if we do it right, they might let me."

"Is that what you want?"

"I don't know. It always has been. For me, Broadway has always been the pinnacle, the ultimate, the epitome of serious acting."

She was honest with him, she always had been. "I'm telling you exactly what I know. I haven't made my mind up yet. I told my agent I had to talk to you first. But . . . Ollie . . . I've always wanted to do a Broadway play, especially one like this."

"What does that mean for us? And what am I supposed to do for two years? Sit out here? I can't leave the office here, I've only been here for a year, and this is an important spot for me, probably for a very long time, if not for good. My kids are all in schools. I can't walk out on them, or uproot them again. They've been through that twice already in a year. I can't do it, Charlie. I can't drop everything and go, no matter how much I'd love to see you do what you want." He had to think of his career and his family too. But she looked agonized. She didn't want to give it up, even for him, and it showed.

"I could commute." But he looked as though he'd been electrified as she said the words, and he leapt to his feet and started to pace the room in silence.

"Don't give me that, Charlie," he finally said. "I've been through that once with a woman I loved. She didn't even start to try to commute. But even if you do, how long do you think it would last? Flying 'red-eyes' from here to there, spending a day together once a week. It's ridiculous, it wouldn't work. We haven't even built our relationship yet, and you want to put it under that kind of strain? I'd rather call it quits now. It would be a lot less painful for both of us, than waiting to do it a year from now. Forget it. I don't want to hear about 'commute.' " He tried to calm down then, and think of her. "Look, Charlie, you have to do what's right for you." He loved her enough to let her do that, no matter what it did to him. He knew he had no right to stand in her way, and if he did, they'd lose in the end anyway. He had learned that lesson the hard way too. "Think about it, do what *you* want." He closed his eyes for a brief instant of crushing pain, but he had lived through pain before, and loss, and despair. He'd survive it again. And he was willing to, for her. "I think you probably should do it. You'd always regret it if you turned it down, and we'd pay the price for it anyway. Go for it, baby . . . go for the brass ring. You have a right to it. You're at the top of your career now. These opportunities will never come again. But don't expect me to commute . . . or believe we can have everything. We can't. Sometimes you have to make choices in life. Just make the right one for you. That's all I want for you." There were tears in his eyes then, and he turned away so she wouldn't see them.

"Are you telling me it would be all over for us if I go?" She looked stunned, and heartbroken too.

"I am. But not because I want to force your hand, or make you stay here for me. I'm just telling you I've been through something like this once, and I can't do it again. It doesn't work. We'll lose in the end anyway. And I can't go through that again. I'd rather wish you well, and kiss you good-bye with tears in my heart. But better now, than in a year or two, maybe even with a kid. And I don't think my kids could go through the loss again in any case. And I have to think of them too. I love you, Charlie. I love you enough to let you do whatever you want to. I'm going home now. You think it out. And call me when it's over. I'll understand . . . honest, I will." His eyes were damp and she was crying. She couldn't believe what he'd said, and yet she understood it. "Just don't let me read about it in the papers first." And then without looking back, he left and drove home to his own place.

Sam was still up when he got there, and he was playing with the guinea pig in the kitchen, as Oliver walked in looking as though he'd been run over on the Santa Monica Freeway.

"Hi, Dad." He looked up with a grin and then stopped, forgetting the guinea pig for once. "What's wrong?"

"Nothing. I had a terrible day at the office. I'm going to bed." He ruffled Sam's hair and went straight up to his room, without saying another word. And Sam ran right up to his sister's bedroom, with a look of terror.

"Something's wrong with Dad!" he reported. "He just came home and he was green."

"Maybe he's sick. Did you ask him what was wrong?"

"He just said he had a bad day at the office."

"Maybe he did. Why don't you just relax and leave him alone? He'll probably be fine in the morning."

But the next morning he wasn't. They all noticed it. He was quiet and pale, and he didn't say a word. He came down late, and he didn't touch his eggs, as Sam looked pointedly at his sister.

"You sick, Dad?" She tried to sound casual. And without meaning to, Sam hit the nail on the head. His father almost flinched at the boy's words.

"You have a fight with Charlie last night?"

"No, of course not." But she hadn't called after he'd left, and he hadn't been able to sleep all night. The terror of losing her was more than he could bear. And at what price. He loved her too much to try to hang on to something he could never have, just as he had discovered he had never really had Sarah.

He left for the office that morning feeling like a zombie, and he almost shuddered when his secretary told him that afternoon that Charlotte was waiting in his outer office. Suddenly he was afraid to let her in, afraid to see her, afraid to hear what she was going to tell him. He felt trapped when the secretary let her in with a look of awe, and he didn't stand up because suddenly his legs didn't feel strong enough to hold him.

"Are you okay?" Charlie looked at him worriedly, and walked slowly toward the desk, her eyes gripping his, her face pale, but no paler than Ollie's.

"You've made a decision, haven't you?"

She nodded, and slumped in the chair across his desk. "I had to come now. It's going to be on the news at six o'clock. The producers of the play made a deal with the network, and they've agreed to write me out of the show by Christmas." . . . Christmas . . . their wedding day . . . almost.

"And you'll do the play?" He could hardly force the words out.

She nodded slowly, with a look of tension in her eyes. "I guess so." And then reaching out and taking both his hands in her own, she begged him, "Can't we work this out? Can't we at least try a compromise? I love you. Nothing has changed." She looked desperate, but Ollie knew better.

"Not now maybe. Not yet. But eventually, it'll just be too much. We'll be strangers. You'll live in New York, with your own life, your play. I'll be here, with my job and the children. What kind of life is that?"

"Difficult, challenging, but worthwhile. Other people have done it and survived. Ollie, I swear I'll do all the commuting."

"How? You have two days off. One day to fly here, one day to go back. What does that leave us? A night at the airport? How long do you think that would last?" He stood up finally, and walked around the desk to face her. "You've made the right choice. You're a talented woman, Charlotte. You have a right to the best."

"But I love you."

"I love you too. But I can't make something work that isn't going to. I've learned that lesson before. The hard way." The scars were too deep, the pain too great, and as he looked at the woman he loved, he knew he had already lost her.

"What happens now?" She looked broken, but she didn't fight him.

"We hurt for a while. We both grow up. We go on. You have your work. I have my kids. We take comfort from that, and eventually it stops hurting." Like it had with Sarah. It had only taken a year of constant agony. Only that. And the prospect of losing Charlotte seemed worse somehow, they had had so much hope and joy and love, so many plans, and now it was over.

"You make it sound awfully simple, Ollie." She looked at him with grief-stricken eyes, and he gently reached out and took her hands in his own.

"That's the only trouble. It isn't."

She left his office a few minutes later in tears, and he poured himself a stiff drink at the bar before going home, to find Aggie and Sam watching the news as they fed Alex dinner. The announcer was just telling greater L.A. that there was a rumor that Charlotte Sampson was leaving her show and going to New York to be in a play on Broadway.

Sam laughed out loud, as Aggie handed the baby another cookie. "That's dumb, isn't it, Dad? Charlie's not going to New York. She's staying here, and we're getting married." He looked up at his father with a broad smile, and suddenly his face froze. Ollie looked glazed as he turned from the TV to Sam and shook his head, as though in a stupor.

"No. I don't think so, Son. She's had a very good offer to do an important play. It means a lot to her, Sam." Aggie and the boy both stared at him, as Benjamin let himself into the kitchen and saw the drama unfolding, without knowing what had caused it. Alex let out a squeal and reached chubby arms up to his father, but for once, no one seemed to hear him.

"Are we going back to New York, too, Dad?" Sam looked both frightened and hopeful, but his father shook his head, feeling as though he had aged a hundred years in a single day.

"We can't, Sam. You're all in school here. And I have an office to run. I can't just pull up stakes and move once a year."

"But don't you want to?" Sam couldn't understand what had happened. But for that matter, neither could Ollie.

"Yes, I do. But I also don't want to interfere in someone else's life. She has her own life to lead, and we have ours."

There was a moment's silence, and then Sam nodded, quietly wiping a tear from his cheek as Benjamin and his father watched him. "Kind of like Mom, huh?"

"Kind of."

Sam nodded and left the room, as Benjamin gently touched his father's arm, and Aggie took Alex out of the high chair and took him with her to check on Sam. It was easy to figure out that hard times had struck again, and Sam was going to take it hard. He had been crazy about Charlotte. But then again, so had his father.

"Is there anything I can do, Dad?" Benjamin asked quietly, touched by the look of grief in Ollie's eyes. But

Oliver only shook his head, squeezed Benjamin's arm, and went upstairs to his own room. He lay on his bed thinking of her all that night, and he felt as though he'd been beaten in a bar brawl by morning.

It wasn't fair that it was happening to him again. It wasn't fair that he was losing her. As he lay in bed alone, he wanted to hate her, but he couldn't. He loved her too much, and the irony of it struck him with full force again in the morning, after a sleepless night, as he threw out the brochures of Bora Bora. He had a knack for falling in love with women who wanted more out of life than just plain marriage. He couldn't imagine ever loving anyone again. And as he stared out the window, thinking of her, he couldn't hold back the tears. He wanted her desperately, but he knew it would never work. He had to let her go, no matter how painful it was to break the bonds that had held him.

He wanted to call her all day, but he forced himself not to. The papers were full of her that day, and for several days, but she never called him. And it was Thanksgiving before he could hear her name without flinching. He longed for her to leave for New York so he wouldn't be tempted to drive by her house, or stop by the studio to see her. She would be gone, to another life, far from his own. Forever.

Chapter 29

The day before Thanksgiving, Sarah arrived to take Mel and Sam to San Francisco with her to see friends. She had even agreed to take Aggie and Alex, and Benjamin was going to get in some early skiing at Squaw Valley. Sarah had finished her book a few weeks before, and Oliver thought she looked well. The odd thing was that when he kissed her on the cheek, she felt like a stranger. He never longed for her anymore, and now her perfume was an unfamiliar smell. The woman who haunted his dreams at night was Charlie. His heart still ached each time she came to mind or he saw her name in the papers.

"When are you getting married, Ollie?" Sarah asked as she held Alex on her knee the morning they left, and Oliver looked startled.

"I thought the children would have told you." His voice was tense and quiet.

"Told me what?" She seemed surprised, as the baby drooled happily all over her clean shirt. Aggie had gone to get the children's things, and Sarah was waiting in the kitchen.

"Charlotte's doing a Broadway play. She should be leaving pretty soon, in fact. And, well . . . we decided that was a better move for her than marriage." He smiled gamely, but Sarah wasn't fooled. She knew him too well. And she felt desperately sorry for the pain she knew he felt. It was different from what she had gone through with Jean-Pierre, but loss of any kind was painful. "Guess I just have a knack for falling for that kind of lady. The smart ones with ambitions of their own."

"You'll find the right one, one of these days, Ollie, you deserve to." And she really meant it.

"I'm not sure I'd have time for her, if I did," he smiled to hide his sorrow, glancing at Alex, "this guy keeps us all on our toes all the time." Benjamin took him from his mother then, and took him out to the car to put him in his car seat in Sarah's rented Pontiac wagon. He hated to leave the baby at all, but Oliver had insisted that the skiing would do him good. And he himself was happy that Sarah was taking the children. The punch of losing Charlie was still too great and Oliver felt anything but festive.

Sarah and the younger children left a little while later, and Benjamin's friends picked him up only moments later. Ollie was alone in the house, trying to get through a stack of bills and mail. It seemed strangely silent, and as Ollie leaned back in his chair, he sighed, as though trying to decide if he liked it. Too quickly, he found himself thinking of Charlie again, and even

Sarah. He wondered if things could ever have been different, with either of them, but deep in his heart, he knew they couldn't. Maybe if they'd done things differently at first, Sarah wouldn't have bolted later, he thought to himself as he sat back at his desk, and then realized it was a foolish thought. She would have done what she'd done anyway. She was meant to be free, and live alone, and write her novels. As Charlie was, with her Broadway play. Megan, in her penthouse in New York. And even Daphne, with the man who would never leave his wife in Greenwich.

It only irked him that Charlie had made such an issue about marriage and children and "real life" being so important to her, and then in the end, she had made the same choices as the rest. Independence. Her play, New York. With a promise to commute that would never have happened, no matter how good her intentions.

It was late that afternoon before he left his desk again, and went to make himself a sandwich. And then he saw her standing there, hesitating, near her car in the driveway. It was Charlie, he realized, in a T-shirt and jeans, with her hair in the familiar pigtails that made her look more like one of Mel's friends, than the woman who had broken his heart and their engagement. She stood there for a long time, staring at him through the window, and he didn't know whether to open the door to her or not. He thought it was cruel of her to come to say good-bye if she had. And then finally, unable to resist the pull he still felt for her, he walked to the door and pulled it slowly open. And she walked up to him looking very nervous.

"I didn't know if you'd be here or not. . . . I was

going to leave you a note . . ." He saw she held it in her hand, but he didn't want to read it. "I guess I should have called before I came by."

"Mailing it might have been a lot simpler." He had nothing left to say to her now. He had said it all. And cried too often.

She looked beyond him then, into the kitchen, as though hoping to see the children but the room was empty and silent.

"How is everyone?" Her eyes sought his, and he nodded, still wondering why she had come.

"Okay."

"I still miss them," she admitted, looking sad and feeling guilty. She had never come by to explain any of it to them. She knew it would have been too painful.

"They miss you too."

"How's the baby?"

"Fine." Ollie smiled. "Benjamin is great with him."

"Where are they all?"

"Away for Thanksgiving." For a mad moment, he wanted to invite her in, but that wouldn't get them anywhere except straight into more pain. And then, with a shrug, he stepped back, and waved her in. "Do you want to come in for a minute?"

She nodded and followed him into the kitchen, thinking how handsome he was, and how much she still loved him. She looked around and slipped the note she had brought back in her pocket.

"When do you leave for New York?"

She seemed to hesitate, as though she wasn't sure what to say to him. She knew how badly she had hurt him, and there was no way to repair it. And now there was so much to explain. She didn't know where to start, or even if she should, as he watched her. "That's a long story."

"You must be excited." He tried to keep his voice noncommittal, but it wasn't. In it were anger and grief and hurt and the love for her that wouldn't go away, no matter how hard he had tried to kill it.

"A lot's been happening," she tried to explain. The last few weeks had been hell for her, but she didn't tell him that. She could see in his eyes that it was too late. She had been foolish to come, and now she knew it.

"Would you like a cup of coffee?" he offered. Part of him wanted her to leave, so he could be alone with his grief again, but part of him wanted her to stay. Forever.

She looked at him long and hard, and despite the pigtails, her eyes said she was not a girl, but a woman. They were the eyes of someone who had paid a price for what she'd done. And then she spoke very softly. "I'm not going to Broadway, Ollie."

"You're not?" He looked thunderstruck. What the hell did she mean? She had told him. And after that he had seen it on the news and read it in the papers. What had changed? And when and why?

"No, I'm not. I'm staying with the show here."

"Wouldn't they let you out of your contract?"

"They would have, but . . ." He waited, stunned, for the rest of the story. "I decided it was wrong to go."

"For your career?" It was barely a whisper.

"For us. Although I guess it's too late now. But it was the wrong thing to do and I finally understood that. I kept talking about how much marriage and family meant to me, and then I was willing to dump everything and run, no matter how much it hurt all of us, you, and me, and the children.

"It was the wrong thing to do. It was too high a price to pay for giving up someone I loved, no matter how much I thought I wanted to do it. It wasn't right, so I turned it down. And even if I don't get any of you back, turning them down was the right thing to do." She smiled a bittersweet smile. "I felt better as soon as I did it."

Oliver looked stunned as he looked at her, and then he grinned. "They must have been furious."

"Yeah," she smiled. "That's the end of Broadway, I guess. But the network loves me." And then, "I was afraid to call you, Ollie."

"Why?"

"Because I hurt you so much. One minute I leave you to go to New York, and the next minute I come back and tell you everything's okay. I couldn't do that to you. That's what the note is about. I thought I'd let you know before you read about it somewhere, and I figured if you wanted to get in touch with me, you would. But I didn't really think you'd want to." She looked as though she expected nothing more from him, but would regret what she'd done till her dying day. And then, to lighten the moment as he absorbed it, she looked around the kitchen for Charlie's cage. "How's my namesake, by the way?" The guinea pig was nowhere to be seen, and Ollie grinned at her, feeling a ten-thousand-pound weight lift from his shoulders.

"He's relegated to the garage in Sam's absence, the noisy little bastard. I have enough trouble sleeping at night, without listening to him play."

She looked more than a little apologetic. "I haven't been sleeping all that well either. I really screwed things up royally, Ollie, didn't I?" Her voice was soft and sad as he nodded.

"Could be." He smiled slowly at her. "Maybe . . . maybe not. It's what you do in the end, that counts in life. We all stumble along the way." They were still standing awkwardly in the kitchen, their lives in the balance, their eyes full of fear and pain and tension. They had so much to lose . . . and so much to gain, depending on what he did now.

"I've missed you, Ollie. I'm going to miss you for a long, long time if you don't forgive me." She loved him enough to come back and ask him to forgive her. "Every day I wanted to call you . . . to come over . . . to tell you I was sorry . . . what a total fool I was . . . how wrong I was to think that the play on Broadway mattered more than you did. It was a stinking decision to make, even if I came to my senses in the end."

"But it was honest," he defended her, "it was what you'd always wanted. You had a right to that, Charlie."

"I wanted you more. I just didn't know it for sure till I lost you. And then it was too late." His eyes told her that it was, and she was sorry she had come then, but he was moving slowly toward her with an odd look on his face.

"Who told you that?" he whispered as he pulled her closer. "Who told you it was too late? And who tells you that you were wrong and I was right? A thousand times I told myself that I could have moved back to New York with you, that we could have moved into the house in Purchase, what right did I have to stand in your way?"

"You had every right . . . you had your kids to think of too. All I was thinking of was myself."

"And now?" He could barely get the words out as he held her. He still loved her so much. It hurt just standing this close to her again.

"Ollie, I love you so much." She barely breathed the words, and then slowly he kissed her. It was all he had wanted to hear, all he had cared about, all he had lived for after she went away.

"I love you too . . . you'll never know how much I miss you. I thought I'd go crazy for a while. . . ."

"So did I." She was smiling suddenly, as he swept her off her feet and carried her through the house while she laughed. "Where are you taking me?" Suddenly she was happy again. She was in the arms of the man she loved. He didn't hate her, and he had been as unhappy as she was. She had been such a fool, but thank God she hadn't left to do the play on Broadway. "What are you doing?"

He marched solemnly up the stairs toward his bedroom. "Taking you to my bed where you belong, until you learn to behave yourself . . . goddamn famous actress . . . don't ever pull a stunt like that again!" He railed as she laughed and he carried her through his bedroom doorway. It looked familiar and warm and wonderful as she looked up into his eyes.

"Ollie, I'm so sorry. . . ." He was still holding her, as though he would never let her go this time, but he smiled at her.

"Don't be. I was as big a fool as you were."

"And now?" She looked up at him, as he deposited her on his bed.

"I figure we're both fools and we deserve each other."

She smiled as she held her arms out to him, and as they lay in his bed for most of the next four days, it was a magical weekend. The kids found her in her jeans and his shirt, barefoot in the kitchen, when Sarah dropped them off Sunday night on her way to the airport. She came in to say good-bye to Oliver, but only briefly, and she looked intrigued when she saw Charlotte, looking tousled and happy in the kitchen.

"Is that who I think it is?" Sarah whispered with a smile, as Oliver walked her to the car. He had tried to introduce them, but Sam and Alex had made so much noise, it was impossible to hear anything, and Charlotte looked faintly embarrassed to be found barefoot in Oliver's kitchen.

"It is."

"Does this mean you're moving to New York?" Sarah looked faintly amused, and pleased for him as she slid behind the wheel of her car. She and the children had had a very good weekend.

"No, I'm not moving to New York." He looked faintly smug, and tried to pretend he wasn't.

"She's staying."

"She is?" Sarah looked impressed, and he smiled at her.

"I got lucky, I guess." This time.

"No, Ollie." She smiled up at him, the past no longer painful for either of them. "She's a smart girl. Congratulations to both of you, or am I premature?"

"A little." He grinned, and they both laughed.

"Good luck then." She waved and backed out of the driveway, and he walked back into the kitchen, still feeling startled as he saw Charlotte with one arm around Sam, and holding Alex with the other, talking animatedly with Mel above their heads, as Aggie made hot chocolate amid the confusion.

"I can't believe how lucky I am," she whispered to Ollie as they sat at the kitchen table.

"I'm the lucky one."

"We both are." She thought of the ring she had had sent back to him and wondered what had happened to it. She glanced at her hand as she thought of it, and as she looked up, she saw that Oliver was laughing. "What's so funny?"

"You are. And in answer to your question, I threw it away." In truth, he hadn't had the heart to send it back to the store, and it was in the safe in his bedroom closet.

"How did you know what I was thinking?"

"Because I'm smarter than I used to be, and I love you." They exchanged a long, slow smile over the baby's head, and Oliver felt as though a miracle had happened. A miracle that had brought her back to him, whether or not he thought he deserved it. "Will you exchange it for a plain gold one?" He wanted to grab her before she changed her mind again, or another play came up, or a film or a handsome leading man. He wasn't even sure he'd be willing to wait another four weeks till Christmas.

But she was nodding in answer to his question. And the look in her eyes told him all he needed to know. She had come back to stay and she would have it all, her life with him and her career, for as long as she wanted. And this time, they both knew she could do it.

She had made her choice. And her choice was to be with him, and the children.

But she had her show too. And an Emmy, and a guinea pig, and the man she loved, three wonderful kids, and even a built-in grandchild. And children of her own, if that was what she wanted. He was ready to give it all to her. He had learned a lot, too, in her absence.

"When?" The look in his eyes was fiery as he took Alex from her lap and handed him to Aggie. And she carried him, and led Sam swiftly out of the kitchen, leaving them alone to settle their future.

"Tomorrow? Next week?" Charlotte was suddenly laughing at him as she answered.

"No later." He scowled as he pulled her close to him, and bent down to kiss her, just as Benjamin walked in, with his ski bag over his shoulder.

"Sorry, Dad," he grinned with pleasure when he saw Charlotte. Oliver gestured over his shoulder, and Benjamin scurried out of the room, still grinning, as Ollie bent to kiss Charlotte again and they both started to laugh.

"Next weekend?" he asked again, amused but getting desperate.

"Tomorrow." She smiled quietly, setting the wedding date they'd almost lost until she came to her senses.

"I love you," Oliver whispered, feeling her heart pound next to him, and almost as loudly.

"I love you too," she whispered back, and in the distance, they could hear the children thundering up the stairs. They were laughing and discussing the good news, and by week's end, it would all be in the papers, and it was, but by then Charlotte Sampson and Oliver Watson were already married and had gone to Hawaii for a week, with her producers' permission. The paparazzi were, predictably, waiting for them when they got home, and snapped dozens of pictures at the airport.

Benjamin and Alex were waiting for them. Benjamin was smiling broadly, and Alex was sound asleep in his arms, happy and peaceful with his daddy.

"I hope ours is as cute as that," she whispered to Oliver as they followed Benjamin to the baggage claim, and he put an arm around his wife, and smiled. He wasn't worried about that. He had it all, the life he had wanted, and a woman who made it all worthwhile. And he knew, without a doubt, that he was the luckiest man alive.

"All set?" he asked, as Benjamin helped him carry the bags. And as they walked slowly outside, a woman came rushing up to them, with a squeal of excitement.

"Aren't you . . . aren't you Charlotte Sampson?"

"No," Charlie shook her head pleasantly with a smile, "the name's Watson."

"Oh." The woman apologized, and disappeared as the threesome laughed, the baby slept, and Oliver and Charlie went home to their children.